A Male Pre
Mount Holyo

£16

A Male President for Mount Holyoke College

The Failed Fight to Maintain Female Leadership, 1934–1937

ANN KARUS MEEROPOL

Foreword by Joyce Avrech Berkman

McFarland & Company, Inc., Publishers

Jefferson, North Carolina

Unless otherwise indicated, all photographs are courtesy of the Mount Holyoke College Archives and Special Collections. In addition, the archive kindly allowed correspondence and other records in their collections to be quoted extensively in this book.

ISBN 978-0-7864-7133-1 (softcover : acid free paper) ∞
ISBN 978-1-4766-0585-2 (ebook)

LIBRARY OF CONGRESS CATALOGUING DATA ARE AVAILABLE

BRITISH LIBRARY CATALOGUING DATA ARE AVAILABLE

© 2014 Ann Karus Meeropol. All rights reserved

*No part of this book may be reproduced or transmitted in any form
or by any means, electronic or mechanical, including photocopying
or recording, or by any information storage and retrieval system,
without permission in writing from the publisher.*

On the cover: Mount Holyoke President Mary Emma Woolley, 1903;
Mount Holyoke President Roswell Gray Ham [undated];
background Mary Lyon Hall, Mount Holyoke College,
South Hadley, Massachusettes, ca. 1900–1910 (Library of Congress)

Manufactured in the United States of America

*McFarland & Company, Inc., Publishers
Box 611, Jefferson, North Carolina 28640
www.mcfarlandpub.com*

To Michael and our children

Table of Contents

Acknowledgments

A good part of this story has been with me for thirty years, from the day my friend the historian/biographer Blanche Wiesen Cook suggested I have a look at the Mary Emma Woolley Papers at the Mount Holyoke Archives. A doctoral dissertation evolved out of that first encounter; then, after a twelve-year interlude in which I put this work aside, I came back to it in September of 2004. Eight years later, with the completion of this book, I can say with certainty that this journey has been a true gift in many ways. Even at the most difficult junctures, when giving up the project seemed the sanest choice, there was always an agreeable, if somewhat peculiar, sense that I was in the company of extraordinary women, alive for me because they tell so much of the story themselves.

My deepest thanks extend to people whose help has spanned the thirty years. Bill Paquette encouraged the first step—the decision to enter the world of Stephen B. Oates through his seminar, "The Art and Technique of Biography," and his Amherst Creative Biography Group. This talented, insightful and witty group—Stephen Oates, Sandra Katz, Dominique Lloyd-Kimbrel, William Kimbrel, Helen Sheehy, Harriet Sigerman, and Will Ryan—has critiqued my work over many years.

Among the faculty whom I have had the good fortune of working with, I wish to thank William Kornegay, Phillip Eddy, Patricia Crosson and Joyce Avrech Berkman.

Archivists Patricia Albright and Elaine Trehub introduced me to the Mount Holyoke Archives. Patricia Albright's expertise and generosity with her time have made the archival work a pleasure.

In 2004, I resumed my research as a fellow at the Five College Women's Studies Research Center and embarked on a five-year research and writing project. I want to thank Amrita Basu and E. B. Lehman, and the "PAWGers." We shared our work while we were research associates and have continued to share our projects through the years. Thank you to Josna Rege, Sarah Doyle,

Danielle Bessett and Mary Elizabeth Strunk for the excellent early insights on how to organize this book. I owe a debt of gratitude to Sally Sutherland, my faculty partner during my year at the Research Center. In subsequent years both she and E. B. Lehman were very helpful in finding me work space on the Mount Holyoke campus, which permitted me to continue researching between 2004 and 2007. I want to thank Archivist Jennifer Gunther King for suggesting I apply for the LITS Scholar-in-Residence post at Mount Holyoke (2007–2008). I am indebted to her for helping to make that the turning point year in which I accomplished a great deal with the assistance of the excellent Autumn Winslow, a graduating senior with superb research and people skills who tracked down numerous sources for me throughout the year.

Joyce Avrech Berkman, whose knowledge and passion for history and belief in the importance of this work, deserves special recognition. At a crucial point, she read the entire manuscript, made helpful suggestions and offered to write the historiographical foreword. Joyce has been an invaluable mentor and friend.

In the course of writing this book, I have had many opportunities to talk about it with enthusiastically supportive family and friends—Kathryn Karusaitis Basham, Adrienne Markowitz, Ellen Epstein Levy, Leonard Berkman, Karen Smith, Bill Paquette, John Anzalotti, Gerald Markowitz, and Chris O'Carroll.

My daughter Ivy read parts of the manuscript, her critical skills and encouragement so helpful and appreciated. My husband Michael has read the manuscript in its several drafts, and I have had the best of times entertaining him with revelations from my research. His technical help in the final stages has been invaluable. My son-in-law, Thomas Ambrose, provided essential assistance in preparing the photographs for publication. To my wonderful family—Michael, Julian, Dylan Ann, Ivy, Thomas, Gregory, Patrycja and Kathryn—I love and thank you for all you do for me.

Foreword

Joyce Avrech Berkman

This work by Ann Karus Meeropol encompasses two stirring narratives and more. It is a heart-wrenching account of the manipulative selection of Roswell Gray Ham to the presidency of Mount Holyoke College in 1937. Her richly textured drama abounds in finely etched character profiles and myriad momentous choices and turning points. At the same time, it offers a fresh and probing new interpretation of Mount Holyoke president Mary Woolley, widely acclaimed for her intellectual acuity and administrative expertise, and whose presidency lasted thirty-six years. No less valuable than these two arresting contributions, we have in Meeropol's work a major contribution to historical scholarship on the situation of educated women during the 1930s, on dominant attitudes toward female leadership and careers outside the home, and on the health of feminism. Crucially, by providing ample evidence of the power of resurgent antifeminism to subvert efforts to select a female successor to Woolley, Meeropol's narrative challenges most scholars' claim of the feebleness by the late 1930s, if not demise, of feminist ideas and rhetoric.

Mining a recently opened treasure trove of documents related to the succession crisis, Meeropol radically reinterprets Woolley's final decade as president. She introduces us to the fiery articulate opponents of Ham's selection and to the resolute dissenters in the wake of his appointment. Indeed, the drive to pressure Ham to rethink his appointment and resign reflects a boldness and breadth of feminist values at odds with other scholars' prevailing historical narratives. Though organized post-suffrage grassroots feminism does not emerge until the 1960s, numerous women of the 1930s refused passive acceptance of Ham as the chosen president. They exercised their will, their minds and their eloquence to oppose and, later, reverse his appointment. College-educated, they came from various walks of life. Their resistance to a male president of Mount Holyoke reveals the presence of a brilliant and eloquent feminist outlook that echoed the rhetoric of the founders of women's colleges and anticipated the fervor and thought of late 1960s Second Wave feminism. In short, Meeropol's compelling research evidence counters scholars' predominantly bleak views of the trajectory of 1930s feminism through her detailing of the push-me pull-you dynamics of the backlash to women's leadership in higher education encountering women's feminist tenacity.

The battle over who would succeed President Mary Woolley unleashed a volley of powerful feelings both within and outside Mount Holyoke. It was no minor skirmish. Woolley, like other women's college pioneers such as M. Carey Thomas at Bryn Mawr and Caroline Hazard at Wellesley College, dedicated her life to preparing women to enter all careers and to become major players in national affairs. (The pioneer faculty represented the generation born in the 1860s and 1870s, commanding academic posts in the 1880s and 1890s and dominating women's colleges until the 1930s.) These path-breaking administrators and faculty of same-sex women's colleges responded to a situation of stark discrimination against academic women, who were barred from entry into the elite male colleges, few admitted into many graduate-level professional programs. Women were excluded from most faculty positions, all administrative posts in male colleges, and denied most administrative posts even in coeducational colleges and universities. These courageous women's college administrators wanted their leadership to set an example that would inspire their eager students. They believed that separate female communities provided essential grounding for the development of female leadership. These same-sex communities would empower young women to enter national affairs with confidence and with the knowledge and ability to transform society, politics and culture. Despite strenuous efforts among some college trustees and some alumnae at both Wellesley and Bryn Mawr to appoint a male president prior to the succession controversy at Mount Holyoke, Presidents Caroline Hazard and Carey Thomas were successful in their campaigns for a female successor.[1] They waged their campaigns before the backlash against separate women's colleges and feminist ambition gained fierce momentum. For them and for Woolley, the choice of a male president loomed as a grenade thrown at their many years of dedicated arduous effort. Ultimately, the significance of the Mount Holyoke succession conflict is the insight it provides to our understanding of the sturdiness of antifeminism and traditional gender and racial beliefs throughout the twentieth century. It also illuminates the resilient undercurrents of feminist ideas and activism that eventually gained ascendancy with Second Wave feminism in the later 1960s.

This work fills a lacuna in the historiography of women and feminism during the Depression. It questions reigning historical narratives and interpretations of women's thought and activity. If you were to look into assigned college textbook narratives of twentieth-century U.S. women for information about female leadership of same-sex women's colleges, indeed, even about women's higher education in general during the Depression, you would find scant information.[2] If you were to seek in these texts a substantial discussion of feminist ideas during the 1930s, you would come up empty-handed. In contrast, if you turn from textbooks to published works focused on women during the 1930s, you will discover this scholarship treats an array of important topics: the plight of working women and their families, women's occupational circumstances, debates over married women working outside the home, the ironic ways New Deal policies discriminated against women but opened avenues for a coterie of remarkable women appointed to New Deal positions, and coverage of a range of women active in a span of labor, political and cultural movements. Yet, although occasional mention is made of women's colleges as the spawning ground for the women who became key social reformers and later New Deal leaders, such as Frances Perkins or Molly Dewson, the women who led these colleges remain offstage, their educational philosophies and the structures of decision making within these institutions virtually ignored. Published in 1983 and continuing as one of the preeminent collection of essays, sixteen in all, on women during the interwar years, Lois Scharf and Joan M. Jensen's *Decades of Discontent: The Women's Movement, 1920–1940*[3] includes not one essay on women educational reformers and leaders. Since most studies of women during the Depression seek to understand their role in both national and international affairs, arenas that engaged Mary Woolley and other female college presidents, the gap in exposition and interpretation is all the more striking. Nor, tellingly, does any essay in the volume address feminist theorizing during the interwar decades.

You may think that surely these experiences of women in higher education and succession battles are treated in histories of women and education. Alas, while we have Barbara Miller Solomon's splendid study of undergraduate female experience and attitudes during the 1930s, including her analysis of controversial issues between students and faculty and administrators during that decade, as well as Patricia Ann Palmieri's thoughtful study of Wellesley faculty and Helen Lefkowitz Horowitz's compelling account of the way the architectural design of women's colleges reflected and reinforced the philosophy of same-sex college education for women, these scholars pay minimal attention to the struggle at Mount Holyoke or to the evolution during the thirties of the rhetoric of feminist philosophy that guided the vision and founding of women's colleges.[4] Other scholars have noted the paucity of studies of women's higher education during the 1930s.[5] The closest we come to a study that hones in on Mount Holyoke appears in a work on women's entrance into the professions from 1890 to 1940. Penina Migdal Glazer and Miriam Slater's

chapter "Professional Scholars in Isolated Splendor" presents cogently the erosion of Woolley's feminist ideals of a separate, same-sex female community of
highly trained rigorous faculty and students at Mount Holyoke. The authors
view the replacement of Woolley by Ham as symbolic of the end of the female
leadership and feminist ideology at Mount Holyoke and the triumph of con-
ventional concepts of womanhood.[6] Glazer and Slater, however, do not
acknowledge at all the forceful resistance to this shift to male leadership. We
lack a book for the 1930s comparable to Linda Eisenmann's *Higher Education
for Women in Postwar America, 1945–1965*.[7] We even lack a comprehensive
and comparative study for the post-suffrage era of the Seven Sisters, the
women's colleges that in 1926 began the Seven College Conference. Further,
we desperately need a study of college leaders that compares the Seven Sisters
with black women's colleges of the period where, strikingly, female leadership
was less contested.

In some respects, Susan Levine's close study of the American Association
of University Women during the interwar years is an exception to the gross
neglect of women educational leaders. Levine notes that during the mid-
thirties the AAUW fostered women's leadership in the public realm, including
that of higher education. Mary Woolley had been president of the AAUW
from 1927 to 1933. The AAUW's general director, Kathryn McHale, was her
fervent ally. Levine offers a brief discussion of the Mount Holyoke succession
struggle, declaring: "No episode more strongly rallied AAUW members in
their efforts to achieve recognition for qualified women than the fight that
followed the appointment of a man to succeed Mary Woolley as President of
Mount Holyoke."[8] Levine writes that many AAUW women took the trustees'
act "as a personal insult to their own accomplishments and to the contribution
women could make to society."[9] As they may well have known, Smith College
president William Allan Neilson, though a friend and admirer of Mary Woolley, recruited men for professorships and favored them for promotions, leaving
some academic departments without women.[10] AAUW leaders launched various campaigns to promote female college leadership but, evidently, as an
organization, separate from its individual members' decisions, refused to take
a position in the Mount Holyoke succession battle. After Ham was appointed
Mount Holyoke president, the AAUW shifted its focus to try to prevent further such calamities elsewhere.

We do have important biographies of individual pioneering women's college presidents. These studies address primarily the decades before the 1930s.
The successors to these presidents have not been subjects of biographies, and
since most successors were also female, despite some strong sentiment among
certain members of boards of trustees for a male president, scholarly discussion
of the succession question for each of these presidents is treated briefly and

carries less historical consequence. Biographies of other key figures involved with the selection of Woolley's successor bestow little insight. Quite shockingly, Kristin Downey in her recently published 2010 biography of Mount Holyoke alumna Frances Perkins, secretary of labor under the New Deal and a staunch ally of Mary Woolley, fails even to discuss Perkins' vigorous and sustained support for Woolley's demand for a female successor to the college's presidency. Downey faintly alludes to the succession battle within the context of a paragraph about Perkins' comfort with lesbian relationships, e.g., Jeannette Marks and Mary Woolley's nearly fifty years' partnership.[11] Although the first published biography of Perkins in 1976 by George Martin accords a chapter to Perkins' energetic support of a female president to succeed Woolley, Martin's discussion is fragmentary and limited by his lack of access to vital documents, particularly those of the board of trustees search committee, which Meeropol here exposes and explores. Martin, moreover, examines the succession issue in relation to Perkins' experience and neglects to place the conflict either within the complexities of Woolley's life or within women's and feminist history of the decade.

Since the defeat of efforts to sustain female leadership at Mount Holyoke was symptomatic of broader moves to deny women public leadership roles and represented a trend that continued until the 1970s, questions about historical patterns of change and continuity during the interwar years naturally come to the fore and are of paramount importance, deepening our comprehension of what Meeropol's splendid action-spiked narrative reveals. During the past several decades, historical scholarship on women and their potential for exercising power during the thirties has evolved from a largely negative view of women's status and the vitality of feminism to one that is far more mixed. Some of the most powerful evidence for the negative view appears from scholars who include positive evidence for women's achievements. None of these studies, however, consider feminist protest at Mount Holyoke in their measure of the vigor of feminism within the nation.

In his early 1970s groundbreaking study of twentieth-century women, William H. Chafe paints a bleak view of women's progress. He charts the decline of career opportunities for women, the tide of antifeminist opposition to women's careers outside the home and internal divisions within the women's movement, primarily over the Equal Rights Amendment and Protective Legislation. Chafe provides an impressive string of statistics that underscores the declining percentage of women gaining doctorates and even holding professorships and becoming chairs of departments in women's colleges. For the first time, female faculty in same-sex colleges faced growing competition from men, though, of course, women could not comparably compete for positions in men's colleges. With a few exceptions, women's colleges no less than coeducational institutions failed to support policies that would enable women to combine motherhood and a career.[12] According to Chafe, feminism "had reached a nadir. Beset by controversy, weakened by a lack of widespread support, and torn by internecine warfare, it had ceased to exist as a powerful force in American society."[13] Susan Becker, historian of the Equal Rights Amendment, agrees, claiming the women's movement by the end of the 1930s was at a "total impasse."[14] Scharf and Jensen, in the early 1980s, likewise conclude that the women's movement was faltering. The Depression, they declare, had "set the motion in reverse ... political careers like other full time careers remained socially unacceptable in a period when women might have challenged male political hegemony."[15] Viewing multiple decades from 1920 to 1970, Lynn D. Gordon writes: "The percentage of women students in colleges, graduate and professional schools and women practitioners in medicine, law, and academia declined or increased very modestly."[16]

Scholars of women during the Depression amass many reasons for the reversal in feminist progress. Analyzing antifeminist policies and attitudes and the decline in appeal of same-sex institutions and networks, they highlight mounting eugenics anxieties about white race suicide, a more militant homophobia, the widespread backlash toward women's suffrage victory, fears of curbs on white male privilege in all realms and, understandably, social reformers' and political activists' preoccupation with economic recovery and the urgency of mobilizing against fascism. Susan Ware reminds us: "So much of the country's attention was focused on the problems of the Depression that women's issues, which were perceived as having little relation to the broader problems of the Depression, were ignored."[17] Yet Ware insists in her brief account of the succession crisis at Mount Holyoke that the choice of Ham was less the result of the Depression than of "changing evaluations of the role that a women's college should play in the modern world."[18] Her comment refers to the fate of same-sex institutions.

Scholars who lament the erosion of feminist values and rhetoric highlight the decline in commitment to same-sex networks and institutions among women themselves, a commitment that had been essential to female power in a world that still discriminated against women and upheld gender stereotypes. Susan Ware's concern over the ebbing of separatism concurs with Estelle Freedman's prior study of the history of female separatist organizations, institutions and networks. Freedman argues that post-suffrage women, in integrating into male-controlled social reform organizations rather than sustaining same-sex associations, lost hold of their feminist values.[19] Ware, as had previous scholars, set forth the preoccupation of college women with heterosexual and personal freedoms along with the increasing marginalization of women who chose careers over marriage and lived in partnership with other women. Unlike college women of earlier decades, young women in the 1930s viewed marriage and raising families as their supreme life mission. Faculty and administrators at women's colleges felt they had become "out of step with society."[20] Helen Lefkowitz Horowitz, in her account of this generational divide, notes, among other disturbing developments, that students became increasingly suspicious of the homosocial and professionally focused lives of female faculty and few viewed them as models for themselves.[21]

A powerful chorus of scholars chimes in on the 1930s decline of the women's movement. Alice Kessler-Harris, in her brilliant study of women and men's quest for economic citizenship during the twentieth century, finds no feminist opposition to the sexist features of the Social Security Act of 1935 and its 1939 amendments.[22] Kessler-Harris argues that only a minority of women pressed for women's equal right to work, and the majority of female social reformers assumed men's economic privilege and a gendered division of labor.[23] In a provocative explanation for the waning of the women's movement, Nancy F. Cott cites Mary Beard's perspective that the curriculum of women's higher education, which was based on the traditional male model, had "deepened the intellectual cowardice of women, making them into spokeswomen for institutional and cultural priorities defined by men."[24] Cott elaborates that Beard's perspective was upheld by two interwar female psychiatrists, Beatrice Hinkle and Olga Knopf. Cott, however, unlike Freedman and Ware, views the source of women's losses in academic and professional spheres as having less to do with women's entry into masculine spheres and mixed-sex associations than with the rise of an individualist meritocracy that inherently serves male privilege far more than women's interests. A fundamental tension prevailed between women professionals' senses of themselves as women and as professionals. The late nineteenth-century professional woman who identified as a woman's rights advocate had given way to twentieth-century professional women, who, believing barriers to their entrance and advancement largely overcome, sought acceptance from their male counterparts and believed a sex-neutral meritocracy held sway. This individualist ethos, not only among educated women, subverted myriad progressive movements for social change. Citing a Barnard-launched survey that unleashed a flood of angry complaints about widespread discrimination against academic women in hiring, promotions, pay, fellowships, and research assistantships, Cott underscores the wobbly state of post-suffrage feminism, as women responded to discrimination and exclusion not through collective feminist protest actions but only through redoubling their individual effort.[25] Much of Cott's analysis of feminism of the interwar years centers on the difficulty for women of saying "we," articulating a gender consciousness and solidarity. Besides the obvious issue of the diversity of women within a plethora of social categories—e.g., class, race, ethnicity, sexuality—as well as profoundly differing definitions of gender equality, the American cult of hyper-individualism played a decisive role in forming 1930s women's resistance to feminism. No wonder, then, that many prominent women reformers of that time felt uneasy with the label "feminist."[26]

Scholars who hold a more optimistic interpretation of the 1930s and shy away from declaring that the 1930s marks the death knell of feminism can muster few women leaders who, like Woolley, publicly and eloquently artic- ulated feminist convictions. Even Ware notes that women's influence within the New Deal reached its zenith in 1936. She bemoans that during FDR's sec- ond term, women's leadership and influence diminished.[27] She discerns no articulate feminist resistance to sex discrimination in New Deal policies or in society at large.[28] Correspondingly, she argues,

> women's participation in government declined because of the failure of their feminist vision...Feminists in the 1930s rarely concentrated their attention on broad questions of women's emancipation or proposed radical restructures of the American economic and social structure. Instead, feminism turned inward in the 1930s.[29]

The guiding lights of feminist thought, Charlotte Perkins Gilman and other turn-of-the-century feminist theorists who developed persuasive analyses of the sex/gender system, had no progeny. As a result, according to Sandra F. VanBurkleo, feminists lacked not only organizational might but also the "ide- ological power" to oppose conservative forces intent on strengthening tradi- tional family values and organization.[30] Nancy Woloch, in her textbook summary, concludes: "Women's activism in politics and government in the New Deal was more a last grasp of progressive energy than an omen of future trends.... By the late 1930s, all varieties of postsuffrage feminism declined."[31] Stephanie Coontz's recently published study for the general reading public repeats the above, concluding that the women's movement had "lost its momentum ... lost its public face."[32]

Despite the weight of so much disturbing evidence of women's losses, most scholars of feminism during the 1930s also include evidence of advances. The mid- to late 1980s scholarship of Nancy Cott and particularly Susan Ware introduce a more mixed picture, indicating numerous examples of female enter- prise and accomplishment and of female refusal to step away from careers as they protest against unequal rewards in the marketplace. Cott emphasizes the vigor of women's organizational activity manifest in the proliferation of groups across a political spectrum from the Daughters of the American Revolution to the Association of Southern Women for the Prevention of Lynching to the National Conference on the Cause and Cure of War. A prodigious variety of women's professional organizations formed as well. Even if most of these women lacked a feminist consciousness and a minority of these associations were decidedly antifeminist, members proudly viewed themselves at last as voters, as first-class citizens. Ware disputes claims that professional women's numbers during the Depression plunged. She argues that the extent of decline varied with profession and, despite increasing discrimination and competition for jobs, women did not experience a "drastic decline" in professional positions, indeed sustaining strength in many of them. Although she admits various areas of decline, women, she argues, sustained strength in a number of professions.[33] Although feminism, Ware acknowledges, was forced on the defensive in the 1930s,[34] she cautions it remained alive through the efforts of individual women and various women's organizations.[35] The decade, she deems, "produced significant feminist accomplishments.... Feminism did survive ... in a healthier state than is usually recognized."[36] In her description of the seventy distinguished women invited to the Speakers Table at the 1940 banquet sponsored by the women's division of the Democratic National Committee, Ware points to suffragist captain Carrie Chapman Catt's hailing Mary Woolley as a "stateswoman."[37] Though acknowledging a decline in the number of women elected to public office from the 1920s to the 1930s, Ware provides a litany of the many women appointed to key positions in government after the election of Franklin D. Roosevelt. She published a probing biography of one of these women, Molly Dewson, head of the Women's Division of the Democratic National Committee.

Sherna Berger Gluck cites her oral histories to document that at least an undercurrent of feminism persisted.[38] A similar mixed conclusion characterizes Estelle Freedman's more recent scholarship. While in her first writings during the 1970s on female separatist networks and institutions Freedman laments the decline in separatism, by the mid–1990s she reaches a somewhat less pessimistic conclusion about the disappearance of these female associations.[39] Although she finds that during the 1920s and even more during the Depression men came increasingly to dominate formerly women's spheres of labor, such as professional social work, female separate reform networks and organizations survived, which "complicates and challenges a monolithic interpretation of the decline of women's moral and political authority after the suffrage victory."[40] Susan Levine's study of the American Association of University Women, mentioned earlier, certainly numbers among the publications that emphasize the persistence of feminist goals.

Synthesizing much of the scholarship on the general history of women's gains and losses as well as the state of feminism and antifeminism in the United States, Kristin Celello concludes that feminism waned in the thirties, but she also holds that "feminists found a place not only in the upper echelons of the federal government, but also in progressive organizations, such as the National Consumers' League."[41] She further maintains that feminist values were prevalent among many working-class women. Cott's conclusion to her study of feminism and professional women's lives epitomizes the precarious balance beam on which current scholars try to secure an interpretive footing: "The trend toward individual accomplishments unrelated to womanhood as such or to gender identity might be read to measure the success of feminism's aims—or the exhaustion of its spirit. Each reading has its truth. That was the dilemma of twentieth-century feminism, to require gender consciousness for its basis while intending to explode gender prescriptions."[42]

"Exhaustion" of spirit is certainly not the story that Meeropol offers us. To be sure, this book makes no bones about the insufficient strength of the forces to stop Ham from becoming president and after his selection to press for his immediate retirement. All the negative influences that scholars rally to explain feminism's flaccid condition in the thirties certainly help us understand the thinking of key players in Meeropol's narrative. Yet this work unearths a stubborn feminist belief system that fueled resistance and laid the groundwork for a future recovery of female leadership at Mount Holyoke and beyond.

Joyce Avrech Berkman is a professor of history and women's studies at the University of Massachusetts, Amherst. She has received the UMASS Distinguished Teacher Award and the UMASS Award for Distinguished Outreach in Scholarship.

Prologue

"With conviction of sin, I am invading what I hope is your vacation with a business matter! It is only because I feel so strongly on the question that I disregard my conscience." So began the letter Mary Emma Woolley wrote to every member of the board of trustees of Mount Holyoke College on July 1, 1935. "The choice of my successor," she continued, "is one of deep importance to me, as you will realize. I hardly need to add that such a feeling is inevitable after giving half of one's life to a work. The choice of a woman for the post seems to me most important from every point of view. I should feel that the celebration of the Centennial of Mary Lyon's effort to open opportunities to women as human beings on an equal basis with men would better be omitted, if a part of that celebration is the installation of a man as President of Mount Holyoke."

Woolley, the venerable seventy-two-year-old president of Mount Holyoke College, was two years away from her retirement in 1937, the year of the college's centennial celebration, and a committee of the board of trustees was already at work on the presidential search. Woolley, who had led the college since 1901, had begun to submit names of accomplished women as potential candidates. There was unsettling talk among board members about the importance of approaching the "question of sex" with an open mind, and it was a well-known fact that several trustees were in favor of hiring a man. However, the search committee had a clear mandate from the full board to find a "suitable woman" or be prepared to explain why it was unable to do so. That April, Kathryn McHale, the executive director of the American Association of University Women, shared with Woolley information that she had just received—confirmation that the succession committee was actively pursuing male candidates.

McHale's news and what Woolley would learn in subsequent months compelled her to write the letter. The presidential search committee appeared to be straying from their mandate. Woolley argued in her letter to the trustees

11

that the issue went well beyond Mount Holyoke: "All over the country, men and women ... are taking a keen interest in this matter and realize that Mount Holyoke's action would count for or against the progress of women more than the action of any other college possibly could. I cannot over-estimate the intensity of the feeling which has already been expressed along this line." The committee had close to two years to find a suitable woman candidate. The public search had already involved the pursuit of two well-qualified women, both endorsed by Woolley. She wanted assurance that the search committee would stay the course and select a woman to succeed her.

On May 18, 1936, ten months after Woolley sent the letter, board president Alva Morrison informed her that in nineteen days, on June 6, the board's nine-member search committee would be recommending the appointment of Roswell Gray Ham to the presidency of Mount Holyoke. Morrison added that the committee had already offered the position to Ham and that he had accepted. Woolley might well have responded in astonishment, "Who?" During the previous year, Ham's name had never appeared on the confidential working list of seventy-plus potential candidates, though more qualified men had. A former officer in the United States Marines, Ham was currently an associate professor of English literature at Yale University. He had published little and could claim no significant administrative experience in academia. One month earlier, he had been a widower with two young sons, but he had remedied this disadvantaged status by marrying into a socially prominent New Haven, Connecticut, family. Although the new Mrs. Ham lacked a college education, she possessed charm and connections, two qualities that, for some members of the committee, considerably enhanced Ham's appeal and made it easy to overlook his meager qualifications.

In a recommendation for Ham sent to Morrison, Yale University's provost had expressed the view that in sending Ham off to Mount Holyoke, "Yale was fulfilling a duty to American education which has become traditional ... that of preparing first-rate young men for our educational responsibilities and giving other educational institutions the benefit." Ham was the second Yale professor in six months to assume the presidency of a major college, the fourth in seven years, although his qualifications paled in the company of Robert Maynard Hutchins, Robert E. Doherty and Alan Chester Valentine.

What should have been—what was expected to be—a smooth and dignified transition within an academic sisterhood had been inverted. A pastoral had changed suddenly into a melodrama and, from several perspectives, tragedy was in the wings. One woman's founding dream and another's decades of extraordinary accomplishment should not have come to such an impasse. And yet, somehow, they had.

Introduction

The official story of the 1937 presidential succession at Mount Holyoke College in which Mary Emma Woolley was succeeded by Roswell Gray Ham acknowledges some opposition surrounding his selection but also asserts that the college community "got over it" and "settled down to cope with the perennial issues of running a college."[1] Ham's presidency constituted a break in a hundred-year tradition of female leadership at the college, and forty-one years would pass before a woman again assumed the presidency. Among those who are aware of this piece of the college's history, the current opinion at the college appears to be that Ham's election represented a power grab by a group of men on the board of trustees who were determined to create a male presidency.

Since journalism is the first draft of history and the *New York Times* has been considered the newspaper of record, it is instructive to consider the *Times'* view of the controversy. Woolley's obituary, published on September 6, 1947, presented the facts as follows:

> Miss Woolley's leaving Mount Holyoke College in June 1937 was not the customary academic farewell to a retiring president. The year before, the Committee of Nine Trustees chose as Dr. Woolley's successor the college's first male president, Dr. Roswell Gray Ham of Yale. Many among the faculty and alumnae were shocked at what they regarded as a terrible break with tradition. A Committee of 100 investigated the appointment and mailed 8400 pamphlets containing their findings to graduates. The Committee charged that the trustees' Committee rejected 70 women for the post and "railroaded" the appointment of Dr. Ham. Charges and countercharges flew for months. Dr. Woolley expressed the view that so radical a change in policy should not have been taken without a consultation with the full faculty and alumnae. She explained her point of view was "not extremely feminist" and that it involved a principle not a prejudice.

The obituary credited Woolley with

> transform[ing Mount Holyoke] in many respects.... In the days when higher education was still unpopular she took that small college scarcely out of its seminary

13

status and brought it up ... to the front rank. She doubled the ... student body, almost quadrupled the faculty, and increased the endowment and equipment to almost ten million dollars. All this achieved without fuss but with infinite tact and labor.[2]

The *Times* also mentioned that, after 1937, Woolley never again set foot on the Mount Holyoke campus.

Former labor secretary Frances Perkins (a Mount Holyoke alumna and member of the board of trustees in 1936 and 1937) said about Woolley: "She was a great woman, perhaps the most influential woman in the world during her period of activity—her influence... always... for establishing the principles of right as a guidepost for the world." Perkins lamented at the time that there was no public opportunity for "recollection, appreciation, and dedication both to her [Woolley] as a human soul and to the causes to which she gave her life work."[3] Such an event would never take place.

Fifty-two years later, in 1999, a wealth of college archival material about the presidential succession fight was made available to researchers. The documents date from 1933 to 1937 and consist primarily of the records of the presidential search committee created by the board of trustees.[4] Morrison, president of the board from 1934 to 1941, gave the papers to the college in 1958, at the end of Ham's twenty-year presidency. Richard Glenn Gettell, Mount Holyoke's president at the time, decided to sequester the material, presumably until those individuals involved with the search committee would most likely be dead. The papers were secured in a vault in the college library until 1968, when renovations forced their removal. They were returned to the president's office and remained there until 1974, when the college hired its first archivist, whereupon they found a home in the College Archives.[5]

The material contained in these records—correspondence, petitions, questionnaires, surveys, lists, clippings, memoranda, notes, press releases, flyers, minutes of closed meetings, reports, articles and speeches—allows for a revealing and nuanced understanding of what actually transpired during the succession fight. The battle reached well beyond the Mount Holyoke community, provoking disbelief, outrage, frustration and a desire to fight for what many believed were the true issues at stake, issues of principle not prejudice, in Woolley's words. It is clear that Woolley and her allies understood the dangers for women's opportunities nationwide as well as internationally. Ham's appointment was merely an example, a particularly dramatic one, of dangerous trends. Woolley and her allies decried the loss for women of this singular opportunity to exercise leadership at the head of one of the nation's most prestigious women's colleges. The argument "best person for the job, irrespective of sex," in the context of the 1930s, was naïve at best, manipulative at worst. A member of the British Association of University Women wrote to the Mount Holyoke board chairman, urging him not to dismiss as exaggeration a comparison of Mount Holyoke's action to the growing intolerance in Europe:

> Fascist dictators early disbanded all independent women's organizations, and discouraged or prohibited the higher education of women. Such crushing out of special groups is contrary to the traditions of America. Yet I submit to you, that the break in the Mt. Holyoke tradition is an action along the lines of the movement in Europe, in that it cuts off one great opportunity for leadership of women by a woman with all that this means to the balance of American thought.[6]

Most American feminists linked democracy with opportunities for women but also recognized the increasing negative effects upon women of the political and economic changes taking place in the United States. No wonder, then, that the Mount Holyoke decision stimulated a spirited and angry response from women and men who saw sex discrimination as a given and who believed in the necessity of "holding the line" against further erosion of leadership opportunity for women. Woolley had achieved the highest position in the separate world of women's colleges, but she could not ensure that position for future generations.

Separatism, the education of women in women's colleges, as a strategic defense against discrimination was increasingly embattled in the 1930s. At Mount Holyoke, the fight that was waged, first to ensure that a woman was selected for the presidency and then, when that battle was lost, to attempt to have the offer rescinded, is a story that exemplifies the times. The attitudes and actions of those involved on both sides of the issue—the board of trustees, the faculty, the alumnae, the students, as well as the feminists at the AAUW and abroad—reveal both how much and how little they understood of the forces at work in the institutions within which they lived.

This story cannot be confined to the events of 1933–1937, dramatic as they are. To understand the context of the struggle at Mount Holyoke, it is essential to understand what the college had become by 1933. How the college achieved its status as an elite liberal arts institution is bound up entirely in the work of the architect of this achievement, President Woolley. Who was Mary Emma Woolley? This book begins with a brief narrative of Woolley's life leading up to her appointment as president of the college in 1901. It then takes up the story of how Woolley, together with a dedicated faculty, created the Mount Holyoke of 1933. Chapters 3 through 6 tell the story of the presidential search, the appointment of Ham, and the fight that ensued. The final chapter tells the story of Mount Holyoke's centennial celebration in May of 1937 after all efforts to reverse the Ham appointment had proven futile. The two-day celebration gave Woolley and her allies a dramatic forum for the "last word." No doubt, they had lost the fight, but they proved unbowed in defeat. The book concludes with an epilogue that reveals both predicted and unanticipated changes put in place by the Ham administration during the years after 1937.

CHAPTER 1

"Who Was the First Woman? ... Miss Woolley!"

—The Brunonian, Brown University

At the age of seventy-seven, two years after her retirement from Mount Holyoke College's presidency, Mary Emma Woolley began to write her life story at the urging of her partner, Jeannette Augustus Marks. Marks believed that Woolley had an obligation to share her exemplary life with other women. She also wanted Woolley to tell the story of the presidential succession fight. For five years in the summer months between 1939 and 1943, Woolley sat at her desk at Fleur de Lys, Marks' family home on Lake Champlain, and dutifully tackled the large brown envelopes filled with letterhead identifying her as president or chairman of numerous organizations. These surplus papers now served as scrap for her drafts. Woolley worked in fits and starts, writing in a bold, open script that filled a page with a handful of words and producing approximately twenty pages by the end of each summer. Like many of the accomplished women of her time, Woolley explained away her eventful life with stories of accidental good fortune and fated choices. "I feel somewhat guilty as I look back," she wrote, "opportunities seemed to come my way and I took advantage of them."[1]

When Woolley finally abandoned the work, she had written seventy-five pages and ended her story in 1900, the year before she assumed the presidency of Mount Holyoke. She titled the manuscript "The History of My Life!" with good humor and a measure of self-mockery. She had recounted nothing of her long, extraordinary tenure at Mount Holyoke, nothing of her

17

extensive national and international work during and following her years as president of the college and not a word about her fifty-year relationship with Marks. These tasks were left for others. This book begins where she left off.

On the morning of December 31, 1900, Woolley woke up in her family home in Pawtucket, Rhode Island, where she and Marks had spent the Christmas holidays. Woolley dressed in a stylish, fitted suit and her white traveling gloves and soon boarded a morning train bound for South Hadley, Massachusetts. Before she left, she placed a note on the dresser in her bedroom for Marks to read when she awoke. It read, in part:

> You can help me to be brave as no other human love can.... Pray for me that I may be strong and wise and brave—God will help me in our work, I know, and I feel that He will soon open the way for us to be together. How happy we should be, beginning the New Year and the new Century together.[2]

About to become the president of Mount Holyoke College, Woolley, at thirty-seven, would be the youngest college president currently in office in the United States. Her official inauguration, a large ceremonial affair, would occur four and a half months later, in May to, it was hoped, catch a mild, sunny day. The tradition of simple, modest ceremony was gone forever as Mount Holyoke succumbed to what Woolley would jokingly refer to as the epidemic of the "new president bacillus." In the previous two years, Yale and Brown universities and Amherst and Wellesley colleges had each held lavish inaugurations. The trustees at Mount Holyoke wanted to claim a place among these elite liberal arts institutions. What better way to introduce their smart, accomplished, attractive new president.

Woolley's selection had not been easily won. In the initial stages of the board's search, a vocal faction had argued that the appointment of a man would finally put an end to a perceived inferior tradition of female leadership. Then, Woolley was a "woman without Mount Holyoke traditions,"[3] a worry for those who feared the loss of the seminary culture. Woolley was an outsider, but her empathy for the college's ideals was genuine. She had accepted the presidency, she said, "after earnest and prayerful consideration, because it seems to me this is the work which God calls me to do."[4] The majority had prevailed. Efforts were already under way "to end the longstanding policy of inbreeding" at the college, and several "frisky" young graduates of Wellesley, Oberlin, Smith and the Harvard Annex were joining the faculty.[5] Mount Holyoke warmed slowly to newcomers. Woolley described to Marks how lonely and homesick she felt during that first week at the college; although the accommodations were pleasant enough, a sunny, spacious set of rooms on the first floor of a college building, she was living in a student dormitory.[6] "I must smile and keep a brave front to the world, this little world, which, I can feel, is watching every mood!"[7]

By the time the gala inaugural arrived, Woolley had succeeded in creating a teaching position in the English department for Marks, who, despite uneasiness about how she would be received, agreed to come.[8] She moved into a suite of rooms three floors above Woolley's, a less than satisfactory arrangement, since the students observed their interactions with great interest.[9] Marks would miss the inauguration because it coincided with her graduation from Wellesley,[10] but with or without her presence, the event could not have been more celebratory. An audience of more than one thousand guests greeted Woolley with jubilant applause when she took the podium. Neither did the weather disappoint. A reporter for the *Springfield Republican* described the day as one of "almost feminine beauty, of moist blue skies with piles of clouds."[11] As if she were speaking to each person individually, her voice confident and embracing, Woolley proclaimed, "The days were over when girls ... were forced to satisfy their intellectual cravings by sitting on the door-steps of the school-house to hear their brothers recite.... Why had women not distinguished themselves in scholarship?" Very simply, it was lack of education and opportunity that held women back. The change that was coming, she said, was so great that one couldn't "predict what [the century] may bring forth."[12] There would no longer be any boundaries that limited what a woman with a trained mind might do. "Perhaps ability in leadership and organization has been more peculiarly the heritage of men, but now the colleges will instruct girls in subjects like mathematics and logic so that they too will develop the power of controlling circumstances rather than of being controlled by them."[13] Feminine characteristics like intuition and insight should never be lost, but they will no longer be subject to prevailing opinion that they are inferior substitutes for the ability to reason. "The sensitiveness to conditions, the ability to feel what one cannot explain by logical processes," will be "entirely freed from the obloquy which now rest upon [them]."[14]

Woolley well knew that there were skeptics in the audience. The three male speakers who followed her ignored what she said and focused on their own issues. They cautioned the women's colleges to keep their enrollments small and to pay especially close attention to what the young women in their charge studied. Amherst College president the Rev. George Harris advised, "Literature, modern languages, music and art should have the right of way rather than mathematics, sciences, economics, and—may I say it?— the ancient languages."[15] Brown University president William Faunce reassured the audience and himself that there was little reason to fear what growth and success at Mount Holyoke might bring. Mount Holyoke had always espoused an ideal that was "frankly feminine" in its commitment to

train women for service in society.[16] He himself could never promote an education that would "destroy the fundamental antithesis of society" so that "all
manly men and womanly women would merge into "a mass of sexless human
beings."[17] Woolley had known these men since her childhood, and her relationship with them was cordial. Years of experience had taught her when to
turn a deaf ear. There were certainly more dangerously influential adversaries
who would deny women, in Woolley's words, "the power of controlling circumstances."

G. Stanley Hall, president of nearby Clark University,[18] was predicting
catastrophe for any young women under the influence of women presidents.
In Hall's view, Woolley was one of a small group of "splendid spinster presidents," of "maidenly preceptresses," who imposed a "denatured intellectual reg-
imen" on the young women in their charge. These women presidents
calculatingly stripped away belief in marriage and family and forced students
to take refuge in "mentality" and career planning, the only consolations left
to them. Hall accused these women of "flagrantly disregard[ing] the grave
dangers of psycho-physic deterioration." When the young women who were
educated in this fashion ultimately realized how "bankrupt, and soul hungry,
and starving" they were, it would be too late. They would likely "throw themselves into some ... highly saturated orthodoxy, swaying over perhaps from
extreme radicalism to Catholicism ... or coquetting with dangerous theories
of social or even family reform, in order to escape from the creeping palsy of
the heart." Hall's solution was simple. Remove all women presidents and
replace them with men. Under male leadership, the women's colleges could
no longer "abjectly" follow "the fashions taken over from men's colleges." The
goal to develop self-determination among women would vanish.[19]

Woolley's commitment to self-determination was decidedly the major
reason for her decision to accept the offer of Mount Holyoke's presidency over
the deanship of Pembroke College at Brown University. She knew how limited
decision-making capabilities would be at Brown. Her experience at Wellesley
College confirmed for her that a true liberal arts education was far more likely
to occur in independent women's colleges where there was opportunity for
"initiative and wholesome freedom" and where utilitarian programs and early
specialization were held at bay.[20]

When the last of the men had spoken, Woolley's father, the Rev. Joseph
Judah (J. J.) Woolley, came forward to give the benediction and deliver the
verse with great feeling: "O the depth of the riches of the wisdom and the
knowledge of God! Unsearchable are His judgments, and His ways past tracing
out!"[21] A reporter observed that "it was a most touching incident.... As he
stood there by the side of his beautiful daughter, he evidently felt that the
benediction had already fallen on himself beyond all measure."[22] It was no

accident that the Reverend Woolley was at his daughter's side at such a propitious occasion. J. J. Woolley had guided with a decisive hand all of his eldest child's education.

Woolley's Early Years

In her effort to write about her life, Woolley wrote with great feeling about her childhood: "If I dwell overlong, ... my excuse must be my pleasure in re-living those days, spent in the happiest of homes."[23] In truth, her childhood was marked by disruptions, conflict and turmoil, all originating in her father's life and career as a minister. When she recalled "home" as "heaven on earth, a place where strife was shut out—and love was shut in,"[24] Woolley was certainly thinking of the genteel home that her maternal grandfather built in South Norwalk and where her mother, Mary Augusta (Ferris) Woolley, gave birth to each of her four children over a period of fifteen years.

Woolley's mother had been living a quiet life in Norwalk when she first met J. J. Woolley in 1858. He had come with his wife, Mary Emma, to assist the pastor of the Ferris family's church. Within three years, his wife became ill and died and J. J. and Mary Augusta were engaged. When Woolley enlisted as a chaplain in the army in 1861, the day President Lincoln called for volunteers, they married half an hour before his departure. Mary Augusta's mother wrote to her own father later that day: "You see there was no time to invite any one or make any wedding. I hope it may all be for the best."[25] Her intuition was correct if she sensed that her daughter's life would be out of the ordinary. J. J. was a restless man driven by convictions and enthusiasms that took over his life and the lives of his family.

He was born on September 17, 1832, one of eight children, in Bridgeport, Connecticut, a city rapidly growing into an industrial center with mushrooming neighborhoods of culturally diverse immigrants. J. J. left school at sixteen, eager for more freedom and less drudgery, and in his late teens experienced a religious conversion. Too impatient for formal theological study, he prepared for a preaching license under the tutelage of a minister and was ordained in 1858 in the Methodist Episcopal faith. He was well suited to the preaching style of the early Methodist itinerants who "went everywhere preaching the Word,"[26] but J. J. was also inclined to marry and raise a family. The Civil War further shaped his ministerial life. His direct experience was brief,[27] but it instilled in him a deep enmity against the senseless waste of war.

When he accepted an invitation to be the "settled pastor" at the Center Congregational Church in Meriden, Connecticut,[28] he switched denominations easily, since he espoused a belief in broad Christian faith that encompassed all sects.[29] The congregation built a comfortable home for the growing Woolley family. When Mary Emma or "May" (named after J. J.'s first wife) reached five years of age, J. J. persuaded a young widow to teach a group of children in the basement of the church. May was a smart and sturdy child who enjoyed books and rough-and-tumble games with her younger brother. A young girlfriend admonished her years later, "I used to try and train your hats and you used to pull them to bits."[30] May had inherited her mother's warm brown eyes and dark hair, but she most resembled her father—with his strong facial features and clear, dark complexion. J. J. cut an imposing figure in his long, double-breasted Prince Albert coat, a trimmed full beard framing his expressive face. May would accompany him as he strode the streets of Meriden, stopping to chat with the people he passed. She was already emulating his easy, interested engagement in the people and world around him.

J. J.'s sense of godliness did not preclude enjoying himself. A skilled and enthusiastic sailor and horseman, he had a special passion for cart racing with newly harnessed colts. Woolley remembered her mother telling her that J. J. did "not know what fear is."[31] May would later describe his seeming recklessness as a form of courage and a sign of his liberality. He always seemed to give "out of proportion to his means, as we see it, perhaps not as God sees it."[32] Religion infused daily home life. Dinnertime was an opportunity for animated and friendly discussion among guests and the family. May recalled: "[N]ever ... did we all hold the same point of view on a political question."[33]

In 1871, May celebrated her eighth birthday, her father his thirty-ninth, and the gentle years in Meriden came to an abrupt end. J. J., looking for a change, had accepted the pastorate of the Pawtucket Congregational Church with little or no hesitation despite the challenges and uncertainties that lay ahead. There was no provision for a home for the Woolley family (the retiring pastor and his family were remaining in the pastorate), nor was there provision for house rent. The Woolleys took up residence in the Pawtucket Hotel, a boardinghouse located at the bottom of Quality Hill, where they would live for three years. Pawtucket Congregational Church stood near the top of the hill, surrounded by many of the grand homes of the wealthy and influential members of the congregation. Boardinghouse life was a challenge for their mother, but May and her brother thrived in its unique aspects. With their arrival, there were six children living in the hotel. Older, permanent boarders welcomed them, and the Woolley children were free to visit these new friends who formed a large, extended family, one that celebrated special occasions together and exchanged birthday and holiday gifts.[34] May was developing the self-confidence and independence during these formative years that would enable her to take bold steps throughout her life.

I have borne insults and slights ... the dagger has been put to the handle into my breast and for more than two years I have buttoned my coat over it. [Reverend J. J. Woolley][35]

J. J. Woolley took on his new life with characteristic energy. Pawtucket was a rapidly growing city like Meriden but twice the size. He soon antagonized the conservative, industrial leaders of the city who were in control of his new church. These men needed the labor that the immigrants provided, but they also feared "foreign" tendencies—socialist and anarchist leanings among the Germans, dangerous superstitions among the "Romanish" Irish and French-Canadians. J. J. shared none of these fears. On the contrary, he spent much of his time visiting in the immigrant neighborhoods, often taking May and her brother along. "Father Woolley," as he was affectionately called, helped organize the Pawtucket Dispensary, a much-needed charity that offered medical care to the poor and indigent sick. When he began to invite the workers and their families to his church's Sunday school and to his sermons on Sundays, several of them ventured to come. J. J. was blurring boundaries in a dangerous way. The visitors sat in unoccupied pews, but these pews belonged by way of rent to families who were required to go through a recently tightened and restrictive process of application for church membership.

In the pulpit, J. J. interpreted "the indications of Providence" in a way that increasingly offended the church conservatives. His sermons stressed personal accountability and social responsibility. May described him as "a sort of father confessor for many people ... he was the friend of more people, of all sorts and conditions, than any one I have ever known."[36] As chairman of the standing committee to review applicants for admission to the church, J. J. proposed that all members, both male and female, be allowed to vote. When the committee voted seventeen to ten to extend the vote to women, all semblance of unity and cooperation evaporated. A number of influential members of the congregation began a campaign for his dismissal as pastor. J. J. was accused of sanctioning "dangerous precedent," of subverting "good order" and destroying the "best interests of the church."[37] Suppressed grievances surfaced and the congregation was divided. J. J. had many strong defenders so that, despite two separate efforts to resign in 1881, the congregation voted each time to reject his resignation.[38]

Torn apart by the loyalty he felt toward his defenders and anger toward his detractors, J. J. wrote in his journal:

> I am moved by deep love for this church ... and by an earnest desire to preserve it from ruin and destruction at the hands of these men and those in league with them.... I have taken all possible steps ... to escape from this trouble.... I have borne insults and slights ... the dagger has been put to the handle into my breast and for more than two years I have buttoned my coat over it.[39]

He made one last attempt at reconciliation at the church's annual meeting in January of 1882,[40] but it ended in acrimony. He proffered charges against his attackers and a trial was set, but he quickly changed his mind and submitted his third and final letter of resignation. The congregation accepted but passed a resolution recommending that the church membership engage in critical self-examination.[41] Worn out by the years of conflict and in a state of nervous exhaustion, J. J. left for Europe with a church companion and traveled for several months.[42]

Mary Augusta took their three children home to South Norwalk. She had suffered a great deal during the eleven years in Pawtucket. Her third child, a daughter named Gracie, died in her first year of life, after which Mary Augusta sank into a depression that did not lift until the birth in 1878 of her fourth and last child, Frank. May took on her mother's responsibilities at the church until 1879, when Mary Augusta was well enough to resume her duties during the conflict that led to J. J.'s resignation. For more than two years, the household remained in a state of chronic crisis. J. J., unable to sleep, paced during the night for months, agitated by his own indecision as much as by the rancor directed at him. One morning, in a rush to answer the doorbell, Mary Augusta picked up her young son, tripped at the top of the stairs and fell to the bottom. The child was not hurt, but she fractured her hip in a frantic effort to break his fall. She prayed openly that neither of her sons would ever be called to the ministry.[43] May was nineteen years old, her brothers sixteen and four, when J. J. finally resigned.

Woolley never spoke about these troubled times. She witnessed the courage it took to live by principles and, although she never spoke or wrote about a connection between her father's principled stand and the battle she fought at the end of her career, there are clear parallels. Through the turmoil of the Pawtucket years, she managed to attend four schools, all at her father's direction. At Providence High School, she described herself as one of a handful of girls isolated in a classroom of boys. Taught by men for the first time in her life, "[t]he contrast," she said, "was a sharp one, and probably just what was needed. Co-educational ... no social life, and no informal 'give and take.'... It was good discipline for the girl who had always known the sympathetic atmosphere of the informal classroom."[44] She was studying hard and performing well until her father's abrupt departure for Europe brought her school year to a premature end.

When J. J. Woolley returned, he moved the family back to Pawtucket and soon agreed to minister to a newly formed congregation that had broken away from the original church during his absence. Nearly half the total membership (123 people) had voted themselves dismissed from the church. This breakaway group convinced him to establish a new Congregational church, one located in the "flats" where the factories were located. In September of 1882, he preached his first sermon to seven hundred people from a makeshift pulpit in the Pawtucket Music Hall Theater.[45] He could easily have enlisted his daughter's help in the extensive church campaign work that lay ahead. It would take three years before the new church building was completed in 1885, but he had different plans for his talented daughter.

Despite the Glamour of Home

In September of 1882, Mary Woolley traveled the twenty miles from Pawtucket to Norton, Massachusetts, where she would take up residence at Wheaton Seminary and join five young women in her class. At nineteen, she was one of the oldest students and among the talented few who came to Wheaton for college-level work.[46] Harvard Annex for women had just opened. Vassar, Smith, and Wellesley Colleges, all single-sex women's schools, were several years old.[47] Woolley would certainly have thrived at any of these institutions, but her father's decision to send her to Wheaton was consistent with his interest in education with a religious emphasis.[48] Woolley was able to transform what some students described as an intolerably monotonous seminary existence into a purposeful time.[49] The boardinghouse years in Pawtucket served her well as she adapted to the seminary's routines and rules. Self-reliant and with some scholarly accomplishment, Woolley took advantage of opportunities for leadership. Good-natured and willing to work hard, she quickly became a popular leader among students and a prized student among the faculty.

When she graduated in June of 1884, Woolley had no plans for the future and, as she said, not the "slightest idea of teaching."[50] Back home in Pawtucket, she was briefly swept up in the activities of J. J.'s new church while, in September, her brother left home for Brown University. The following year must have felt long and unsatisfying. When Wheaton offered her a temporary position teaching mathematics the following September, she seized the opportunity. Over the next six years, Woolley would accept one-year appointments to teach Latin, history, and rhetoric, and every second year she was replaced by a newly-hired college graduate. In the summer of 1890, Woolley and three other Wheaton teachers joined a group of Smith College faculty for a two-month trip to Europe. This was her first taste of the adventure of an Atlantic crossing and train travel through new countries. She was entirely smitten. The high-spirited, intellectual companionship of the group and the direct contact with British culture made a heady combination, and when she returned home, she proposed to her father that she pursue a degree at Oxford University.

Once again, J. J. had a plan of his own. It was not the larger world she envisioned for herself at Oxford, but she gave him no argument. Woolley would be an undergraduate in the first class of women admitted to Brown University, the only institution of higher education in Rhode Island and one with the distinction of denying women an education. Brown's policy had become increasingly indefensible as the number of "exiles," women enrolled in out-of-state colleges, steadily rose.[51] Newly elected president, the Rev. Elisha Benjamin Andrews, quickly took on as a personal project a campaign to convince the university corporation, the faculty, and the students that the addition of women to Brown was in their interest.[52] Meanwhile, J. J. had joined a group of twenty parents in a petition that demanded a guarantee that the women admitted would "pursue the same course of study ... on the same condition as the young men."[53] In September of 1891, the university accepted women as candidates for all degrees and women graduates were admitted to classrooms. No provision was made for undergraduate instruction, nor could a female student earn a university degree. Andrews succeeded in creating an undergraduate class of seven young women whose task was to prove that women were capable of competing on equal terms with men. It was clear that the group needed a fearless leader for support and inspiration as they negotiated the hostile world of the university. Woolley was her father's and Andrew's choice.

How did Woolley feel about this plan? After nine years at Wheaton, she had come to embrace the seminary's concept of educated women as part of a long, continuous "undying existence." The women of the past were "watchers in the heavens above"[54] in "God's great school of Destiny." There could be no "going back."[55] The responsibility of the educated woman was to further the education of all women. During Woolley's last year at Wheaton, John F. Jameson, a newly hired history professor at Brown, had invited her to attend his lectures. Woolley joined the class "without bashfulness and without forwardness, quite as if it had been her daily habit ... as if she were unconscious of traditions to the contrary." Jameson was delighted with Woolley's "excellent good sense, right feeling and perfect manners" and her "careful, exact, intelligent, judicious work"[56] and concluded that "no young woman could have been found better for the purpose."[57] Woolley resolved to join the little group of seven women, which included two teenagers, one just fifteen years old.

One evening on a train ride home to Pawtucket, Woolley told a friend that she had decided to attend Brown rather than finish her degree at a woman's college because she "wanted to come in contact with men's minds."[58] No doubt she also saw the opportunity to shepherd her classmates through the chilly, sometimes hostile, mocking world of the university. She told them early on, "It depends on us in a very large measure whether there is ever a woman's college in Brown." She told her classmates to look straight ahead as they walked across campus and to appear not to notice the male students.[59] When the women took exams, she advised them to work hard to make themselves "oblivious to the presence of men." This way, they would not compromise their test performance.[60] Woolley herself maintained an emotional aloofness toward the many men, most of whom were eight to ten years younger, with whom she came in contact. When asked about the attitudes of the men toward the women students, she simply reported, "I do not know how they felt. I can tell you how they acted. During the four years I received nothing but the utmost courtesy."[61] One of her classmates, a young woman who transferred from Smith College, described a different experience, one in which two women in her class were "objects of [the professor's] unpleasant witticisms and the boys embarrassed us by enjoying it."[62]

Woolley was fortunate in that she entered Brown with advanced standing and was privileged to study with some of the best and most receptive faculty.[63] President Andrews handpicked the faculty that taught the all-female classes, but the classes initially had no official connection to the university. The women who ventured up College Hill to attend classes with the university men did so primarily because there were insufficient numbers of them to justify the duplication of courses in all-female classes. By the following year, 1892, the group of women had grown to fourteen freshmen, nine sophomores, nine graduate students and twenty-two special students, "women of maturity and culture, teachers and others who worked to supplement their knowledge."[64] As the number of women grew, *The Brunonian* published jokes about the "strong smell of brimstone in the vicinity"[65] of the Benefit Street building where they held classes and gathered to socialize.

In the spring semester of 1893, Woolley submitted a major research essay to *The Brown Magazine*, a publication under determinedly male control. The essay was accepted,[66] and the magazine was soon inundated with submissions from other women students. The following year, Woolley joined the editorial board and became responsible for her own department, "Etchings," which contained her own lively prose portraits of literary characters.[67] In 1893 as well, Woolley was elected first president of the Alpha Beta Fraternity, the first organization for women at the university whose goals were "to promote the mental and moral development of its members and to further social intercourse."[68] Extemporaneous speaking was the fraternity's first activity, and Woolley, who excelled at this, addressed the group on the repeal of the Silver Bill, advocating the regionally unpopular political view for the free coinage of silver.

President Andrews, trained as an economist, also held that position—one that would put him at the center of a dispute with the trustees of the university. Influential members of the corporation argued that Andrews' political views were interfering with their ability to raise funds. When a committee asked him to stop making his views public, Andrews declined and submitted his resignation, stating that he could not acquiesce in the request "without surrendering that reasonable liberty of utterance ... in the absence of which the most ample endowment for an educational institution would have but little worth."[69] Andrews' resignation in 1897 provoked strong protest, his supporters asserting "that the action ... had struck a blow at academic freedom, and that freedom, not money, is the life-blood of the university." Woolley was one of the forty-four alumnae (of a total of forty-nine) who participated. Ultimately, the corporation unanimously adopted a conciliatory, appreciative stance suggesting that their intention had been "simply to intimate that it would be the part of wisdom for [him] to take a less active part in exciting partisan discussions and apply [his] energies more exclusively to the affairs of the college." Andrews withdrew his resignation, but not without making his feelings clear. He wrote: "The studied effort ... to produce estrangement between the Corporation and myself I deeply deplore. On my side it has had no effect."

The short-term outcome of the Andrews affair was a happier one than the outcome of J. J. Woolley's conflict in the Pawtucket church. The lessons, however, were similar. Andrews had been chastised for going beyond the narrow self-interest of the university, the Reverend Woolley for challenging that within his congregation. Both men refused to compromise their rights and values, and both men dealt with their adversaries with remarkable willingness to reach conciliation. Andrews became a second powerful influence in Woolley's life. She, too, would be criticized for "exciting partisan discussions" and not applying her "energies more exclusively to the affairs of the college."[70] Toward the end of her long career, her political opinions and broad commitments would rankle influential members of her board of trustees. However, unlike her father and Andrews, Woolley was not permitted to define her actions and beliefs as matters of principle. No matter how often she argued that she stood on principle, her adversaries would use her gender to argue that her concerns were, by nature, reduced to the personal. Her resolve strengthened in the face of insult and ridicule, and she would never waver in her conviction that the fight she waged at the college was grounded in principle, never a matter of personal grievance.

Andrews was a great man in Woolley's eyes, a man who lived by a code of high ideals and personal self-restraint. "Don't be afraid to stand alone—to be the only one,"[71] he told his students. When Andrews put an opportunity in her path, she took it. He invited her to his home to meet the president of Wellesley College, Mrs. Julia Irvine, who, with the remarkable ex-president Alice Freeman Palmer, was in the process of transforming Wellesley into a secular institution dedicated to scholarship of the highest caliber.[72] Irvine and

Palmer were looking for talent, and Woolley impressed them both. As for Woolley, she had never met a woman like Palmer. At age forty, Palmer had already significantly influenced the quality and direction of women's education at four elite institutions: the University of Michigan, Wellesley College, the University of Chicago and Harvard University.[73]

A Pleasurable Excitement[74]

Woolley impressed Palmer with her accomplishments at Brown.[75] There is no doubt that if Woolley had elected to pursue doctoral studies she would have produced outstanding scholarship. Her master's thesis was the proof. Jameson said she was as good as the best history graduates in the country, and he was prepared to help her secure a fellowship for further graduate study. Woolley did not abandon the idea of earning a doctorate, but she was willing to postpone that pursuit. She was impressed with Wellesley, with its faculty of outstanding women, and, after the hardships at Brown, she welcomed the material comforts and physical beauty of the campus. Wellesley promised professional challenges and a potential for influence greater than the work she had done at Wheaton and Brown.

There was much about the female community at Wellesley that Woolley found both attractive and familiar. She was in full sympathy with Palmer's directive to students that each of them must at all times exemplify the new college woman: "Remember, girls, that You are Wellesley College."[76] She agreed with Palmer that favorable public sentiment was critical in the struggle for women's higher education and that the development of group loyalty among women college students was essential. Palmer practiced what she called "heart culture," a personal and sympathetic interest in each of the students. She knew all their names and kept a book in which she jotted down notes to familiarize herself with every new student.[77] She emphasized the "cooperative method," group loyalty in the administration of all college affairs. This, she believed, was how Wellesley could achieve the goals of true scholarship, love of learning, and a full life of work and leisure. For this to occur, students and faculty had to participate in governance and accept responsibility for the success of the college.

Woolley's experiences at Wheaton and Brown had taught her the importance of female leadership and the necessity of collective activity. It was Palmer's ideal for Wellesley that would most influence the direction of her professional and personal life. For almost five years, Woolley would share in the life of this all female intellectual community, a diverse group of scholars educated at a variety of institutions. They introduced new methods of instruction that included inquiry and discussion, a change that pressured those who relied on recitation and rote practice to re examine their methods. Irvine's presidency marked the end of evangelical conservatism at the college. The library opened on Sundays, the number of Bible, Greek, and Latin classes was reduced, and faculty were no longer required to teach the Bible. Sixty-seven new required and elective courses were introduced into the curriculum, and faculty who could or would not accept new standards for instruction either were not reappointed or were pressured to resign. Irvine was criticized by some for her single minded focus. One faculty member described her "handling of situations and individuals [as] ... masculine; it had, as the French say, the defects of its qualities."[78] Woolley would mimic Irvine's radical reform measures in the earliest years of her presidency at Mount Holyoke. Indeed, in the words of a faculty member at Mount Holyoke, "those were the heart-break days."[79] Faculty were given the choice of taking a leave of absence to do graduate work or resigning, hence the "heart-break" of change.

As Wellesley changed, the biblical history department was in desperate need of modernization.[80] Woolley accepted the offer to take on that department and immediately faced the daunting reality of what she was expected to accomplish. The entire class of 243 freshmen was her responsibility in the required year-long Bible course. Woolley had never attended a theological seminary. Her rigorous scholarship was in American history, not Greek, Latin or Hebrew. As she had done at Wheaton, Woolley would have to engage in intensive study. She put aside her scholarly interests and immersed herself, later recalling a naïve, unworried attitude toward her new responsibilities.[81]

She was philosophically committed to substantive study of the Bible in undergraduate education and was critical of the tendency at many colleges and universities to relegate the study of religion and the Bible to a curricular minimum. She emphasized the need for a formal department, citing the success at Chicago University, suggesting that the formation of departments like Chicago's and Wellesley's was in response to "the realization that ignorance of the English Bible was increasing and threatening the very foundations of sound learning."[82] Her intention was not to focus on the philosophy and history of religion nor on biblical criticism. Unchallenged Christian faith was fundamental to Woolley's educational ideal.[83] Her father's influence was evident in Woolley's activities beyond the Wellesley campus. She was committed to creating an effective Christian Association both at the college and in the local community.

On Thursday evenings, Woolley led prayer meetings, practicing a kind of lay ministry for local young women in a village meeting room, and it soon became one of seventeen sites for Bible circles held in college buildings and in the village.[84] In the classroom, teaching replaced ministering, and Woolley had no difficulty separating the two. One of her students commented that she could find "no trace of personal bias."[85] Woolley was concerned about the feelings of a Jewish student in a New Testament class and asked if "the situation ever made [her] uncomfortable." The young woman responded that everything "was quite all right." Years later, this student recalled, "What she [Woolley] said was interesting to me, as my attitude toward the New Testament course was entirely impersonal. It was just a nice little job, and one was out for any information on pretty much anything."[86]

In Woolley's second year at Wellesley, Wheaton offered her the principalship of the seminary and Smith College offered her a teaching position. She turned down both offers.[87] Wellesley was too attractive a place to leave so soon. Woolley was in the company of an extraordinary group of women. Her colleagues included, among other notable scholars and progressives, Mary Whiton Calkins, Vida Scudder, Katherine Coman, Emily Green Balch, Katherine Lee Bates and Ellen Hayes. Several of the women brought their activism into the cloistered world of the college. These progressives were conscientious teachers who believed in the superiority of the young women they were educating. Their task, as many of them saw it, was to teach an ethic of responsibility, to awaken in the students, who represented less than 1 percent of the American female population, the desire and the ability to improve society.[88]

During Woolley's years at Wellesley, "home" remained her parents' house in Pawtucket. Marriage appeared to hold no interest for her. Perhaps she approached marriage with the same equanimity that her colleague Vida Scudder did when she wrote that "as I had always serenely suspected without regrets, [it] was not for me."[89] The focus of Woolley's emotional attachments had always been her family and her life at Brown, and Wheaton had not changed this. At Wellesley, however, she entered a different world, a female community in which close relationships between women were common. Scudder called the affection that she felt toward many of her students a "spiritual maternity," estimating that thirty to forty students had entered her "inner mansions." As the young women matured, the intimacies "ripen[ed] into equal fellowship."[90]

Woolley, too, nurtured relationships with students. Years later, they expressed their love and admiration for her. "I admired and loved her as we all did."[91] Another spoke about Woolley's "dynamic forthgoing personality and her deep human sympathy."[92] A third recalled "her quiet way of speaking, her soft friendly eyes as she looked into yours. I always felt I could go to her and discuss my troubles or joy."[93] Woolley had many friends, but she shared intimacies with no one. Her devotion to her mother was, by her own description, the most deeply felt love she had known. She was attentive to her mother's smallest needs, called her "Blessed Little Mother" and spared her difficulties and worries as much as possible. Woolley had learned, as had her mother, to "keep [the] nerves under."[94] She lectured herself, "Mary Woolley, your father was a soldier and he never faltered under fire. Now pull yourself together."[95] Her father had also taught her never to turn back once she had begun on a definite course. When, for the first time in her life, she felt drawn to a young woman whose feelings seemed mutual, she found herself on such a course.

Jeannette Augustus Marks was a twenty-year-old freshman who enrolled in Woolley's first required Bible course. The articulate, high-strung young woman quickly made herself known in class, her pale hair and light eyes prompting a classmate to call her a pre–Raphaelite beauty. Woolley herself was youthful and trim at thirty-two. "In the day when the Tailored Woman was just emerging, she was Par Excellence It," one student recalled.[96] At ease in the classroom, Woolley had, according to one student, "a superb collection of stories." Another remembered that "[s]he told us of the stupid blunders we made in the geography and spelling of names and places in Palestine; and yet with such a sparkle in her eyes and with humor."[97] One wrote about her "warmth and kindness ... her power to make the individual feel that she counted. [She had a] teacher instinct which did not assume a very great intelligence or training on our side of the desk in the lecture room."[98]

Marks was emotionally on edge and responded quickly to Woolley's warm manner. Her mother had just died in a sanitarium that August, one month before the college term began, and Marks' family seemed to be falling apart. Her younger sister rushed into marriage, and her father, absorbed in his own troubled affairs, was threatening to withdraw his financial support.[99] Marks' single hope was to study literature and pursue a writing career,[100] and she feared having to leave Wellesley. She was accustomed to lonely weekends at boarding school and had learned to make herself a welcome guest in other people's homes. Woolley was one of the first faculty at Wellesley to invite her for the weekend, and the affectionate, good-humored atmosphere of the Woolley household was both tonic for Marks and a reminder of her own situation. Over the course of the next three years, Woolley invited her frequently as her affection for Marks grew.

In Woolley's second year at Wellesley, the college began a search for a new president and Palmer lobbied for the appointment of a man. She argued that the college's advancement was now hampered by exclusively female leadership, but tradition held,[101] and the trustees searched instead for a well to do, cultured woman with good social connections. Wellesley was in financial straits and desperately needed to build an endowment. For the third time, Palmer assisted the board in finding a president (in this case a compromise). Caroline Hazard was a woman who met most requirements.[102] Woolley had been granted a year's leave to pursue doctoral work, but after discussion with Palmer, she changed her plans. It was Palmer's expressed preference that Woolley stay to help Hazard in her first year. Woolley was "entirely willing to defer [her] absence from Wellesley for a year,"[103] and Hazard was delighted to have her support. In deference to the knowledge and skill of the college faculty, Hazard gave the departments full autonomy in making educational policy decisions. Woolley was appointed to a new key administrative position as head of College Hall, the residence of between two and three hundred students and was also promoted to full professor. Marks was taking a fifth year to finish her degree, an additional incentive for Woolley to stay.[104]

At College Hall, Woolley supervised an experiment in student government in which selected members of a House Council met with her once a week, while the whole council met once a month to begin a student initiative in governing the "Home Organization" of College Hall. In an article she wrote for the *Wellesley Magazine*, Woolley suggested that the women's colleges were in a unique situation:

> The friends of student government at Wellesley feel that there is a wide field for it here, but they do not ask for a belief in its efficacy as a panacea for all ills; they wish only for the cordial support of faculty and students, that the plan of organization now being tried may have every opportunity to prove itself a source of real strength to the college.[105]

The students were enthusiastic about the system, and College Hall functioned better than it ever had. Woolley continued to live there and take her meals with the students. Personally, she had no strong objection to this arrangement, but an increasing number of faculty were unhappy with a tradition that virtually directed faculty to live among students for the purpose of close supervision. In response to persistent faculty protest, the trustees voted a $300 increase in salary for those faculty who preferred to make off-campus arrangements for housing. A serious housing shortage on campus was part of the motivation, and twenty-seven faculty members chose to move off-campus. Thirty-nine faculty, including Woolley, continued to live among the students, providing a "strong nucleus for elevating influence."[106] Judging by student reaction to Woolley, this was successful: "I admired and loved her as we all did, and used to think wistfully that I wished I could ever hope to be lovely and charming as she seemed to me."[107] A senior whose room was next to Woolley's often visited with her and remembered how ardently Woolley spoke about the importance of women's involvement in national and international affairs.[108]

While at Wellesley, Woolley had her first encounter with the controversy of domestic science as a field of academic study. Courses would include household management, sanitation, hygiene and child care, and some faculty believed that "something ought to be done in that direction."[109] Opponents, Woolley among them, vocally and insistently objected to the addition of any courses that diluted the academic focus of the college. The issue would become a persistent part of the debate over goals in women's higher education, and Woolley would face the issue head-on at Mount Holyoke. A colleague at Wellesley asserted:

> The unwillingness of college faculties to admit vocational courses to the curriculum is not due to academic conservatism and inability to march with the times, but to an unclouded and accurate conception of the meaning of the term "higher education."[110]

In December of 1899, Woolley was presented with two almost simultaneous offers. Brown University offered her the position of dean of the Women's College while Mount Holyoke College offered her its presidency. "December...," she wrote, "was a critical month, the most critical, probably, in my life.... That I decided as I did I have never regretted."[111] She abandoned the plan to take the postponed leave to pursue a doctorate. Then, despite her strong ties to Brown University and to its new Women's College, she chose the greater challenge. She was ready to break away from the familiar world at Wellesley and to give up a scholarly career. In a sense, becoming the president of Mount Holyoke completed the circle of influence in her educational and professional life. The early Wellesley had been modeled on Mount Holyoke Seminary. Mount Holyoke was nurtured in its beginnings by Wheaton Seminary, and now Woolley would attempt to model Mount Holyoke College, still much influenced by its seminary past, on the academic excellence of Wellesley. Wellesley's President Hazard declared that, in Woolley's new role, "all her abilities will have free play."[112] The Mount Holyoke trustees made their formal offer on January 4, 1900. Woolley accepted eleven days later and negotiated a starting time for January of 1901. In September, she wanted to visit and study the educational systems of the women's colleges of Oxford, Cambridge and London.

In contrast, Marks' future after graduation was entirely uncertain. She had no family home to return to and no plans for graduate study or employment. She spent her last two years at Wellesley in an increasingly agitated state.[113] Marks had come to rely on Woolley's steady friendship. After Woolley accepted the Mount Holyoke offer, she began to travel throughout the country visiting Mount Holyoke alumnae groups to establish the connections essential for the work ahead. Her absences from Wellesley heightened Marks' sense of insecurity. One evening in March, Marks cried in desperation about her uncertain future, telling Woolley that she depended entirely on her love, and "entrusted" her life to her. Woolley was overwhelmed and unable to answer. She later wrote to Marks:

> I was frightened. I felt almost like saying that you must not, that I could not, dared not, take the awful responsibility. I do not feel so now—God is first, both

of us are in His hands—but as far as human trust can go, I joy in the realization that you have given yourself to me in this way. I have put my life into your hands, dearest, for the great overpowering love of which I had never dreamed before, has come to me and nothing can ever separate us, my other and better half.[114]

Woolley and Marks formalized their love with an exchange of a ring and a pearl pin, and a few weeks later, Woolley wrote to Marks about the revelation of their love for each other:

Your coming is my rest and refreshment and delight after my hours of work or "Sassiety."... Oh! my dear little girl, do you not know, can you not understand, that you do just as much for me as I can possibly do for you? I want to be what you think that I am, Jeannette the fact that I love you makes me wish to be more in the world ... you are an inspiration to me, dear, as well as my greatest comfort.... Does it seem possible that it is only a few short weeks since we have felt that we could say all that we feel without restraint or constraint? Two such proud ladies, too, each one afraid that she felt more than the other and determined to keep her own self respect!... I am so glad that it is not a sudden "possessing," Jeannette, that for five years it has been coming surely to pass and that for almost three years I have realized that you were very dear to me, never as dear, however, as you are today.[115]

They spent the summer apart, Woolley in Pawtucket and Marks in Philadelphia, and wrote to each other almost daily. "If only the separation need not come!" Woolley wrote:

It will be so hard this coming year first the ocean between me and all that I love, and then the new work among strangers!... Besides, we cannot afford to be separated! We should be bankrupt in the stationery and postage line!... I cannot grow reconciled to the thought of being away from you. God in his Providence has given me this love when I most need it, when I am about to take up crushing responsibilities.... Do you realize what it means to have you, the heart of my life, to talk with you as I would with my own soul, to have nothing hid, to feel that we are one?[116]

In September, Woolley sailed for England with her cousin while Marks headed back to Wellesley to begin graduate study. Ten years had passed since Woolley's first trip to Britain. This time, she was the honored guest of the colleges she visited.[117] For three months, she observed and studied the methods and problems of women's education. At Surrey, she attended a formal reception and joked in a letter to Marks about the luxury and pomp of the affair: "You would have screamed could you have seen me—parading arm in arm with the principal between 2 lines of students—on dress parade." She joked about imagining Wellesley's faculty "in decollete gowns," and about the many servants and told Marks that she could acquire a taste for an English college president's life.[118] After visiting one English friend, she wrote that the woman had a "beautiful home, a very fine husband (notice the order!)."[119] Woolley's close friend

Lida Shaw King, who would become the dean of the Women's College at Brown,[120] was traveling with the group, and Woolley confided in her about her love for Marks. "Dear old Lida ... she knows of my great love for my Dearest and yet seems to understand my love for her is just the same as it was before this supreme love came into my life." Marks was jealous of Woolley's affection for King, but Woolley reassured her that another woman had "come to have the first place [in King's heart] as you have in my heart."[121]

Woolley spent a harrowing few days in a winter storm during the return crossing before the ship ultimately ran aground in New York Harbor. Unfazed by the experience, Woolley was becoming an enthusiastic, tireless traveler. During the remaining days of December, she anxiously anticipated the short train journey from Pawtucket to South Hadley, Massachusetts, the home of Mount Holyoke College.

CHAPTER 2

"Mount Holyoke *Is* Miss Woolley!"

—Smith College president William A. Neilson

Woolley woke up in South Hadley on January 1, 1901, the first day of the new century. It would be several months before her official inauguration, when Wellesley's President Hazard would welcome her to the very small world of women college presidents—a world in which each woman "must literally work out her own salvation, along the line of her highest powers."[1] Board of trustees president Judson Smith[2] would assure the audience that the elaborate inaugural event entirely befitted Mount Holyoke. He was proud of the college's recent growth,[3] asserting that standards of admission and graduation equaled those of the elite women's colleges. He and his fellow trustees were irked by critics, most recently by President M. Carey Thomas, who had disparaged Mount Holyoke at Bryn Mawr that fall. The trustees composed a terse note asking Thomas to "state the definite facts," and she had promptly replied, enumerating the weaknesses she observed—the college's small endowment, the small number of faculty, the granting of credit for technical work in art and music, the recent separation of the preparatory department from the college (in 1893) and the lesser and inferior quality of academic work accomplished by the students because of obligatory domestic work.[4] Thomas was not wrong. Mount Holyoke faced major challenges in its efforts to achieve the highest standards. In order to bring Mount Holyoke to undeniably equal status with the other elite women's colleges, Woolley would have to significantly increase the college's endowment, upgrade both the faculty and the student body, improve the curriculum, and remove the domestic work system that was a hallmark of Mount Holyoke's education. A broader challenge for Woolley was the need to advocate publicly for the higher education of women and to promote the value of college training against persistent, destructive prejudice that too much education damaged women's health and compromised their nature. Woolley's

37

Mount Holyoke President Mary Emma Woolley, 1903.

third challenge stemmed from her belief that, beyond academic training, a college was obligated to inculcate in its students a deep sense of social responsibility. Her last major challenge was a personal one. She wanted to create a home for herself and Marks at Mount Holyoke.

In meeting her first challenge, it was important that Woolley not be defensive about the college's idiosyncrasies and limitations. In 1901, Mount Holyoke life still had a monastic quality. Discipline was enforced through a self-monitoring system of public confession of transgressions. Missionary influence remained strong and, unlike at Wellesley, there was virtually no expression of social or political ideas. Bible study permeated the community. Competition between students was downplayed. There was some dissent, as evidenced by an editorial that appeared in the student magazine.

> We are told that woman is incapable of detaching herself from the personal point of view and of maintaining an argument for the sake of an abstract principle. Hence any form of competition arouses personal feelings—usually of resentment and antagonism ... the hearty handclasp between victor and defeated on the battle grounds of men is rarely to be found in rivalry of women.[5]

At the end of Woolley's career, this persistent prejudice would be a problem for her. She was unable to persuade her critics that her actions were based on principle and that personal feelings played no role in her decisions.

Woolley did not focus on the conservative impulses that worked to keep Mount Holyoke at a standstill. She was sensitive to Mount Holyoke's history of struggle and isolation, its students typically characterized as "all embryo missionaries in shawls, woolen gloves and hymn books."[6] Rather, she emphasized its progressive elements, linking founder Mary Lyon's ideals and the school's accomplishments in a historical chain whose end one couldn't "dare to predict." Student obligation to perform domestic duties provoked strong criticism. Lyon's intention had not been to teach housekeeping skills, but rather to develop a cooperative spirit among the young women as well as a homelike environment in the school. "Might not this simple feature do away with much of the prejudice against female education among common people?" she had argued.[7] Perhaps, but not in the world of higher education, where it became one of the most criticized aspects of the college. Woolley worked slowly and judiciously and only succeeded in eliminating the practice in 1913. She encouraged the students to be proud of the aspects of the college that set it apart from other colleges. "U. T. H." ("uphold the honor") became a code that disallowed ridicule of domestic work, quiet hours or missionary service, because these traditions made Mount Holyoke an honorable and democratic institution dedicated to service to the world.[8]

Woolley at Work

Woolley kept a large black leather-bound memorandum book on her desk and filled the pages with her daily obligations. She accepted virtually all invitations to speak and subscribed to several news clipping services so that she could stay abreast of current events. She took full charge of her office, assumed the responsibilities of inviting speakers, managed an increasingly extensive correspondence, and planned her many trips. Religious activities on campus, especially Sunday evening Vespers, were among her favorite duties. Woolley spoke at morning chapel, and if she missed one day "a slight wave of disappointment" passed over the chapel.[9] She used chapel time for "food for thought" and "quiet reprimands." Woolley told the young women to "do a kind deed, never criticize, never complain, and never abuse."[10] One student said, "I have only to think of Miss Woolley to feel a strengthening of my backbone,"[11] a reference to Woolley's superb posture as well as a measure of the effectiveness of her advice.

Mount Holyoke President Mary Emma Woolley at her desk, 1904.

She was the guest speaker at a seemingly endless round of luncheons and dinners of college alumnae. She spoke about the value of college training for women over sweetbreads and squab on toast, about women in the professions over caviar and lobster. She was remarkably adept at revitalizing a speech she had given many times before and joked to friends that "few arts [were] more difficult than the attempt to speak a graceful word when there is nothing to say!"[12] A refined and genuinely kind woman, Woolley added the gracious style of Wellesley's academic culture to the work ethic of Mount Holyoke. The major event of the year for each alumnae association soon became a visit from Woolley.[13] This was more than a social event. The college relied heavily on alumnae financial support, and Woolley had to cultivate loyalty.[14] Woolley told the women that alumnae should be "just what loyal, loving daughters mean to the mother" and gave them three points of advice—"to give kindly judgment," to bring any weaknesses to the "attention of those who can correct them" rather than discuss among themselves or, even more harmful, discuss with outsiders, and "to keep in touch and so in sympathy" with the college.[15]

Fund-raising was a constant in Woolley's life, and it was a task she thoroughly disliked. In a letter to Marks, she described her feelings about an event in Albany: "Tomorrow at luncheon I expect to feel like Wellesley [their dog] when he goes through his 'stunts' to get something to eat."[16] The college needed large gifts to build its endowment, but women were not in control of wealth, including their own, the way men were. Woolley had to emphasize the importance of many small gifts, but she firmly believed that without a successful appeal to individuals and organizations outside of the college, Mount Holyoke would not grow. She joked with the alumnae that a good policy for a college was to befriend the lawyers of the rich,[17] and she criticized the lack of giving to women's colleges: "[I]n no case does the entire endowment equal the single gifts frequently made to men's colleges and universities."[18]

Meanwhile, in the world beyond Mount Holyoke, women's education was under constant attack. Adversaries kept old questions alive. Did college "unfit" women for the home? Did college women lose their desire to marry and raise children? Did they permanently injure their health, including their reproductive capacity, because of the overstrenuousness of college life? Wasn't it true that "women have a peculiar power of taking out of themselves more than they can bear" and, therefore, wasn't college the worst environment for young women?[19] Woolley developed detailed, provocative speeches that she delivered over and over again. She asked her audiences to think rationally on the issues. She published articles in numerous publications.[20]

Unlike her colleague Thomas, who asserted that the college woman was faced with a clear and unfair choice between celibacy and a life of servitude, Woolley was mild in her assurances that college women did marry. The important difference, she said, was that they married by choice, not out of necessity. In fact, Woolley knew that college women married less frequently and had fewer children than women in the general population. The number of educated women remaining single was on the rise.[21] When critics of women's education voiced concerns about fitness for the "home," Woolley noted that they generally meant the home managed by wife and mother. In her earliest speeches, she emphasized the narrowness of this focus: "A great many women must make their own home life, if they are to have it at all."[22]

Woolley recalled visiting Pawtucket thread mills as a child with her father, watching girls her age "stamp, sort and pack the spools with marvelous swiftness."[23] She said opportunity, not any innate specialness, was what distinguished her and other college women from the factory workers. Married college women who were supported by their husbands were fortunate, but the ability to earn one's living was essential whether or not one had to put that ability into practice. She expanded the definition of home to include the many "cheery, charming homes" of unmarried, professional women who became cultured and efficient at college.[24] Because college training developed both resources and resourcefulness, young educated women were not desperate to marry: "Every woman lives her life in relation to herself as well as in relation to others, and what she is in herself determines to a large extent what she will be to others."[25] Woolley assured her audiences that the educated wife creates a well ordered home and that she gladly applies her mastery of intellectual activities to the management of family and home. She becomes an "intelligent sharer" in the lives of her husband and children.[26]

> Her "bread and butter" does not depend upon it—she can by her own efforts provide the staff of life and even add an occasional piece of cake. And this takes from the thought of marriage its utilitarian character and emphasizes the ideal relationship. It may be a heterodox position to take, but it seems to the speaker that for the common welfare the question of quality of marriages is far more important than that of quantity.[27]

Jeannette Augustus Marks, c. 1895

Woolley's references to "cake" and quality versus quantity suggest a little of her impatience with this topic.

Her frequent allusions to a single woman's need to create her own home were deeply personal. She had succeeded in bringing Marks to Mount Holyoke, and eventually (in 1909) the college would build a President's House in which she and Marks would live, but it was never the home that she, and especially Marks, desired. Public profession of their love was out of the question, and the boundary between their public and private lives at Mount Holyoke would always be unclear and troubling. Disguising the intensity of her feelings for Marks would become a major challenge for Woolley. In public, Woolley adopted a cordial formality toward Marks, greeting her warmly, as she would any colleague. She begged Marks to understand the necessity of this. A "perfunctory How do you do?" and "Good-bye in the company of so many" had to be enough. She told Marks that what she wanted to do was to "take you into my arms and kiss you.... What shall I say to you, Dearest, when the room is full of people?"[28]

> I knew that such love existed—but no friend had ever before come into my life as you have come into it.... Few people ... are so rich as to have such a love, such a lover—David said of Jonathan—"Thy love for me was wonderful, passing the love of women"—Dear Heart—Thy love for me is wonderful, passing the love of men.[29]

For a measure of privacy, Woolley rented a hotel room in Springfield where Marks would join her when Woolley returned from official trips.[30] Marks complained bitterly about the artificiality of this arrangement. She wanted "no shadow of concealment in their relationship" and told Woolley,

> that I should appear to the slightest degree insignificant in your eyes to other people is a matter of bitter concern to me ... anybody seeing [the dignified dependence of two people who love each other] is the better for it.... I despise conventionality; courtesy is another thing. I would not take a kingdom for proof at the dinner table as well as in the quiet of our bedroom that you depend upon me. There is no gift equal to the dignity you can confer on me in that way.[31]

They would not have a real "home" until Marks retired in 1941, when she joined Woolley in Westport, New York, at the Marks family property.

Woolley did not permit the limitations imposed on her personal freedom to interfere with her fierce advocacy for women's self-determination. She seized upon every opportunity to bring this issue into the public discourse. Society simply could not ignore the issues that the increased independence of some women provoked. In relation to work, women had to be counted as individuals; they could no longer be defined as exclusively female:

> The opponents of higher education are right in their fear that it means something more than the opportunity to study Calculus or to read the Greek dramatists in the original. It has introduced into many a household the startling and novel question, "If John Jones has a right to become a dressmaker because he prefers it, why should not Jane Jones become a doctor, if she prefers that?"[32]

The college woman did not view her work as "a temporary expedient" until marriage, although she was not averse to marriage. If a professional woman remained unmarried, she might be fortunate enough to still have her childhood home or she could join the groups of women who were "forming homes for themselves." Unmarried or married, every woman was entitled to remuneration because "her part in building up and providing for the home has as distinctive a value as any other work in the world.... What she receives for personal use is not a donation, a charity; she is truly a wage earner."[33]

In answer to the charge that women's colleges sacrificed the physical well-being of students to promote the intellectual, Woolley argued that an entirely opposite situation prevailed: "There is an interrelation that physical vitality helps the development of mental strength and that a 'level head' promotes a strong body."[34] Critics who were preoccupied with life within the women's colleges had a peculiarly misguided focus on what was really a larger societal concern. Woolley reinforced her argument with data from the reports of the resident physician at Mount Holyoke, which confirmed that students either maintained good health or made significant improvement while at the college.[35] A professor at Brown University had given her advice when she began teaching at Wellesley: "Do not be too much concerned about the general welfare of your students. Girls are good enough as they are." Woolley incorporated this piece of advice into her talks, mocking what she called a "gallant, masculine attitude." "As women," she said, "we may be allowed both to establish an ideal for our girls and consider how we measure up."[36]

The year 1912 marked the seventy-fifth anniversary of the seminary/college as well as the end of the first decade of Woolley's presidency. She had already accomplished her major goals for Mount Holyoke. With the support of the trustees, she had implemented a ranking system along with a salary scale. She had upgraded the faculty through both an aggressive hiring policy and a liberal leave policy that encouraged faculty to engage in advanced study, research, and teaching at other institutions. Faculty were given the choice of taking a leave of absence to do graduate work or resign, and for some, it seemed a dictatorial policy. In the words of a faculty member who lived through that period, "those were the heart-break days." Some faculty would hold on to deep resentment for decades over the pressure to pursue further education and degrees.[37]

Woolley's goal in granting leaves was more comprehensive than the earning of advanced degrees. Consistent with her desire to increase their knowledge and experience as well as to renew their energies, she encouraged faculty to pursue new interests. In 1905 she proposed the creation of a fund to finance "Sabbatical years":

> The importance of these "Sabbatical years," so called, is very great. The profession of teaching is exhausting, mentally as well as physically, and an instructor, in order to do her best work, must stop and be recreated. She needs to become again a student, not only that she may come into touch with the progress made in her own line of work, but also to gain a broader outlook, that education which is to be found in studying under the men and women who are making history in the literary and educational world; in seeing new places and hearing new things; in taking in, instead of always giving out. The instructor who has this new lease of life, brings quite as much back to the college in the way of buoyancy and a broader outlook as in the increase of knowledge. There has been no definite pol-

icy at Mount Holyoke, but leaves of absence have been granted to those who have asked for the privilege. It is for the interest of the College, as well as for that individual, and there should be a fund of which the income could be used for the continuance of part salary to members of the Faculty who have been granted leave of absence for study.[38]

In 1912, the fifty new faculty members whom Woolley had hired since 1901 and who had remained at Mount Holyoke possessed a higher percentage of Ph.D.'s than the eighty-three faculty hired during this period who left the college.[39] Woolley's greatest dissatisfaction was that, after ten years, she had still not been able to adequately increase faculty salaries, which remained significantly below those of other elite colleges.[40] An ambitious goal of raising $2 million had been set in 1911 to guarantee major improvements in salaries.[41] Despite persistent talk about the "'unwisdom' of the president raising money at the expense of time and energy,"[42] the task fell to Woolley most of the time.

Just as at Wellesley, there was interest among some students, faculty, and trustees in domestic science as a field of study.[43] Woolley was firm in her resistance: "We have no courses in domestic science; we do not try to train our students in the practical details of 'keeping house.'"[44] The priority in education was to develop leaders and thinkers in society. Male students prepared to specialize in the public world of politics, economics, education and religion, and there was no logical reason why female students who did the same should be forced to assume twice the preparation by specializing in domestic science as well. Women students would be penalized for "their double relation to the home world and to the world outside of the home."[45] In 1910, she took on the controversy in her speech at the inauguration of President Marion Burton at Smith College. The danger facing women's colleges, Woolley said, was "not that of 'excessive mentality,' as President Taylor [of Vassar] once expressed it," but rather "the influence of the outside life and its standards." To give a humorous twist to this serious subject, she utilized a presumed African American dialect, a technique she would use occasionally with no apparent regard for its racist implications:

> It is not my intention, Mr. President, on this auspicious day to "breed a coolness in de congregation," if I may borrow the negro preacher's objection to preaching on the ten commandments, by my introduction of this controversial subject. The value of vocational training, of the skill, the expertness, the saving of time, of money, of energy, even of life itself, by knowing how to do, can hardly be overemphasized. But in every vocation the men and the women who are the leaders, are the ones who can think. This is the "bedrock" of college education, and if we take our stand here we shall not be in danger of losing our footing in the shifting sands of opinion with regard to the place of vocational training in the undergraduate course.

Acknowledgment of this goal, Woolley pointed out, did not require universal agreement on a "definition of woman's sphere" or on the necessity of equal suffrage.[46] Fears of where equal opportunity in education would lead turned on these very issues, but Woolley took a strategic position by focusing on education.

She believed in the academic freedom of scholar teachers. From the beginning of her administration, individual departments had the power to make decisions about allocation of subjects and materials used within courses. Once Woolley established strong leadership within departments, the heads of those departments took on the responsibility of searching for faculty candidates. "The personnel of a department tends to perpetrate itself be it excellent or mediocre," she asserted. Woolley presided over faculty meetings efficiently, keeping discussion in focus and resolving conflicts among the faculty with sensitivity and good humor. According to her secretary, if there was a problem of any sort, "all assumed Miss Woolley would have the answer of 'what to do' and she always did!"[47]

While Woolley worked to upgrade faculty, she also upgraded the standards for student performance. During her first year in office, Mount Holyoke and Wellesley accepted invitations to join the College Entrance Examination Board (CEEB), a policy-making organization that included, among other colleges, Harvard, Yale, Bryn Mawr, and Smith.[48] Woolley would later become the first woman to head the CEEB.[49] In 1915, Woolley met with the presidents of Smith, Vassar and Wellesley to consider a new entrance method. They all agreed to eliminate the certificate system and began comprehensive examinations in June of 1916. Mount Holyoke would remove all certificate privileges by 1918 and begin comprehensive exams in 1919 when a board of admissions took over the work of entrance requirements.[50] The comprehensive examinations were to be "a test of the quality of the applicant's scholarship and intellectual power" while examinations in all subjects would continue as an alternative measure.[51] The plan, as conceived by the heads of the four colleges, was similar to the one adopted by Harvard, Princeton and Yale Universities. Mount Holyoke was accepted into Phi Beta Kappa in 1905,[52] and in 1907, during elections held at Pembroke College, Brown University, Woolley was elected the first woman senator of Phi Beta Kappa, leading all the candidates with 143 of 157 votes.[53] By 1911 a total of ten Mount Holyoke graduates were recipients of fellowships for graduate study,[54] and by May of 1913 thirty-seven students had received Mount Holyoke fellowships.[55] Board president Smith's premature portrayal of Mount Holyoke's student accomplishments was becoming a reality.

Woolley sought to develop student responsibility and leadership from the beginning of her presidency. The Students' League had been in existence since 1898, but the organization had no legislative power and simply attempted to enforce the rules set down by the faculty. The honor system of students' self-reporting of rule violations (Lyon's method) had been replaced by a proctor system. The proctors, who were usually students themselves, kept track of offenses, enforcement consisting of a mandatory visit after three offenses to the chairman of the house in which the student lived.[56] Students were, as yet, unfamiliar with the exercise of any independent authority and many shared a fear of too much independence. A student editorial articulated this sentiment: "[An] extreme of independent, democratic spirit [is] to be guarded against." Too much independence will create "self-sufficiency" and "undue self dependence."[57] In 1904, Woolley created an opportunity for the students. Representatives from the Mount Holyoke Students' League traveled to Wellesley to participate in a newly formed conference on improving student government, where they shared ideas and common problems with students from Bryn Mawr, Cornell and Vassar Colleges. This was the beginning of the Woman's Intercollegiate Association for Student Government and, through Woolley's efforts, Mount Holyoke became a charter member in 1906.[58] Fourteen years later, in 1920, an article titled "Rules, Regulations and Revolution" appeared in the same student publication. "We have had our share of externally imposed discipline," it read, "of living under rules and regulations; now we need the training of experience, the self imposed discipline, the self regulated life."[59]

The policy of domestic work as part of student life brought the severest criticism from outsiders, but students and faculty within the college felt differently. One month before Woolley's arrival, college faculty and students in the classes of 1901 and 1904 responded to a questionnaire designed by a faculty member to discover their sentiments about the usefulness of domestic work. The response was overwhelmingly positive, the reasons reflecting an appreciation of the original intent of the system. The students said that the system "gives a sense of responsibility for the comforts and happiness of other people," "instills regard for rights and privileges of workers," and "teaches that we are not exempt from labor."[60]

The faculty valued the intellectual, social, moral, and economic advantages of a system of cooperative work. The survival of the system begun in the seminary, the only domestic system of its kind currently in existence in the colleges and universities, was a strong argument for keeping rather than eliminating it. Faculty said that cooperative work promoted "common brotherhood" more quickly than in the classroom, that it taught "respect for labor," promoted "sympathy between classes," brought college life "nearer to family life," saved money and trained women to become "better employers." "Unselfishness, thoughtfulness, promptness and independence of action" were all learned attitudes and behaviors that faculty attributed to the domestic system.[61] Within a decade, the faculty who were most strenuously in favor of domestic work had retired, and a forum for discussion opened.

Woolley and the trustees formed a committee in 1911, and, after two years of deliberate investigation, assembled arguments in favor of discontinuance of domestic service.[62] The board was persuaded by the report, and in May of 1913 domestic work was voted out of existence. This policy decision was of a piece with the efforts of the elite women's colleges to emulate the male elite. It was also consistent with the changing nature of the student body and with the attitudes of the families who sent their daughters to Mount Holyoke. The student body had, on average, grown wealthier. By 1916, high heels, silk stockings and silk dresses had become acceptable attire in classes.[63] There was some sentiment that, within the student body, poorer students were judged by their lack of wealth. This manifested itself in social pressure on students to not live and work in the cooperative houses and not seek remunerative domestic work.[64] Woolley was concerned about students of lesser means, but she opposed the suggestion of a sliding scale for fees based on the ability to pay, agreeing with the board that there should be no class distinctions within the college.[65] What she failed to recognize was that a slowly increasing uniform fee became, in effect, a subsidy for those families who could afford to pay more and a hardship for those who could not. The changing student body ultimately meant a changing alumnae group. By the mid–1930s, the alumnae group included many women who embraced individualism and saw no need for solidarity. For them, feminism was an antiquated embarrassment. These women would play a crucial role in sustaining the trustees' decision to hire Ham.

In 1916, Woolley agreed to participate in a study of the living conditions within women's colleges. The report would become one component of a larger work on the corporate life of the woman's college, and the subjects included Mount Holyoke, Smith, Wellesley, Vassar, and Bryn Mawr. Woolley reported that the service force was not hired through an employment bureau but rather through independent sources which provided an informal network of recommendations. Staff received no written contracts or training; no tipping was permitted, and no summer provisions were made for staff. In response to a "welfare" question on the survey: "Do they [workers] resent it [welfare work] as ostentatious display of superior to inferior?" Woolley responded "yes." Mount Holyoke, she said, "does nothing and the maids do not desire it." There were sixty-seven women in service in 1916, 98 percent "country girls" from Ireland, France and Poland, one-third of whom were under the age of twenty-five. They lived in the residence halls and worked daily from 6:00 a.m. to 2:30 p.m. and again from 5:00 to 7:30 each evening, with one afternoon off per week as well as every other Sunday. Wages ranged from $4.75 to $8 per week, with an allowance of one week's pay in an emergency or illness.[66]

Apart from occasionally giving the workers complimentary tickets to college events, Woolley made no mention of any other effort on the college's part to draw the women into the academic or social life of the college, nor did she convey any sense that the close college community was ideal for a social experiment that might address some of the problems progressives had identified: how to increase the opportunities of the less fortunate, how to train skilled workers, and how to give more meaning to work. Although her father would have applauded such an endeavor, Woolley separated the outside world from the insular college. She encouraged settlement work by Mount Holyoke students in the city of Holyoke and in the "summer house" for workers in South Hadley but went no further to minister to the young women workers at the college.[67] If she had been inclined to do so, she would have found little support within the college community as the early view that domestic work "teaches a certain class of girls that no one is too good to work"[68] slipped into the past.

Woolley began her work toward collegial unity and cooperation among Mount Holyoke's American "daughter colleges," Mills, Rockford, Western and Lake Erie,[69] in the earliest years of her administration. Her reputation as a visionary leader and problem solver grew rapidly, and soon after Mount Holyoke was accepted into the Association of Collegiate Alumnae in 1912, Thomas was asking Woolley to allow her nomination for its presidency:

> You are the one person, I think, who could be unanimously elected, and your election ... after the reorganization would signalize among other things the new, broader policies of the Association.... Personally I am coming to believe more and more in what can be done by organized effort. I am anxious that those of us who have been presidents of women's colleges in these days would unite to help the young college women of the country to direct their energies where they are most needed. Under you as president we can do this in harmony and with enthusiasm.[70]

Woolley waited until 1927, when the ACA had evolved into the American Association of University Women. During the intervening years, she initiated and participated in unifying efforts that would primarily benefit Mount Holyoke. In 1915, Mount Holyoke joined with Vassar, Wellesley, and Smith in the Four College Conference, whose primary purpose was to cooperatively seek ways to secure endowments for women's colleges that equaled those of the men's.[71] The colleges' relatively poor endowments presented major obstacles to advancement and demanded an enormous amount of administrative attention.[72]

A World beyond Mount Holyoke

By the early 1920s, Woolley had successfully met three of her challenges. Mount Holyoke College had achieved equal status with other elite colleges. Woolley and others had succeeded in marginalizing the most hostile opponents of women's higher education, and Marks was teaching at Mount Holyoke and living in the President's House.

Woolley's fourth challenge was to instill in young college women an idealism and a sense of mission that would prompt them to put their skills to work for a better world. The early years, devoted to developing student interest in suffrage, settlement work, and peace activism turned, in the twenties and thirties, to an effort to persuade students with newly acquired political rights to use them constructively. There was urgent work to be done if peace and unity in the world were to be achieved. Woolley argued that women's "constructive" instinct made "every woman in favor of a league of nations."[73] She responded to all requests to speak on behalf of President Wilson's League, "a call to the colors!" whenever she had spare hours.[74] By the end of 1919, American support for the League had eroded and Mount Holyoke students, listening to arguments in favor of the League at college and arguments against at home, had drifted into an apathy that greatly concerned Woolley. At a meeting of the Association of American Colleges in Chicago, she warned:

> [W]e are very proud today to carry the memory of the year 1917 because then we showed the world that we were ready to stake all for an ideal. We are very proud to look back to the year 1918 when we proved that our deeds spoke even louder than our words. I wonder whether we shall look back as filled with pride upon the year 1919. I fear not.[75]

Meanwhile, Woolley's college schedule was more demanding than ever. She joked, "Between the attempts to organize the world and the alumnae, life is somewhat strenuous."[76] The years ahead became, in her words, "a killing Business."[77] What the college needed was a large gift of $500,000 or more, and Woolley's job was to create interest among wealthy outsiders. "[P]reparing the ground," she said, involved "the inevitable talk to a group assembled in front of their open fire!"[78] Politics often mixed with talk of money, and Woolley had to censor her opinions, always careful not to offend potential donors or trustees. When Board President Skinner attended one function with her, Woolley "took a wicked satisfaction in having [Skinner] hear what he [the host] had to say about the League of Nations (emphatically favorable)."[79] Tired of being away from home, she told Marks: "[A]ll the more as the arbiters of my destiny intimate that they expect me to be 'on my job' continuously.... This Juggernaut is relentless."[80] In May of 1921, in Georgia and on her way to Ohio and Pennsylvania, she complained, "I have grown tired of hearing of the poverty of millionaires!"[81]

She returned to Mount Holyoke for the twentieth-anniversary celebration of her inauguration and the announcement of a $100,000 endowment of the president's chair to be named the Mary Emma Woolley Foundation.[82] The China Educational Commission of the Foreign Missions Conference of North America invited Woolley to participate, but even though the campaign fund had already reached $2.5 million, she did not expect the trustees to release her from fund-raising. The trip would require a six-month absence from the college. To her surprise, the board decided that she should go. She had allies among the trustees who welcomed an opportunity for Woolley to have influence in a larger sphere. Later during the 1930s, some board members would use Woolley's frequent absences from the campus as evidence of poor leadership and an indication of a need for dramatic change in the college's administration.

Woolley was most concerned about leaving Marks. She told her: "I feel pretty 'heart achy' at the thought of leaving you.... Ah me! I fear I was not cut out for a 'career,' but for a 'stay at home!'"[83] "What I care about most of anything in the world is your well being just as I care most about you. It almost kills me to think of being away from you.... If you say the word, I will say I simply cannot go."[84] In the end, Woolley did go. She headed first for Japan aboard the Canadian Pacific steamer the *Empress of Asia* and then on to China for six months of respite from college concerns.[85] China's central government was on the verge of collapse. Peking (Beijing) closed the city gates nightly against raids from northern troops while Woolley and her commission engaged in conferences and committee meetings whose purpose was to create an educational scheme for China. In her free time, she slipped away to visit shops, climb the Great Wall, and indulge in Chinese foods. Woolley saw in China a nation struggling to maintain its fragile independence while Japan and the European colonial powers cynically sought to gain advantages for themselves: "If only the rest of the world will give her [China] a chance to find herself and interfere only by the helping hand!"[86] Just as in her wholehearted support of the League of Nations, Woolley's hopes for China reflected her endorsement of the idealism in Wilson's foreign policy. Woolley never acknowledged or perhaps never understood that the "helping hand" of Wilson's foreign policy constituted a less obvious form of interference.[87]

Back in the States, Woolley was once again swept up in fund-raising obligations, college activities, conferences, and organizational work. After attending a conference in New York of the Women's Foundation for Health, an organization that existed "on a shoestring" and whose situation Woolley called "wearisome like beating the air," she explained to Marks why she didn't withdraw her support: "I stay in because I feel that I have no right to get out, when the work they are doing is good and the workers so devoted." On the same New York trip, she was obliged to attend a dinner at which representatives from seven colleges, along with several lawyers, discussed the best methods for colleges to guarantee bequests. About this she told Marks: "I am tired of trying to interest 'wealth' in worthy causes! Today's 'jobs' are not peculiarly to my liking."[88]

In 1924, Woolley was unanimously elected to the American Council of the Institute of Pacific Relations.[89] Business, financial, and political leaders, university presidents and "unofficial diplomats" (individuals who represented neither governments nor private interests) came together to study "the factors that underlie racial contacts and the adjustment of conflicting interests—the possibility of creating a new type of international community in the Pacific region based on mutual understanding."[90] The Institute was a controversial enterprise. The U.S. State Department believed that the Institute would make a bad situation worse between the United States and Japan. Business interests objected to the Institute's meddling in affairs beyond their competence; the press dismissed it as an idealistic venture, and organized labor saw nothing good coming of it.[91] In spite of the suspicion and skepticism surrounding it, the Institute grew through the 1920s, and Woolley became an enthusiastic participant. She had come to the attention of Edward C. Carter[92] during his search for "able women who have interests in the educational and international field who have some kind of contact with the Pacific." Unhappy with the "great preponderance of males" within the Institute, Carter told the chair of the Pacific Council, Stanford University president Ray Lyman Wilbur, that a "definite search" for women was essential:

> In international affairs in this country there seems to be a tendency for certain organizations that are stressing their role as objective students in international affairs to largely limit themselves to men; and, on the other hand, there seems to be a number of organizations made up exclusively of women who are taking either a subjective or what seems to be a purely idealistic attitude to international relations. Their separation by sexes cannot conduce to realism in international progress.[93]

When a colleague of Carter's recommended Woolley, he described her as "the only outstanding woman" in his opinion. "She knows a good deal about the Far East, and while very liberal in her views is highly regarded by all elements in our Institute, and is not classed, as are many other women, as sentimentally enthusiastic."[94] Woolley accepted the vice chairmanship of the research subcommittee and quickly sent off an initial short list of prominent women who, she assured Carter, were not "sentimentally enthusiastic."[95] Woolley did not share Carter's view of women's organizations as "subjective" and "idealistic." Rather, her skills in negotiating the male world were in play. Her goal was to bring as many women as possible into the Institute, and she succeeded in recruiting several. The committee work was time-consuming and involved travel to Honolulu in 1925 and again in 1927. In November of 1927, she was elected to membership in the Institute's National Council and board of trustees. She acknowledged that her "exceedingly full" schedule made it impossible for her to meet all her obligations, but she did not want to quit the Institute, hoping instead to find some way to improve her attendance at meetings.[96]

That year, Woolley also agreed to serve "for a limited time" as president of the AAUW.[97] She now had, as she said, "two full-time 'jobs,'"[98] but she could not say no to the opportunity to head an organization whose membership exceeded thirty thousand women in more than four hundred local branches.[99] Recognizing the enormous amount of work that needed to be done, Woolley persuaded the board of the AAUW to create a permanent administrative position at the national headquarters in Washington, D.C. Two years later, in 1929, Kathryn McHale became the first general director.[100] The structural changes initiated by Woolley would prove highly successful. She argued that

> the Association's structure was intended to resemble that of a university. The role of general director ... "corresponds roughly to that of college president while the national president's duties are more like those of a chairman of a board of trustees.[101]

During McHale's twenty-year tenure, she would unify and strengthen the national organization. One of her significant achievements was to

> consolidate the Association's research and publication activities. The new headquarters staff developed resource materials, research guides, and study aids for AAUW branch use, conducted research projects and collaborated with numerous other educational, women's and reform organizations on research and lobbying. The Association quickly developed a

General director of the American Association of University Women Dr. Kathryn McHale, 1930s.

reputation for producing high-quality professional materials, for which there was a growing demand.[102]

After the 1936 decision at Mount Holyoke, the Association would assign a researcher to investigate.

McHale shared Woolley's interest in developing internationalism within the organization. For Woolley, "the problem of the century" was international in scope:

> first, the increasing need of international experience and understanding on the part of students and scholars from all countries; and second, the especial need of American students to acquire an international consciousness which shall leaven our national egocentrism, without lessening appreciation of our great advantages and opportunities. The ignorance of the average British student whom I have met about America is appalling. But the oblivion of the average American student touching Europe is more so and more dangerous because less often stirred by a lively curiosity.[103]

Woolley wanted American women to be full participants in the International Federation of Women. While she found kindred spirits among the AAUW leadership, women who believed in the importance of international dialogue and who were involved in peace and anti-militarist organizations, the Association also had a strong conservative strain within its membership. Some AAUW branches were committed to removing pacifists from key committee positions, especially from those committees whose purpose was to influence congressional opinion.[104]

Meanwhile, Woolley closely followed the progress of the Sacco and Vanzetti case in Boston and joined a petition campaign for a retrial. In a telegram to the governor, she argued for clemency:

> There are many thinking people who believe them innocent. There are many more who are not convinced they are guilty. Their execution while there is a shadow of a doubt as to their guilt would be a tragedy for Massachusetts and a blow to confidence in American justice.[105]

This and other public actions brought Woolley negative media coverage and the attention of professional anti-communists, and soon her name appeared in a pamphlet titled *Red Revolution: Do We Want it Here?*[106] The author sent it to all the chapters of the Daughters of the American Revolution, which led to Woolley's expulsion from the Massachusetts chapter, an action that she accepted with equanimity. She was pleased that her home chapter in Pawtucket, Rhode Island, did not succumb to the hysteria.[107]

In April of 1928, Woolley cast aside convention as president of Mount Holyoke and publicly announced her support for Herbert Hoover in his presidential campaign. A local newspaper reported: "In taking this stand Miss

Woolley broke the academic tradition of Mount Holyoke College, whose head has always held herself aloof from partisan politics."[108] Woolley was regularly in the news. By 1931, she had begun her third consecutive term as president of the AAUW. The Sixth Conference on the Cause and Cure of War, organized by nine national women's organizations, was held in Washington, D.C., that year, and Woolley was a principal speaker. It was time, she said, to demobilize the "war machine" and mobilize "peace machinery."[109] The following March, *Good Housekeeping* ran profiles of "America's 12 Greatest Women" and Woolley was third among them. She was asked what the future held for women:

> First of all they will be human beings. Marriage and motherhood are all-absorbing for a time—but think of the years after ... women are left to rust out their lives in discontent and bitterness.... Motherhood seems like an unanswerable problem for the ambitious woman with a great work to do.

She was asked what the solution was. "Change the business world's attitude toward [motherhood]," she said. The interviewer noted that Woolley's eyes were those "of a happy woman, of a woman satisfied, fulfilled. She had loved her work and seen it count."[110] The interviewer was mistaken about Woolley retiring from public life. She had hoped to retire from Mount Holyoke in 1932, shortly before her seventieth birthday. "The attainment of that age ... seemed a sufficient reason," she wrote. However, the board of trustees persuaded her to remain in office at least until 1934, following the wishes of the majority of the faculty and alumnae.[111]

The Board Begins to Change

Woolley had strong allies among the trustees, Boyd Edwards perhaps the most insightful and worldly among them.[112] In his mid-fifties, Edwards was a minister and headmaster of Mercersburg Academy in Pennsylvania. In the fall of 1930, Woolley and Edwards had corresponded about a proposal from newly returned trustee Howell Cheney to reorganize the board of trustees, a plan that had been discussed and tabled prior to his return.[113] Cheney, a Connecticut silk manufacturer and a member of the Yale Corporation, had previously served on Mount Holyoke's board from 1912 until 1925 and had a reputation for independence and fair-mindedness. This time, he brought a second Yale contact onto the board. Edgar S. Furniss was a political economist who quickly became known as the outstanding educator among the trustees, a man to be deferred to. In his early forties, he was an ambitious scholar who had met with early success, having just been appointed dean of the Graduate School at Yale. One historian described Yale's graduate school under Furniss as a "teeming

Mount Holyoke Commencement 1924. Back row, left to right: Joseph Skinner, chairman of board of trustees; Russell Wicks, pastor of the Second Congregational Church, Holyoke, Massachusetts; Boyd Edwards, Mount Holyoke trustee and headmaster of Mercersburg Academy, Pennsylvania. Front row, left to right: the Honorable Henry Morgenthau; President Mary Emma Woolley.

rookery of scholars,"[114] any one of whom would be a huge asset to an institution fortunate enough to hire him. Furniss, who was married to a Mount Holyoke graduate, had little to no interest in the scholarship of women, nor did he have an understanding of the depth of intellectual activity at Mount Holyoke or of faculty accomplishments. He was, however, interested in finding work for Yale graduates. He would soon place himself at the center of a brewing conflict over who would succeed Woolley in the presidency.

When Cheney reopened the question of reducing the size of the board, Edwards volunteered to resign,[115] but Woolley persuaded him to stay on. He was an important ally, his willingness to share his insights with Woolley too valuable.[116] That fall, he advised her that the trustees no longer took her annual report seriously. Woolley's long-standing practice of submitting the completed written report for the board members to read on their own was now working against her interest. He recommended that she take time with the trustees and "give us the flavor" of how she felt about what should be given priority. Edwards eloquently conveyed his respect and affection for Woolley as he warned her of the trouble that lay ahead. The board, he said, had grown used to

> the greatness of your service both to the college and to the wide world.... We take it for granted a good deal like the rising of the sun in the morning or the falling of rain or the light of the stars ... we count on [it] vitally but never notice adequately unless we have a poet's soul or maybe a drought.[117]

Then, in March of 1931, Board President Joseph A. Skinner, a Holyoke businessman who had served on the board since 1905 and as president since 1912, announced his desire to retire. A significant era was ending. For nineteen years, Woolley and Skinner had assumed major responsibility for the board's decisions. Decisions were typically made without question unless Woolley herself raised one. The task of selecting Skinner's successor would not be simple. Skinner delayed his resignation while Edwards sent letters to all the trustees asking for three choices of candidates. Cheney recommended Woolley. Edwards disagreed. He felt that the new president of the board needed to provide continuity over the transition to a new administration and that "a good man" was needed to provide good business sense.[118] The board decided on trustee Henry K. Hyde, a choice that Woolley was pleased with. Hyde's geographical closeness to the college and his "singular poise" and "conciliatory spirit and firmness" gave her confidence that he would be able to handle the trustees.[119] Hyde was already a strong ally of Woolley's.[120] His leadership would be important as the board was changing and becoming increasingly assertive. Edwards and trustee Edward White[121] shared the view that the board was plagued by "snap judgments and hair-trigger business procedures" in addition to "cheap gossip" that was hurtful to Woolley:

There are those ... who are interested in giving the impression of difficulties in the situation and they probably are not altogether scrupulous and certainly not sportsmanlike. One of the unhappy things about such a situation is that it sets us all to suspecting this one or that one.[122]

When Edwards agreed with White about "hair-trigger business proce-dures" and "cheap gossip," he was alluding primarily to the influence of trustee Henry Plimpton Kendall, a graduate of Amherst College, whose mother and sister were Mount Holyoke alumnae. Kendall was a highly successful Boston-based textile manufacturer and a devoted follower of Taylorism,[123] who had succeeded in merging a dozen cotton mills into a new corporation, sufficient proof for him of the superiority of his business practices and judgment. A large, balding man, brash and opinionated, he thoroughly disliked Woolley and was not averse to making his sentiments known. He criticized her leader-ship style, her relationship with Marks, and "a good deal of what [Woolley] stood for."[124] Two other Boston businessmen joined Kendall on the board in 1926, William James Davidson , who was a close friend of Kendall's, and Elbert Harvey, who would soon become board treasurer. The following year, Kendall persuaded investment banker Alva Morrison, another Boston connection, to become a trustee and to immediately join the board's Finance Committee.

With Hyde at the helm, Woolley still hoped that the board would con-tinue in the tradition set by Skinner. The trustees had routinely supported her activities outside the college. She, therefore, accepted the invitation from the Laymen's Foreign Missions Inquiry, which involved a four-month trip begin-ning in January of 1932. She planned to be at the college during the fall term when her presence was most critical.[125]

"Protests Heard in Capital on Ground Mt. Holyoke President Is Pacifist"[126]

Then, in December of 1931, just before Woolley was scheduled to leave, plans were swept off the table when President Hoover offered her an appoint-ment as the sole American woman delegate to the Conference on the Reduc-tion and Limitation of Armaments in Geneva.[127] For Woolley, this was the most important work she could be asked to do, and she immediately sent a letter to each trustee describing the offer. Hyde was wholeheartedly supportive. Then, Woolley was pleasantly surprised when the trustees uniformly congrat-ulated her and expressed the hope that she would accept. Even Kendall gave his approval.[128]

Woolley had not been the first choice in the selection. Judge Florence

Allen, at that time serving on the Ohio Supreme Court, was the unanimous choice of all the major women's organizations, but she was a Democrat and President Hoover complained that his Republican friends in the Cabinet would demand to know why he couldn't find a Republican woman. Uncertain about Hoover's real interest or ability in persuading his committee to appoint a woman, Carrie Chapman Catt and her colleagues on the National Committee on the Cause and Cure of War wasted no time finding an alternative. They recommended Woolley as their single choice without consulting Woolley herself. When Catt did approach Woolley, she strongly urged her to accept the offer if made. "[I]t is the highest recognition of women that has yet been made," she told Woolley. "You stand as the united choice of the women of this nation and that is a wonderful thing."[129] Woolley received an urgent, confidential telegram from Dorothy Detzer of the Women's International League urging her to give permission to recommend her. A few weeks earlier Woolley had written to Hoover urging the appointment of Judge Allen, and she would not agree to her nomination until she was certain that Allen was not a candidate.[130] When Woolley was assured that that was the case, she enthusiastically accepted and wrote to Catt: "On the thirty-first day of December it will be thirty-one years since I began my work here [at Mount Holyoke] and, in that time, I have had one year's leave of absence!"[131]

There was great celebration among the progressive women's groups. For Woolley personally, it was an opportunity to step into a much larger arena as "a vigorous and able feminine advocate for peace," in the words of an AP reporter.[132] Woolley called it the "fulfilling [of] a lifelong ambition."[133] Pacifist and peace groups had won a seven-month campaign to gain representation on the American delegation. The National Council for Prevention of War released a statement calling the appointment "the most important ... yet given a woman in this country."[134] When word got out, Woolley's life changed dramatically. She was a national figure. "The whole country has received a magnificent Christmas present in your appointment," wrote Ellen and Mignon Talbot, two Mount Holyoke faculty members.[135] Letters of congratulations poured in and Woolley answered them all. The message was consistent. This was the greatest of honors, and women around the world would be following her every move in Geneva. Mount Holyoke historian Viola Barnes, who would later support the appointment of a male president and assist Woolley's opposition, congratulated Woolley "on the splendid honor which has come to you! It is pleasant to know that there is in the national presidential chair a man with the discernment to pick the ablest woman in America for the post.... We are all very proud of you."[136] Woolley was inundated with advice. Reporters pressed her for interviews, and the trustees publicly applauded her high-profile appointment, recognizing the positive publicity for the college. A *Boston Globe* reporter who interviewed Woolley wrote admiringly of her gracious and commanding style[137] and the slow, pleasant way she told him, "War is an anachronism." Another reporter wrote approvingly: "Unlike many other women in public life, Miss Woolley has never dressed in what is regarded as mannish fashion."[138]

One week before Woolley left for Geneva, activist and educator Annie Nathan Meyer[139] sent her a copy of the *Weekly News* published by the New York League of Women Voters. Amid articles about discriminatory dismissal of married women and the fight to raise the minimum age when children can leave school was a commentary that began:

> Now what does Mary Lyon think? Mary Lyon, who endured criticism and ridicule and poverty, whose heart was sick long years with hope deferred in that modest little attempt of hers ... to found a seminary.... That her successor ... has been chosen by the President of the United States as the first woman to sit in on a great international peace conference.... We are proud of the choice the President has made.[140]

At the same time, ultra-conservative organizations had concerns about Woolley's pacifist convictions and some campaigned to remove her from the delegation. "Only the Pacifists, Socialists and Communists are for complete disarmament," the acting president of the National Civic Federation wrote to Woolley. Even limitation of arms required safeguards, he reasoned, so that civilized countries did not place themselves in a "position where they can be overrun by the Red armies of Soviet Russia and the hordes of Islam."[141] Negative press that focused on Woolley's politics did not derail her appointment, but she did have to assuage the concerns of Mount Holyoke alumnae who heard members of the Massachusetts DAR accuse Woolley of "the Red variety" of pacifism. The day before she left for Geneva, Woolley took the time to write a response to an alumna affiliated with the Commonwealth Fund:

> It may not be necessary for me to tell you that I am not an atheist; not a believer in the dissolution of the family group; not an advocate for Bolshevik immorality; not a member of any clubs or leagues that would promote red causes and overthrow the United States government and its ideals.

Woolley listed the numerous organizations "working for internationalism" that she was a member of and ended the letter with a statement of her belief that Sacco and Vanzetti were "really executed because of their political views." She reiterated that she was "not in sympathy with Communism" but did believe that "if a man is not guilty of murder, he should not be executed because of his political theories."[142]

Woolley left South Hadley for Geneva midday on the 19th of January. Twelve hundred students lined the driveway of the President's House and cheered as she climbed into a car accompanied by Marks and two others. Woolley would be away from the college for at least six months but felt confident that Academic Dean Harriet Allyn would do well as acting president. Allyn was well liked and had solid administrative skills and diplomacy.[143]

In Geneva, a spacious three-room suite with two bathrooms and three telephones became Woolley's temporary home. In this world of politicians and career diplomats Woolley was a novice, but she took on her responsibilities with characteristic confidence. She asserted that "no one worked harder to understand the problems confronting the Conference."[144] Journalist and humorist Will Rogers sought Woolley out and found her "the outstanding novelty" of the conference. "'Doc' and I got along great," he wrote. "It's no joking matter getting the world to disarm. Maybe a woman can do it. It's a cinch men can't. So good luck to you 'Doc.'" He found her "very likeable, broad in mind and body, feet and plenty of 'em right on the ground.... You would like her," Rogers told his readers. "She is not the type for a college president at all."[145]

Expectations ran high among the women's peace organizations. One organization that Woolley worked closely with wanted her to have "the privilege of materially advancing the peace and stability of the world."[146] A representative of another organization told her: "You ... are the spokesperson for the longings, no, the demands, of peace seeking American women. Do we lay too heavy a burden on you? But we know that you have already chosen it."[147] Woolley's former Wellesley colleague, national president of the Women's International League for Peace and Freedom Emily Greene Balch, took a more realistic approach:

We shall all look to you for help to the cause of Peace in many ways, but I hope you will not be burdened by a feeling that people are expecting more of you than is possible. I, at least, fully understand that such an official position carries with it limitations as well as opportunities.[148]

Woolley quickly understood the reality of the situation. The European papers were reporting a behind-the-scenes

Mary Emma Woolley in Geneva, 1932, "Talking to America" broadcasting news of the disarmament conference.

agreement between members of the French and American delegations that put the United States in a position to take no initiative toward disarmament. The composition of the American delegation, experts from the State, War and Navy departments, belied a commitment to disarmament or reduction in arms. Thus, the leadership of the Women's International League argued strenuously for a change of focus by replacing the current delegates.[149]

Woolley was the unofficial representative of the scores of peace organizations who sent petitions to the conference, petitions gathered by house-to-house canvassing in cities and towns in fifty-four countries. She was the only woman on the five-member Committee on Petitions, and it fell to her to guarantee a formal and official presentation of the millions of signatures. She not only succeeded but also got extensive coverage in the media, prompting Catt to assert that "no one in all the world has any excuse for not knowing that eight million people have asked the world to disarm."[150]

Millions of Americans listened to Woolley's radio talk over the Columbia Network. Catt told her how "splendid, optimistic and cheerful her commentary was," how "different from the temper of all that men have given"—each one so fearful of political fallout.[151] Woolley gave her listeners brief glimpses of the meetings, ending the talks with the optimistic assertion that "we are thinking peace—not war, and we are determined to succeed." She would not acknowledge her discouragement or a sense of hopelessness. She was assigned to two committees beyond the Committee on Petitions: the important Budgetary Control Committee, where she "stood out as long as she could for a minimum of armament expenditure," and the Moral Disarmament Committee, which she quickly understood was seen as a "somewhat unnecessary appendage to material disarmament."[152]

Japan began bombing Shanghai virtually on the eve of the conference, and although Woolley saw "pessimists grow on every bush," she persisted in searching out like-minded delegates. She persuaded one fellow delegate to include in his speech a statement asking for "an absolute prohibition of lethal gas and bacteriological warfare."[153] She irritated another when she simply closed her eyes and told him, "You don't understand; there is a new spirit in the world. Besides, the President told me to work for the maximum of reduction, and I propose to work for that."[154] By March, the inertia created by the caution of delegations following orders from governments had seriously eroded Woolley's optimism. She found the actions of experienced diplomats incomprehensible. "Granted that nationalism was in the saddle and rode mankind, realistic thinking should make clear the fact that the only safe and sure policy for the future of the individual nation lies in maintaining the sanctity of treaties."[155] Woolley was "stirred by the small powers" that strongly advocated League of Nations intervention over Japan's aggression in Manchuria and "depressed by the 'big'" nations whose political and economic self-interest so obviously dictated their positions. She witnessed the United States "on the sidelines." The nation's refusal to join the League was one of the "keenest disappointments of [her] life," she said, "a disappointment personal in its intensity."[156]

Powerless because she was not participating in the actual negotiations, she was angry "that certain influential delegates have such connection with the steel interests that any real progress toward reduction in armaments must be made by over-powering their opposition."[157] She wrote to Marks asking her to sell all of her DuPont investments. "I am seeing so much of the evil of manufacturing munitions and the insidious way in which the private manufacture works against disarmament."[158] She shared with Marks the unending frustrations she experienced as a woman: "I must be effective, but not aggressive; womanly but not womanish; equal to social obligations but always on hand for the business ones; informed, but unable to take my pipe and join other 'pipers' in the corridors."[159] "Men and politics are both queer!"[160] She was convinced that if women ran the conference, they would simply apply to other nations the restrictions that had been placed on Germany at Versailles. Woolley was asked by a fellow delegate to begin a massive telegram campaign urging Hoover to allow the delegation to "go far in a liberal policy."[161] The administration was "holding our thumbs." She wanted to be "allowed off the leash."[162] "Unless this Conference accomplishes something," she wrote, "it will stand before the world as the most striking example of a reduction ad absurdum."[163] She succeeded in collecting what she called "a marvelous collection of human documents" and sent a portion of them to Hoover.[164]

When the conference adjourned, there were no specific agreements to limit or reduce armaments, and Woolley had come to agree with the Soviet delegate Litvinov when he argued that "governments still believed in war as an instrument of national policy and that they preferred to talk to each other, even of peace and international solidarity, when armed to the teeth."[165] She was extremely disappointed in the outcome of the conference and in her own ineffectiveness. Privately, she expressed outrage and frustration over the refusal of the powerful nations to see "that the way of safety lay in disarming down to Germany before Germany demanded arming up to them."[166] She refused, however, to let the experience in Geneva change her attitude toward the work that needed to be done. She believed that public opinion, mobilized through the successful campaigns of the women's and peace movements, had influenced Hoover and it was his Plan that had reinvigorated the conference sufficiently to pass the Benes Resolution. "Not to have failed ignominiously is almost a triumph," she concluded. It was the first time in world history that fifty nations had come together to discuss vital issues.[167]

The plan was for Woolley to return to South Hadley in time for commencement, but she felt that she couldn't leave Geneva. In June, she wrote to the trustees: "I am sure you will agree with me that I must not be a 'slacker.'" To the graduating seniors, she wrote: "It will take all the moral courage of which I am possessed to be cheerful over here in Geneva."[168] It had been a difficult time at the college. Allyn wrote to Woolley as early as April imploring her to "make very few engagements away from the college next year—from every point of view I think it is *most important* for you to be at the college!"[169] Woolley returned in July, but rather than embracing the affairs of the college, she hit the ground running in response to numerous invitations to share her experiences in Geneva. She was consumed with the need to keep hope alive, her own as well as others, and she used her celebrity to that end. Woolley wrote to Hoover in August, offering to travel to Washington at a moment's notice to report on the conference, but while he responded with praise for her efforts, her tact and her understanding, he expressed no interest in her offer.[170]

While the conference continued to limp along, Woolley relied on detailed weekly reports, four pages single-spaced on ledger-size paper, that she received from Laura Puffer Morgan, the AAUW representative who was also working for the National Council for Prevention of War. In September, Morgan told Woolley that everyone in Geneva was asking if she was returning. "You know what we all hope," she said. In October, knowing that she couldn't return, Woolley wrote to Morgan: "I feel that my future is on the knees of the gods ... I am trying to be helpful to the cause!"[171]

The Disarmament Committee of the Women's International Organizations wanted a full American delegation reassembled with Woolley as part of it. When in February of 1933 part of the delegation did return to Geneva, there was still hope that Woolley would join them. In March she wrote to one of her fellow delegates: "I feel as if I were divided at least into two parts: one busily at work here: and the other living in spirit, if not in body, at Geneva."[172] Though she continued to travel to cities throughout the country speaking to large groups, she was also turning down invitations. She had to acknowledge that the college was not being given "the right-of-way which it deserves." When the conference reconvened in April, Woolley was not invited to return. The United States had assumed a passive role in Geneva, its two-person delegation a mere token. When she corresponded with President Roosevelt in September of 1933, he told her that while he wanted her to continue to serve on the delegation, he couldn't say when it would be necessary to go to Geneva.[173]

British delegate Margery Corbett-Ashby, a brilliant, world-renowned feminist/activist, left Geneva in January of 1934, terminally discouraged about the outcome of the conference. She wrote to Woolley: "I have missed you there so badly through the dark days."[174] Woolley stepped up her activity, reading Geneva material daily. Well-informed with the help of Morgan's extraordinarily detailed newsletters, she met briefly with Roosevelt in March, urging "super-vision" and "control" on the part of the American government.[175] As a last-ditch effort to stall the breakdown of the conference, three women representing the 45 million women in forty countries who made up the Disarmament Committee of the Women's International Organizations, composed a letter in May of 1934 addressed to twenty of the heads of delegations. The letter urged them to "make a supreme effort to bring the Conference to a successful conclusion."[176] The appeal had no impact. For Woolley, the failures of Geneva loomed large. She continued to accept speaking engagements until the summer of 1935. In June, she wrote to Morgan that she would take the summer months "to help the 'reservoir' fill up again ... this is certainly an anxious time, but the time in which to work harder to make human beings realize that we must find a way out." She told Morgan that the college demands were "heavier this year than ever before." What weighed most heavily was the recent news from McHale. At this very early stage in the search for Woolley's successor, the designated trustee committee, mandated to select a woman, was actively interviewing men.[177]

CHAPTER 3

The Seeds of Suspicion

From 1930 to 1933, the years in which Skinner resigned from the board, Hyde was elected and Woolley traveled to Geneva, the cast of characters on the board of trustees that would play prominent roles in the presidential succession fight was assembling. The transformation began with the election of Cheney and Furniss in 1930. Three key men, Kendall, Davidson and Harvey, had joined earlier, in 1926, but had little influence until after 1930. Between 1928 and 1932, three more male trustees joined the board. All of these men were motivated to move Mount Holyoke away from the college culture established by Woolley over her thirty-six-year tenure as president.

They began to challenge the administration of the college, focusing first on the college's finances and its faculty governance. The arrival of these men onto the board coincided with the beginning of the Great Depression, which, from 1931 onward, would put tremendous pressure on the college's ability to meet its expenses, thereby giving ammunition to those who sought reasons to criticize and opportunities to effect change. In April of 1931, Treasurer Harvey shared his opinion with Woolley's ally Edwards that the Education Committee failed to carefully scrutinize faculty appointments. In Harvey's view, the members had been deferring too much to Woolley. He wanted to hold the committee accountable to the trustees, requiring that it give a "thoroughgoing survey to the faculty situation in every aspect before recommendations are made." He assured Edwards that this was not a "veiled attack against Miss Woolley." He told Edwards that he had great respect for Woolley, but "there are two or three individuals in the faculty and administrative group whose presence is hardly for the best interests of the college and that a change is not likely to be made until we have a vital and independent Education Committee." Marks on the faculty and Harriet Newhall in the administration, both living with Woolley in the President's House, were undoubtedly two of the three. Harvey was assuming that because Marks and Newhall were personally close to Woolley, they wielded inordinate power within the college, an erroneous assumption.[1]

66

Woolley's institutional ideal was one in which faculty leadership was paramount, and this was clearly not what Harvey and other trustees envisioned for the college's future. Kendall, for one, with his business background and admiration for Taylorism, clearly saw the model of a faculty-run university as highly inefficient and backward. What mattered to him was that college administrators and trustees assert their leadership prerogatives. The idea that the faculty could be leaders was as foreign to him as envisioning a committee of his employees telling him how to run his business.

What Harvey did not realize when he attacked the Education Committee was that Edwards was the chairman. Harvey had neglected, he told Edwards, "to look the matter up" and had "not the slightest notion."[2] Edwards made eloquently certain that Harvey knew where he stood on Woolley, on the committee and on Harvey's concerns:

As a rule, I believe the head of an educational institution knows more about the personnel and the personal relationships and the hot spots and the danger spots in the institution than almost anybody can on the outside or even on the inside … furthermore it is well known that psychologically speaking if a person who is looking for trouble approaches different members of a faculty asking questions that gives opportunity for fault-finding that is almost certain to run into criticisms of the administration.

About Woolley, Edwards had this to say:

I am for her absolutely all the time and everywhere. The time passed many years ago when Miss Woolley's standing in the educational world depends in any sense upon the attitude of a board of trustees towards her. On the contrary the standing of the board of trustees in the educational world will be conditioned by their attitude toward Miss Woolley. It is not Miss Woolley who is being judged but ourselves. We are expected to use our best judgment and give her the benefit of our opinions about questions that are vital to the welfare of the college. All that pertains to the character, capacity and usefulness of Miss Woolley is practically at this moment set in bronze for an enduring record. We must not permit the fouling of a stream that has flowed so clear and strong and full for a human generation. It does not need to be done and everything vital in the situation can be absolutely protected and conserved without any such thing happening.[3]

Harvey, embarrassed by his misstep, could only agree with Edwards, yet he persisted in asking for an opportunity to talk about campus issues, even though they were "quite likely … wholly of the nature" that Edwards described.[4] Edwards told Harvey that if he believed there were issues at the college important enough for the trustees to become involved in, then the individual trustees who had the information had an obligation to bring them out into the open. Otherwise, Edwards warned, "we shall talk about them behind our hands and give some people who do not hear the true facts the impression that there is something subtle and insidious working underneath."[5] Edwards had to be aware that these tactics were already surfacing, tactics designed to create the false reality that there were serious problems at Mount Holyoke, only solvable by new, tough leadership.

Woolley had many allies on the changing board, men and women who had no desire to impose radical change and who believed that Woolley ranked among the best college presidents in the nation. Her most loyal supporters among the men, in addition to Edwards and Board President Hyde, were White, James Speers, a New York City businessman, George Dwight Pratt, a Springfield businessman, and William Horace Day and Rockwell Harmon Potter, two Connecticut ministers.

During the same month, April 1931, when Harvey attempted to sow seeds of suspicion with Edwards, the *Springfield Republican* ran a story announcing Woolley's impending retirement in 1933. Woolley refused comment, and the trustees refused to be individually quoted. The source of the story was a mystery. Local alumnae immediately organized an open letter of protest to alumnae throughout the country demanding that Woolley "be retained in the presidential office until the observance of the Centennial in 1937."[6] Trustee Cheney drafted a letter intended for the Alumnae Association in which he referred to Woolley's "'repeated expression' of a desire to retire." When he shared it with Woolley, she rejected his characterization and reminded him that although it had been her strong desire to retire in 1932, she had agreed to the board's wishes to remain until 1934. She had never made "repeated" statements about wanting to retire.[7] Woolley sought trustee White's opinion of Cheney's actions. He told her that he believed she "had no stronger friend on the Board than Mr. Cheney." In private communication with Marks, Woolley referred to the "'masonic' character" of the board.[8] Beyond Kendall, who was so bluntly oppositional, Woolley was not certain who among the trustees shared his views.

The Nominating Committee on the board of trustees, a committee that until recently had not functioned, had three members, Davidson, Kendall and Mrs. Susan D. Arnold, an alumna trustee from the class of 1899 and an ally of Kendall's. With the new interest in activating the nominating committee, Speers and Edwards objected to the small size and its composition.[9] They moved to enlarge it to include themselves and the Reverend Day and recommended that Cheney join as chairman. Cheney had previously expressed concern that committees in general were being formed too haphazardly and reporting irresponsibly. As if to prove him correct, while Cheney was absent from a meeting because his wife was ill, Kendall unilaterally appointed Arnold to the chairmanship. Edwards was furious and told Woolley that sooner or later somebody was going to have to stand up to Kendall.[10] "That particular man's usefulness in the Board is very questionable, in view of his temper, aggressiveness and lack of reticence."[11] Edwards wrote to White as well, observing that it was "impossible to prevent leaks in a group of this size.... There are those, I think, who are interested in giving the impression of difficulties in the situation and they probably are not altogether scrupulous and certainly not sportsmanlike."[12] The now active Nominating Committee quickly brought two new trustees on board—Paul Hazlitt Davis, "a brilliant and aggressive businessman," and Alva Morrison, an urbane Harvard-educated Boston stock-broker with a "genuine interest in cultural and educational matters."[13] A year later Kendall succeeded in adding Hartford banker Maynard Hazen.

Newhall, as secretary to the board of trustees, was present at all board meetings and described to Edwards some troubling actions after he had left a meeting early. Edwards told Newhall that she and Woolley had to "get used to the kind of people that you have to deal with, then having to deal with that kind of people becomes less disturbing simply because you are aware of the psychology in the case."[14] In this, Edwards would be proven woefully mistaken. As with Plunkitt of Tammany Hall, whenever they saw their opportunities they took them.[15] While Woolley was away in Geneva, Morrison, as head of the Finance Committee, called an all-day meeting with the heads of all the academic departments and informed them that there would be appropriation reductions for the 1931–1932 academic year. There was discussion of possible faculty layoffs, prompting Latin professor Blanche Brotherton to write to Edwards. She was concerned that the most recent hire in her department would be let go, and she offered her own money to save the colleague's job:

> I know if Miss Woolley were here our particular case would not be questioned.... Ratification in the past has been absolutely automatic—trustees meet in March and hirings happen as early as January—here was a college with a president whose word was never broken, whose decisions were upheld by a harmonious board of trustees.[16]

Indicative of this changing board's agenda, the Nominating Committee appointed Furniss to head the 1937 centennial committee despite significant sentiment among the trustees that he was not the best choice. Furniss accepted the position, a decision he would later regret.

When Woolley returned to the campus in September of 1932, she was pleased to inform the trustees that Dean Harriet Allyn had stretched the college's scholarship funds to their limit while Dean Mary Ashby Cheek had shown "great ingenuity" in making it possible for students to do paid work on campus. Despite the pressures generated by the Depression, the college had finished the year in the black and, most important, "without lessening academic strength."[17]

By the end of that year, the board of trustees decided that "in consideration of the appointment of President Woolley as delegate to the Disarmament

Conference," the majority of the trustees wanted Woolley to remain at the college past 1934. There were rumors that President Hyde had informally told Woolley that the board wanted her to remain until the centennial in 1937.[18] Such a request would have made sense in the context of the college's endowment shrinking and enrollment in danger of declining. Woolley's popularity among the alumnae and her national and international prominence would have been seen by the trustees as important assets.

The mood on campus did not reflect Woolley's description of a positive state of affairs. Faculty distrust of the trustees was increasing. Several faculty members chose to bypass the Faculty Conference Committee (FCC), the faculty's official representative body, when they decided to distribute a petition directly to each of the trustees demanding a thorough investigation of the business practices of the Comptroller's Office. Woolley chastised the faculty signers for failing to go through appropriate channels and for creating undue publicity. In the fall of 1933, Hyde and Woolley agreed to meet with the FCC but insisted that the comptroller himself be present. There is no evidence that anything substantial happened at the meeting, and events soon made the issue of faculty insubordination moot.[19]

Hyde died unexpectedly on November 18, 1933, and with his death the balance of forces within the board between Woolley's allies and opponents would shift dramatically. A new board president had to be chosen, and Woolley shared her preference with Edwards in a private communication. Morrison, she thought, somewhat resembled Hyde in his "poise and good manners." "Wisdom, tact, forbearance and firmness" were the qualities she sought, and she hoped that he possessed them.[20] Edwards' "spontaneous" response was that Morrison was too much "under the influence of Mr. K[endall]. There is something there to be considered." Did Woolley feel this way as well? She told Edwards no, and he appeared to withdraw his objections when he added a positive observation of Kendall's recent behavior on the board. Edwards observed that Kendall had "undergone a great change."

> I think he has come to realize that there is a certain strength and wisdom in the administration of the college beyond what he had originally estimated. He is such a useful man that that particular development in his case seems to me to be auspicious.[21]

However, he did not base his vote on this new perception. While he told Woolley that her preference should be "the controlling factor," he chose to vote in absentia for Cheney, not Morrison, at the March 1934 meeting.[22]

Morrison won handily and immediately lobbied for a new trustee who would serve on the Finance Committee. Woolley countered with her own recommendation, a New York lawyer who was a trustee of both the Chapin School for Girls and the Union Theological Seminary. Lansing Reed was the son of a prominent Congregationalist minister in Springfield, Massachusetts, and his wife's father, an Episcopal bishop, was known as the "Banker Bishop" because his fund-raising efforts "invariably developed with Midas-like magic." Someone with Reed's background should have been an ideal candidate. However, he would be a Woolley ally and the board preferred Morrison's choice, Rohl C. Wiggin, a Boston banker and vice president of the Caribbean Sugar Company.[23]

Woolley would finally welcome a strong ally to the board the following June. Frances Perkins, class of '02, who had been appointed just one year earlier by President Roosevelt to serve as the first secretary of labor, agreed to become a trustee—one of only two women serving elected ten-year terms during this crucial period.[24] Perkins' appointment to the cabinet had provoked outrage and derision in some quarters. The press reported that "business men ... pulled out chunks of their hair in frenzy; labor leaders ... uttered low guttural sounds"[25] at the realization that "Ma Perkins" was in such a powerful position in government. Despite the enormous demands that came with her presidential appointment, Perkins decided to weigh in on the historic decision at Mount Holyoke. The path to her extraordinary career in public service had begun at the college. She felt indebted, and she also had great respect and affection for Woolley.

Young "Fanny the Perk" was at once a formidable intellect and leader and a lighthearted, witty girl as a student at Mount Holyoke. She began her studies in science, but it was Professor Anna May Soule's course in political economy that set her on her path. Soule was a young, innovative teacher who brought her students to the factories in Holyoke to observe workers and objectively report on workplace conditions. Soule's students organized a chapter of the National Consumers League and, in Perkins' last semester, they invited the imposing Florence Kelley, national secretary of the League, who spoke passionately about the need to abolish tenement sweatshops and child labor. A Socialist and former anarchist, Kelley was divorced and raising children alone. Jacob Riis also came to speak, and Perkins read his book, *How the Other Half Lives*. These were transforming experiences for Perkins. At her graduation from Mount Holyoke, Perkins' mother said about her daughter, "She's a stranger to me."[26]

Woolley, in Perkins' view, was a woman of "marvelous ability, strong personality and great talent." If she was also "a little stiff-necked and a little old-fashioned," it was of no consequence. Perkins believed that Woolley's successor should be a modern woman with great potential, capable of navigating the new social world in which Woolley and her colleagues were somewhat uncomfortable. Perkins was aware that some trustees found Woolley "difficult," men in business, for example, who argued with her that limited resources be spent on advertising and publicity for the college. These men compared the generous entertainment budget and gracious lifestyle of President Stanley King and his wife at nearby Amherst College to the meager social facilities at Mount Holyoke and concluded that Mount Holyoke's image would be immeasurably improved "if a man were President who had a nice wife who could entertain visiting dignitaries and trustees and would be the charming hostess."[27] Perkins observed those she called "the other-side trustees" beginning to take action and realized that an all-out struggle lay ahead.

These "other-side trustees" had other motivations for changing Mount Holyoke beyond Woolley's unwillingness to spend money on advertising and entertaining. Several were critical of her "feminist" work, in particular her heavy involvement with the AAUW, a "second job," as Woolley herself described it. Some were critical of her high public profile, specifically her prominence in the work for peace. When Woolley was attacked in the press as liberal, pacifist and 'un-American,' they saw it as unacceptable exposure for the college. Although there was little public talk or criticism of Woolley and Marks' relationship, there was an undercurrent of disapproval and dislike of Marks based in part on a sense of her favored status. Marks' thin-skinned and argumentative nature, her feminist and radical politics, and her intimacy with Woolley all contributed to the criticism. There was also talk about the absence of "normal" family life in the President's House.

In addition, many trustees, Kendall perhaps the most prominent among them, strongly opposed the model of faculty self-governance that Woolley had always nurtured. They resented the faculty's forceful, oppositional responses to what these trustees felt were their prerogatives. The overriding goal of the broadest coalition of "other-side trustees" was not necessarily to appoint a man to succeed Woolley but to make sure that whoever was appointed would have the toughness, even the "ruthlessness," to discipline the faculty. A sub-group of trustees affiliated with Yale had a more specific goal. For them, Mount Holyoke offered opportunities for employment for its "rookery of scholars." A Yale man in the presidency would virtually guarantee a continual source of jobs at a time when there was great concern over unemployment.[28] From these various perspectives a consensus would emerge that male candidates for president should be seriously considered, if not preferred.

In July of 1934, the trustees who would serve on a search committee for the presidency had not yet been selected; nevertheless, the *Holyoke Transcript* ran a lead story about Woolley's alleged successor, the Reverend Boynton Merrill, forty-three years old, a medical doctor, married with three children, and a trustee of Wellesley College.[29] Board President Morrison criticized the paper for its erroneous reporting, asserting that there was no truth to the story, and blamed the newspaper for not checking with the college.[30] The *Transcript* claimed that it had a source from "the eastern part of the state." Woolley and others wanted to investigate, but the effort died. The source was never discovered. Alumna trustee Rowena Keith Keyes, a writer and teacher with a Ph.D. from New York University (and a classmate of Perkins), heard about the news story through a chain of angry communications from faculty and friends. She told Morrison that she was "aghast" to receive a letter from an angry alumna who was so distressed by the news that a man was to be the next president of Mount Holyoke that she immediately dropped her "small support of the alumnae association."[31]

The story galvanized the full board to focus more closely on the succession. Woolley agreed to remain in office through the centennial celebration in 1937, giving a newly formed search committee more than two years to carry out a successful search. Keyes, meanwhile, found herself "meditating a good deal on the reasons why she hoped a woman would be chosen," since the issue had been "thrust" into her thoughts.[32] She sent Morrison a confidential letter in which she touched on the sensitive issues that percolated just below the surface at the college. One of the most persistent criticisms of Woolley had been her willingness to grant Marks special privileges. "I know," Keyes wrote,

> that there has been much annoyance growing out of the presence of a certain favored member of the faculty and her methods. Frankly I have been one of the most impatient about that situation. Yet I think that the tendency to say "that's what you get from having a *woman* at the top" is unfortunate. No *perfect* president will ever be found, and favoritism, founded perhaps less on sentiment and more on self-interest, has been known among *men*.[33]

Keyes also refuted the criticism of Woolley for her absences from the college, absences unrelated to fund-raising but, rather, related to working as "a warrior for peace" and as a spokeswoman for organizations.[34] These outside affairs were not distracting, Keyes argued. In fact, it was "more likely to be characteristic of a man than of a woman." Furthermore, "men of great power in leadership, were not found in great numbers among college presidents." She didn't believe that any male president ranked as high as Woolley, with the possible exception of President Neilson at Smith. She confessed that she had "never been personally drawn" to Woolley and had been "very much irritated by her at times." This, however, should have no bearing on how valuable Woolley's career and accomplishments had been to the college and to the world. These alone, Keyes believed, "should lead naturally to an endorsement by the trustees in the form of the selection of a woman to succeed her." Keyes preferred a young woman.[35]

It is clear from Keyes' early efforts that she was aware of sentiment on the board for replacing Woolley with a man. Was the story in the *Holyoke Transcript* deliberately planted by someone who was "testing the waters?" To the extent that the college appointed an outstanding person of either gender, such an individual would naturally take on activities that extended beyond the college. As the college community had long recognized throughout Woolley's career, and as Keyes stated in her memo to Morrison, such contributions to national and international issues enhance the stature of the college. What Woolley's critics neglected to acknowledge was that, by making certain that her successor focused exclusively on college affairs, they were taking a real risk that the college would be led by a mediocrity.

When Mount Holyoke opened in September of 1934, Woolley told Edwards that "everything seems propitious from the human point of view." The freshmen class was a good size; the dorms had been renovated with new bathrooms; the heating plant was nearly completed; library construction had begun. A new master's program for prospective high school teachers that stressed both academic preparation and training in pedagogy was one year away from inauguration.[36]

Time magazine chose to tell a very different story of the college that year. "Large, florid President Woolley" presided over Mount Holyoke, a "famed feminist and warrior for peace who crowned her labors in 1932 as the only United States woman delegate to the unsuccessful Geneva Disarmament Conference." The college itself provoked "testy gentlemen [to] snort 'rib factory' and "Protestant nunnery.'" The young women students were "always studious, always hard up ... little changed" by the Depression. They "dress drably and, under the large, stern shadow of Mary Emma Woolley, lead rather drab lives." The sarcastic and mean-spirited tone of the article angered Mount Holyoke students who publicly repudiated it.[37] They saw their college as "forward looking and alive," and as a gesture of solidarity a large group serenaded Woolley after chapel. It is not clear how this gratuitously humiliating portrait of Woolley and the Mount Holyoke students came to appear at this critical time.

In October, Board President Morrison selected four individuals to join him on the search committee—Cheney, Kendall, Keyes and Mary Hume Maguire, the youngest alumna trustee.[38] Keyes was not Morrison's first choice. Lottie Bishop, an alumna trustee who worked as an executive secretary at Yale, had said no. She told Morrison that she and Cheney and Maguire overlapped too much in terms of their similar contacts.[39] (Bishop, described by the Yale dean she worked for as a woman who "lived for the institution and ran her part of it with an iron hand," would eventually accept a place on the committee.[40]) Maguire quickly assumed a unique role on the five-person committee when Cheney suggested to Morrison that Maguire's

> work would be done more effectively for herself and with less chances of embarrassment to the committee if she were given the formal title of "secretary" to the committee and if outside of the committee no mention of the nature of the

Left to right: *Top*—Henry Kendall, trustee, Boston industrialist; Alva Morrison, chairman of board of trustees, Boston stockbroker. *Bottom*: Howell Cheney, Connecticut silk manufacturer, trustee of Mount Holyoke College, member of the Yale Corporation; Rowena Keith Keyes, alumna trustee, principal of Girls' High School, New York; Mary Hume Maguire, alumna trustee, tutor at Radcliffe College. Original members of the committee of nine.

appointment were made than simply that she was serving as secretary.... Possibly when you send her out it would be well to give her letters of introduction to specific individuals under your name.

Maguire was to be the committee's investigator, her job to get "the real scoop" on each of the potential candidates.[41]

In October, the Alumnae Association and the search committee jointly mailed seven thousand survey questionnaires to alumnae about the search. Their stated goal was to elicit suggestions for possible candidates, but they neglected to include an explicit question about sex preference. Only 278 questionnaires were returned and the committee chose to interpret this small response as indicative of indifference about the choice. The truth of the matter, which later became clear, was that the typical alumna had few suggestions, if any, for candidates and therefore did not respond. Of the 278 returns, 177 alumnae did specifically say that they preferred a woman, even though they were not asked the question. The failure to ask the alumnae about any sex preference could be construed as a deliberate effort to avoid a potentially overwhelming response. The small response by the alumnae would figure very prominently in the official defenses developed by the trustees and alumnae who supported Ham's appointment.[42]

Meta Glass, president of Sweet Briar College, Sweet Briar, Virginia, 1925–1946, president of the AAUW 1933–1937, offered the presidency of Mount Holyoke College.

Morrison paid a visit to Woolley in November 1934, a month before the committee's first meeting. She asked him if he was prepared for a "lengthy and exceedingly frank communication" about her successor. She had two women to recommend. The first was her friend and colleague Meta Glass, a woman, she said, who would bring distinction to the position. Woolley listed her attributes for Morrison. Glass was a Democrat, her brother was the senator Carter Glass, and her sister had been appointed to a post by President Roosevelt. Glass was also Woolley's successor as president of the AAUW since 1933, a Latin and Greek scholar with a Ph.D. from Columbia University and president of Sweet Briar College since 1925. Glass was fifty-four years old, not as young as Woolley would have liked, but she proposed that it was "better to have the right person for a shorter term than longer with someone about whom one has reservations."[43] Morrison's reliable good manners must have gotten him past the instinctive recoiling he

Marjorie Hope Nicolson, Dean, Smith College, offered the presidency of Mount Holyoke College, Smith College Archives [Used by permission of Smith College].

felt at the prospect of a New Deal feminist with so many Democratic connections as the new president of Mount Holyoke.

Woolley's second recommendation was Marjorie Hope Nicolson, the academic dean at Smith College who worked with Woolley's colleague and friend President William Allen Neilson. Nicolson, to whom Mount Holyoke had awarded an honorary degree in 1933, was forty-two years old and had been dean for five years. A brilliant scholar, a prolific writer, an exceptional teacher and public speaker, she was also Neilson's "right hand." She had earned her doctorate at Yale in two years and left with no regrets, feeling that "she had learned little enough." She described her major professor, a leading authority on Shakespearean and Elizabethan literature, as a "scoundrel" in his "pedagogical misogyny."[44] "Miss Nicky," as she was affectionately called by students at Smith, shared Woolley's views on the role of the liberal arts college. ["May] it never be of use to anyone, if 'use' means merely vocational training," she wrote.[45] Her field was seventeenth-century English literature, with particular interest in tracing the effect of scientific discoveries in physics and astronomy on the imaginations of the writers of the time. She began her most innovative work at Smith, essentially creating a new discipline that concerned itself with the interrelationship between science and literature. Nicolson's courses on Milton and on science and the imagination were among the most popular at Smith and well-known among other colleges.[46]

Nicolson saw clearly what was happening in the 1920s and early 1930s to women trained in the professions. "What do we say to the women who follow us? We do not pass on the torch of opportunity." Opportunities for women peaked in the mid–1920s, but in the past decade nothing could be taken for granted, not education and training, not professional appointments after earning an advanced degree. "[More] than one Cassandra-voice of warning" predicted that women would encounter fewer and fewer open doors, she wrote. Nicolson had an answer to the strongest argument against women's higher education—because women did not engage in original work and made few contributions to the important fields of music, math, and philosophy, it was legitimate to not hire them. Women could not engage in this work, she argued, for the simple reason that they had no wives. Men achieved their status, she pointed out, less through real qualifications than through social contact. Women routinely assisted men in their research, copying and editing projects throughout men's careers. "History will show," she said,

> that the greatest contributions to knowledge (at least quantitatively speaking) have been made by those men who had acumen enough to marry students whom they themselves had trained, students young enough to appreciate the honor, old enough to accept the responsibility....
>
> Here is the matter in a nutshell: it is entirely possible to be a scholar and a gen-

tleman, but it is hard to be a scholar and a lady.... We don't mind the absent-minded professor, so long as he is a man—his undarned socks, his unkempt hair and his spotted clothes may seem even picturesque. Translate the description into the feminine world and shudder at those women who deny their sex.[47]

Nicolson herself was a victim of this double standard. Several Mount Holyoke faculty were concerned that Nicolson was not sufficiently "well-groomed." Nicolson was aware that her more informal and spontaneous style felt unconventional at Mount Holyoke, even though she did not view herself as unconventional. When a reporter visited the Smith campus for a story, he made no reference of unkemptness. Rather, he was charmed by Nicolson. Apparently expecting something quite different, he found a youthful, spirited woman with humorous clear blue eyes and a "winning smile." In his words, she was, reassuringly, "in no sense of the word a blue-stocking."[48]

Nicolson's irreverent humor, her brusque impatience with convention and her seeming lack of religiosity led Woolley, who did not know her personally, to share some concerns with Morrison, whom she trusted to keep in confidence. Woolley told him that while Nicolson had the advantage of being younger, she also had the disadvantage "of being less cultivated in manner and personality." Woolley had what she called some "side-lights" on the issue, "some criticism at Smith College," and suggested that Morrison not submit Nicolson's name to the committee until he had done some investigating, including enlisting the help of his wife. Woolley told him: "Having put on my thinking cap, with regard to names, I will not take it off!"[49] Several of the trustees had also begun thinking about candidates. Kendall was investigating several men, and he was also at work on a questionnaire for candidates that included the following questions: "Is he businesslike in personal finances? Has he an income above salary? [What is] the Health basis of his wife and self. If a man, [what is the] personality of his wife, her family background, social qualifications, tact and ability to play the game with her husband."[50] Cheney recommended two male ministers from the Boston area.[51] Woolley knew nothing of this.

On December 16, 1934, Kendall reserved a private dining room at the Boston Chamber of Commerce for the first meeting of the search committee. He emerged at that meeting opinionated and dominating, and it became apparent that the committee would be endorsing a search for candidates of both sexes from the beginning. As Maguire cited examples of women in leadership positions as proof of women's successes, Kendall brought up disparaging arguments to emphasize how the choice of any woman would be an inferior one. There was little to no talk of the successes at Mount Holyoke over a century of female leadership. Afterward, Keyes confided to Morrison that she felt "a little sad over the apparent enthusiasm of the committee about having a man." She came away concluding that she was the only one of the five-member committee who strongly felt that "a suitable woman is to be preferred to a suitable man" and that the responsibility was falling to her to find "if possible one or two women whom I can whole-heartedly endorse." This early interest in considering men was clearly a violation of the mandate from the full board, but Keyes chose not to make an issue of it with Morrison. As for Morrison, he chose not to assure Keyes that Woolley had already recommended two outstanding women candidates.

Kendall's self-assurance made Keyes fear that he might influence the committee "more than the irrefutable character of his argument." She admitted to Morrison that during the meeting she had come "under the spell of his sureness, wondering if [she] were all wrong," but that, with time for reflection, she realized that his arguments were specious. She recalled that his judgment about a former college administrator had been wrong and decided that she "need not look upon him as infallible." She felt the need to express admiration for Kendall, telling Morrison that she could appreciate Kendall's usefulness to the committee. Keyes had composed what she called "A Statement of Consideration Indicating the Advisability of Choosing a Woman as President to Succeed President Woolley upon Her Retirement"[52] and wanted it sent to all the members of the committee. The statement urged them to consider no men as candidates "unless it can be conclusively demonstrated that no suitable woman candidate exists." Morrison deftly avoided endorsing this. He left it to Keyes to send copies to Kendall, Cheney and Maguire. Morrison's response to Keyes' concern that Kendall might unfairly influence others was to subtly criticize her own advocacy and assert his own "objectivity":

> Those of us on the committee who are trying to approach this very difficult problem with an open mind should be careful to consider all the factors involved and not allow ourselves to be influenced by any individual on the committee who has a strong conviction.[53]

A week later, Keyes wrote to her classmate and fellow trustee, Perkins, looking for an ally:

> This is to ask you to help me.... I am the only one on the committee who believes heartily that if a really suitable woman for the position can be found, she should be preferred to a man. We all agree that we must first look over possibilities among both men and women, but the others either waveringly or (in the case of the very emphatic Mr. Kendall) strongly prefer the idea of a man.[54]

Perkins answered immediately with strong support for Keyes' position as well as a recommendation of how the committee might broaden the scope of its search:

> We should try to get a woman of the world with worldly experience, and that is more often denied to ... great scholars because of the necessity of attaching themselves so completely to academic life. I don't mean ... that scholarship is a handi-

cap, but merely that I don't think it should be particularly emphasized ... in this Mid-Century where women need very much to learn to respond to leadership of other women, a college aided by a vigorous and inspiring woman is one of the ways in which they can learn.[55]

Over the next two months, the faculty began to weigh in with opinions and suggestions. As early as February, Newhall was worried about Morrison's seeming desire to speed up the process. He had already expressed impatience over how much time he was devoting to college trustee matters. No meeting had yet been held to consider candidates; the data from a preliminary survey had not been organized. Nevertheless, Morrison told Newhall that he was "pressing for a decision at the earliest possible date. The present crisis in our financial outlook demands prompt action." He went further. If a choice could be made, the college "would not be justified in jeopardizing the possibility of getting an acceptance ... by imposing conditions."

Clearly, Morrison was suggesting that Woolley agree to retire that June if a candidate were selected. Newhall, who believed that an early retirement would be "disastrous from every point of view, as well as unfair under the existing circumstances," assured Morrison that she, for her part, would make every effort to increase enrollment.[56] Morrison spoke to Woolley about this possible scenario, and she did not openly reject the idea.[57] Keyes felt strongly that the approach should be different. Woolley should turn over "a 'going' institution" to her successor by clearing up any financial difficulties with the help of the trustees and the alumnae so that "she may go out in glory—not defeat." Keyes believed that Woolley would respond to "that psychological appeal.... [S]he does like glory," Keyes told Morrison. "If she really goes to work, she may need until 1937 to do the cleaning up."[58]

Rumors began to fly through the college community. There was, in the words of David Adams, the chair of the FCC, "a general feeling of anxiety and unrest among the faculty." There were rumors of trustee actions to economize, about proposed renovations at the expense of the academic budget, about "forcing" Woolley out despite her agreement with the trustees that she would stay until June of 1937. Adams asked for a "frank and friendly talk" between Morrison and a large, representative group of faculty. The FCC was simply asking the board to keep good faith with the agreement made in 1932 to appoint two non-voting faculty representatives to the succession committee.[59] The whole faculty was actively responding to Maguire's request that all members of departments submit suggestions of qualifications as well as specific nominations. Helen Patch, French professor and secretary of the FCC, had told the faculty that "we are assured of careful consideration"[60] by the trustees, and, in good faith, two-thirds of the faculty responded, many with long, thoughtful opinions and suggestions.

Chair of the zoology department Ann Haven Morgan, dubbed the "electric Professor" because of her boundless energy, composed one such submission. In Morgan's view, the accomplishments and influence of Woolley were absolute justification for continuing the tradition of female leadership at Mount Holyoke. Morgan nominated Frances Perkins. If women were trained to be leaders, they must have opportunities to use their skills. Universities and men's colleges offered no opportunities, and since the Depression more men had been seeking positions in women's colleges. Morgan proposed a study of the hiring practices of men versus women in leadership in women's colleges. Finally, she was confident that "the first ranks" of women were available while "the first ranks" of men chose men's colleges over women's. Pragmatically speaking, women also cost less.[61]

Historian Ellen B. Talbot submitted a comprehensive list of suggestions with a somewhat different focus. The new president should definitely be a woman for reasons that Morgan cited, but she should also be "deeply interested in public questions—international relations, social justice.... It would be a grave misfortune for our future students if this were not the case." Talbot warned that what had worked so well with Woolley as president, her leadership style to not "exert her authority in opposition to the opinion of a considerable majority of the Faculty," would not work in the future. The president currently had the right to decide many issues without consulting the faculty. Talbot proposed that a plan be developed to define the relationship of the faculty to both the board of trustees and the president: "Faculty should have by right, not courtesy, a larger voice in the affairs of the college."[62]

Midwesterner Rogers Rusk, an associate professor of physics, had been at the college for just six years. Admitting that Woolley's presidency had been very strong, he went on to describe her as a leader "of the social-religious type with some leanings toward the older humanistic spirit of things." He believed that the focus should shift to college leadership, "rather than [a] search for world figure." He also suggested that it was time

> to help correct one of the greatest complaints heard from coast to coast outside of the college, and well recognized within ... over-feminization. The time is past when Mount Holyoke can afford to be known by anyone ... as a woman's world—run by caprice and whim.

A male president would solve the problem. The college needed, according to Rusk, "more of the healthy aspect of family life, with a sufficient male representation on the faculty to avoid the criticism of the outer world."[63] John M. Warbeke of the Department of Philosophy and Psychology shared Rusk's views. It was "a matter of general knowledge that the standing of the College has been adversely affected by its reputation as a 'female seminary' or 'Protes-

Ann Haven Morgan, professor of zoology, "doing fieldwork."

tant nunnery'" in which "the conviction [is] that men judgments are relatively insignificant ... in the councils of the College."[64] Rusk and Warbeke shared the view that even a one-term administration under male leadership would significantly help the situation.

Their opinions were shared by only a small minority. Two-thirds of the faculty, 75 percent of professorial rank, responded with lengthy descriptions of qualifications and references in the event that their nominees became serious candidates. Over the next two months, the search committee received these long, full statements, and the recommendations were almost exclusively for women. Then, the board of directors of the Alumnae Association met in February and produced a report that hedged on the issue of sex:

> The Board in general seemed to feel that the question of sex should be approached with an open mind—fitness for the task being the primary factor and sex of secondary importance. Preference of the Board so far as expressed seemed to be for a woman.[65]

By early May 1935, the trustees had a list of seventy-one suggested candidates from sources both within and outside the college. Thirty-eight of the candidates were women.[66]

The issue of faculty representation on the search committee remained unsettled. The faculty wanted what was commonly done in other colleges and universities—non-voting representation. The trustees could not agree, and Adams suggested to Morrison that the cause might be the "extensive changes in the personnel of the Board since 1932."[67] Morrison denied that the board had changed in any significant way. Then in early April, the board made the decision to deny the faculty any representation on the committee and Morrison explained the board's reasoning to Adams: "No two members of the faculty could represent the faculty as a whole.... Anything like a referendum to the faculty after a decision has been reached (or nearly reached) would be in the nature of the case impracticable."[68] This was clearly a move to exclude faculty input.

Morrison was also in the process of denying a faculty request that an advisory committee be formed to address the growing animosity and suspicion felt by the faculty toward the trustees. He told Alzada Comstock, professor of economics and sociology, that an advisory committee was not "practicable," just as the notion of a referendum to the faculty was "impracticable." He suggested that the faculty continue to submit proposals to the trustees, while Comstock told him that he was underestimating the seriousness of the situation, that his suggestion would only make matters worse: "We [the faculty and trustees] have reached a point where we should use last resorts ... the opportunity for friendly faculty-trustee cooperation" was lost. "I don't think a day has passed this week without someone's coming to talk over the desirability of resigning.... The sudden, sweeping trustee actions have made the situation critical." The board had abolished tenure for associate and assistant professors without informing chairmen of departments, cut salaries while money was being spent on soundproofing dining rooms, and rescinded offers already accepted by graduate assistants in the science departments without notifying the chairmen. Comstock urged Morrison to come see for himself. The situation was "pointing towards catastrophe."[69]

At the end of April, Morgan wrote to her colleagues a second time. This time she urged the faculty to express their opinions about the choice for president and to do it quickly. She enclosed an article she had written that would appear in the next *Alumnae Quarterly*, but in the meantime she encouraged faculty to write letters to either the FCC or the search committee.[70] As a concession, the trustees had agreed to invite two faculty members, Helen Patch and Elizabeth Adams, Morgan's protégé and good friend in the zoology department, to the trustee meeting in Boston on April 27. Patch and Adams would be speaking on behalf of the faculty. It was essential that the faculty make their opinions known. Morgan began her article in the *Quarterly* with the question

> What shall we ask of the next president? ... of first importance that the president should be a leader whether of promise or proven power in scholarship and human relations rather than a business executive.... The president of Mount Holyoke should be a woman.... There are women to be found now who can guide Mount Holyoke College with ability and distinction. But beyond that as women they can keep the best of tradition, yet build new and broader ways for women's understanding and scholarship in the future.[71]

Morgan sent Morrison a copy of her alumnae letter along with a copy of the article. He responded quickly to her: "We feel that you are laboring under a misapprehension. The endeavor of the trustees' committee has been to search the entire field."[72] A day later, Perkins, already alerted to the committee's bias by Keyes, sent Adams a telegram: "Prefer woman beyond all question."[73] A week later, trustees interviewed two candidates in separate hotels in Washington, D.C.—Meta Glass, Woolley's first choice, and Henry Wriston, president of Lawrence College in Wisconsin. Wriston was one of the seventy-one candidates on the "working list."[74]

A pattern was emerging in which the male members of the search committee were conducting interviews that Keyes and perhaps Maguire were unaware of. Maguire did approve of the committee's early decision to open up the search to both men and women and disagreed with those women who believed that the committee would "naturally" select a man unless the choice was restricted to women only. "The women are too modest," she said. She, herself, was "proud to find how many splendid women candidates there are after the century of educational opportunity and training."[75] After four months of searching, Maguire still wanted the new president to be a woman, not, as she said, to uphold Mount Holyoke tradition or because of a duty to the sex, but because she held on to the belief that the committee could find "the best."

In early May, in response to Morgan's entreaty, letters began to pour in. Faculty and alumnae wrote to Morgan, to the Faculty Conference Committee and to Morrison. The overwhelming sentiment expressed in these letters was that the Conference Committee should "bend every effort to influence the trustees to choose a woman." The writers urged the search committee to not be misled by the small response to a letter sent to the alumnae in the previous fall.[76] Most alumnae had no definite suggestions for possible presidential candidates, but they had no doubt that a qualified woman could and should be found. The letters reflect how well the writers understood what was at stake in this decision:

I have just heard that there is a possibility of a man being chosen to succeed Miss Woolley.... If Mount Holyoke is to produce in the future her present quota of such women (scholars) I believe the stimulus and inspiration of a woman president is absolutely essential.[77]

It is with surprise that I heard that the nomination of a man, rather than a woman, was even considered ... it should be a woman who will see women's problems from a woman's point of view.[78]

We are much more likely to find the right kind of leadership for Mount Holyoke in a woman than in a man.[79]

I think that only a woman can have the astute perception of educational needs for women which must guide the administrative officer of the oldest and pioneer women's college in the United States ... assuring you that the alumnae of Mount Holyoke follow present events there with continued interest, and assuring you that we shall also support the new president if these fundamental principles are preserved.[80]

If any woman's college is to grow, it must give a woman the chance to be president and must recognize the fact that most women marry and not insist that a future president be an unmarried woman.[81]

Were it not for women's colleges with women presidents and women heads of departments I wouldn't have even a faint hope [of getting a position to teach in 1936]—and there are hundreds of others in the very same position.[82]

Women's colleges should confirm and not weaken important professional positions for women.[83]

If the women's colleges do not offer their higher administrative posts to suitable and suitably trained women, that career will be closed to them; which will inevitably react on the work of the women's colleges themselves.[84]

Letters continued to pour in. Alumnae were making up for their failure to respond during the previous fall. Only one month had passed since McHale had told Woolley she had proof that the board had been interviewing male candidates.[85] She was asking Woolley for guidance in the matter:

> Knowing that the Association would regret very much losing any of the gains it had made in the recognition of women if the presidential tradition of Mount Holyoke were ever broken, I am writing to ask if you have any suggestion about what the AAUW might do in the matter.[86]

Woolley, who had been kept in the dark about "unofficial" interviewing of male candidates, told McHale:

> [I]t would be impossible to over-emphasize my feeling in regard to the importance of having a woman as my successor, and the attitude on the part of some Trustees, which they put in the form of "the best person possible regardless of sex" troubles me greatly.[87]

She suggested that individual members of the Association write to the committee members and that McHale contact Cheney directly. McHale enlisted the help of Dr. Esther Richards, a Mount Holyoke alumna and associate professor of psychiatry at Johns Hopkins University, and asked her to recommend women candidates.

The AAUW was already documenting negative trends for women both nationally and internationally in the context of the Depression and the rise of fascism in Europe. McHale wrote a letter on the economic status of women that appeared in the *Journal of the American Association of University Women* on May 31. It began:

> Like a rising tide, the subject of discriminations against women increases relentlessly in importance. Within the past few months requests have come to Headquarters as never before for information on discriminations against women, for facts on trends in the employment of women, for material on the relative status of men and women engaged in doing the same work.

McHale also reprinted the Resolution on the Employment of Women adopted by the Council of the International Federation of University Women in 1934 at the Budapest meeting. The Resolution read in part:

> The International Federation of University Women strongly deprecates the tendency increasingly evident in the majority of countries by new regulations to debar women from careers for which they are well qualified, whether on grounds of sex or marriage. It considers that such regulations are inimical to the family which is itself the foundation of society; and desires to affirm its profound conviction that it is only by permitting and encouraging women to play a full and responsible part in the intellectual life of their country that the civilization and the prosperity of future generations may be developed on a sound basis of general understanding and enlightenment.

The Council used statistics and anecdotal evidence to confirm increasing obstacles to women's opportunities.[88]

At Mount Holyoke, in response to the call for recommendations, names of women poured into the search committee. Among them were Richards, Perkins, McHale, Janet Howell Clark from the School of Public Health at Johns Hopkins, Dr. Mary Ely Lyman of the Union Theological Seminary and Professor Eunice Schenck at Bryn Mawr. Meanwhile, Glass and Nicolson, Woolley's two recommendations, were being discussed. No one on the search committee shared Woolley's view that Glass was the best and strongest candidate, and it was left to Woolley to pursue a rather reluctant Glass, who was committed to her work as president of Sweet Briar College.[89] The committee's concerns were that Glass was too old at fifty-five and too much like Woolley. Glass' work as Woolley's successor to the presidency of the AAUW was a further liability. Concerned about Glass' minimal interest in leaving her current position, Woolley informed the committee that, despite her earlier concerns, she had come to believe that Nicolson had the "real stuff." The "sobering job" of the presidency, Woolley said, would dampen any inclinations Nicolson might have to indulge in "lack of caution."[90]

Meanwhile, faculty representatives Adams and Patch came away from the April trustees' meeting feeling frustrated and angry. They had numerous complaints, and Adams immediately shared them with Morrison. Too few faculty members were part of the candidacy pool, and those who were had been relegated to a "B" list. There was too much defeatist talk among the trustees on the committee about Mount Holyoke "slipping" with no evidence to back up those assertions. There was too much talk of the new president having to "effect a rescue" and "pick up the pieces." There was an "overemphasis on material aspects" of the college. Finally, there was a troubling lack of interest in squelching the rumors about Woolley being "forced out" of the presidency before the mutually agreed-upon 1937 date.[91]

Morrison merely listened, focusing instead on the existence of a lengthy list of candidates that the committee had created. He promised to send Adams that list, informing her that the trustees' committee was in agreement that the college could not afford to take a chance in choosing someone "from another institution who we believe has administrative ability and yet who has not had an opportunity of proving it in a large way."[92] Nicolson, he said, was the "front-runner" among the women candidates. What he didn't mention was that trustee Davis, Morrison's friend on the full board, was researching Harry Gideonsee and Dean Chauncey Boucher, both at the University of Chicago. Davis was also waiting for the okay from Morrison to "lay all the cards on the table" in a talk with Chicago president Hutchins. Cheney was suggesting that the search committee look at the Reverend Daniel Bliss from Boston and the Reverend Charles Taylor at Harvard University. These men, too, appeared on the trustees' working list of candidates. Davis was not on the search committee, but he was working hard "behind the scene." Keyes was kept out of the loop.

Based on his own and Maguire's "investigations," Kendall had expressed his opinion at the April meeting that Nicolson would attempt to make Mount Holyoke over in Smith College's image, that her allegiance was to Smith and President Neilson. Kendall predicted that one of her first actions would be to hire male faculty in large numbers, replacing female faculty in senior positions. Keyes, apparently forgetting her earlier conversation with Morrison about the unreliability of Kendall's opinions, began to doubt her initial enthusiasm for Nicolson. When Keyes and Elizabeth Adams found themselves together in the ladies' room during a break in the meeting, she shared her Kendall-inspired fears with Adams. Later, disturbed by the damage she might have done by raising doubts about Nicolson, Keyes, once again trusting that Morrison would keep their conversation confidential, sought him out after the meeting to share her worries about Kendall's opinions and her reactions to them.

Keyes decided to write to Adams the next day. She attempted to explain that "Mr. Kendall gave a coloring to things that was really false—not intentionally but through his peculiar set of mind." She was sorry that he, "with his lack of judgment, rather 'queered'" Nicolson for the trustee committee. Keyes wanted Adams to know that she "as the only unmarried woman on the Committee, the only entirely self-supporting woman," was the "strongest advocate for a woman president—if a suitable woman would be found." Keyes had begun to recognize the danger inherent in searching for "possible shortcomings" in the women candidates and already felt herself caught up in a "diligent and rather discouraging search for 'the perfect candidate.'"[93]

Adams promptly replied to Keyes, revealing that she had thought a good deal about Nicolson's desirability as a candidate. Adams fully appreciated Nicolson's extensive experience as dean and acting president at Smith and believed it "probably essential at the moment in 'handling the trustees.'" Nicolson's innovative scholarship, intellect, public-speaking skills, and youth were all desirable qualities. Her "assumption of Mount Holyoke's low estate" and her possible inclination to significantly increase the number of men at the college were negatives, but they did not outweigh the positive. As for the criticism that Nicolson was known for her "abruptness, tactlessness and impersonality," Adams suggested that these behaviors "may be only occasional aspects of the decisiveness and directness which seem strong assets." On the matter of her lack of grooming, a concern for some, Adams felt it "should not be given undue importance." She bluntly told Keyes: "I should frankly prefer working with Miss Nicolson than with some of the masculine paragons described!"[94]

Morrison did not follow through on his promise to share the list of candidates with Adams. She had to approach Maguire and ask for it.[95] Although there were seventy-one names on the "List of Candidates Suggested," not surprisingly, the nominated members of the faculty and administration were not included. Adams herself had been nominated numerous times as a most desirable candidate, more often than any other member of the college.

Sometime during the same day of the April 27 trustee meeting that Adams and Patch attended, Morrison, Kendall and Furniss privately arranged to interview Roswell Gray Ham. Ham was not on the official list of candidates and was unknown to all but Cheney, Morrison, Kendall, and Furniss. It is unclear if Maguire knew of the interest in Ham at this point.

In early May, Cheney and Morrison each met with Nicolson to assess her attitude toward Mount Holyoke. The search committee wanted to ascertain whether she would accept an offer. Nicolson now had Woolley's unequivocal endorsement and much of the faculty's. "Time is of the essence," Morrison told Cheney.[96] They both came away with the impression that she was unwilling to commit. Cheney felt "reasonably certain" that Nicolson would turn down the offer. He told Morrison that Nicolson

> has evidently been making enquiries, or has of her own knowledge come into a pretty exact understanding of the state of affairs at Mount Holyoke and feels doubtful about the advisability of injecting herself into a situation which she believes is going to be a very difficult one for a woman to handle.

"The gist of her conversation," Cheney told Morrison, "was that we really need a man."

Cheney found Nicolson to be a "frank individual" and "was rather bound to take her at her word—always recognizing that where a woman is concerned one may be entirely mistaken." Cheney had just had a meeting at Yale with Furniss and the provost, Charles Seymour, and was pleased to report that they had "unearthed the names of four men who are at least worthy of our investigation." He included Ham in the four and added another associate professor of English as well as two men from the education department. None of the four were on the official list. He suggested that Maguire begin to investigate these men.[97]

Cheney had earlier expressed some reservation about the way in which he and others were maneuvering the search. He was not totally immune to the arguments in favor of a woman president, acknowledging that not selecting a woman would "discourage the professional advancement of women scholars." The argument, he said, could be "stretched to cover the whole field of women's professional development." Further, not hiring a woman would undermine Mount Holyoke's accomplishments, implying by the decision to hire a man that "women's education has fallen short."[98] He shared with Morrison that, while Nicolson was not the "ideal appointment,"[99] he could be "influenced by the opinion of the alumnae or the faculty if [he] was convinced that it was expressed soberly without relation to another question, and without hysteria." He remained skeptical, however, of this actually being a possibility.

While he acknowledged that the "only solid argument" for hiring a man was "one of personal opinion," Cheney was certain of the correctness of that opinion:

> [A] man can and should assume the full leadership and responsibility not only for the educational but for the business direction of a college.... A woman is at a disadvantage in business management and yet a divided responsibility is never ideal.... Further, when it comes to altering important major policies which have their percussion on individual interests or establishing new principles, a man can generally act more impersonally and with more authority than can most women.[100]

Morrison met with Nicolson on May 22and offered her the presidency. She was non-committal in her response and asked for time to consider it. Morrison told Keyes that he still held out hope that she might accept.[101] As the days passed, Cheney solicited a letter of recommendation for Ham from the Yale provost and held on to it waiting to hear from Morrison. After a conversation with Kendall, Cheney wrote to Morrison in the hope that Morrison had "ascertained that Miss Nicolson will not accept, as I believe that this will materially clear our pathway for a better selection." He enclosed Ham's letter of recommendation.[102] Morrison told Cheney that he could not give "the assurance which now apparently you would like, that she is not to be the next President of Mount Holyoke." Ham, Morrison agreed, "would seem to be well qualified for the job,"[103] but they had to wait.

In early June, Nicolson spoke frankly in a letter to Morrison about her preference for the academic community at Smith, which had "the impersonality of a university." Nicolson, despite her purported belief that a man was needed at Mount Holyoke, was not fazed by the prospect of difficult academic or administrative challenges. What did concern her was the sense she had that there was a "poor fit" between her personality and Mount Holyoke. She turned down the formal offer with no misgivings.[104]

Neilson was traveling at the time, and Nicolson wrote to him about what had transpired for his "travel enjoyment." The Mount Holyoke trustee committee, she told him, had conveyed to her in their offer that they originally had misgivings about her but had grown "assured" that "a certain levity of spirit in [her] will disappear in their chaste groves of Academe." She joked: "I doubt not they are correct." Nicolson told Neilson that she turned to the "Holy Word of Scripture" for direction, as she was sure he would do in a similar situation. After several joking interpretations of verses, she settled on one that convinced her the search was over. The lines were familiar, but she had

never so fully comprehended as when [she] felt that [she] was about to be separated from [Neilson] by force. This henceforth (until the next time) becomes my
motto until the day of your retirement, and in these words I hope to take leave
forever of the enemy. For a day in *thy* courts is better than a thousand. I had
rather be a doorkeeper in the house of my Lord Than [*sic*] to dwell in the tents
of—RIGHTEOUSNESS—forever.[105]

This mocking letter from Nicolson remained discreetly between them. Soon
the trustees of Mount Holyoke would be seeking her advice.

The alumnae were now aware that the search committee might well select
a man among the candidates, and many began to write to the trustees in protest.
The letters, like those of the faculty, contained thoughtful argument about
the inroads into women's fragily held positions, emphasized educational priorities including scholarships, faculty salaries and scientific equipment, and
criticized misplaced priorities in spending on buildings and campus amenities.
Amy Rowland, director of the Cleveland Clinic and currently an alumna
trustee, wrote a personal letter to the presidents of all local clubs urging them
to declare themselves in favor of a woman. Six clubs took immediate action.

At Commencement that June, the talk among the alumnae was all about
the presidential succession. Maguire was approached by a few women who
were concerned about the scandal of an open controversy and wanted to see
a response to Morgan's *Alumnae Quarterly* article. Maguire and the head of
the Alumnae Association, Maude Titus White, were in agreement that, above
all, they did not want a public controversy that would "rouse emotions on any
one aspect of our problem." Maguire hoped to gain the confidence of the alumnae by reassuring them that the "matter is being conducted with the greatest
care, and best intelligence of which we are capable, that priorities will not
influence our decision." Most important, "no one clique will run in a candidate." The editor of the *Alumnae Quarterly* published Maguire's lengthy statement in the summer edition, including a description of the search committee
members and what Maguire called "the general method and scope" of the
search.[106]

Increasingly agitated over the direction the search was taking and grieving
over the sudden death of her beloved brother Erving, Woolley threw herself
completely into the work that she needed to do. On July 1, she wrote the following letter to every member of the board of trustees. "With conviction of
sin," she began,

> I am invading what I hope is your vacation with a business matter! It is only
> because I feel so strongly on the question that I disregard my conscience. The
> choice of my successor is one of deep importance to me, as you will realize. I
> hardly need to add that such a feeling is inevitable after giving half of one's life to
> a work.

The choice of a woman for the post seems to me most important from every point of view. I should feel that the celebration of the Centennial of Mary Lyon's effort to open opportunities to women as human beings on an equal basis with men would better be omitted, if a part of that celebration is the installation of a man as President of Mount Holyoke. The importance of this action is not limited to Mount Holyoke. All over the country men and women interested in the recognition of women are taking a keen interest in this matter and realize that Mount Holyoke's action would count for or against the progress of women more than the action of any other college possibly could. I cannot overestimate the intensity of the feeling which has already been expressed along this line.[107]

Woolley wrote to Maguire the same day to set the record straight. Maguire had asked her pointedly about her plans for the upcoming school year, and Woolley wanted Maguire to know that travel plans would be adjusted as necessary, that she fully realized "the large amount of work to be done and its importance." In March, Woolley had canceled a goodwill trip to South America sponsored by the AAUW and the YWCA and had also decided against attending the biennial of the AAUW in Los Angeles in June. Instead, she wired her report as chairman of the International Relations Committee. Woolley told Maguire that she was "practically giving [her] summer" to college matters while offering Maguire "many good wishes for [her] own summer."[108] Woolley was always gracious but never the fool.

Trustee Reverend Pratt called Woolley's letter to the trustees "an inspired and soulful appeal" and suggested that Morrison send a personal letter to each of the trustees endorsing Woolley's wishes. Once everyone understood that Woolley and Morrison were in agreement, so went Pratt's logic, the search committee would focus its efforts solely on finding the right woman.[109] Morrison ignored Pratt's suggestion, and the summer passed with discussion among the committee members about several candidates on the official and "unofficial" list. One was a favorite of Woolley's, Anna Cox Brinton, dean of Mills College, a highly successful administrator and world traveler who, along with her husband, Howard Brinton, played key roles in the development of Quakerism in the United States. She was a social activist (active in the American Friends Service Committee throughout her life) as well as a leading member of the American Classical Society. During the 1930s, the Brintons gave numerous talks on pacifism, embracing controversial issues such as the Mooney-Billings case.[110] Alumna trustee Lottie Bishop suggested that Morrison travel to California to interview Brinton. She had sent Morrison a photo, which he found "not particularly prepossessing," and he told Bishop that he hesitated to spend money on a trip to the West Coast "on the mere possibility that she would prove to be the right person."[111] No one pressed the issue and, unsurprisingly, Brinton's name soon dropped off the list and out of discussion.

Morrison did make an effort to speak with Marguerite Hearsey of the English department at Hollins College. He also looked at the documentation on Mary Ely Lyman, a distinguished scholar, excellent public speaker and graduate of Mount Holyoke, who was married to a professor at Union Theological Seminary. A popular candidate among many alumnae, she was another favorite of Woolley's. Woolley proposed to the trustees that since Lyman's husband was a good deal older than she and was planning to retire within a year or two, a move to South Hadley would pose no work-related problems for the marriage. Meanwhile Kendall, speaking for himself and Cheney, told Maguire that they felt that "most of the women have been eliminated." Maguire, not ready to concede, told Morrison that she hoped all three men, Morrison, Cheney and Kendall, would visit Dean Margaret Morriss at Pembroke College of Brown University. Morriss should appeal to Cheney and Kendall, Maguire suggested to Morrison, because they "both seem susceptible to feminine charm!"[112] Meanwhile, Kendall's independent pursuit of Gideonsee had come to an end when it became clear that Gideonsee had no desire to leave the University of Chicago to take on the presidency of Mount Holyoke.[113]

CHAPTER 4

"The Die Is Cast"

—Board of trustees president Alva Morrison

When Morrison discovered that alumna trustee Harriet L. Thompson had been urging alumnae to write to the search committee about their preference for a woman president, he promptly wrote to her to put a stop to it. "There is nothing to be gained," he told her, "and possibly even something to be lost, in further organizing this kind of agitation."[1] He sent a copy to Woolley. The fall of 1935 began with a flurry of activity within the search committee. A typed memo came across Morrison's desk with the names of two recommended male candidates who were not on the official list. One, a Robert M. Strong, had five listed attributes. He was dean of freshmen at Dartmouth College, youthful at thirty-five years old, formerly secretary to Dartmouth's president and the director of admissions and possessed a charming wife. The second, William Eddy, had three attributes. He was a professor of English at Dartmouth and formerly at Princeton, and he, too, had a charming wife. Morrison corresponded with Woolley and Kendall on the same day in October. He was updating Woolley about a woman candidate whom Stanford University's president had praised as one of the university's "most promising scholars"[2] until, on closer investigation, he had to report that the woman was "not fond of people." The search committee decided to pursue her no further. "There is always some new way of spoiling what you think is a good picture," Morrison commented to Woolley. "I am finding this to be true in the search upon which I am now engaged."[3] It was this search that Morrison was discussing with Kendall. Morrison neglected to tell Woolley who the candidate was or why there might be a "spoiling of a good picture." Julius Seelye Bixler had been added to the working list and was currently the committee's most promising male candidate. A professor of theology at Harvard University and a former Smith professor, he was recommended by Neilson, who gave his "complete endorsement."[4]

A well-liked, affable man, Bixler was youthful at forty-one years old, held

95

a Yale Ph.D. and an impeccable pedigree. His grandfather, Julius Seelye, had been president of Amherst College, and his granduncle, L. Clark Seelye, was the first president of Smith.[5] Kendall urged Morrison to talk with Nicolson as well as Neilson, reminding Morrison that she had recommended that Mount Holyoke find a man. Nicolson understood "the Mount Holyoke situation.... I think her slant on him for that job ... would be quite as valuable as Neilson's. We mustn't make any mistakes in that situation," he warned. Kendall liked Bixler, and Kendall's wife was "very much impressed" with Bixler's wife. She was, in Kendall's wife's estimation, "distinctly a lady, talked intelligently when it was proper to talk, and held herself in reserve at other times." Kendall had already asked Bixler "the definite question" as to "how his wife would function and whether she would be happy in a situation like that," and Kendall reported that Bixler had said "unqualifiedly she would fit in very well."[6]

Morrison telegrammed Cheney. Both he and Kendall were "favorably impressed" with Bixler, and Morrison urged Cheney to make every effort to come to Boston to meet him before the November trustee meeting. Morrison, Keyes and Maguire were meeting in South Hadley in a few days, but Morrison would neglect to inform them of the Boston plans.[7] Cheney met with Bixler and, although he found him quite likeable, it was evident to Cheney that Bixler lacked administrative experience. Moreover, Bixler appeared to "belittle ... the need for any definite training or experience in administration." Cheney doubted whether Bixler had "sensed the significance of [Harvard] President Eliott's definition of an essential qualification of administration as being 'the willingness to give pain.'" Cheney had a greater concern. How could the search committee, at this early stage, inform the full board of trustees that "we could not carry out their mandate of securing a woman if possible." It was clear to him that this was the trustees' position as of the last board meeting. It was also still unclear when Woolley would step down if a candidate accepted an offer this early.[8]

Meanwhile, Keyes remained determined to fight for a woman candidate and was able to persuade the committee to consider Eunice Schenck, graduate director of Bryn Mawr and a popular candidate among the Mount Holyoke faculty and prominent alumnae. That fall, Kendall and Cheney met with Schenck, and Cheney described her as "the best possibility we have as yet interviewed in the case of women." She possessed, he said, "genuine scholarship, administrative ability, and attraction in spite of her great homeliness." He shared these thoughts with Morrison in the same letter in which he discussed Bixler and the problem of the trustees' mandate to hire a woman.

On the same day, November 5, that Cheney wrote to Morrison about Schenck and Bixler, Elizabeth Adams wrote to all five committee members, Cheney, Morrison, Keyes, Maguire and Kendall, reiterating her conviction that Woolley's successor must be a woman. Frustrated and angered by the committee's stonewalling, Adams informed the members that "opinions are being expressed freely by alumnae and non-alumnae since the question of President Woolley's successor has been given open publicity by the questionnaire sent out to all graduates of the college." She reminded the trustees that she and Professor Patch had made clear to them that the position of the faculty and "prominent alumnae" was that a woman must succeed Woolley. Lest the trustees believe that because some individuals espoused the opposite view the two positions might cancel each other out, Adams elaborated on the larger issues at stake.

First of all, appointing a man would deny some qualified woman one of the most important positions open to women. Second, the whole goal of women's colleges was to "equip women for leadership." An appointment of a man would be a betrayal of Mount Holyoke's very reason for existence. Finally, she told them that while

> this choice may satisfy the expressed preference of some alumnae, faculty and trustees who desire a "change" [it] will not counteract the effects of the choice. It is both ironical and serious that these persons are apparently so little aware of the unique contributions of Mount Holyoke's presidents as women that they wish to change the character of that leadership.

She ended in a conciliatory tone, expressing the hope that the trustees would "bulwark the faith in women's education and leadership" by selecting a qualified woman.[9] Adams was far too astute to not recognize that among those who were intent on appointing a man there were trustees who wanted to change the character of Mount Holyoke's leadership as an outright rejection of Woolley's unique contributions.

Only Keyes and Kendall answered Adams. Morrison, Cheney and Maguire chose to ignore her. Keyes attempted to reassure Adams that Morrison, Cheney and Maguire felt as she (Keyes) did. They did not prefer "a man as a man." Only Kendall wanted that. Keyes told Adams once again that she was firm in her advocacy for a woman president.[10] Kendall played his hand craftily, telling Adams that he thought that when they had met in Boston she and her colleague Patch "agreed that we should pick out the person who could do the best job ... regardless of whether it were a man or a woman." Didn't Adams hope that a woman could be found "who would be entirely competent?" It was his belief that this was the "attitude of the committee," but "some of the committee feel that Mount Holyoke, at the present time, needs some qualities which a man is more likely to contribute than a woman." It was his hope that, whatever the final decision, "the faculty will accept it as the best thinking on the part of the trustees.... You have the perspective from within and our committee has the perspective from without," he told

Adams. "The benefit of both viewpoints should be sought and seriously considered."[11]

The following day, Morgan sent off a letter similar to Adams, and Cheney was moved to respond. He told Morgan that he "frankly regret[ted]" her letter because it contained nothing new and was clearly "based either upon some gossip ... or upon a feeling that the trustees are not giving serious consideration to the arguments which have been advanced so many times." He disingenuously told her she would "be performing a service to the Committee" if she submitted the names of the "qualified women" she knew,[12] while he complained to Morrison that Adams' and Morgan's letters left him "quite irritated." "This letter writing by members of the faculty," he said, "and perhaps more particularly by members of the faculty committee appointed to serve with us in a confidential capacity, cannot possibly serve any useful purpose." He suggested that Morrison tell the two women this,[13] and Morrison agreed. Cheney's reaction "coincide[d] precisely with [my] own," Morrison told him. It was time to call a full meeting of the committee.[14]

Meanwhile, Cheney, Morrison and Kendall continued to make inquiries about Bixler's presidential potential. The results were mixed. One source observed that "Mrs. Bixler was the real administrator and executive in the home and family affairs. She seems calm and steady and firm, when events seem to disturb him overmuch." Another offered assurance that "while [Bixler] has never had great executive ability, because he is so exceptional in every way, there seemed to be no doubt that he would be an effective executive."[15]

Morrison telephoned Nicolson asking for her opinion. She described Bixler as "impatient with the minutiae of administration and impatient at committee meetings with the technical side" of things. He would be fine, she said, with "good support from a Dean," likely thinking of her own close relationship with Neilson, his successful presidency made possible in part by Nicolson's outstanding work as his "right hand." Bixler, she said, had "a certain nobility and grandeur of character which make him admired and trusted by all.... We love him at Smith." His wife, she added, is a "delightful person" and his home has been "a social center in which people of every class and opinion were equally welcome the distinguished and the undistinguished the conservative and the liberal." Bixler was not entirely what the three men were looking for. Morrison shared his concern with Nicolson that Bixler might have difficulty handling the "considerable adverse feeling ... aroused against him," but she assured him that she had "no fear in that direction."[16] Morrison decided it was time to send copies of the correspondence to Keyes.

Meanwhile, Keyes was heavily involved in activity created by the list of women candidates that, good to their word, Adams, Morgan, Woolley and others had given to the committee. Maguire made immediate inquiries about several women, and both she and Keyes kept Morrison informed. By the end of November, the faculty had submitted forty-two names for consideration. All but a handful were women.[17]

Eunice Schenck emerged as a particularly attractive candidate because of her close relationship with Mount Holyoke. As director of the Graduate School of Bryn Mawr, she had shepherded numerous Mount Holyoke students through the program. Bryn Mawr president Marion Park advised Keyes to have Morrison talk to an informant who knew Schenck very well, but Morrison passed the task to Maguire. The contact spoke very favorably about Schenck, and Schenck herself was enthusiastic about her possible candidacy. Maguire quickly objected to Schenck's "keen interest." Keyes defended Schenck against Maguire's negativity, citing Schenck's excellent administrative experience and her clearly positive feelings about Mount Holyoke. In Keyes' view, Schenck seemed "to have a natural and perfectly justifiable interest in going a step higher," an approach that Keyes fully understood as a single professional woman herself. Schenck would also make "a better president because she approached it with certain affection as well as ability." President Park gave Schenck the highest praise. If she [Park] were "to die tomorrow," Schenck would most definitely be one of two people considered for the presidency of Bryn Mawr.[18]

When the committee met as a whole at the end of November, Keyes came away utterly frustrated and, predictably, sought out Morrison. She believed that he was sympathetic to her concerns and spoke openly, apologizing for being "a trial to the committee." She told Morrison that she had "sincere respect" for her fellow committee members because of their "disinterested desire to do the best for the college," but she couldn't accept the opposition to Schenck. She was too "well fitted for the position" to allow three men on the committee (Cheney, Kendall and Morrison) to cause the selection of a man "for a women's college whose individuality has included for 100 years a woman president." She didn't mention Maguire's peculiar negativity toward Schenck. She asserted that the selection of a man was against "the expression of a majority of trustees that the Committee should be able to show that no suitable woman could be found." It was also against "the sentiment of the most thoughtful letters of the alumnae" and against "the request of the faculty." A point of discussion during the committee meeting had been the presumed necessity for a "confidante—a wife" for the incoming president. Keyes had sat through that discussion in angry silence, preferring to vent her feelings in a private letter to Morrison. "Don't you suppose Mary Lyon faced as big problems as these,—and got along without a wife? Is it not assuming a good deal to think a few of us know so much better what will work out for the best?"[19]

Morrison granted Keyes the Mary Lyon point, but then, taking on an

almost supercilious tone, he began to lecture her on the burden of responsibility they must assume. The committee must do, "not what others think we
should do, but what our own minds and consciences dictate.... After all that
is the responsibility [thinking and deciding for others]." Keyes needed to recognize that the committee had "made a more thorough study of both situation
and candidates than those who are outside the Committee and who are trying
to influence our opinion." Morrison sent Keyes a copy of a memo of his conversation with Nicolson about Bixler. He then sent copies of his and Keyes'
exchange to Maguire, Kendall and Cheney.[20]

Cheney saw Keyes' letter as "a good deal of a facer," an attack, and com-
plimented Morrison on his self-control and "dignified and quiet reply." He
decided not to send Keyes a three-page memorandum he had just written on
the problems involved in the selection of a president of Mount Holyoke College. Keyes, as he told Morrison, was "in a state of mind where perhaps it would
rather set her in her purpose rather than move her from it." Cheney suggested
instead that Morrison sit down with her and "let her argue it out." She might
"get it out of her system" and "might approach the problem more from the
rational and less from the emotional point of view."[21] Cheney's goal was to
successfully undermine Keyes' efforts to promote women candidates before
the committee. Keyes, through no action of her own, had become, by Cheney's
definition, a woman not "of sober opinion" but one prone to "hysteria." How
had she accomplished this? Loathe to engage in open conflict, Keyes made a
miscalculation in choosing Morrison as a confidante.

In early December, one issue was finally put to rest. Those members of
the committee who favored installing a new president in 1936, with Woolley
returning only for the college centennial in 1937, heard from Woolley. She
made it clear that she would not return for the centennial under those circumstances.[22] Meanwhile, Cheney sent his three-page memo to his fellow committee members, all but Keyes.[23] It was a very different document from the
five-section brief that Keyes had asked Morrison to send to the newly formed
committee the previous January.[24] Now, almost a year later, Cheney had produced a memo on the problems of selecting a president without mentioning
the issue of male/female preference. His memo earned the highest praise from
Morrison, who couldn't imagine an analysis "more complete and well balanced."[25] Cheney identified the weaknesses that had developed within Mount
Holyoke and blamed the closeness of the community for its isolation—out of
touch with "the world of ideas developing outside, and the world of social
interests which have so concerned some of the other women's and most of the
men's colleges in the East." Cheney's "world of social interests" was far from
Woolley's world of social reform and peace organizations. For the most part,
Cheney was looking to make Mount Holyoke a more hospitable environment

for male influence, for links that would open up opportunities for male academics and, secondarily, for opportunities for Mount Holyoke girls to socialize with young men, potential husbands, from the men's colleges.

His criticism that the college neglected broad and new intellectual ideas was not only incorrect. It also contradicted his praise of Mount Holyoke's sound scholarship. He had to acknowledge the college's significant work in scientific research, which he lamely described as "keeping abreast."[26] He attributed the college's weakness to the development of "too close a community," missing entirely the strength inherent in a community of scholars. Mount Holyoke students were, he wrote, "equal in intellectual ability and capacity with that of any other women's college," but the student body was "less well-known except in the lines of teaching and research."

Beyond teaching and research, however, Cheney did not attempt to cite opportunities open to highly educated, intellectually superior women. Yes, Francis Perkins had just become the first woman member of the president's cabinet, but the reality was few and diminishing opportunities for professional advancement. Keyes, herself, was proof of this. She had earned a Ph.D. in English literature from New York University and was teaching at a New York City high school. A new administration "must take hold of Mount Holyoke's pressing problems," Cheney pronounced, citing "the ingrowing tendency of the faculty and its isolation as a community [which] has seriously hampered it in its abilities both to get together as a unit, and to inspire the student body." Contradictory in his criticisms, he gave no evidence to support them.

Cheney praised Woolley as "a tremendous asset in holding public interest" while he criticized her for the school's administrative weaknesses, citing financial troubles and her inability to "meet the serious problems growing out of the Depression" or to hold the faculty "to any continuous policy." These vague charges had little to do with the fiscal reality at Mount Holyoke. There was no dire news about student enrollment or any sacrifice of academic excellence.

Morrison disagreed with Cheney about withholding his memo from Keyes. He wanted Keyes to see it. Keyes had asked Morrison to meet in New York to "talk over the problem" of the search committee, and he wanted to present the memo to her.[27] Keyes' plan was to discuss the two candidates Bixler and Schenck, as well as trustee Furniss, who Keyes feared had inordinate influence on the search committee members. She argued for Schenck when she and Morrison met and continued the discussion in a letter:

> [I]t strikes me that you and Mr. Bixler have a certain fine-ness of perception which makes friction especially hard for you, but that he has perhaps less of the business-man to balance that quality and that his position as Mount Holyoke President would be even more difficult than yours,—shut up with his troubles in

South Hadley. While sensitiveness is not a matter of sex, I think perhaps women are often more inured to friction, and that Dean Schenck in particular ... has probably acquired a "coating" that would be a great help.... The other idea is that in considering Mr. Furniss' preference for a man in this position, it is necessary to recognize his definite bias against women in "careers" of any sort.

Keyes had personally experienced Furniss' bias in meetings. She found it impossible to miss "his frequent references to women's doings in a slighting way even his wife."

[Furniss'] attitude is so different from that of any others (except Mr. Kendall) as to women's capabilities that I don't think he's a very safe guide. Of course you may say that I too am biased,—the other way! But whereas he tends to think that women are in general "unfit,"—I do not feel that way about men, but merely that for this critical situation, this particular woman [Schenck] is better even than this very fine man [Bixler]—or than most men.[28]

Keyes was especially concerned about Furniss because Morrison and others had begun discussion of adding new members to the committee to break the stalemate that prevented them from making a decision. Keyes was right to be concerned. On December 26, Morrison sent telegrams to Furniss and three other trustees, inviting them to join the committee. Furniss' acceptance was a given. This time Lottie Bishop, who was open about her preference for a male president and about her dislike of Woolley, accepted. Kendall's friend Paul Davis, president of the Chicago Stock Exchange, said yes. Helene Pope Whitman, class of '04, a married alumna new to the full board, was the fourth

Others from the Committee of Nine. *Left to right*: Lottie Bishop at reunion parade 1931, alumna trustee, executive secretary at Yale University; Paul Hazlitt Davis, trustee, Chicago stockbroker; Edgar Furniss, trustee, chairman of Committee of Nine, dean of the Graduate School (later provost) of Yale University.

new member. Morrison told the four that because the committee had narrowed the choice to two candidates, expanding it to nine members was essential: "[T]he correct decision is so important." Three of the four new members were strongly in favor of a male president and would certainly help Cheney with his stated goal to "move [Keyes] from her purpose" and pressure her to give up her "emotional attachment" to the idea of hiring a woman.

Keyes still saw Kendall as the major opposition to hiring a woman. In early January, she proposed to Morrison that the division in the committee between her strong support for Schenck and Kendall's strong support for Bixler be presented before the full board. "If I were a minority of *one*, I should still feel that Schenck is the better 'bet' that I should wish to go on record with the trustees as so believing."[29] She likely held out some hope that the other less vocal trustees could be persuaded by evidence and argument. There is no record of Morrison's response to Keyes' proposal. It was never addressed, nor was the full board ever consulted about the Schenck/Bixler impasse. In early February, Mount Holyoke historian Viola Barnes shared with Furniss the fact that in 1852 the trustees of Mount Holyoke Seminary had offered the principalship to a man, Professor Albert Hopkins from Williams College. Furniss sent the information to his Yale colleague Ham, who remained an unacknowledged candidate. Furniss' note read: "Here's the evidence that trustees of an earlier day were as guilty as are we of preferring the masculine influence at the College."[30]

Meanwhile, Woolley held on to the slim chance that Glass might be persuaded to accept and the committee obliged her with a formal proposal to Glass. On March 10 Morrison met with Glass to discuss the offer. He described the encounter to Furniss the following week:

> After a day spent with Miss Glass at Sweet Briar[31] I came away with the haunting fear that, while she is a lady of great charm, she may be lacking in an essential qualification of administration which is now greatly needed at Mount Holyoke and which Mr. Cheney has referred to (quoting the late President Elliot) as "the willingness to give pain."[32]
> In my conference with Miss Glass she expressed a wish to talk with Miss Woolley, which of course I encouraged. But as a drowning man clutching at a straw, I sought to suggest some other person who could give her a clear conception of the ruggedness of the task, which awaits her in academic administration at Mount Holyoke. I think she discounted somewhat my remarks on this aspect as being the viewpoint of a "business man."[33]

Morrison felt like a "drowning man clutching at a straw" when Glass asked to confer with Woolley. What did he fear?—that Woolley might persuade Glass to accept. He had suggested to Glass that she meet with Furniss. She never did, but if she had, Furniss had assured Morrison that he definitely

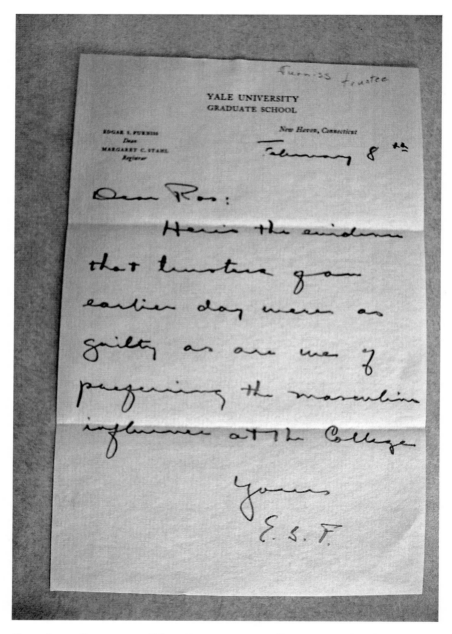

Cover letter from trustee Edgar Furniss to Roswell Gray Ham dated February 8 [1936] describing the contents of an enclosure that is evidence that in 1852 the trustees of Mount Holyoke Seminary offered the principalship to Albert Hopkins.

would have emphasized "the darker side."[34] Woolley tried to persuade Glass. She traveled to Washington, but after a three-hour discussion, had no success. Glass was not interested. She focused on her commitment to unfinished work at Sweet Briar College as her primary reason and officially declined the offer at the end of March.

Those trustees who were determined to appoint a man had appeared willing to gamble on an offer to Glass. Olive Copeland, Woolley's secretary for eighteen years, until 1937, gave a plausible explanation. She knew that the committee had offered a very low salary "to a really distinguished woman— so low that she felt it was intended to warrant a refusal—a real insult!"[35] Copeland saw this as clear evidence of bad faith. This "distinguished woman" had to be Glass. Nicolson had no complaint about the salary, if the trustees, in fact, had gotten that far in their discussions with her. Millicent Carey McIntosh, headmistress of the Brearley School, who also allegedly was offered the presidency, was married with young children and well situated in what was the beginning of a promising career. In any case, she did not believe that she had been made a serious offer.[36] Thus, Glass, the oldest and most distinguished of the three, likely understood that the offer was "intended to warrant a refusal."[37]

Around this time, an alumna named Anabel Stone Budington at Oberlin College sent an urgent letter to the secretary of the Alumnae Association. Budington regretted that she had not sent a strong recommendation for Mildred McAfee, the thirty-six-year-old current dean of the Women's College at Oberlin. She knew that Wellesley College, engaged in its own presidential search, was very interested in McAfee and that Oberlin would "be miserable to lose her." Budington wanted Mount Holyoke to "have an equal chance" with McAfee. There is no evidence that the Alumnae Association responded in any way to Budington's appeal. In fact, McAfee's name had already appeared on an anonymous, undated list of potential candidates with a comment written in the margin next to her name: "eliminated almost at once as undesirable." Wellesley's trustees felt differently. They hired McAfee that spring after an eighteen-month search that considered close to one hundred women candidates.

On April 1, Furniss complained to Morrison that the committee was "back at scratch again." Notes flew back and forth as the men brainstormed about numerous men, and on April 18 Furniss brought up Ham again. Furniss had news about him. Months earlier, Ham had been unmarried, a widower with two sons, but he had recently remarried, and Furniss assured Morrison that the new Mrs. Ham was "a very charming lady." Nine days later Morrison, Furniss and Kendall interviewed Ham, and the following day they sent a letter in support of him to the entire committee. In a separate letter to Cheney, who was not at the interview, Morrison told him that Furniss planned to bring Ham's name before the full committee. He urged Cheney to meet with Ham as soon as possible. "We were all favorably impressed," Morrison said. Of utmost significance, Morrison told Cheney that Furniss had established that Ham "would accept the call."[38]

Meanwhile, Woolley and others continued to submit names of strong women candidates, Mary Ely Lyman and Esther L. Richards among them, and Morrison responded with slightly different versions of the same letter—"I regret to say ... that her name has been carefully considered, and I am quite sure that the Trustees' Committee would not reach a favorable decision as to her candidacy." In Richards' case, one of the top women on the list, Morrison went further: "After very careful consideration the Trustees' Committee has been unable to reach a favorable decision in regard to her." As early as January, Bishop responded to a letter from Adams, who was recommending Lyman and Schenck: "Frankly ... neither of them fits my ideal for the office under consideration."[39]

With Ham "in hand," Morrison, who was eager to be done with the search, was less inclined to be "patient" with Keyes. He responded to a letter from her with a frank statement of his position, his tone condescending as he spelled out his version of the committee's actions. Keyes had said that his earlier letter to her "seems to imply that while a thorough search has been made for a woman, no such search has been made for a man." Morrison was curtly dismissive. "I do not mean to "imply this" but to state it for a fact," he told her. He then proceeded to lecture Keyes like a schoolchild:

> Let me review the sequence of events. Mrs. Maguire made a most thorough and painstaking survey of the entire field. I think that she rounded up more than one-hundred possibilities. The leaning of the committee was towards a man and Wriston was a possibility, but we could not agree. This was about a year ago. The committee then decided to direct its efforts toward the selection of a woman, and I have since personally interviewed eleven women candidates ... and only one man.... Out of the eleven candidates, the committee agreed upon two, both of whom declined.
>
> What I meant to say in my letter was that an effort commensurate with that which we have exerted to find a woman should now be directed toward finding a man. A clear majority of the committee favors this procedure.[40]

He sent a copy of the letter, humiliating in its tone toward Keyes, to all the members of the expanded committee. If Morrison "personally interviewed eleven women candidates," there is no record of these meetings with the exceptions of those with Nicolson, Schenck, Glass and McIntosh. He and others on the committee had independently approached several men about their availability as candidates. Though Morrison proposed a concerted effort on the part of the committee to find a man, he told Cheney on the same day that he had decided not to pursue any more leads because he was so favorably impressed with Ham.

On May 2, Whitman, the new alumna trustee on the expanded committee, sent a curious letter to Morrison, assuring him that this "first offence," an assertion of her opinion and position, would be her last. She told him that she strongly preferred a woman, preferably an older one who would not stay long enough to become a "benevolent despot." She did not wish to meet with Ham because she doubted that most "first-string" men would consider becoming head of a women's college. However, as a new member of the committee she felt that she had no right to stand in the way of what the original committee wanted. She assured Morrison that if a man were chosen, "there will be neither grumbling nor after-claps from the member from the free and sovereign State of South Carolina!"

In his response to Whitman, Morrison felt no compunction about putting Mount Holyoke in the worst possible light. He told her that

> the conviction has been steadily growing in the past few months that the only thing which can save Mount Holyoke is a strong masculine administration. I use the word "save" advisedly. The college is over-feminized and in this day and age when there is an increasing tendency among young women to go either to co-educational institutions or to institutions like Barnard and Radcliffe where men predominate in the faculty where sooner or later this growing reputation of over-feminization will inevitably result in a declining enrollment.[41]
>
> You have what I believe to be a majority of our own trustees who would not send their daughters to Mount Holyoke for this reason. If our own trustees feel like this, what about the outside public?
>
> The quickest and most effective way to overcome this difficulty is to place a strong man at the head.
>
> ...I have been strengthened in my conviction by the opinion of two of the younger outstanding candidates in our list of women; one, Marjorie Nicolson who declined the post, and the other Millicent Carey McIntosh who is so situated that she could not accept but on whom our committee could undoubtedly have agreed. Both of these women say emphatically that we should choose a man for next president of Mount Holyoke.[42]

Neither Nicolson nor McIntosh had said "emphatically" that Mount Holyoke needed a male president. Rather, in conversation prompted by Morrison and others, they chose to not disagree. Whitman, too, chose not to dispute Morrison's assertions that young women preferred institutions where men "predominate in the faculty," that Mount Holyoke was hopelessly "over-feminized" and that the quick, effective cure was to put "a strong man at the head."[43]

Ham Is Chosen

On May 18, Morrison informed Woolley in writing that in three weeks, at the June 6 meeting of the board of trustees, the committee would be recommending Ham's appointment to the presidency.[44] Stunned by the audacity of the committee in making such an abrupt and, in her view, ruinous decision, Woolley resolved to persuade the full board to reject the recommendation. The mandate from the board remained clear—to "secure a woman if possible" or to "show due cause" if not. The list of accomplished and potentially available female candidates remained long and untapped. Woolley wrote to the trustees a second time, this time in strong protest rather than measured appeal. Keyes answered mournfully in a long letter, arguing that once the committee offers had been rejected by Nicolson and Glass there remained only one woman, Schenck, whom she could support. Keyes told Woolley that Ham was "head and shoulders above any woman left in the field except possibly [Schenck] ... for whom a majority would not vote." In defense of her new attitude, she added: "I may say that Mr. Kendall was not present at our last deliberations, and that his opinion influenced none of us directly as far as I know.... I want to assure you that no pressure from members of the committee influenced me. It was the pressure of the situation as I saw it." Morrison, Cheney and Furniss had clearly succeeded in moving Keyes "off her position."

On May 21, Woolley notified the FCC that the trustees were about to appoint a man to succeed her. The committee took two immediate actions. They prepared a questionnaire polling the entire faculty on preference for a man or a woman and sent a telegram to Morrison asking the trustees to delay any action until the results were in. Morrison responded by telegram the following day:

> Trustees' committee has been fully cognizant views of faculty ... these views have been given full weight in deliberations of committee for more than year.... Nothing useful can be accomplished by poll at this time ... such procedure is likely to make Mount Holyoke luaghling [*sic*] stock among women's colleges especially if it receives newspaper publicity.

Almost belligerent in his irritation, Morrison wanted to know how the faculty had learned of the committee's decision a day before the "confidential report" had been made available to the board of trustees. He told the faculty representatives that, "if after knowing and calmly considering all the facts," they still wanted to address the full board, they could do so at the executive session on June 6.[45] The FCC shot back an answer. The information, they told Morrison, came from

> members of the administration who were deeply disturbed at the prospect of so marked a change in policy at the very moment when the College is about to

memorialize a century of successful achievement under the leadership of distinguished women.

The FCC "deeply" shared the administration's concern and now felt obligated to "secure further consideration of the larger question of Mount Holyoke's attitude toward and confidence in the leadership of the American college woman." The committee disclaimed any knowledge of the identity of the male candidate. Their goal, in light of faculty opinion, was to urge the trustees to continue the search for a woman. They had immediately sent out the faculty ballot in order "to determine the exact present state of faculty opinion," reassuring Morrison that there need be no cause for "alarm as to the danger of unfavorable publicity." Preliminary returns showed that

Mount Holyoke President Roswell Gray Ham (undated)

the vast majority of faculty preferred a woman. The final results, 106 of the 123 questionnaires returned over the weekend, revealed eighty-seven votes for a woman, eleven for a man and eight with no preference. Maguire was sent to meet with the FCC, which attempted to impress upon her how clear the "present faculty point of view" was on the issue and to "open the way for a greater measure of earnest cooperation."

Three days later, on May 26, Morrison rejected a request from the FCC for a meeting with the entire search committee. "The die is cast," he telegrammed, "as far as the Committee of Nine is concerned." The nine trustees were scattered throughout New England and New York and could not be brought together for a meeting. He reiterated that the proper place to present the faculty case was at the June 6 meeting.[46] The FCC conceded and devised a plan to report the results of the faculty poll, to ask for a delay of the final decision, and to strongly recommend that the trustees resume the search for a woman.

On May 29, Keyes wrote to Elizabeth Adams. She felt the need to justify the radical change in her position. Though she supported Schenck, she told Adams:

> I honestly believe that Mr. Ham would make a better president for our manifold needs than she would.... I am inclined to think that the more as women we say "Always take the best *person*, regardless of sex," the more in the long run, we shall promote women's causes.

Keyes continued defensively: "[I]t seems to me rather petty to distrust the judgment of the nine committee members and be willing to make a tragedy out of a change no more radical than it was to change from 'Seminary' to 'College.'" On June 3, three days before the board meeting, Keyes wrote to Woolley for the second time. She pleaded with her to accept the decision of the search committee and to use her power and influence to exercise "true leadership ... in uniting trustees and faculty." Keyes warned Woolley of the potential damage to the college if distrust of the committee's decision spread. Faculty were, she said, "almost violent in their feeling.... My belief in your *bigness* makes me think that, weighing all this, you may be able to reduce the *importance* you now conscientiously place on your own point of view."[47] Keyes might have been describing her own situation. She had "conscientiously" held her "own point of view" for many months, increasingly isolated as her fellow committee members pressured her to back down. She failed to understand the difference between one's own point of view and a matter of principle. Perkins would not forgive Keyes' betrayal.[48]

Keyes' capitulation is unfortunate testimony to Morrison's influence over her and his ability to gain her confidence. She had often asked Morrison not to share her views with the other members of the committee and trusted that he would not, likely believing that she and Morrison had a special relationship. Even at this late date, Keyes was suggesting to Morrison that they persuade the trustees to vote by mail ballot in order to avoid conflict. She also suggested that, in the interest of harmony, Kendall be persuaded to stay away from the June meeting. Morrison ignored both suggestions.

On June 4, two days before the board meeting, Pratt, who was a longtime member of the board, wrote to Furniss to warn him of the "considerable friction" that Ham would encounter were he to accept the trustees' offer. Ham, Pratt said, should be informed of this:

> [E]ighty-seven out of one hundred and six members of the teaching faculty of Mount Holyoke College have voted in favor of a woman as president to follow Miss Woolley.
> ... had the alumnae been asked for a direct vote as to whether they preferred a woman or a man for president they would undoubtedly have voted by an overwhelming majority for a woman.

You may also know, as I do, that eleven members or possibly twelve members of the Board of Trustees want a woman, while twelve or possibly thirteen want a man. With these facts in mind, would it not be a very kind thing on your part to impart this knowledge to Professor Ham, who is a friend and a member of your faculty, ... I am of the firm opinion in which Mr. E. N. White of Holyoke, a brother trustee agrees, that you ought to let Mr. Ham know this before the trustee meeting on Saturday.[49]

Pratt's and White's hope, which they withheld from Furniss, was that Ham would readily decline the offer if he were made aware of the controversy and potential conflict that lay ahead. Neither Pratt nor White had been informed of Ham's determination to take the presidency or of Furniss' determination that he succeed in doing so. Furniss kept Ham apprised of the unrest among the faculty, administration and alumnae. On the day Pratt wrote to Furniss, Perkins, who had been "simply stunned" by Morrison's notification,[50] attended a dinner in Washington, D.C., with Richards, who, at that time, was the chair of the Educational Policies Committee of the AAUW. Perkins told Richards that she was heading up to South Hadley for a board of trustees meeting where she fully "expected a great argument."[51]

CHAPTER 5

The Board Decides

It was a cooler than usual morning in early June of 1936 when the board of trustees met in executive session on the Mount Holyoke campus. Located on the top floor of the college library, the large meeting room was comfortably furnished. Tall casement windows cast light on the dark wood-paneled walls. A raised fireplace dominated one end of the long room. The Reverend Henry A. Stimson, for whom the room was eventually named, had retired only months before this historic meeting. A trustee of Mount Holyoke from 1894 until 1936, Stimson was a staunch advocate of women's higher education despite his strong anti-suffrage beliefs. Part of Stimson's legacy was a substantial collection of anti-suffrage material that had found a home in the college library. Stimson had made his own contribution to the literature. "[G]iving women the ballot," he wrote, "would at once add greatly to the number of ignorant voters, and the mass with which every reform movement has to deal with would become so much more obstructive, making the situation so much more difficult than it is now."[1]

Twenty trustees were in attendance, thirteen men and seven women, plus Woolley in her ex officio status. Six trustees would be voting in absentia. Maguire was appointed secretary. As planned, seven members of the FCC were present, their presentations first on the agenda. At her request, Woolley would not be present to hear the faculty statements.[2] We can surmise that Woolley chose to do this so that no member of the board could accuse her of influencing, by her presence, any of the faculty who made presentations. She was sequestered in a small anteroom until the last faculty member had spoken.

Emma Perry Carr, chair of the chemistry department, began the proceedings by stressing to the trustees the results of the faculty poll. Given the clear mandate to hire a woman, she asked how the board could not postpone its decision.[3] Six members of the faculty followed Carr, each in turn expressing strong opposition to the trustees' action. Abby Turner, head of the physiology department, cautioned, "Institutions are living things with personality. A change to a man would lead to a change in the sense of the college." English professor David Adams warned, "Don't surrender Mount Holyoke's distinction." For economics professor Amy Hewes, the board's decision constituted an unacceptable loss of female leadership. "The status of professional women," she said, "is in a critical situation at this time.... A woman symbolizes in herself the ideal towards which students might strive." Hewes was well aware of Mount Holyoke's unique status among the women's colleges in hiring female faculty at the professorial level. Several of its most distinguished faculty were approaching retirement, and Hewes believed it essential that the college remain a female-led institution to prevent backsliding under male leadership. Morrison was already thinking along the same lines. In the article he prepared for the August *Alumnae Quarterly* announcing Ham's appointment he would emphasize that the fact that the new president would be charged with replacing so many senior faculty

> was a material factor in [the] decision to elect Professor Ham. His work at Yale, his association with education on the Pacific coast, and his researches in England have brought him into familiar and confidential relations with educators in both countries. When making the very critical replacements necessary during the next decade he will thus possess the distinct advantage of a broad and notable acquaintance.[4]

Morrison was not referring to the elite women's colleges when he commended Ham's "broad and notable acquaintance" from which he would draw those "very critical replacements."

Latin professor Caroline Galt called the search woefully inadequate. Incredulous over the board decision, she stated that "1600–1700 women graduate annually from the so-called 7 Colleges.... [It is] inconceivable that from these numbers no woman can be found suitable." Elizabeth Adams, who, along with all other faculty, had been summarily eliminated as a presidential candidate, once again emphasized the 82 percent of the faculty who had voted for a woman as the next president. She challenged the trustees to answer the central question that no one had been willing or able to answer: "Why is a change necessary at this time?" Dean Harriet Allyn, a potential candidate also eliminated by the trustees' blanket edict, described how, at first, she had had no preference for a man or woman. Now, she said, "I stand strongly for a woman," and gave three reasons why—the strength of faculty opinion for a woman, the reality that women did not have equal opportunity and losing the leadership of such a prestigious institution for women would constitute a serious setback, and, finally, since "one must gamble with the choice in any case—it is a safe bet if we gamble on a woman." Allyn was the last to speak, after which the faculty quickly withdrew. Unaware that Woolley had decided to absent herself, Carr later recalled how much she resented Woolley's exclusion. Woolley, she reported, had been kept waiting "before being called by her own trustees to confer with them on one of the most important issues of her whole administration."[5]

It was Woolley's turn to speak as soon as she entered the room. Missing was the collegiality that was second nature to her. Her warmth and humor, familiar to everyone at the meeting, were markedly absent. Woolley was resolved to deliver a sharp protest that reflected her anger, determined that her objections not be interpreted as a reaction to personal insult. She imagined a steel rod running the length of her spine.[6] One month shy of her seventy-fourth birthday, Woolley possessed remarkable vigor, her voice still filled with ministerial power as she gave the reasons for her protest:

> [F]irst, the principle upon which Mount Holyoke was founded, that women as human beings have an equal right with men for the development of their powers and an equal right to opportunities for service: second, that the progress of Mount Holyoke throughout the last one hundred years has been under the leadership of women, to whom recognition is due: third, that a change in policy with regard to the presidency of Mount Holyoke would mean striking a blow to the advancement of women, the seriousness of which can hardly be over estimated.
>
> The faculty of Mount Holyoke have given unmistakable evidence of their desire.... Surely no expression of opinion should have greater weight than that of the faculty to whom is due in large measure the progress of an institution.
>
> To sum up I can imagine no greater blow to the advancement of women than the announcement that Mount Holyoke celebrates its Centennial by departing from the ideal of leadership by women for women, which inspired the founding of the institution and which has been responsible in large measure for its progress.

Just as no discussion followed the faculty presentations, there was no response to Woolley's statement. Maguire immediately gave a summary report of the history of the search. The committee, she said, had considered more than one hundred candidates "drawn from all parts of the country." The most difficult challenge had been to establish a "yardstick" to measure qualifications. The candidate had to be a scholar, a "person of imagination and good judgment in these times of confusion and experimentation," a person of "achievement" in "vigorous good health, a fine speaker and of a deeply religious nature," a person "to inspire and lead." Maguire reminded the trustees that each had been provided a written report on the specifics of the search, including the unsuccessful offers to three women candidates[7] and the reasons for the recommendation of Ham. Without discussion, committee chair Furniss then put forward a motion to offer the presidency to Ham, while informing the trustees that, in his opinion, the selection of Ham was "not second to any woman interviewed by the Committee." As evidence, he praised Ham for his effective leadership as chairman of freshmen counselors at Yale, a position Furniss amazingly likened to that of a deanship or presidency.

Furniss' motion galvanized those trustees in opposition. Pratt said that he had listened carefully to the issues raised by the Faculty Conference Committee and concluded that "since the faculty has asked for a delay, it is only reasonable to grant it." Perkins followed Pratt, briefly restating Woolley's and Hewes' arguments before adding her own:

> This choice has more than academic implications.... It would cause great disappointment among women who have tried to further women's education. In the depression, women have lost professional opportunities and we don't want opportunities closed permanently in education.... The prestige of Mount Holyoke will suffer from such a choice.

She argued that a "sufficient canvas" had not been made, noting that the relatively unknown McAfee had just recently gained "immediate distinction" when she was appointed president of Wellesley. Those on the committee who had been instrumental in the disappearance of McAfee from the "working list" of candidates sat impassively while trustees in opposition continued to

Frances Perkins and Mary Emma Woolley on Mount Holyoke College campus on Founder's Day, 1934.

speak up. Dean Florence Purington, class of 1886, urged the board to reconsider: "Eighty percent of the faculty feels so strongly. We must pause. Is there not some hope in prolonging the search?" Alumnae trustee Thompson, who had earlier been chastised by Morrison for eliciting alumnae opinion on the question of sex, told the trustees, "I represent the alumnae of the Middle West. They want a woman. There will be damage to our prestige in the outside world if we appoint a man." And just before the board adjourned for lunch, the Reverend Potter, a trustee since 1912, made a strong personal appeal. "I do not want to commit myself," he said. "Is not delay possible?"

When the board reassembled after lunch, Morrison took the floor, prepared to take on the opposition. Alumnae and faculty, he asserted, shared "a peculiar devotion" to Mount Holyoke and were, therefore, not as likely to hear or recognize criticism as those who were more "detached." He claimed that he himself had begun the search process from a "detached" position, that his "slant" had been financial from the beginning. Make no mistake, he told the trustees, Mount Holyoke's endowment was most assuredly small, and in order to build up both the endowment and enrollment an effort had to be made to give the college more prestige. In his travels, Morrison said, he was naturally in contact with many people and had been made uniquely aware of a "serious matter." He had discovered that the world beyond the college viewed Mount Holyoke as "'over-feminized.'"

As proof that this was truly a serious problem, Morrison referenced a confidential report from a large foundation that gave gifts to colleges. The report contained two pieces of bad news for Mount Holyoke. "Colleges," he claimed the report said, "run exclusively for women were declining" and "Mount Holyoke was the most feminized of all the women's colleges." Things needed to change. Morrison told the trustees, "Some women see [how] and could correct it." However, "a man could do it better and more quickly." A woman president had to be distinguished, and there was no guarantee that the committee would be able to find a distinguished woman. Morrison warned, "We cannot afford to take a risk.... The world will see [Ham's appointment] as a forward step." He assured the trustees that he had not ignored the concerns of the women on the search committee. Some of them, he said, "had started with the same view as the faculty," but after they studied the facts they had changed their minds. He reminded the full board that the recommendation from the search committee was now unanimous. Thus, Morrison dispensed with Keyes' long, solitary struggle on the committee with a few facile words. To hear him tell it, there had been no need for discussion, no need to work hard to move Keyes "off her position." The women had simply changed their minds when confronted with facts.

A flurry of approving comments followed. Hazen said that what he wanted was "the best individual." He would have been "glad if it had been a woman," but now the board had no choice but to endorse the committee's recommendation. Keyes asserted that, yes, she had initially wanted a woman for president but now emphatically did not want "a second-rate woman before a second-rate man." She reported that only one woman [Schenck, whom she did not mention by name] was currently a viable candidate, but she had the support of only three of the nine members of the committee. For Keyes, Ham had become "almost an ideal candidate, adequately prepared and equipped with a kind of ruthlessness." She had been persuaded by Furniss, Cheney, Morrison and Kendall, impressed by the importance the men attached to a presidential candidate's "willingness to give pain." Keyes now wanted no delay. There was, she said, "an increasing fever in the College" and a quick decision was essential to quell the agitation within the faculty. She feared a vote of no confidence from the board. "How can you trust any Committee at any time if you can't trust the Nine?" she challenged the trustees.

Perkins, responding to Keyes, repeated Adams' question: "Why is the situation so pressing?" "Why does it require ruthlessness?" Keyes did not respond, conceding to Morrison, who had a great deal to say about this. President Woolley's frequent and lengthy absences from the college had put the management of the college "into the hands of the faculty," and he illustrated this with an example of a personal experience. When the Mount Holyoke trustees recently endorsed a renovation program on campus, the faculty made it very clear that they wanted Morrison to make a special trip to the college in order to explain and justify the program, as he described it, "item by item." Morrison, despite his great irritation, did what the faculty had asked. He was well aware of increasing trustee–faculty conflict and now warned the trustees, "Delay this decision" [about Woolley's successor] and "the new president will be chosen by the faculty. If the trustees wish to surrender their responsibilities, all right. But we must realize what we are doing."

Keyes had warned of an "increasing fever in the College." Some trustees were experiencing a fever of their own as they reacted to Morrison's prediction. Massachusetts businessman Philip L. Warren, new to the board that year, worried that "indecision is the worst thing that can happen.... We could lose our best candidate." Cheney reiterated that "three times ... we have gone to a woman.... The choice now is will you have a first-class candidate or a 'suitable woman?'" Harvey told his fellow trustees that "the present administration has failed to deal decisively with trouble in the faculty." He, like Morrison and Keyes, characterized "the situation as urgent. A proper selection had been made. Delay could only cause trouble," he warned. Then Speers, an attorney on the board since 1925, abruptly dissented. He asked if any of the three women candidates could be approached a second time. He told the trustees that he had done some research on his own, asking the head of the General Education Board if men were better fund-raisers than women, and had been told that sex made no difference. Speers hoped that the committee would see fit to keep the search open until a "suitable woman" could be found.

Speers' suggestion provoked Kendall, who, until this moment, had remained silent. The committee, he said, was "carefully selected." At least half of the members were involved in higher education. The committee had "exhausted its resources" and a delay would mean nothing less than a "repudiation" of the committee's work. Kendall's antagonism toward Woolley's administration was no secret, and the meaning of his warning that Mount Holyoke was at a "crossroads" was not lost on the trustees. White disagreed, ignoring Kendall's dire predictions. At first, White told the trustees, he had thought that sex would not matter, but now he firmly believed, after listening to Woolley and the faculty, that the college must have a woman president and that a delay was essential. Alumna trustee Whitman, who had promised Morrison she would not protest if a man were chosen, now objected to the questioning of the committee's decision. She warned that if the college "must have a woman," the board needed to "adopt a different standard." New York attorney Frank Clayton Myers, also a new trustee, worried that even though "all [his] emotions [were] for a woman, ... judgments based on feeling are likely to get us into trouble." He, therefore, supported the "strong" committee. Committee member Bishop simply asserted that "[w]hen the faculty got the facts they would accept the committee decision."

Perkins jumped in again. The committee, she declared, had "not made a sufficiently conscientious search of all woman candidates in the country." They had been laboring under the false assumption that a woman candidate had to have already achieved great distinction as a college leader. Perkins proposed that the committee "modify its standard" and look for a woman "with experience in other fields" who could then be given the "technical academic advice" necessary for running a college. Maguire, increasingly irritated by the challenges to the committee, took the floor. By what right did they "put into Mary Lyon's mouth what her policy would be in 1936? ... The Board should not be frightened by faculty reaction." Women have the right to opportunity, Maguire asserted,

> only when [they] earn it. What makes so many women bitter is that many opportunities are reserved for men whether they earn them or not. If there is no outstanding woman of achievement whom we can secure, then we must drink the bitter draught.

If Keyes and Maguire were prepared to do this, then why not Perkins, Woolley and the others? These had to be Maguire's unspoken thoughts.

Early evening was approaching. The trustees, weary and increasingly impatient, had been meeting for nearly the entire day. The nine members of the search committee had come prepared to stonewall discussion, unified in the effort to convey an extreme sense of urgency as justification for Ham's nomination.[8] They put pressure on troubled trustees. Any disagreement over the decision constituted a vote of no confidence, they were told. At this late hour, trustee Potter was still determined to slow down the process and, to accomplish this, he made a motion to accept the report as "one of progress", only. His motion would require the committee to continue its search and, when ready, convene the full board for a "final consideration." White seconded the motion, and the trustees proceeded to vote by closed ballot. The motion failed fourteen to five. The six absent trustees were not able to vote on that motion.

Furniss immediately moved that Ham be invited to accept the presidency. Harvey seconded the motion, and the trustees voted once again by closed ballot. The motion carried eighteen to eight. This time, the absentee ballots counted in the vote.[9] Apparently, one of the trustees who had voted for delay had switched and now voted to offer the presidency to Ham. Since the board's rules required a two-thirds majority for major decisions, the opposition had come within one vote of blocking Ham's appointment. Cheney moved that the board "extend a unanimous invitation to Ham." Keyes seconded and the motion carried. It was done. Hours of opposition and cogent argument had not changed the outcome. Roswell Gray Ham was to be the next president of Mount Holyoke College.

Woolley had come prepared for this. She submitted her resignation on the spot and in a brief dissenting statement told the trustees that this action was "a very serious thing to do without an overwhelming demand on the part of the faculty, alumnae and undergraduates and without an overwhelming majority of the Board." Perkins, who may have known in advance of Woolley's plan, immediately asked her to reconsider. This dispute "must not be personal," she said, and argued that it would be interpreted that way. Cheney expressed concern that Woolley's resignation would only confuse matters more. Keyes added that "[it] would certainly work harm to Mount Holyoke." Whatever Woolley's true desires, she was quickly persuaded to withdraw her resignation. Her concern that others would interpret her actions as personally motivated as well as her deep loyalty to the college may well have influenced her decision.

The meeting adjourned at 6:00 p.m. After seven tension-filled hours, the outcome for Woolley was a devastating defeat. Perkins accompanied Woolley home, where Woolley collapsed into a chair, utterly exhausted and ready to share a drink. Later, Woolley would tell a colleague: "I feel so ashamed that it should be Mount Holyoke!"[10] Well beyond the insult and sense of personal failure, Woolley knew that this decision meant the loss of hard-won "ground" in the fight for women's leadership opportunities. She could not grasp the thinking of the majority of trustees, including, most painfully, the four alumnae on the search committee, who were not persuaded that female leadership was essential at Mount Holyoke. Woolley had never imagined that it would be abandoned at the college. For her, ground won must never be lost.

Initial Protests

Morrison had notified the press about Ham's appointment two weeks before the meeting. The *New York Times* was prepared to report the decision on the following day, June 7, and Morrison received his first letter of angry protest, posted that day:

> I can't tell you with what regret I read the announcement in today's Times of Professor Ham as Miss Woolley's successor ... surely men have everything in this very man made world and it seems as though the presidency of Mount Holyoke might go to a woman. Is it possible that the majority of answers to the questionnaire sent to alumnae were in favor of a man? Surely the faculty were not in favor of a man—or don't trustees bother with faculty? Whatever Professor Ham is, I regret the move exceedingly. There are plenty of men's colleges and coeducational institutions for his ability, places not open to women. Is it possible that Miss Woolley favors the appointment of any man to her position? I can't imagine it. Mount Holyoke—that bulwark of women's rights—under a man! Surely there are women in this country capable of going on with Miss Woolley's work. I weep.[11]

Morrison responded several days later:

> [T]he Trustees' Committee of which there were nine, and on which there were four Alumnae representatives, one of them an ardent feminist, were unanimously and unqualifiedly in favor of Professor Ham's appointment.... The view of the faculty and of Miss Woolley were carefully weighted by our Committee, and the most conscientious effort was made for more than a year to have the choice conform to their point of view.[12]

The characterization of Keyes as "an ardent feminist" and the assurance that the faculty's and Woolley's views "were carefully weighted" and "the most conscientious effort was made" to find a woman were Morrison's formulation of the distortions he felt necessary in order for the trustee decision to move forward unchallenged. Morrison at this point had no inkling of how often he would be repeating those words.

On June 10, Elizabeth Adams, already furious about the ongoing trustee-driven campaign designed to undermine the college's reputation with allusions to mismanagement, slipping standards, an old-fashioned culture lacking in social prestige and a recalcitrant and "over-feminized" faculty, sent "An Open Letter to the Trustees of Mount Holyoke College" to be read by all trustees, faculty and alumnae. Three days later, she sent the same letter to the *New York Times*, the *Springfield Republican*, the *Boston Transcript*, the *Hartford Courant* and the *Holyoke Transcript*. The press called Adams' letter a "scathing indictment ... that came at the end of a week of smoldering anger and resentment on the part of some of the faculty and alumnae."[13] Adams was demanding that the trustees explain their action:

> The inevitable reaction to the choice of a man for the presidency of Mount Holyoke is the question "why?" ... From the fundamental biological qualifications, the best person to head a college for women is a properly qualified woman and to head a college for men is a properly qualified man...
>
> It is reported that the nominating committee approached at least three of approximately forty women on the list of possible candidates, without success. However it is inconceivable that among the more than twenty thousand women of eligible age, graduates of the "Seven College Group," to say nothing of those from universities and from other colleges for women, there is no woman of achievement or promise who could fill this presidency.

Adams challenged the value of the questionnaire that the trustees sent to alumnae:

> The number of replies to the questionnaire was small. This can be explained in part by the fact that direct questions, such as: "Do you wish to have a woman as the next President of Mount Holyoke?" were not asked. Neither was adequate information on the subject given in an accompanying letter. It is probable that under either of these conditions many who felt that they could not state qualifications or suggest candidates and many who disregarded the matter entirely would have replied.

She singled out for criticism the alumnae trustees for behaving as they did:

> Why have even the alumnae trustees voted away a unique birthright of Mount Holyoke Women? The statement issued to the press by the board of trustees says, "The appointment of a man to the president of Mount Holyoke College represents in some respects a break with tradition; but the college as a pioneering institution, has always been ready to depart from tradition when such a course seemed required by existing circumstances." What are the "existing circumstances" that require this departure?

Adams also wanted it well publicized that the college was not in financial difficulty and that enrollment was not a concern:

> Efforts have been made to discover why Mount Holyoke cannot be headed by a woman; whether the problems to be solved and the decisions to be made are

impossible for a woman's intellect and power. Women are reputed to be poor at business. But according to a published report, the question of business administration is not now an issue.

She reported that applications for admission in the fall of 1936 were 10 percent higher than in the previous year:

> The education given at Mount Holyoke equals that given to women in any other college or university. Her curriculum is sound and progressive. The record of Mount Holyoke women commands admiration and respect. The achievement of her faculty is distinguished.

Adams formulated the most critical question:

> Do the trustees also plan some change in the standards and character of Mount Holyoke that can only be achieved by a man? Both the tangible and, to some extent, the intangible property of Mount Holyoke is in the hands of her trustees.

If Mount Holyoke did indeed need help with its financial management, why was Ham the trustees' choice? It made no sense. Ham was an associate professor who had never worked in the business world. She ended with a demand for answers from the trustees, emphasizing once again the complicity of the four alumnae on the committee:

> It is the right and privilege of the faculty, of the alumnae and of the public to know what the "existing circumstances" are that compelled a committee of the trustees on which there were four alumna trustees to recommend a man for the presidency of Mount Holyoke when there are properly qualified women available. These groups can neither evaluate them nor help to rectify them, if they need rectification, unless they know what the circumstances are.[14]

The press sought out the trustees for a response to Adams' letter. "I have nothing to say," said Morrison. Several trustees said that they planned to ignore Adams and her questions. When asked to comment, Ham said, "I think I had best keep quiet, and let this remain a difference of opinion between some of the faculty and alumnae and the trustees." One trustee commented with utter confidence, "The vote was decisive. You might say we had enough votes to override a President's veto in Congress."[15] How surprised he must have been, then, by the outpouring of angry protest that immediately followed the trustees' decision.

Committee member Bishop reported: "[W]e soon learned how many feminists Mount Holyoke had; I was cut dead on the street [in New Haven] by a classmate and received a tower of correspondence which was sent on to Mr. Morrison."[16] One of those letters was a rejoinder to Morrison's June 11 letter:

> You are no doubt wishing by this time that you had never heard of Mount Holyoke. In my previous letter I spoke of faculty wishes and Miss Adams gave me

the figures I lacked. I feel strongly on the way trustees in general ignore the faculty on everything except salary cuts. I have boasted that Mount Holyoke trustees were less ruthless than most and yet in one of the most important matters that have come up they ignore faculty and alumnae wishes.... May I ask why men were interviewed at all? If you canvassed all the able available women without success, wouldn't it have been wise to say so to the faculty and alumnae before actually appointing a man? I prophesy a decline in alumnae interest. Those of us who have followed even superficially the downfall of the movement for women's advancement in Europe regard this with dismay. It's not equality of the sexes—it's a part of a definite move to discredit women and what they have accomplished.[17]

By mid–June, Morrison felt the need to send a mailing to the entire alumnae group informing them that the trustees would "employ dignified normal channels" to provide "the excellent reasons" for their choice:

Professor Roswell Gray Ham of Yale University will become president of MHC upon Miss Woolley's retirement at the end of the next academic year. The Trustees wish you to know the considerations which determined their selection and the excellent reasons for complete confidence in the individual chosen, but will employ dignified normal channels for conveying this information.

The ill-advised tone and choice of words further provoked alumnae already informed by Adams' critique. "It would seem," wrote one, "that for a distinguished alumna to ask for an explanation of an unwarranted act is not 'dignified' or 'normal.' The use of these two adjectives is symptomatic, I should say of a kind of mental dry rot ... at a time when uniformity is highly prized."

It is interesting, to put it mildly, for the alumnae of a college founded by the vigorous efforts of a woman, kept alive by women, and given further vitality by the outstanding achievements of a woman who has become an international figure, to be told that all intelligent women are dead. Obviously nothing else excuses the recent action of the trustees of Mount Holyoke College.

I am glad that I now know whom to tell that which I intimated in my letter of thanks to Professor Adams and that he has indicated so neatly what can be expected of male leadership.... I trust that Miss Adams will continue to agitate the waters, however, since I could not respect any teacher at a college who would do less.

What I intimated I shall now make explicit. I shall not renew my Alumnae Fund pledge. I shall not, in my capacity as a high school teacher, encourage any promising girl to go to Mount Holyoke.[18]

Adams' public challenge to the board worried some alumnae who complained in letters to Morrison, Adams and Woolley about the bad publicity for the college. Could Adams be irrational enough, one alumna asked, to suggest that "the jobholders dictate who should be chosen as their boss" or that Ham might withdraw to avoid "undertak[ing] a job with a hostile group?"

> To a mature and liberal alumna, the very fact that such a letter as yours [Adams']
> with the, at least, implied backing of 87 out of 123 members of the faculty, could
> be sent out at all would be the very first reason why the new president should be
> a man. If Mount Holyoke has become such a feministically-inclined place by rea-
> son of its present faculty that they feel the decision must be made about a new
> president on sex lines *and* in favor of a woman, I think you have the answer there
> to the trustees' phrase "existing circumstances.".... I am sure that the opinions of
> the trustees and loyal alumnae with wider outside interests than many of the fac-
> ulty, are more likely to be correct as to what Mt. Holyoke needs in its chief exec-
> utive officer than the collected opinions of department heads for some of whom
> the appointment of a man as president may mean the handwriting on the wall.
> The objectors to the choice are too much in the position of the very ill person
> attempting both to diagnose and prescribe for his disease.... Just what result you
> expect to accomplish by your letter I do not see.

Ham's withdrawal, this alumna believed, "would be a calamity that would
intensify the ridiculous position in which the college is placed by reason of
[Adams'] letter and its accompanying publicity, and which many loyal alumnae
deeply resent."[19] By the end of July, Adams received sixty-nine similarly critical
letters from alumnae distressed by the negative publicity, many filled with
invective and ridicule even as they expressed fears of public ridicule. She also
received 240 letters in support of her position, including the following from
an alumna who was "not particularly concerned as to whether Dr. Ham under-
stands women. What he can mean to undergraduate women seems to me more
important":

> Perhaps no one who has not been at Mount Holyoke under Miss Woolley can
> understand what her womanliness has meant to hundreds of us. I hope that I
> have chosen the right word, for it seems to me that the implications are deeper
> than the superficial qualities incidental to sex.... I know that the fact that I left
> Mount Holyoke with a greater respect for religion, with a stronger sense of world
> citizenship, and with some vision of the strength and dignity possible in the life
> of the individual was due in part to the leadership of a woman who spoke as one
> having authority. I am proud of the academic standing of the college and anxious
> for its continuance. We have proved ourselves worthy competitors of men, but as
> we grow stronger will there not be greater emphasis on the problems and talents
> peculiar to women? Certainly if that should be, the reason for having a woman as
> president will be more than a matter of tradition.[20]

Those opposed to Ham's appointment hoped to convince the board to reverse
its decision.

On June 14, eight days after the board meeting, Woolley received a call
from Furniss, informing her that Ham was scheduled to be in Amherst to
receive an honorary degree the following day and that he would also like to
visit Mount Holyoke. It would seem that Furniss, Ham, and the committee
were prepared to deal with the opposition by ignoring it. Woolley wrote to

Marks in mid June describing a meeting with trustees. It "went well," she said, with "no reference to 'the succession.'... I felt that I had a steel rod in place of my normal spine, but I suspect that that feeling will continue."[21] Numerous alumnae were writing to Woolley, split "about half and half" over the trustees' action. Most were trying to absorb the implication of the decision. One alumna with connections to Yale told Woolley that "everyone in New Haven was astonished" by the choice:

> It is a mystery to me and to most others to whom I have talked of the matter, how the trustees came to pitch on this Mr. Ham ... one man, a Yale professor of high standing, said to me: If I had known they were bent on getting a man from Yale, I could have told them of ten who are much better fitted for such a place![22]

There is no indication that Woolley ever used this and similarly damning information against Ham personally. She would, throughout the long fight ahead, argue from principle, denying the importance of the impact on her personally. She was adamant that her June 6 statement appear in the *Alumnae Quarterly*. Alumnae needed to be informed so that they could increase their visibility and pressure on the trustees. Woolley saw no possibility of Ham voluntarily withdrawing. "As for any withdrawal of acceptance or resignations of Trustees, the 'Horoscope' has no such indication!" she wrote to Marks.[23] Getting Woolley's statement into the *Alumnae Quarterly* would prove surprisingly difficult. At first, the editor, Florence Clement, refused to publish it. Meanwhile, hoping for a wider audience, Woolley sent a copy to her colleague and friend Esther Caukin Brunauer, an associate in international education and secretary to the Committee on International Relations at the AAUW headquarters, though she realistically doubted that the AAUW journal would publish "anything controversial about a college in the Association."[24]

Brunauer decided to write a lengthy letter directly to Furniss, informing him of the widespread national and international effort under way to remove women from influential positions. She told Marks that she did not expect the letter to have much impact on Furniss, head of the graduate program at Yale and demonstrably antagonistic toward women's issues, but perhaps "an accumulation of these sentiments might."[25]

Her reasoned argument began:

> The choice of a man to become President of Mount Holyoke at this time amounts to an assertion that a hundred years of collegiate education for women has failed to produce women of sufficient scholarly attainment and administrative capacity to be entrusted with the executive posts of important educational institutions. One does not need to look very far to realize that such an assertion is false, but the implication that your committee believes it to be true gives much support to those who are striving today to eliminate women from positions of influence in our national life. It may be true that there are today few women with

long experience as college executives available for the post at Mount Holyoke, but men college presidents are not always obtained by transferring successful executives from one institution to another. Regardless of sex, there is almost always some uncertainty as to how a new president will develop, and I submit that the proportion of successful presidents among the women heads of colleges is very high. A scarcity of already successful women college presidents for the filling of the Mount Holyoke vacancy does not seem to be a valid reason for turning away from women entirely to appoint a man who, whatever his potentialities may be, is as untried as many of the women whose names must have been before the Committee....

I have seen a whole nation of women put back two generations under a philosophy that accords them neither the status of individuals nor the right to gain economic independence. (I spent all of 1933 in Germany.) Moreover, I have come across in many parts of this country evidence of a movement to eliminate women from posts of importance and influence. To see Mount Holyoke College waver in its faith in women is a serious disappointment, indeed.[26]

British journalist Maude Meagher reinforced Brunauer's arguments in a letter to Woolley. "It seems," she said, "a matter of *international* interest to women, and they should know about it." Meagher was beginning a campaign to spread the word and expected the British Association of University Women to be in close contact with associations in Europe.[27]

Meanwhile, Woolley quietly worked behind the scenes, encouraging and assisting those who were organizing to pressure the board to reverse its decision. In early July, Amy Rowland,[28] a friend and ally of Woolley's who had served on the board as an alumna trustee until 1935, brought together her local alumnae association. The group immediately began an organized petition campaign that gathered and sent more than seven hundred signatures to the board. The librarian of the Holyoke Public Library, Frank G. Wilcox, wrote a letter that ran in the *Holyoke Transcript* with the headline "Librarian Wilcox Revives Protest." When Woolley wrote to thank him, he offered to do more:

In fact I had small hope of reviving the protest and wrote mainly to relieve my feelings by giving expression to my sense of the outrage committed. At the same time, if responsible parties were thinking of "reviving the protest," I would not regret giving them ... encouragement.

Wilcox had written a longer, more detailed statement beyond the published letter and encouraged Woolley to use it

in any effective way with or without my signature. I am not for one moment seeking your confidence in the matter ... but if I were to chance to come into touch with anyone who is sufficiently informed about the affairs of the college to be a trustworthy advisor, I would be glad to submit this later communication to his or her perusal and judgment.[29]

Woolley sent Wilcox's article and a copy of his letter to Rowland.

In September, Woolley publicly endorsed President Roosevelt for re-election, a decision she might have kept private had the board not appointed Ham. The *New York Times* headline read: "Dr. Mary Woolley Backs Roosevelt Breaks Lifelong Republican Allegiance to Support His Foreign Policies."[30] The article noted that she would soon be delivering a nationwide radio address in support of the Democrats. She was seen about campus wearing an FDR pin.[31] Since the majority of board members were staunch Republicans, some of whom were vehemently opposed to Roosevelt's policies, Woolley's actions undoubtedly were perceived as a bold rebuke.

Florence Allen, the highly respected Circuit Court judge who, had she not been a Democrat, would likely have been President Hoover's first choice appointee to Geneva,[32] had written a strong protest to each of the trustees in June and now followed up with a second letter in August:

> I feel certain that women everywhere look upon Mount Holyoke not as just another college for women, but as a college holding a unique place in the woman movement.... There is a distinct and widespread conviction that Mount Holyoke College should continue to have a woman at its head. I think I speak for the leaders in women's activities everywhere.[33]

Kendall wrote to Maguire before answering Allen. "I am getting tired," he said, "of this sort of thing. I am going to be positively rude rather than just rude in the next replies." True to his word, he accused Allen of sending him an "inauthentic" letter, one that was clearly "not spontaneous":

> The Trustees have regularly received a letter from some alumna about each week for the past few months, with very slight variation in language. I should like to ask you if these letters, and say your letter, were written at the suggestion of any member of the administration or faculty of Mount Holyoke College.... There is no question, if one can judge by appearances, that many of the ... letters [in opposition] were not spontaneous. With equal force I think those that were complimentary were spontaneous.[34]

Kendall was not alone in his accusations. Bishop, in an exchange of letters with Morrison in early November, told him that the letters she had been receiving had been stimulated by "one or more individuals." Morrison agreed that the letters he was receiving in opposition "clearly indicat[ed] some point of origin which is stirring up studied protest."[35] The trustees on the search committee were imagining a conspiracy among a small group of malcontents.

Meanwhile, Clement, the editor of the *Alumnae Quarterly* who had at first refused to print Woolley's protest, was pressured to relent by the college administration. Perkins, eager to publish a statement of her own in which she gave her reasons for opposing Ham's election, was successfully thwarted by Morrison, and the *Quarterly* was closed to all communication regarding the controversy. The Alumnae Association officially closed ranks. As for Woolley's statement, Morrison reassured Ham that the *Alumnae Quarterly* was "planning to reduce its presentation to the least possible terms." This was a necessary compromise

> because of her [Woolley's] position as Pres [*sic*] and because many of the alumnae will be much less disturbed to find it there, than to find it omitted. The alumnae's personal regard for Miss Woolley is so strong that we feel only by the acceptance of her statement can we retain their loyalty to the College and the Alumnae Association.

Morrison concluded gratuitously: "[T]he publication of this statement will in the long run react only against Miss Woolley and is therefore most unfortunate."[36] When the *Alumnae Quarterly* came out and Woolley's statement finally appeared, the editor included the disclaimer "print[ed] at her [Woolley's] request." As Morrison had promised, its impact was further diminished by a nearly unreadably small type size and its obscure placement at the end of the issue in the "Comments and Discussion" section. The *Quarterly* was devoted to an enthusiastic welcome to the new president.[37]

Clement wanted to include an interview with Ham in the upcoming November issue and contacted an alumna who had been following the controversy with great interest. Esther Price, a 1913 graduate, had assisted Rowland at the Cleveland Clinic early in Price's career and she openly acknowledged her strong dislike for Rowland. Most recently, Price held a salaried position as assistant national Director of the Girl Scouts but had left complaining of the strong Catholic influence and "the whims of the board women." Currently unemployed, she was looking for a project, and when Clement approached her she readily accepted.[38] In the first of several contacts with Ham, she assured him of her wholehearted support, telling him that Adams' letter was "ridiculous," a "tempest in the teapot—only unfortunately it was Tempest in the Tribune and the Transcript." She hoped that "as a Californian and a marine" he had "a sense of humor and good old-fashioned 'guts'" and would "pay no attention to a 'noisy minority' " that talked confidently about his declining the appointment. "For goodness' sake, don't withdraw," she urged him:

> If there's anything Mt. Holyoke needs, it's just what you can bring—a good healthy Western breeze, a normal family in the President's house, and a masculine point of view. All families have fathers, and most daughters seem to prefer them to mothers.... If Elizabeth Adams and Mary Emma Woolley had had a few more men in their lives, they wouldn't go off so haywire.[39]

Price went on to make erroneous assertions that would be repeated again and again by those who supported the board's decision. She told Ham to "laugh ... off" Adams' claim that 80 percent of the alumnae were "against" him. Adams, she said, based this on 211 questionnaires returned out of a potential pool of eleven thousand graduates. What Adams had actually said was that "60 percent of the replies indicated that the president should be a woman or suggested only women as candidates." Price was clearly combining the 20 percent who expressed no preference with the 60 percent in order to make Adams' statistics look, in her words, "cockeyed." "And the 90 percent faculty," Price mocked Adams, "or whatever figure it was she thought looked pretty, is pure fiction." Price's proof of this was an interview with English professor Ada Snell, who assured her there were no more than three faculty "who were definitely opposed," an absurd assertion in light of the evidence presented by the members of the Faculty Conference Committee at the June 6 board meeting.

Price also told Ham that she had spoken with several of the administrative staff: "[T]hough they all seem scared of their lives to say what they think (which is a nice state for a college), the strong intimation was that the majority were your way." It was Price's opinion that the controversy "boils down to some kind of a fight between the faculty and the trustees." Ham, seen as "the trustees' choice," was simply the scapegoat as the faculty "vent[ed]" their "hurt feelings" against the trustees for ignoring them.[40] Price was mistaken. It was decidedly not "hurt feelings" but rather mistreatment over a period of years that had fostered the faculty's animus and suspicion toward the trustees. The faculty trusted Woolley, but she was leaving. Price did not bother to find out that faculty representation on the search committee, even ex officio, had been denied and all internal candidates had been summarily eliminated early in the process.

In October, Price wrote to Ham telling him of Rowland's work in organizing the petition campaign. Claiming to "know her like a book," Price told Ham that Rowland was an agitator who could cause trouble:

[She] has gotten all of her currents ... flowing against the November trustee meeting and you as an individual ... there isn't anything Miss Rowland won't do to get what she wants. She's frightfully clever and a lot of people don't see through her ... I'm sure she's responsible for Judge Allen's bombardment and for several other women in public office, not alumnae. She's a pretty good politician and it's an open question just how much she can stir up.... It may all tie into J. Marks, though I'm not sure of that tie-up. Miss Woolley herself is still making statements that are amazing—such as that the trustees have asked her to resign three times.[41]

Price had not spoken directly with Woolley and was merely reporting gossip.

The Board Meets Again

On November 5, the trustees again assembled at their regularly scheduled board meeting, this time in the spacious, well-appointed New York Room in the Student-Alumnae Building. Morrison opened discussion with a reference to "some protest" in the form of letters and telegrams about the trustees' action in June. He stated that ex-trustee Rowland had just presented him with a "monster petition protesting the action taken and asking for reconsideration."[42] Perkins, ready to move to receive the petition and to reconsider the June 6 decision, had to wait while Morrison reported several facts that he considered highly significant. He told the trustees that the petition contained 779 signatures, only 160 of which were from Mount Holyoke alumnae. Of the 160, only 14 were recent graduates. Further, he wanted the trustees to know that the letters of disapproval were closely matched by letters of support.[43] The facts that Morrison reported about the petition were inaccurate but, more significantly, misleading. Morrison failed to share some essential information with the trustees. A lengthy cover letter addressed to Morrison from Rowland explained in detail the intent of the accompanying petition and the scope of participation. Rowland made it clear in her letter that the petition "was not intended to test [the alumnae] feeling as much as that of the public at large." Accordingly, she stressed the diversity of the signatories:

> Among the signatures, 77 colleges are represented; 24 states, and 192 communities. Among the signers are 181 men. There are included philanthropists, physicians, lawyers, bank officials, businessmen and women, social workers, college deans; members of the faculties of various colleges and other institutions; principals and members of the faculties of secondary schools, clergymen and parents, many of whom have daughters approaching college age.

Morrison dismissed the petition because most signatories were not alumnae. Rowland, by contrast, argued that the opinions of these outsiders—especially such a distinguished group—were significant. The ability to collect so many signatures in only four weeks was strong evidence of widespread sentiment that Ham's appointment should not be a closed issue. Further, Rowland's signature count did not match Morrison's. Not only did he understate the number of signatures (779 names as compared to Rowland's report of 1,045), but his characterization of the alumnae signatories was also misleading. Rowland reported 216, not 140, signatures "representing 56 classes since 1872."[44]

After the petition (without the cover letter) was read, Perkins moved "to receive and accept the petition and to consider the action taken by the Trustees on June 6, 1936, in electing Dr. Ham to succeed to the presidency of the college in 1937." Before Perkins could say a word in support of her motion, Warren made a long speech in which he re-iterated Morrison's reasons for dismissing the petition.[45] Cheney, at his most diplomatic, supported Perkins' motion, saying that he welcomed any new evidence—"any considerations that bring fresh light on the question." Keyes, angry about the ongoing protest, challenged Perkins: "Reconsider really means to reverse."[46] Perkins clarified that it would take another motion to cancel June's decision. Her goal was to bring the issue before the board, and she was well prepared to do so. The alumnae protest, she asserted, was "far too broad and strong to be understood merely through petitions." It was not only alumnae but concerned individuals all over the country who opposed this decision. She spoke with reason and passion:

One feels it everywhere. And I feel that it is of extreme importance that we should remember that the alumnae have been the principal supporters of the college and are likely to be in the future. It is my belief and opinion that the members of the Board of Trustees who are legally entitled to control and develop the financial policy of the college have not begun to make so strong and important a financial contribution to its development and extension as have the persons who are the alumnae....

I have been very much interested and stirred by the discussion of the meaning of education which came forth in the Harvard Tercentenary exercises which many of you had the opportunity to attend and I think that running throughout all of those discussions, when you came to the more realistic expressions, you got the expressions that self-education is the only education which really matters, and that the individual brought to the great fountain head cannot be made to drink but his will to participate and his belief in self-education is really what is the primary action necessary for continuation of education in this country in its highest sense.

I believe that these alumnae are very sincere and interested, and that they have associated with them in the country women who are graduates of other institutions or who have come into the group of scholars by the disciplines of life as well as education, who have agreed with them that a great enterprise for the education of women must be based on this expression of self-education and that it is very important now in these days that the power and capacity of women to develop leadership in the field where they develop it themselves is of tremendous importance in furthering higher education both for men and for women. That in so far as we deny in this college the capacity of women in the United States of America graduated from any of our institutions, trained in the techniques of education through all the institutions open to them, in so far that we deny that there is a woman the product of these institutions who is competent to be the head of Mount Holyoke College, we deny the validity of our claim to be trustees, directing this college in this way.

I was consistent in my action last June. I have the greatest respect for the opinions of those who did not agree with me. But as I have reconsidered the whole action in the weeks since, I have come to an even greater belief that a very serious mistake was made, particularly since as I look into the life and career, scholarship, etc. of the gentleman selected—he is not a great genius, not a scholar, but a man of ordinary capacity who is not an outstanding leader in any field. We have set aside in our consideration women who have equal capacity at least and I feel therefore that this matter should be considered again. We ought to take very seriously into our thoughts the possibility of making a correction at this time.

Maguire asked Perkins to describe how she would proceed, and Perkins obliged with a straightforward, "It would seem very simple." The faculty "are primarily the institution," and the faculty had made it clear that they didn't want Ham. Many alumnae didn't want Ham and, by now, Ham must know this about both groups. "I am sure Mr. Ham is a gentleman ... I think that a mere indication to him that his retirement ... would be desirable would be sufficient." Perkins recognized that Ham had the legal right to fight, but she did not expect that he, as a scholar and gentleman, would "consider matters in that light." Furniss, likely sensing the dangerous direction that the discussion might take, moved that the trustees resolve into a committee of the whole "to entertain a motion for discussion of this matter."[47] Hazen immediately moved to reaffirm the vote taken in June and Keyes seconded.

Woolley then took the floor. You, she told the trustees, have no idea of the "depth of feeling and extent of the feeling which has been aroused throughout the country" and other countries as well. She had been traveling for five months since the June meeting and this had given her numerous opportunities to consider the decision from an impersonal point of view. She knew nothing of the petition until that morning[48] but was not surprised that it encompassed "a cross section of public opinion." The topic had been brought up wherever she went. The issue had become "very much bigger than the question of Mount Holyoke College." Speaking directly to the male trustees, she asked if this had been done at any of their colleges, how many alumni would "simply quietly accept it and say, oh well, it seems best to put a woman in as president?" She reminded the trustees of the procedural problem that was created when the vote was taken on the same day that the nomination was introduced. Even at faculty meetings, an issue was raised and then voted on at a later meeting. The hurt she told the trustees would "always leave its scar," but her criticism of the process and decision was much more impersonal. If the decision was not reversed, Woolley concluded, "I should feel that something unjust to the traditions of Mount Holyoke and the cause of women had been done, and done in a way which is more worthy of Nazi-Germany than of the United States of America."

A heated discussion about the alumnae followed—what they wanted, what they knew, what their role should be. Keyes told the trustees that she was deeply disappointed when the committee was unable to find a woman, but that she did not believe in alumnae votes and petitions. Alumnae should not be in the business of running a college. Keyes, using Price's phrase, called the whole controversy "a tempest in a teapot." She said she had heard from many alumnae who agreed with the decision, dismissing those in opposition as "the violent ones." "We live in a world that is as it is.... We can hardly expect that young men are going to prefer a woman president, or even want to consider it, and we know that girls want either a man or woman according to individual tastes." Because the "field of women is greatly narrowed," it is more difficult to find a woman than a man. Keyes complained that the hard work of the committee should not be minimized. Reversing the decision would mean abandoning leadership of the college to the alumnae. The arguments put forward by Woolley and Perkins now appeared irrelevant to her, and Keyes made no mention of her personal ordeal on the committee.

At this point, Pratt spoke up, strenuously disagreeing with Keyes:

> First, last and forever, as long as I am on the Board of Trustees, I am for a woman.... I feel that it has fitted into my qualifications on the Board ... and to the alumnae who are the stockholders of the college.... We must do what is best for them.

Pratt was much impressed with Perkins' arguments both in June and now in November, and his only concern was that the board act legally. He acknowledged that it was not going to be easy "to get out of it." He wanted Ham to turn down the offer. Speers agreed with Pratt. He, too, had voted against the June action and still believed it was a mistake. Ham had to be made aware of the "antagonism." It was the only way out.

Morrison reminded everyone that the alumnae had had their chance to make their opinions known and only 10 percent had responded. There was, he asserted, "no ground at all for the statement and ... no evidence that the alumnae do not want the vote to go through." He went further, claiming that the letters in support of the trustees' action outnumbered those opposed. "Dr. Ham may know of it," Morrison suggested, knowing full well that Ham was in regular contact with Furniss and himself and that they assured him the protesters were no more than a handful of malcontents. Pratt, Speers, White and others on the full board were kept in the dark about this.

Thompson, who was more aware, would not be cowed by Morrison's aggressive stance. Chastised by him in 1935 for encouraging women to write to the trustees, she now made it clear to the board that she had been careful "not to agitate at all" about the June decision: "Everyone knows where I stand, and I am proud of it. I have been careful not to condemn or advise." The only alumna trustee to vote against the motion to elect Ham, Thompson had received over 250 letters. She turned to Morrison and told him, "I have had as many as you have had." Alumnae continually asked her to explain the action of the board, but she could not. "There is no question that the majority of the alumnae are disappointed ... and are anxious to have you reconsider this action."

Potter, who had sat silent and listening, now dropped a bombshell on the entire assemblage. On June 6, it was Potter who had proposed that the Ham decision be referred back to the committee for further investigation. He began, "I feel that I owe to the President of the Board a personal statement because I have learned a good deal since I came into the room." When his motion to delay failed after the long discussion that day, he had made the fateful decision to cast his vote for Ham despite his strong personal opposition. He wanted now to explain to everyone what his reasoning had been: "[I]t was clear that it was the purpose of the Board to proceed to the election of Dr. Ham.... I wanted to support whoever came." Potter had just come to realize that it was his vote that explained the discrepancy in votes. Woolley and those in opposition believed that nine votes had been cast in opposition, making the two-thirds majority vote impossible.

Realizing that his vote "might have blocked the election," Potter addressed the trustees:

> [I]f I did the wrong thing, I am sorry but I did it feeling—because as a member of the Board I have respect for the judgment of the Committee and because having expressed myself on the question of procedure and the majority of the members present wanted him elected, I thought I should assent to it as I will if he should come here.

It was this expression of solidarity from the unhappy Potter that Maguire, Cheney and others would later seize upon to support their arguments for unity against the alleged destructiveness of dissent. But Potter hadn't finished. He had been speaking with alumnae and "friends of the college" and found only "a few in favor of the action that was taken, but the total number is negligible." He warned that

> a marked disaffection among the alumnae and a substantial disaffection among the faculty, to say nothing of it here, would seriously impress that impact upon the general public which is the source out of which come the resources to carry it [the college] on.

Potter concluded, "I am inclined to think myself that if Mr. Ham is as wise as the Committee says he is, he will be as wise as the gentleman back in 1852." Potter was referring to the offer of the principalship of Mount Holyoke Seminary to Albert Hopkins, an offer Hopkins chose not to accept.[49]

One can only imagine Woolley's reaction as she learned that Potter could have stopped the appointment of Ham had he not changed his vote in June. As the meeting progressed, those intent on resisting any efforts to get Ham to resign urged the necessity of unity and emphasized the impossibility of reopening the search. None of the Ham supporters responded to Woolley's criticism about procedure or to any other criticisms of the June decision. Maguire, ignoring Potter's true position, gave him credit for having "hit the nail on the head. We must have unity." Cheney challenged the trustees, "Are you going to accept your individual responsibility and are you going to get behind those who assume this responsibility?"

Cheney and Perkins had exchanged words earlier in the day. Perkins accused the search committee of acting in an un–American way, and Cheney, taking strong exception to the criticism, told her that the important thing was that a decision was made, whether one agreed with it or not. Now he told the entire board, "There cannot be any question of our determination to carry on." In a transparent attack aimed at Perkins and Woolley, Cheney stated *his* determination to carry on in the face of what he called the "thoroughly repugnant" decision made the day before with the re-election of President Roosevelt. His was a much more bitter pill, he said, than the pill those who opposed the trustees' decision were being asked to swallow. He made dire predictions of the outcome if the board reneged on its agreement with Ham. What would the educational profession think of the college? How would the board approach new candidates? Who would be willing to come to the college? "It is unthinkable," he warned. Trustee Davidson, the father of seven daughters and originally in favor of hiring a woman, now believed the board "should let well enough alone." Who would take on the responsibility of finding another candidate? Keyes raised the specter of "plung[ing] the college into chaos" if the decision was made to give Ham the option of turning down the offer.

Purington, who had voted against Ham in June, ultimately gave Ham's supporters the arguments that appeared to carry the meeting. Purington was initially extremely unhappy about the outcome of the June meeting, but she came to believe that the situation could not be remedied. Who would find another president? The alumnae certainly could not do it. She could not imagine another committee of trustees willing to take on the work. And who would be willing to be president after such a debacle? She had made up her mind to work for unity and "to accept the situation and to make the best of it." Cheney seized upon what he called Purington's "glowing common sense analysis" of the situation. He hammered away at the idea that trustees had a duty to stand by the decision and to demonstrate loyalty to the college.

No one disagreed more eloquently than Perkins. Once again she emphasized the importance of the faculty: "The faculty make the institution." She predicted that if Mount Holyoke went ahead with the "leadership of a non-distinguished young man," the college will soon become "an uninteresting place.... [W]e have no right," she said, "to continue as trustees if we honestly believe that there is no woman in the country who is competent to be the president of the college." Ham should be approached "in a very considerate and courteous way" and told, as White had suggested, that there was dissension on the board, that some trustees believed a mistake had been made, and that Ham should not accept the nomination. If the board did not take this action, it would continue to be criticized and the college would suffer. Day, unwilling to support repudiation of the offer based on procedural failings, now was willing to suggest that "the whole matter" be brought to Ham.

The discussion turned to how much Ham knew about the discord within the college community. It was easy for Furniss to supply the answer. He told the trustees that Ham's knowledge of the situation was about equal to theirs. Furniss told the trustees that what they were dealing with was "a small minority of vigorous protesters and a large number of people who are indifferent and some who favor." He reported that Ham had a "tremendous number of letters, expressing cordial approval and offering every support." Furniss did not tell the trustees that Ham had no intention of turning down the offer. Ham had made that clear when the controversy began in June.

The discussion had gone on for hours. Several of the trustees worried about the outcome of a vote taken at the end of the meeting. Speers asked if it was necessary to vote. "I wish we could leave it and not put it on record." Pratt asked that the meeting be closed, obliterating it from any official record. Hazen seized this opportunity to let the board's controversy end in silence. "I am perfectly willing to withdraw my motion," he told the other trustees. The minutes of the discussion of the Committee of the Whole ended with the withdrawal of Hazen's motion and the minutes were sealed. The trustees moved back onto the record with a Report from the Committee on Buildings and Grounds.

The Dissenters Mobilize

The next day, November 6, the Alumnae Association, with 175 members present, endorsed the September decision of the Alumnae Council that supported the closure of the *Alumnae Quarterly* to any potential controversy. The official statement read: "The Alumnae Association and its clubs, committees, and individual members would with all good will give their heartiest support to the coming regime." Among the eighteen dissenters present at that meeting[50] were Rowland and Caroline Smiley, an alumna from the class of 1912 (therefore a classmate of Price) and an outspoken activist who had spent her formative years in India.[51] She was currently the co-publisher, together with her life partner, the British journalist Meagher, of a Boston-based magazine called *World Youth*.[52] Smiley charged that "the whole affair savored of fascism and dictatorial rule."[53] With the official alumnae organizations now completely closed to dissent, Smiley joined forces with Rowland and prepared to take their case to the world outside the college.

Later in the month, Price's interview with Ham appeared in the November *Alumnae Quarterly*. She showed him the piece before she submitted it, and he was pleased.[54] "There is far more than the usual curiosity about our new president," she began, "for feminist opposition has given him the tremendous advantage of being silhouetted against the searching light of controversy.... Being of strong caliber, he stands out the more effectively against such a background." Indeed, when she saw Ham for the first time in the Taft lobby at Yale, Price had been most impressed by his size: "He look[ed] the college president—over six feet, broad shoulders, strong features. Presence, dignity and abounding vitality [were] his." At dinner with Ham and his wife, Price was taken with the "awfully human" qualities of Mrs. Ham, a "small" woman who gardened, golfed and played tennis, a woman who would "never try to interfere in administrative matters as some presidents' wives do."

Price had asked Ham how he came to accept the presidency. "Because," he said, "it is a challenging position, and I like challenge.... There seems to be some fear complex abroad about me, that I'm going to turn the place upside down." He told her he planned nothing drastic. Price asked him about his attitude toward the higher education of women.

"I see woman as the housekeeper of civilization, of the world's culture.... They nurture culture, extend its influence, in their home, in their community—whether they go into the professions, or the very responsible business of marriage. Does that answer your question?" Ham asked.

"Quite," Price said. She brought up the controversy, calling it the "faculty-trustee rumpus." "They say you're the trustees' man," and Price detected "real annoyance" on Ham's face.

"That's not true," he said. "I don't think the trustees want someone they can handle. If they did, they certainly shouldn't have chosen me."

Price chose to interpret "the light of humor playing over" his face as he said this as a sign of his ability to see things "quite dispassionately," a "tremendous advantage of coming from the outside, not only of Mount Holyoke, but of the women's college group." Thoroughly impressed by Ham, Price described her feelings as she left the Yale campus: "Three words kept humming through my mind—vitality, flow, growth. These are his watchwords."[55]

Price was not altogether pleased with her interview/article. Well aware of "the jumpy pulse of the *Quarterly* readers and the feverish temperature of the faculty," she couldn't include any of the "finer points" she had discussed with Morrison about trustee and faculty preference for Ham. Her goal had to be to "play up Mr. Ham as a strong, sane, impartial administrator." She had spent a week on the Mount Holyoke campus and concluded to Morrison that "J.M. [Marks] and her cohorts [were] still busy" and "M.E.W. [Woolley] [was] still very fit. If only we could induct Mr. Ham now!"[56] She knew that faculty opposition to Ham's appointment was based in part on rumors that had begun within days of his appointment in June when Ruth Fairchild, the wife of a

Yale professor, came to Mount Holyoke to warn the faculty about him. Price had heard the story repeatedly but had no details and during the interview with Ham had chosen not to mention it.

Price was correct that Woolley and her allies had not given up. On December 12, Bernice McClean, a 1926 alumna currently working at Hunter College in New York City, wrote to Woolley and enclosed the text of a petition to the Mount Holyoke trustees that was being circulated among alumnae. She noted in her letter:

> The action of the trustees and its acceptance by many members of the college have been profoundly disheartening, but your contributions to Mount Holyoke and to women's progress are permanent. I believe that the reactionary attitudes revealed during the past few months are a part of the depression and post-depression confusion of values.[57]

Woolley wrote back in support of the petition and included a letter from a newspaper editor who offered to publish opinion pieces on "the Holyoke presidential situation."[58]

Meanwhile, McHale and Richards of the AAUW were meeting with Perkins to discuss a radical proposal. The plan was for a select group of alumnae including Perkins and Richards to approach Ham and directly ask him to resign. Perkins believed it was important to confront Cheney, Furniss and Morrison as well as Ham, but she also believed that the "academic, logical, dignified approach had failed and would continue to fail with those men." Instead, the group should be "militant, interested in 'scratching,' in no sense ladylike in their statements concerning what they were going to do about the future of Mount Holyoke College under a man president if Mr. Ham did not see a reason for resigning."[59] McHale reported this discussion to Woolley. She told her that Perkins did not believe the appropriate pressure could be accomplished by academics like Richards or women like herself: "It would be ludicrous for Dr. Richards and herself [Perkins] to be chained to the gates of Mount Holyoke College as the Woman's Party might dramatically and justifiably behave." Instead, Perkins suggested that "a specific selection of militant representatives of other organizations should be encouraged to carry out [the] suggestion."

McHale told Woolley that she agreed with Perkins' position that "Mount Holyoke College should be made to suffer until the trustees are convinced that the support of women can only be gained when the tradition of Mount Holyoke College in the matter of a woman president is carried on."[60] Woolley agreed that the strongest possible influence would have to come from organizations outside of Mount Holyoke. She put McHale in touch with Rowland and Smiley, who were preparing to release a major publication. Their plan was to take the protest to both the alumnae and the media.

CHAPTER 6

The Question of Solidarity

Rowland and Smiley, evoking the long arm of history, titled their document "The Case of Mary Lyon vs. the Committee of Nine." Dubbed the Broadside, it was designed to attract attention. Twelve separate charges against the trustees, described in detail, framed Woolley's June 6 protest to the board, the centerpiece of the page. In late January of 1937, Rowland and Smiley's group, self-identified as the Committee of 100, mailed 8,400 copies to alumnae and the press in response to the closing of the *Alumnae Quarterly* to controversy and the board's refusal to reconsider its June decision at the November meeting. The Broadside attacked the search committee's conduct during the presidential search and its repeated attempts to stifle dissent. Headlines leapt off the page in bold type: **"Was the Committee of Nine Packed?" "Railroading It Through the Board," "Alumnae and Faculty Opinion Disregarded," "They Could Not Find a Suitable Woman!" "Is It Too Late to Act?"** A resounding "NO" followed.[1]

The Committee of 100 urged alumnae to consider changing their wills, withholding money from the college, and calling for the resignation of the trustees who were on the search committee. They reasoned that the resignations of those responsible for selecting Ham would invalidate Ham's contract, allowing the search for a woman to resume. In the meantime, it would be a simple matter to select an acting president from the pool of administrators at Mount Holyoke.[2] In line with the strategy proposed by McHale of the AAUW, the Broadside recommended that alumnae clubs "withhold centennial and other funds until satisfaction is obtained.... It is understood that others are watching developments, intending to withdraw bequests if a man is inducted."

The Broadside charged that the offers to three women—"one college president, one college dean, and one married woman with a family and head of her own preparatory school"—were not real offers because "[i]t was generally known beforehand that none of these three would be able to accept because of responsibilities already undertaken." In support of the charge that

1837—The Case of Mary Lyon vs. The Committee of Nine—1937

Was the Committee of Nine Packed?

1934. The Board of Trustees appointed the following Committee on the Succession to the Presidency, 5 members:

Mr. Alva Morrison
Miss Rowena K. Keyes
Mrs. Mary Hume Maguire
Mr. Howell Cheney
Mr. Henry P. Kendall

Note: Of that number Mr. Kendall was known to be strongly opposed to the election of a woman. Only Miss Keyes was at that time in favor of a woman president.

1936—Spring. The Committee on the Succession to the Presidency added to their Committee:

Miss Lottie Bishop
Mrs. Helene Pope Whitman
Dr. Edgar S. Furniss
Mr. Paul H. Davis

Note: In answer to a letter in July, 1935, Miss Bishop and Dr. Furniss replied that they were absolutely in favor of a man rather than a woman president.

Yale in South Hadley

Three members of Mount Holyoke's Committee of Nine are connected with Yale.

Howell Cheney—Yale Corporation
Lottie Bishop—Secretary at Yale
Dean Furniss—Yale Graduate School

Excerpt from letter of Charles Seymour, Provost of Yale, to Board of Trustees of Mount Holyoke while Mr. Ham's candidacy was under discussion:

"It he were made head of Mount Holyoke College, I think that his services to American education would be enlarged. . . . After all, Yale as a great educational institution of America will in the long run profit thereby."

Rushing It Into the News

June 4, 1936. Publicity announcing Mr. Ham's election was given to the College Press Bureau by Mr. Morrison two days *before the election was held.* The Press Bureau was instructed to get the story into the telegraph offices of all key cities of the country to await wired confirmation.

Railroading It Through the Board

From the letter of a Trustee who voted for Mr. Ham:

"It was moved that the report of the Committee of Nine be referred back to the Committee for restudy in order that the change might not be made with such haste. This motion was lost. . . . I think it was hardly recognized that the other members of the Board had not known the nature of the report within two weeks of that meeting and then only through a manifolded copy of it which had been sent around. I felt that we had not had opportunity for adequate discussion of the matter in the light of the announcement of the change proposed. . . .

"I am clear that our action in electing him in June was precipitated. . . ."

June 6, 11 a.m. Miss Woolley and members of the Conference Committee of the Faculty made formal protests before the Board against the possible election of a man for the Presidency.

4 p.m. Miss Woolley protested again.

Late afternoon. Nine members had asked for delay, which was refused. One member was swung over at the last minute, thereby giving the minimum necessary vote: 16 to 8.

Wills Being Changed

Already women have changed their wills because they are not in sympathy with the idea of a man-elect to the presidency of Mount Holyoke. It is understood that others are watching developments, intending to withdraw bequests if a man is inducted.

Miss Woolley's Administration

Endowment, Mount Holyoke College (i.e., "productive funds")

May 31, 1901 .... $568,723.39
June 1, 1926 .... $4,676,886.99

Growth of Student Enrollment

1900-1901 550
1935-1936 1,017

Growth of Faculty

1900-1901 54
1935-1936 123

(Figures from Comptroller's Office and Registrar's Office.)

President Woolley's Protest

Letter to the Board of Trustees

June 6, 1936.

The letter which I wrote to each member of the Board of Trustees, under date of May the twentieth, gives the reasons for my strong feeling with regard to the appointment of a woman as any successor in the presidency. These reasons, as you may recall, are as follows: first, the principle upon which Mount Holyoke was founded, that women as human beings have an equal right with men for the development of their powers and an equal right to opportunities for service; second, that the progress of Mount Holyoke throughout the last one hundred years has been under the leadership of women, to whom recognition is due; third, that a change in policy with regard to the presidency of Mount Holyoke would mean striking a blow to the advancement of women, the seriousness of which can hardly be overestimated.

There are other factors which deserve consideration. If the College were a college for men, would the possibility of appointing a woman as president be given a moment's consideration? Certainly not without an overwhelming demand for the change, a demand from the faculty, alumni and undergraduates. The faculty of Mount Holyoke have given unmistakable evidence of their desire, 87 members of the teaching faculty out of 106 voting for a woman. Surely no expression of opinion should have greater weight than that of the faculty to whom is due in large measure the progress of an institution.

No opportunity has been given for an alumnae vote on the question of choice between a man and a woman, but judging from the individual comments from all sections of the country and from the petition signed by a large number of New York alumnae, one assumes that a large majority of alumnae prefer a woman as President of the College.

The opinion of thoughtful persons outside the College and outside its immediate constituency should not be underestimated in its influence upon the future development of the College, and that feeling strongly supports the policy of choosing a woman as President of Mount Holyoke.

To sum up, I can imagine no greater blow to the advancement of women than the announcement that Mount Holyoke celebrates its Centennial by departing from the ideal of leadership by women for women, which inspired the founding of the institution and which has been responsible in large measure for its progress.

(Signed) Mary E. Woolley

College Supported By Women

1. The largest individual gifts Mount Holyoke has received have all been from women:

   a. The Mandelle Bequest $750,000
   b. Mrs. E. R. Stevens 480,137
   c. Mrs. Willis James 100,000
   d. Mrs. Kennedy 50,000
   e. Miss Fox, Boston 50,000

2. Gifts from Alumnae $1,868,500
3. A woman gave $350,000 for the new chapel, and has promised money gifts totalling one million dollars. This was done because of personal devotion to Miss Woolley.

Alumnae and Faculty Opinion Disregarded

Faculty vote: 87 for a woman; 11 for a man; 8, "sex not a factor."

Action of clubs in favor of a woman.

May, 1935. Six clubs wrote urging the appointment of a woman: Springfield, E. Connecticut, Hampshire County, Franklin County, Urbane and Champaign.

Nov. 1935. Two clubs wrote in favoring a woman: Western Maine and Long Island.

(Above information from Mary Hume Maguire's letter.)

May 26, 1936. New York petition for a woman.

June 4, 1936. St. Louis Club presented resolution demanding appointment of a woman.

Note: There is no record of any club having expressed itself as wishing a change to a man president.

Nov. 5: 1,045 general signatures of protest sent to Board. Ruled out by the Board because signatures other than alumnae were included.

Protest of Indianapolis Club.
Protest of Detroit Club.
Protest of Minnesota Club.
Dec. 1936. Special protest of prominent alumnae all over the country.

Note: The President of the Board was asked, before Mr. Ham was elected, whether an alumnae vote of preference would have any influence with the Board. He replied that an alumnae vote of preference would make no difference in the Board's decision.

They Could Not Find a Suitable Woman!

Qualifications of Women Considered:

Rejected: (70 women "disqualified")

One woman College President.
One woman Dean of Graduate School.
Two Deans of Women.
Two women Heads of important Preparatory Schools.
Two important Government Executives.
Several internationally known women scholars and writers.

Three women were asked: one College President, one College Dean, and one married woman with a family and head of her own preparatory school. It was generally known beforehand that none of these three would be able to accept because of responsibilities already undertaken.

Tell It to the Marines

Mr. Ham's qualifications:

Instructor at the University of Washington.
Instructor at the University of California.
Lieutenant and captain in the Marine Corps during the war.
An authority on English literature of the 17th century.

At present:

Associate professor at Yale.
Lecturer at Albertus Magnus (a college of 115 students conducted by Dominican Sisters in New Haven).

(Facts given in Mr. Morrison's message in the August "Quarterly.")

Quarterly Bans Miss Woolley

Shortly after commencement Miss Woolley sent for Florence Clement, the editor of the *Alumnae Quarterly,* and asked that the *Quarterly* publish her statement made to the Trustees on June 6, giving her reasons for wishing to have a woman as her successor. Miss Clement refused. Miss Woolley remarked: "Do you not think it is going rather far to refuse the President of the College admission to the *Alumnae Quarterly?*" Miss Clement continued to refuse.

When the Executive Secretary to the Board of Admissions heard of this, she went immediately to see Miss Clement and Miss Higley, the Alumnae Secretary. The Executive Secretary told them that they would be criticized by all responsible men and women if they continued to refuse to admit Miss Woolley's statement to the *Quarterly.* Her position was strong, both as an alumna and as an officer of the College. The result was that Miss Woolley was allowed to print her protest in the *Quarterly,* but it was buried in the back pages, front space being given to Mr. Morrison's eulogy of Mr. Ham.

Quarterly Closed To Alumnae Opinion

Sept. 26, 1936. The Directors of the *Alumnae Quarterly* met in New York and decided not to print any letters or articles of protest. This decision was made despite the fact that throughout the summer the officers of the *Alumnae Quarterly* in refusing protests for the August *Quarterly* had been writing to those who sent in articles and letters that these would be published in the November issue.

Nov. 6. A Meeting of about 150 Alumnae Members in South Hadley passed a resolution to accept the decision of the Directors of the *Quarterly* to close the *Quarterly* to all contrary opinion. No previous notice given. Vote not unanimous.

Note: Have the alumnae forgotten that they support the *Quarterly* and therefore have the right to be heard?

Is It Too Late to Act?

NO. MR. HAM HAS NOT YET BEEN INDUCTED AS PRESIDENT OF MOUNT HOLYOKE COLLEGE

1. On the evidence given above, the Trustees who composed the Committee of Nine should be asked to resign. Although Mr. Ham now holds a legal contract, the resignation of his original sponsors would naturally be followed by his withdrawal. The case is moral, not legal.

2. If you are interested, write individually to the address below, or call your club together. *Clubs can withhold centennial and other funds until satisfaction is obtained.* All reports should be sent to the Secretary of the Committee for Investigation, in order that material can be presented to the Board at the most effective time. Time is short; work quickly.

3. Until the election of a new woman president, an acting president will be available from among the administrative officers of the College. One of them has already served as acting president during Miss Woolley's mission in Geneva.

Amy F. Rowland (former Trustee), Chairman, Cleveland, Ohio.
Carolyn D. Smiley, Secretary, 118 Myrtle Street, Boston, Mass.

For the Alumnae Committee for Investigation.

Keep this sheet for reference. We have proof in hand for every statement made on this page.

The Broadside, "1837—The Case of Mary Lyon vs. The Committee of Nine—1937."

the decision was "railroaded" through the board at the June 6 meeting, the Broadside quoted part of a letter from an unnamed trustee:

> I think it was hardly recognized that the other members of the Board had not known the nature of the report within two weeks of that meeting and then only through a manifolded [*sic*] copy of it which had been sent around. I felt that we had not had opportunity for adequate discussion of the matter in the light of the monumental character of the change proposed.[3]

The publication of the Broadside shocked most alumnae and trustees. White, the head of the Alumnae Association, had warned Morrison after the alumnae council meeting in early November that she believed Smiley was "exploiting our difficulties for her own benefit to make a name for herself in feminist circles." This was White's interpretation of a conversation she had had with Smiley in which Smiley had told her "she'd been making investigations ... when the alumnae 'knew the real issues' she was certain there would be an 'overwhelming vote for a woman president.'"[4] White sent Morrison a copy of Smiley's magazine, *World Youth*, as evidence that Smiley was a radical and a troublemaker. She added: "I think I'll subscribe, just to keep an eye on it. Do you notice the list of advisors? It looks like dirty work at the cross roads to me."[5]

Purington knew that Rowland and other alumnae felt "their desires were entirely disregarded" during and after the November 5 meeting. She recommended to Morrison that some "conciliatory message should go from the Board" to both Rowland and Smiley.[6] Morrison ignored the suggestion. Contemptuous of the protest and convinced that the election was now a "closed issue," he sought the public support of the trustees who were opposed to Ham. He failed to persuade them to submit a minority report accepting the election. Morrison had given up all hope of getting Woolley's support. He complained about having to reply to Rowland and to the other protesters who had signed the petition, telling Alumnae Association president White that he was "getting really tired." He did not want "to continue forever a discussion of the Mount Holyoke presidency."[7] Despite White's warning, Morrison was probably among those who were taken by surprise when the charges in the Broadside hit the newspapers.

He had to respond immediately. On January 30, he told a reporter from the *Sunday Union and Republican* that the choice of Ham was a "closed issue." White, when questioned about the alumnae, minimized the significance of the opposition, and Ham, when asked about his reaction, told the press that he was "disregarding any actions by [dissident] alumnae groups because they represented a small group.... I have accepted the election, and that's all there is to it."[8] On February 1, Morrison wrote to Ham, telling him how angry he was that the *Holyoke Transcript* had printed the Broadside "almost in full." He assured Ham that he, White and others made certain that their views got into the press to counter the charges and, as proof, sent Ham clippings including one quoting White, "Mount Holyoke Alumnae Head Defends Choice."

Newspapers ran with the story of the protest, the headlines variously serious, trivializing or mocking. "Mt. Holyoke Won't Be Ruled by a Leatherneck from Yale," "No Men Wanted," "Male Head of Holyoke Stirs Up Big Rumpus," "Mere Man Is Cause of Fuss," "Male, Female Battle Rages at Mt. Holyoke," "A Man at Mt. Holyoke? Never! Cry Graduates," "First Male as President Arouses Mount Holyoke," "Dr. Roswell Ham Is Not Excited," "Ham Calm in Storm."[9]

Woolley claimed not to have seen a copy of the Broadside until it arrived with a letter from an alumna (Ruth Waldron) who was upset about the damage the publicity could do to the college. The alumna urged Woolley to release a statement that would put an end to the opposition:

> A few people are doing incalculable harm to our college by circularizing alumnae with printed matter which is at once misleading in fact, sensational in tone, and disloyal in intent. Whatever has already occurred, the outstanding fact now is that this sort of thing is destructive to our college in every sense.... Inasmuch as your name has been used freely, and because your influence is so deep and wide, I venture to suggest that a statement from you would save us all the reputation of Mount Holyoke, our own joy in the Centennial party, and that "unity of spirit and bond of peace" which is so essential to real achievement.[10]

Woolley answered promptly to express her strong disagreement. The issue, she said, was larger than Mount Holyoke. The accusations in the Broadside were, as far as she knew, "accurate."

> The copy of the flier enclosed in your special delivery received yesterday morning is the first one that I have seen—in fact I did not know that it was being circulated until yesterday. I understand that it is being sponsored by many prominent alumnae as well as by Miss Amy Rowland of the Cleveland Clinic, a former Alumna Trustee and Carolyn Smiley of World Youth.
>
> To the extent of my knowledge the statements on the flier are accurate. They are not only accurate but they also suggest a trend which has been markedly unfortunate for women in European countries and in England. Although the women of America have been somewhat more fortunate nevertheless there are many instances even in this country today of "fraternal" decisions to replace women by men. For the sake of other women, if not for ones [sic] sake, noblesse oblige dictates that these evidences should not be ignored.
>
> It must seem superfluous for me to say to the alumnae of Mount Holyoke College that the conditions under which my work at Mount Holyoke is closing are not those toward which I had looked forward.

Woolley ended with a characteristically personal note: "It is a pleasure to have your daughter in college and I hope that I may some time during the year see you."[11]

Waldron's response to Woolley suggested that Woolley's cogent argument and respectful tone had made an impression. She remained fearful that "if undue criticism should force resignations, the result could only be to render the offices of President and Trustee undesirable in the eyes of the kind of men and women who are needed in South Hadley." However, Woolley's larger view of events had impressed her:

> If this new appointment should really be a manifestation of a trend, similar to the trend toward nationalism which we all recognize and deplore, it would be a matter of sincere regret to all of us who believe in enlightened womanhood. It is hard to see our world take a backward step even after a long succession of forward ones.

Waldron still insisted that "real worth in personality," regardless of sex, should not be overlooked in spite of "reactionary trends."[12] She was expressing an opinion shared by many alumnae.

On February 3, the *Boston Transcript* published a copy of a letter that Woolley had written to an alumna supporter of the Committee of 100 in which Woolley attested to the accuracy of the Broadside and its wider implications.[13] A reporter from the paper telephoned Woolley asking for a statement about Ham. She refused to make one but confirmed the accuracy of the story. The following day, while Woolley was in Boston to speak at a centennial celebration for the minister Dwight Moody, she agreed to an interview with the *New York Times*. The headline would read: "Dr. Woolley Joins Attack on Dr. Ham." Woolley had told the *Times* reporter that "the election of a man as her successor set a precedent which might have reverberations for women throughout the world." The issue, she said, was "broader by far than Mount Holyoke itself," explaining that her point of view was "not extremely feministic." It "involved a principle not a prejudice." There was "nothing personal in this situation." She was, she said, "speaking without emotion." Ham, according to the reporter, was surprised that Woolley had "joined the group in re-opening the issue."[14]

Other newspapers picked up the story. The *Herald Tribune* carried the headline "Dr. Woolley Leading Rebellion against Dr. Ham at Mt. Holyoke." The *Tribune* story took Woolley's general statement that the Broadside was accurate and included the accusation that "a 'packed' committee of trustees selected [Ham]." The reporter had attempted to interview four trustees. Keyes was quoted as saying, "I don't think I ought to comment. I was on the committee and you can imagine what my sentiments are." Speers, believing that Woolley would not have made inflammatory statements, told the reporter, "There must be some misunderstanding. I do not wish to make any comment." Myers was cautious. "The situation is unfortunate. I do not think I had better say anything at this time." Cheney refused comment: "I don't wish to be quoted. I have nothing to say."[15] The *Springfield Republican*, in quoting Ham, captured the "public face" that Ham and the trustees were attempting to wear: "Her [Woolley's] statement is unexpected. Miss Woolley has been extremely cordial to me."[16]

Woolley did not want to lead the protest against the board decision. In fact, she took the position that it was up to the alumnae and concerned people outside of the college to put sufficient pressure on the board to reverse course. She made it clear internally to the trustees that she believed they had violated at least the spirit of correct procedure by insisting on a vote at the board meeting at which the search committee's report had just been presented. She had also clearly stated her opposition to Ham's appointment in the statement she read at the June board meeting and had insisted on its publication in the *Alumnae Quarterly*. When newspapers began to attribute statements to her that originated in the Broadside, she quickly issued a statement to the press and telegrammed Morrison to set the record straight. The telegram read:

> Recent reports in the press have attributed remarks to me that I did not make—I have consistently maintained the position of favoring a woman ... but I have made no statement to the public and with the exception of a single interview concerning the principle involved in changing the presidency from a woman to a man, I have given no interview.[17]

The *Republican* article predicted that Mount Holyoke College faced a "Wide Open Fight" when the Alumnae Council met on March 6. The article noted that this would probably represent "the last ditch effort to force [the] resignation of Ham and eight trustees." Official Mount Holyoke, the board of trustees and the Alumnae Association, in the persons of Morrison and White, sprang into action. White telegrammed the United Press in Boston: "Difficult to believe reports in morning papers that Miss Woolley supports action of a small group of insurgent alumnae who are more interested in feminism than in Mount Holyoke. I have utmost confidence in integrity and unselfish service of our trustees."[18] Morrison added the information from Mount Holyoke historian Viola Barnes that Mount Holyoke Seminary had offered the principalship to a male in 1852. The current board of trustees was, therefore, not breaking a precedent. White also wrote to Ham that day. She expressed at great length her outrage over the attack on the trustees and apologized to Ham and his wife for all the "unpleasantness." She also informed him that she had written to Smiley asking for the names of those on the Committee of 100. "I presume," she told Ham, that "we'll have trouble at [the March alumnae council meeting] unless we can reach all clubs convincingly." She had talked to Smiley months earlier in Boston but was unsuccessful in her effort to persuade her to stop "her threatened campaign." White told Ham that she (White) had a plan to bring an ally to the alumnae meeting, a woman who had heard Smiley tell

White that she was more interested in feminism than in Mount Holyoke. White would have her "speak from the floor ... to put the facts before the councilors." "I like a good fight," White told Ham.

Morrison, for his part, reported to White that developments in Boston had been "popping" all week. He felt it was "safe to say [Smiley] has received more disapproving letters than support." The letter-writing campaign on the part of the "feminist faction," which exercised "great effort" to get names on Rowland's November petition, had produced a small enough response from trustees and alumnae alike that Morrison encouraged White "to ask for complete records pro and con of the returns" from [Smiley's] Broadside. White would be on "perfectly safe ground," and Smiley would refuse to cooperate because she knew that "the record [would] undoubtedly prove her effort to have been futile and even ridiculous." He urged White to come to Boston to meet with Smiley. "Nothing could be better than to make known to alumnae club presidents the returns" from the Broadside. Morrison was "still waiting for a constructive statement from Woolley which [he hoped] may repair so far as that is possible the damage done by the unauthorized publication of Woolley's 'letter to an alumna,'" the letter confirming the accuracy of the facts in the Broadside.[19]

In an interview on February 8, Ham presented what was emerging as the official position on the opposition. He criticized alumnae and others who opposed his appointment as "more interested in feminism than in the good of Mount Holyoke." Mary Lyon, he asserted, "was not a feminist. She was used to working with men.... Besides, the fight for feminism is over now." When he was asked how the controversy had affected him, he dismissively joked that "it has helped my scholarship. I have acquired a philosophical attitude." He added insult to jest when he assured the interviewer that he understood the upset over his appointment: "It was as if Yale University had appointed a new president who had not graduated from Yale." But this was a college for women, not Yale University, and Ham reminded the interviewer that "the fact must always be kept in mind that women's main vocation is marriage."[20]

In an earlier February interview, Ham had told the press that letters of support exceeded letters of opposition by twenty to one and he cited this approval as ample reason for not resigning. The agitation over his appointment, he asserted, had nothing to do with education of women. "It's a pity," he said, "that an alien discussion to the principles of education should be brought up."[21] This would become a recurrent theme in Ham's public stance— the protesters were caught up in what he called a "side issue" while the important matter, "education," was never their concern. It appears that he was not reading the letters in opposition. If he had been, he could not have missed the detailed and cogent arguments about why the controversy had a great deal to do with issues of education.

The following letter to Ham had arrived only a week after the board's June 6 decision:

Dear Mr. Ham:

Please let me introduce myself ... as a Yale Ph.D. in English and a Mount Holyoke AB. As the only Yale PhD on the English faculty here, I feel in a peculiarly appropriate situation to write to you, now that you have become our president-elect.

I write this letter because of the repercussions following your appointment ... We have a tradition, you see, of the widening of opportunities for women....

...We don't teach or preach feminism: we have never thought of it as something to be taught. All we want at Mount Holyoke is the right to use what brains the Lord gave us. Our graduates marry and/or have careers, just as men do. Many on the faculty are scholars, women and men; and the women could, if given the chance, teach with equal honor at Yale. But they have not that chance, and they must, if they are not to atrophy intellectually, continue to have that chance at Mount Holyoke and its sister colleges.

So long as the men's colleges maintain a closed door against women on their faculties, so long as opportunities for women are limited, our response to your appointment is natural.[22]

This letter and others written long before he could claim weariness at persistent, pointless protest or before he could claim to find feminist ideologies everywhere in the opposition give the lie to his and his supporters' dismissal of the opposition.

British journalist Meagher[23] sent Ham a copy of a letter she had written to the board in October, which emphasized the reality of inequality in opportunities for leadership:

There are only a few leading educational posts in America for which a woman would even be considered, however high her qualifications for leadership. By its decision, the Board has lessened this small number by a very important one. Individuals whether men or women, need and should have in prospect the attainment of reward if they are to give their best work; men no less than women, would be discouraged if they knew that the highest posts were closed to them on grounds of sex....

The argument of "the best person for the place, irrespective of sex" could only be valid if it worked both ways. It does not.[24]

When McHale read in the *Boston Globe* that "Mr. Ham's big durable he-man personality and solid scholarship would be a fine tonic for the spinster management of Mount Holyoke"[25] she quipped to Smiley that endocrinologists would better understand that statement than educators. "I think the time has come for a crusade by women and for women," McHale told her, and asked Smiley for clippings from the *Globe* and copies of the Broadside to send to interested women. McHale was discussing further strategy with historian Mary

Beard, among others, while continuing to recommend that women withhold money and withdraw their daughters from the college. The AAUW could not discuss any official action until the March convention meeting. "The tragic figure in all of this is Miss Woolley," McHale told Smiley.

> It is incredible to think that vicious statements are going around about her. When I consider what Miss Woolley's disinterested service has been and then realize that she is going out of Mount Holyoke a person without honor in her own college, and without a suitable income, it alarms me.[26]

The "vicious statements" that McHale alluded to were part of the ongoing whispering campaign against Marks that had stalked her throughout her life at the college but had now taken on an especially hostile tone. The philosophy professor Warbeke, who had earlier made clear his strong preference for a male president, now felt at liberty to write to Ham about Marks, calling her "a little Rasputin in the situation back of the main power, a distinctly pathological character whose pronouncements however are extremely mighty with authority."[27]

An example of the extreme animus that existed toward Woolley and others opposed to Ham's appointment came in a letter to Morrison from Whitman on February 8. Whitman, while serving on the search committee, had originally told Morrison that she did not want to meet with Ham because she preferred a woman and doubted that most "first string" men would consider becoming a head of a woman's college. Now, fully in support of the committee's decision, she filled her letter with invective against Woolley, Smiley and Perkins. After the publication of the Broadside, Whitman had received a slew of what she called "scathing" letters from outraged alumnae. She described them to Morrison as "the most reserved and mildest sort of women." They urged her to not, "under any circumstances, resign" from the board.

Already appalled by what she called the "feminist uprising," Whitman was further enraged when she had heard that "Miss Woolley was 'leading the fight.'" Whitman told Morrison:

> I thought we had at last gotten to Hecuba, but my feelings were too much for mere words.... She [Woolley] may not believe it, but no amount of varnish will ever restore the gloss to her reputation.... How *can* she say that her letter which inadvertently got into print was "misinterpreted" by the press? ... The "denial"— even if convincing—could never catch up with the accounts in papers all over the country. It was so inconspicuous in the NY papers I almost missed it entirely.

Whitman promised Morrison that she would make the arduous trip north from South Carolina to attend the March meeting, much to his relief. He had begged her "not to fail us," and she would not disappoint.

Whitman had contemptuously referred to Woolley's effort at clarification, her special delivery letter sent to the trustees about the early February newspaper stories, as the "Woolley crawl which is, I think le dernier cri of its ilk." Smiley, in Whitman's view, did not care what happened to Mount Holyoke. She suggested to Morrison that Smiley might "organize a sit-down strike with Miss Perkins as backer" during the March meeting.[28] Whitman's insinuation that Woolley had deliberately planted the letter was further indication of how willing some people were to personally accuse the protesters of the worst intentions and behavior. Price responded to the Broadside in similar fashion. She wrote to Morrison:

> Am so sorry you had this fresh flare-up from la Rowland. But my memories of her in Cleveland are most unpleasant—brilliant but lacking in fundamental integrity.... I suppose every alumnae body has its pernicious members, but it's mighty unpleasant to have them in your own college family.[29]

Contrary to Price's assessment, there is every indication that Rowland, a highly regarded editor and associate in the biophysical research department of the renowned Cleveland Clinic in Ohio, was also an outstanding member of the college community. She had just left the board of trustees after serving for seven years. It is possibly no coincidence that Price, Whitman and White, who expressed themselves so viciously in their attacks on Woolley, Marks, Rowland and Smiley, were targeting women in life partnerships with other women.[30]

Maguire took a different approach to "the controversy which the militant feminists [were] forwarding so vociferously." She told Ham that she was relying on his sense of humor and assured him that "the alumnae [were] not such a bad lot." Maguire claimed embarrassment over a "small group of misguided women" and was eager "to have everyone realize that Miss Woolley has accepted the situation." The others, "more than our share of fanatics and insane women," many of whom held "the minority opinion that Yale has sinister purposes in South Hadley," were, Maguire believed, part of an "episode [that] seems so utterly ridiculous and fantastic in this day and age." She assured Ham that "Miss Smiley has and will receive the most fiery denunciation."[31]

Meanwhile, Smiley was writing to alumnae clubs calling into question the board's management of the college's finances. Morrison, forced to take some action, called a meeting with Woolley and Hazen.[32] The three met on February 16, along with Board Secretary Newhall, whom Morrison wanted present. Newhall was vocal in her opposition to the board's decision, and Morrison, along with others, distrusted her. He told Woolley, Hazen and Newhall that the ongoing agitation would soon affect student enrollment. He criticized Woolley's published "letter to an alumna," which, by endorsing the Broadside, put in question the integrity of the trustees on the search committee. Woolley carefully pointed out that she had made a distinction between fact and opinion in her letter. She had only affirmed that the information was "accurate." Her comments were not meant to endorse opinions expressed in the Broadside. Morrison asked Woolley if she would make a statement of unity urging faculty, alumnae and students to cooperate with the trustees. This would indicate that she "really cared about the college," and he hoped that she would do this "sincerely." He proposed that she allow the release of a statement that he had already prepared.

> That although Miss Woolley disapproves, as she has repeatedly stated, the appointment of a man to the presidency of Mount Holyoke, and has in no way altered her stand for the emancipation of, and equal opportunity for, women, she nevertheless recognizes that the election of Dr. Ham is an accomplished fact and that further and prolonged protest can only be injurious to Mount Holyoke College: that consequently she is conferring with Dr. Ham concerning budget problems and appointments for the coming year and is cooperating to further the success of his administration; and finally that she expects alumnae, faculty and students similarly to support him.

Woolley refused. She told Morrison and Hazen that this was a fight for equal rights and, as she had said repeatedly, the issue was much larger than Mount Holyoke. She could not "cut the ground from under her staunch supporters." She had warned the trustees that their decision would bring widespread protest, and now there was nothing more to say. It was out of her hands, "taken up by men and women all over the country—many with no connection to the school." In an added "punch," Woolley proposed that anything she said would have no effect, reminding them that in June, when she made her protest to the trustees, it "definitely" had had no effect.

If Woolley was concerned about "letting down" the alumnae, Morrison challenged, hadn't she "let down" the trustees when she agreed that the committee was "packed?" Woolley reminded him that she had not been aware of the Broadside until she was contacted by an alumna who had received one in the mail. Once again, Woolley denied that she had ever made a statement about the committee being "packed." The trustees, she told Morrison and Hazen, had made two major mistakes. The first was to push through so radical a change without full knowledge of faculty and alumnae sentiment. The second was to allow the vote without a larger majority in favor among the trustees. "How, Mr. Hazen, would you feel if a woman were suddenly made president of Williams College without alumni consultation?" she asked.

Morrison, defeated in his effort to move Woolley off her position, needed to report the outcome of this meeting to "a small group with whom he was in conference." He mentioned Rowland, Smiley and Richards in his first draft, implying that Woolley had referred to the three women at the meeting. Woolley had not, and she objected when she saw the draft. Woolley wrote her own three-page report and sent it to Morrison. She demanded that the names of the three women be removed from the final copy, and Morrison complied. When he sent Hazen copies of the exchange with Woolley, Hazen wrote back and blamed the "mean" head cold that sent him to bed for a few days on the "chilly" reception they had gotten from Woolley. He had already told Cheney, Furniss and Potter of the meeting, opining:

> This subject of women's rights is a monomania with Miss Woolley, I fear, and her judgment of proportion seems to be warped. In her mind evidently the issue transcends all matters such as the good of the college, her own obligation to her job, etc. It is indeed pathetic.[33]

Morrison agreed: "Doesn't the record look perfectly incredible when put down in cold type? Your conclusion is the only one which can be correctly drawn from it." He told Hazen that he was anxious to meet with Cheney and Furniss. The question was whether they should include Potter, since he had failed to "deliver" Woolley, the only motivation for involving Potter in the first place.[34]

Newhall had not been silent during the meeting. She told Morrison and Hazen that the news of Ham's appointment "had come like a thunderbolt to the alumnae in June" and that it had taken the women time to react. Because the *Quarterly* was closed as a forum for discussion and protest, the alumnae were "obliged to take this way," a public protest through the Broadside. Morrison told her that the *Quarterly* simply could not have contained any controversial material alongside the endorsement of Ham. Newhall disagreed. There "could have been dignified articles on both sides," she told him.[35] Newhall's outspoken criticism of the trustees was apparently the last straw for Morrison. Coming from the secretary to the board of trustees, such insubordination must have infuriated him. Morrison discussed Newhall with Furniss and the others soon after the meeting and followed up with a letter to Newhall in which he cited a series of concerns that read like accusations. Furniss didn't believe this approach went far enough. He preferred to dismiss her from both of her positions:

> Perhaps I am entirely too aggressive in this matter, although I do not think my attitude is colored with vindictiveness. It seems to me, first, that we are quite within our rights to challenge her fitness to go on acting as Chairman of the Board of Admission, and second, that it is quite preposterous for us to allow her to continue to serve the Trustees as their secretary.[36]

Morrison prevailed and sent the letter, and Newhall promptly replied.[37] Her tone was respectful as she answered each charge. No, she did not assist Smiley in creating the Broadside, nor did she know anything about it until she saw Miss Woolley's copy. No, she had never told any alumnae group that Ham's election was "railroaded." She was "consistent in trying to refuse to discuss the affair ... when publicly asked some very embarrassing questions." Newhall told Morrison that she continually reminded groups of alumnae with whom she met that she was "traveling in the interests of enrollment" and, as secretary of the board of trustees, she could not discuss the issues. As for the controversy over the endowment and accusations of financial mismanagement, when asked by alumnae, she consistently claimed ignorance of the facts. One alumnae club had requested that she provide them with printed reports for the past five years. She had given them the reports, but there had never been any discussion in her presence. After responding to Morrison's specific charges, Newhall wrote an uncompromising statement of her position:

> I have been consistent also when questioned by individuals—alumnae and others—in saying that I was deeply disappointed in the election of a man and that I did not understand how the trustees could have taken that action nor how they could have done it in the way that they did—disregarding the traditions of the college, the expressed wish of Miss Woolley and the faculty, and the general feeling of the alumnae in so far as it could be inferred. I have said this also to several members of the Board and do not feel that it is in any way inconsistent with my office as Secretary of the Board.

Newhall also pointedly reminded Morrison that she was not present at the executive session on June 6 when the election took place, nor were the records of that session filed with her as secretary of the board. "You will remember also," she wrote, "that there are trustees and ex-trustees who disapprove the action of the Board."[38]

Morrison responded a day later on March 4. He was "glad" to be able to "deny the rumors," but he remained uncertain about her understanding of the restraints placed on her in her position on the board: "You did not specifically give me the assurance for which I asked, but I assume from the tone of your letter that in the future the Board of Trustees will have your full cooperation with respect to any of its decisions."[39] Furniss would not have his way. Morrison, more the diplomat, abandoned any plan to remove Newhall. She remained board secretary through the June 12, 1937, meeting, the last meeting of Woolley's presidency.

On February 11, three days after Ham's interview was published in the *New York Times*, the *New York Herald Tribune* published a lengthy response. It was written by Elizabeth Porter Wyckoff, a 1909 graduate of Mount Holyoke, a writer and supporter of the Committee of 100. Wyckoff took exception to Ham's assertion that the dispute was "alien" to the issue of women's education. "[T]he tendency to consider any expressed opinion ... as the work of headstrong and willful women," she wrote, indicates how the trustees truly feel about the ability of alumnae to think independently. Wasn't

this the primary goal of education? She accused both the trustees and the officers of the Alumnae Association of engaging in a "policy of suppression and
censorship of what may or may not be a minority of the alumnae." It was clear
to her that many of the trustees wanted a man from the beginning based on
their choice of only three women, "all of whom were an educator [*sic*] of emi-
nence, well established in positions of responsibility, and embarked on work
which they were understandably reluctant to relinquish." Why Ham? There
was nothing in Ham's "modest academic record" to recommend him ahead of
the many women who were associate professors with Ph.D.'s with similar or
greater qualifications. Wyckoff went further. She accused the trustees and
alumnae officials of deliberately withholding information about the numbers
of letters of support or protest that they had received.[40]

At Smith College, Nicolson observed the controversy in silence until she
became aware of the circulating Broadside. She told Morrison that she was
"appalled" and felt compelled to speak out on the matter as it pertained to
her. She had sympathized to some extent with the Mount Holyoke alumnae,
but "it's all gone" now, she told him. She was angry about the allegation contained in the Broadside that the offer to each of the three women candidates
was "a mere empty gesture." It took away, she said, "the pleasure and the recognition we all must have felt."[41] She wrote to Smiley, chastising her and the
Committee of 100 for "spoiling" their cause with this charge, and challenged
her to show the proof that Nicolson was not in a position to leave Smith College at the time of the offer. "I had hoped," she told Smiley, "that women had
developed beyond the stage where it was necessary to think in terms of men
versus women, as it used to be in the past." Nicolson informed Smiley that the
trustees "put every possible pressure upon [her] to accept the position.... Mr.
M [Morrison] was particularly insistent and had he had his was [*sic*], a woman
would today be the next president of Mount Holyoke."[42]

Nicolson also wrote a warm, appreciative letter to Morrison and enclosed
her letter to Smiley. She gave him permission to make use of it as he saw fit,
provided it didn't get into the press. Nicolson believed without a doubt that
the board had made her a legitimate offer and that she was their preferred candidate. She had had no hint that board members might have preferred a man.
No one, she told Morrison, with the exception of her "intimate friend" President Neilson, knew "the whole story" of her reasons for refusing the offer.
(Neilson, who had great admiration and affection for Woolley, when asked by
the press for an opinion on the demand for Ham's resignation refused to be
drawn into the controversy.)

Nicolson reminded Morrison that she had told him she "did not at that
time wish to be president of anything," that she had "already refused several
offers of the sort, but [he] could not have known that in advance."[43] On the

contrary, information about any offers that Nicolson had received could very easily have found its way to the Mount Holyoke search committee. Lines of communication between colleges throughout the country were open and "buzzing" constantly with news of searches and candidates. There is no doubt that several members of the committee at Mount Holyoke began the search with a strong preference for a man, contrary to Nicolson's belief that with the exception of one trustee [Kendall], the others "laid stress on their desire to find a woman." Any trustees who preferred a man and knew of Nicolson's rejections of other offers would have viewed the Mount Holyoke offer as a reasonable gamble.

Nicolson was apparently unaware of Kendall's efforts to frighten both the search committee and the Mount Holyoke faculty into opposing her. She found Kendall's reasons for wanting a man both "sincere and cogent" and yet "felt no prejudice in him." Thoroughly charmed by the self-assured and diplomatic Morrison, Nicolson was certain that he had been sincere in his representation of the board's desire to hire her. "No one could have been kinder," she told him, "or brought more pressure to bear upon a woman ... you paid me the honor ... of suggesting your preference for me ... you were so persuasive that you almost succeeded in my case!" She went further and told him: "Men have always shown the most candid appreciation of anything I have done; and I have no quarrel with the other sex!"[44]

Smiley responded to Nicolson and conceded that if the Committee of 100 had been "wrong" in its accusation, then it was guilty of an "honest mistake." She insisted, however, that the charges in the Broadside reflected the reality of the situation more accurately than did Nicolson's opinion, even without "proof." A few months after the exchange with Morrison and Smiley, Nicolson gave a major address at the University of Michigan's centennial celebration in which she attacked the growing trend, nationally and internationally, of declining opportunities for professional women. She was, she said, part of a generation that

> came late enough to escape the self-consciousness and the belligerence of the pioneers, to take education and training for granted.... [We] came early enough to take equally for granted professional positions in which we could make full use of our training. This was our double glory.... It never occurred to us at that time that we were taken only because men were not available.[45]

The fight at Mount Holyoke to keep women in leadership could have been instructive. The success of yet another "fraternal decision" to replace women with men was the reality there, but this strangely eluded Nicolson.[46]

Glass, the second woman who was offered the presidency, refused to comment publicly on the charge that the offer was based on the assumption that she would refuse. The third woman, Millicent Carey McIntosh, found herself at the center of a confusing and ultimately embarrassing situation. Susan Kingsbury, the chairman of the AAUW Committee on the Economic and Legal Status of Women, interviewed McIntosh in mid–February.[47] Kingsbury was investigating the events leading up to and after the appointment of Ham and was doing so with Woolley's full cooperation.[48] McIntosh knew about the charge that the committee was dishonest in its professed interest in finding a woman. Therefore, when Kingsbury told her that she was "one point in the evidence" against the trustees because they offered her the job with full knowledge that she would not accept. McIntosh responded, "They did *not* offer it to me because they knew I would *not* accept it."

Kingsbury reported what McIntosh had told her, and Morrison contacted McIntosh as soon as he got word of it.[49] He told her that she was technically correct in that a full vote of the trustees was the necessary procedure after a candidate had agreed to be considered. However, he assured her that when he came to see her in New York in April of 1936, knowing that she had "strong ties in New York," he was hoping that she might be tempted by such an important position. "I well remember," he wrote her,

> your emphatic statement that you could not possibly consider it and the manner in which you showed me the picture of your small children as proof of that fact. I accepted your statement as being distinctly not a mere feminine "No" inviting further argument.

Millicent Carey McIntosh, head of the Brearley School in New York City 1930–1947, allegedly offered the presidency of Mount Holyoke College.

Thus, Morrison's explanation for not pursuing McIntosh any further was that he understood her "no" to be final, not a feminine ploy to invite pursuit.[50]

McIntosh ignored this rather blunt insult and told him that she "had not realized that [he] made ... a definite offer." She reminded Morrison that he had told her the committee would agree to offer her the presidency if they thought there was any chance that she might be interested. "I did not realize," she told him now, "that you were serious about what you said." Morrison then revealed to McIntosh that she was in the same situation as the other two women. The trustees had not made an offer to any one of the three women, "for the very simple reason that each signified an unwillingness to accept such an offer." He asked McIntosh to make a statement that would "clear the record" and thereby force Kingsbury to retract the charges. Morrison told McIntosh that it would be a "tragedy" if indeed her misunderstanding of his intentions stopped her from pursuing the position. McIntosh reassured him that was definitely not the case. She was far too committed to her life in New York and to her work at the Brearley School.

Soon after their meeting, Morrison sent someone (probably Maguire) to see McIntosh to inform her about the Mount Holyoke situation from the point of view of the trustees. She was shown the Broadside. The next day, she wrote to Morrison to tell him how "deeply shocked" she was by what she was told: "I feel so concerned ... that I am prepared to do anything on earth I can to stop Miss Kingsbury from publishing her article. I am planning to go over all the material tonight, and to write her as soon as I can." Her trustee visitor also offered McIntosh the opportunity to serve on the Mount Holyoke Board of Trustees, an offer she declined. "I should give anything if I could accept," she told Morrison, "especially under the present circumstances." Morrison was simultaneously in contact with Nicolson. He telegrammed her to let her know that he was preparing a "statement of facts" to be distributed to forty-eight alumnae clubs. He asked for permission to include a copy of Nicolson's letter to Smiley, which she was glad to give provided that it be kept out of the press.[51]

McIntosh told Morrison that she "never should have made [the] statement if [she] had not seen the account in *News-Week*, in which the names of three other people were mentioned so that I thought I was out of the picture." The headline in *News-Week* read: "Dr. Woolley Openly Opposes Male Successor." A photo of Woolley was captioned "Miss Woolley called it a 'trend'" and a photo of Ham was captioned "Dr. Ham said it was a 'side issue.'" Nicolson, Glass and Jane P. Clark of Barnard College were identified as the three women to whom the presidency had been offered. McIntosh was not mentioned.[52] The *News-Week* writer had originally intended to focus on the opposition and Woolley's allies, but Price "got wind" of it, as she said, and called the editor. Price wrote Ham about how she influenced the final piece:

> I found they were going pretty much by la Rowland's statement, and some trustee down here who isn't playing cricket with Morrison. I don't know who it is, but have a hunch it may be Speer.... I told her that unless she wanted a biased story, she'd better get in touch with Mrs. White, Rowena Keyes ... and then I said that I was perfectly willing to go on record as having wanted a man from the beginning ... because it was only a healthy swing of the pendulum after so long an era of feminist sway.[53]

The *News-Week* writer wrote a reasonably well-balanced article despite Price's efforts. Price took credit for the references to "more pipe smoking males" as a welcome addition on campus and to many people remaining "silent out of deference to Miss Woolley." She disclaimed responsibility for recalling "the gossip" (a reference to Woolley and Marks' relationship) or for "digging into Mary Emma about her absences from S.H." Marks, who was identified as Woolley's "intimate friend who lives in the President's House in an apartment called 'Attic Peace,'" was given ample opportunity to comment on the legitimate objections to a male president, particularly the obvious loss of opportunity for women who can only rise to the top in women's colleges. Price could not resist telling Ham what she desired when the controversy came to an end: "Mr. Morrison ought to get a D.S.O.," she said, "and Jan Marks a damp little hummock in the swamp along with a few bull-frogs. She's had too much 'Attic Peace.'"

In this letter to Ham, Price finally decided to raise the issue of the negative rumors about Ham and his relationships at Yale, especially the information provided by Ruth Fairchild the previous June.[54] "Have you any inkling," Price asked Ham,

> of why Prof. Fairchild of Yale and his wife so definitely oppose you? I think the way Ruth has broadcast her opinion that Yale had wished on Holyoke something they didn't want has a lot to do with the faculty antagonism to you.... Apparently within a week of your appointment Ruth Fairchild rushed up to college and burst in on a group of faculty who till then at least wavered in your direction, and painted a very bad picture of you. It was most unfortunate.[55]

There is no record of Ham's reply, if any, to Price, nor is there any revelation of the specific complaints that the Fairchilds had against Ham. There was, however, a persistent undercurrent of rumor that circulated throughout the Mount Holyoke community. One alumna who wrote to Elizabeth Adams in late February told Adams that while "an effort has been made to keep the individual man out of the controversy, it seems impossible to do that." She recounted that at a recent meeting "everyone had heard some disturbing thing about him from as many different sources."[56] She told Adams a story relayed to her by a "very sane and well balanced" woman who was not a Mount Holyoke graduate. Ham had arrived at the annual convention of the Deans of Women in New Orleans. "He was quite a trial from the beginning," this dean reported, "arriving 36 hours early and expecting to be taken care of, had no ticket or reservation and when it was time to seat him, there seemed to be Holyoke people at every single table and they would not have him." She observed that he "spoke quite freely of the attitude toward himself and seemed determined to fight the thing through." Ham, in her estimation, was ready and willing to "contribute his share in doing the college harm" while it was the alumnae who were taking the brunt of the criticism. This experience with Ham led her to conclude that he was just the sort of person I have suspected all along he was—a very mediocre indi-vidual, of whom Yale may possibly be glad to be rid, and one who is sufficiently enticed by the prestige ... of being a college president ... to hang on even though it has been evident for a long time that he was not welcome.

Her reaction was corroborated by a distinguished alumna who had also attended the New Orleans meeting. She wrote to Morrison in July, having postponed the "unpleasant task" of expressing her concern for Mount Holyoke under the leadership of someone "who exhibited such poor taste at his first public appearance in a group of college officials." When one dean gave Ham her seat at the banquet, the women remaining at the table found him "a ridicu-lous braggart" who "monopolized the conversation." He apparently remarked, "All this publicity is hard on the college but good for me." The deans in general were unfavorably impressed.[57] In reality, the publicity was not so "good" for him. Ham, Morrison and the officials in the Alumnae Association were receiv-ing a good deal of negative mail in response to the publicity in early February. Morrison had confidently, back in November, characterized the vast majority of alumnae who opposed Ham's appointment as women from the early years of Woolley's tenure. The truth was that the letters reflected a much wider group of alumnae and included the most recent graduates. Ham received the following letters in February and March of 1937:

[from an alumna, class of 1912]

> Your comment in the press that the large majority of alumnae at the Nov. meet-ing of the Association were in favor of accepting the situation as a closed issue is true. But those who can go to such a meeting on a week day in mid November are not in my estimation a fair cross section of our alumnae. No professional women can attend. The hall was packed with homemakers, many of whose inter-est are very limited. I was able to attend for the first time in my graduate life and was amazed at the methods used in conducting business.[58]

[from an alumna, class of 1926]

> ... either you took a great deal on faith or else fully cognizant of opposition were prepared to withstand it. your resignation will constructively terminate the pres-ent regrettable but inevitable controversy.[59]

[from a recent graduate, a doctoral student in zoology at the University of Chicago]

> The aim of the college has been and should be the intellectual and personal development of the individual. It is not and should not become a fashionable polishing school for "damsels" as you have implied, and ineptly called the stu-dents, to the press.
> The persons who have frankly and openly objected to your election are those whose reputations in their fields have brought jobs and fellowships to the rest of us. They were not allowed time to speak beforehand.[60]

[from an alumna/professor, class of 1910]

> I understand from the newspapers that you are not cognizant of the extent of
> alumnae disapproval of your appointment to the presidency of Mt. Holyoke Col-
> lege. I feel that we who disapprove of your appointment have been responsible
> for that impression as, apparently, we have been less vocal than those who have
> informed you of their approval. I am, therefore, personally informing you of my
> disapproval of your appointment and my reasons for that position....
>
> I particularly regret the fact that the Board of Trustees and the Committee of
> Nine have acted in such a way as to lose the confidence of a large body of the
> alumnae. And I believe that that lack of confidence in the action of the Board of
> Trustees and of the Committee of Nine is more widespread than either you or
> they realize as many of those who share this point of view feel that to protest
> now that the appointment has been made is not only futile but undignified and
> not quite sportsmanlike, a feeling which I understand although I do not share.
> This lack of confidence was expressed quite unanimously, for instance, by all of
> the Detroit alumnae present at a recent general club meeting although only
> about half were willing to protest the action of the Board for the reasons
> expressed above.... Nor do I feel that you meet the qualifications necessary for the
> leadership that Mt. Holyoke needs. You are a scholar in a very narrow field and
> so little known outside that narrow field that when I ask our own university
> English faculty whether they have heard of you, the typical reply is, "Why no,
> but then my field is not Dryden." You have had no experience in the administra-
> tion of a department, let alone a College. Your experience in the education of
> women has been very limited and not typical. Your experience with the broader
> aspects of education has been too limited to fit you for the administration of a
> college like Mt. Holyoke at this time. Particularly do I feel that the field of educa-
> tion at present has need for vigorous leadership by individuals who are familiar
> with and have actively participated in healthy, present day trends in education
> and who bring to the interpretation of those trends a broad vision and a new bal-
> ance.[61]

As this writer observed, a substantial number of alumnae saw protest, at
that point, as futile, undignified and "not quite sportsmanlike." The rules of
the game, apparently, were not expected to be fair. The publicity resulting
from the protest of the Committee of 100 brought forth a second wave of
support for Ham. This time it was an angry reaction to the protesters' willingness to bring Mount Holyoke's conflict into the public square. Alumnae
expressed embarrassment over the public nature of the protest. Their unhappiness over the outspokenness of women who opposed Ham's appointment
led some Ham supporters among the alumnae to abandon civil discourse.
Looking at the totality of letters received by Ham, Woolley, Morrison, Adams,
White and the trustees on the search committee, it is fair to say that cogent
argument was overwhelmingly the strength of those opposed to the election
of Ham, while assertion and histrionic name-calling were the province of those
in support of the board's action.

[from a woman who had been a Mount Holyoke student for one year]

Holyoke has suffered from too many women for years, and the one ray of hope that I have when I learned that a man was to be president now seems to fade! ... My husband says our four daughters are not going to college if he can help it. Too many horrible examples of misfitted women, mostly college graduates abound![62]

[from a married alumna/teacher, class of 1931]

It seems to me that a militant attitude about careers for women is now quite unnecessary.[63]

[from an alumna, class unreported]

I consider all this fuss ... made by a handful of antiquated females outrageous, as well as undignified. It makes me awfully ashamed of Mount Holyoke. My daughter went to Smith and I often visited her there. No college is prouder of its man presidents than Smith, and I, for one, would prefer any man to any woman for Mount Holyoke no matter how outstanding that woman might be.[64]

[from an alumna, class of 1913]

[T]hink nothing of this deplorable Amazon uprising! Command me.[65]

[from an alumna, class of 1921]

[A]lleged champions of tradition, feminism and the like are really betraying their own inadequacy and the attendant insecurity imminent upon reorganization. An outgoing tide is apt to have a goodly bit of refuse on the beach; I admire your fortitude in assuming the task of "cleaning up."[66]

[from an alumna, class of 1930]

There's no disgrace likely to come upon our fair college and its womanliness quite equal to the shame of being known as the hot bed of fussy and militant (I don't know which is worse displaying both, we're awful) femininity. We of the more recent classes (mine was 1930) are aghast at the unseemly behavior of our elders.... I'm ashamed of us.[67]

[from an alumna, class unreported]

As a Mount Holyoke alumna I wish to express to you my embarrassment at the controversy which the militant feminists are forwarding so vociferously. The whole episode seems so utterly ridiculous and fantastic in this day and age that one scarcely knows what to do about it. I have protested to the committee against their actions, which I feel are making Mount Holyoke the laughing stock of the educational world.

Unfortunately I am not a woman of wealth and influence, but at least I can be counted as one more on the side of common sense and dignity.

I feel sure that the majority of Mount Holyoke women are not pleased by this re opening of the issue. We all wish to be gracious to Miss Woolley, who is an old woman now, but who has no right to dominate all of us.[68]

It was almost impossible for those who knew Woolley to imagine her "old." Until recently, her energy had seemed limitless. At Geneva, just three years earlier, Woolley had been tireless. Now she was often weary and heartsick over the unfolding events. Woolley suffered a mild heart attack in early February and was forced to rest for a brief period. Mid-month she received a letter from an alumna[69] that contained an intriguing proposal. It began with the assumption that while some alumnae and members of the college community currently objected to a male president, no one until 1936 had objected to a woman president. Thus, if the goal was to keep Mount Holyoke united, there had to be a woman president. Ham had signed a contract in good faith, and therefore should not "be penalized for the mistakes of the college's own Board of Trustees." The solution that the alumna proposed was that the Mount Holyoke women who were opposed to Ham's appointment raise enough funds "to provide for the maintenance of Dr. Ham and his family either for a minimum of two years or until he can reasonably be expected to find another position." She recommended that "contribution toward this fund be considered a vote *for the unity of the college as well as for courtesy to Dr. Ham*." If the fund was raised from a large proportion of the college it would be "an impressive indication of sentiment." Ham, she fully expected, would take the money and "proffer ... his resignation without its becoming necessary to take any action which might cause bad feeling, such as ousting the present Board of Trustees." The writer pledged $1,000, half to be used for "the circularizing of the college and alumnae" and the remaining $500 to be the first contribution toward the fund for Ham. Woolley thought well enough of this very civilized, if unrealistic, proposal to forward the letter to Rowland, but there is no evidence that Rowland pursued the idea.[70]

Rowland was hard at work in an effort to mobilize support for a last-ditch effort at the March Alumnae Council meeting. She and her supporters were facing both an offense organized by official Mount Holyoke and a willingness among many who had initially opposed Ham's appointment to now ally with his supporters. Purington was one of the latter. Her change of heart is evidenced in a letter she sent to Morrison in late February. Having accepted Ham's appointment as irreversible, she now actively joined his supporters:

> I was so pleased ... with Miss Nicolson's letter to Miss Smiley ... some similar ... statement covering the most important charges and misstatements is needed to answer the questionings of those who do not know what to believe and to silence those who know better. Could such a statement be written and mimeographed for distribution among the councilors. There is time before March 5. What do you think? The councilors represent all the alumnae groups and could carry back the information to their groups. Miss Rowland will be on hand and I hear that Miss Smiley will be in town although not a member of the Council....

> The thing that has troubled me most for the past two days is the attempt to stir up the students to take sides against the appointment of Dr. Ham. Of course this has been railroaded by some members of the faculty and staff—it is not difficult to guess who. I am informed that the insurgent group is small but there is some talk of a student meeting for discussion.

Purington, in her "guess who" comment, was predictably blaming Marks among others for fomenting dissent. She agreed to attend the student meeting to present the trustees' position, but she was not looking forward to the March 5 meeting and felt certain that neither was Morrison.[71]

The student newspaper had editorialized in favor of ending the controversy over Ham's appointment,[72] but protest surfaced in a letter published on February 19. Theresa Howley, a senior, had perhaps been inspired by an open letter addressed to the student body from Holyoke Librarian Wilcox. Wilcox's letter, which had also appeared in the *Holyoke Transcript* two days earlier, lucidly summarized the important points at issue in the controversy. He chastised both students and alumnae who had initially opposed Ham's appointment for their apparent willingness to now give up support for the principle of female leadership "for considerations ... of propriety." Most of these young women seemed to be, he wrote,

> pathetically unconscious of the significance of the ... conflict.... The ease with which multitudes of women ... could be tricked into surrender of their principles, and could then be tricked again into allowing themselves to be used to prevent exposure of the trickery, gives me the first doubt I have ever harbored of the success of the higher education of women. I had supposed that, whatever college training may or may not do for one, it teaches the wisdom of cultivating the open mind and the courage to look squarely at both sides of any issue.

He suggested that the students read Wyckoff's February 11 letter. The issues raised there might inspire "the brighter minds" to consider "whether loyalty of an institution invariably means loyalty to its governing body, even when that body has proved false to its trust and betrayed the confidence reposed in it."

He challenged the students and alumnae on the question of solidarity, suggesting that in terms of intellectual attitudes there were three sexes: "the masculine, the feminine, and the intermediate." He described the "intermediate" group as largely made up of married women who "transfer their allegiance from the feminine to the masculine side as regards most issues." On issues related to equal opportunity and equal pay (as opposed to access to the vote) these women do not make common cause with their unmarried sisters. "This is the principal reason," he asserted, "why women's rights are so hardly won and so hardly held."

Wilcox's final point was that far more was at stake than "the sex of the president." The rights of the faculty, the students and the alumnae had "been thrown into the discard." In particular, the right of the alumnae to be fully represented had been "betrayed, by its elected representatives on the Board of Trustees.... How is it," he challenged the students,

> that you ... of Mount Holyoke can so precipitously abandon allegiance to her traditions and ideals in favor of a man not yet your president who comes nonchalantly trampling them under foot? Is it true, indeed, that all women are fickle; or did you just not understand?[73]

Howley seemed to be responding to Wilcox's call to action. She wrote:

> "Feminism," some of the trustees call it. All right, Feminism! ... The whole voice of the women of our country today may be heard deploring the fact that women have no status in Germany under Hitler. We are fighting for the rights of German women while doing nothing about our own. Does this show a thinking mind? Are we trying to make an end to our last hundred years of progress? ... we are all standing back afraid to fight for that which we really want—a woman successor to Miss Woolley—because of the "publicity" we might arouse, our college is becoming a subject of ridicule throughout the country.... Don't be an ostrich! There's going to be a fight! Let's face it. Let's show the world that the spirit of Mary Lyon still lives in us! Let's have a woman president at Mount Holyoke! Let's be feminists!

One week later, on February 27, Howley and a small group of students distributed a three-page document throughout the campus. "An Appeal from Facts" challenged students to consider the question "Why should Mount Holyoke, the first and foremost in women's education, lead the return to the subordination of women?" Students were urged to get involved—to educate themselves, to help formulate a coherent student opinion and to support the group of student protesters who planned to present their grievances at the trustee and alumnae meetings scheduled for March 5 and 6. Six students were listed as members of the committee, and they asked for signatures to a petition that supported their action.[74]

White was outraged when she saw the document. It included the promise of a debate between herself and Esther Richards from the AAUW. "How ridiculous and what rotten taste!" she exclaimed to Morrison.

> I hope the students don't believe any such rot.... Let them rave! What can they do? Nothing at all as long as you and Dr. Ham sit tight.... I think the agitators went pretty far when they put my name on the flier ... don't you?...My husband was furious. He has gone to Florida without me. I wouldn't leave this fight for anything! Yours to the finish, Maude.

Morrison reassured her that "this last raid on the student body comes from a very few students ... all in the Department of Drama," again an implication that this was Marks' doing. Rumors flew that Marks was forcing her students to write letters in opposition to Ham, threatening to fail them if they didn't comply. Some trustees wanted to press charges and get Marks fired.[75] There is no evidence that Marks threatened or coerced her students or manipulated any student protest. She had always been a popular teacher and remained so. Given her general outspokenness, she might well have discussed the controversy with students.[76]

Howley contacted Morrison asking to meet with the entire board of trustees on behalf of the student committee. Morrison told her that he would be glad to receive "an accredited representative or committee" and then confided to White: "I think there is no change [*sic*] that she [Howley] can get her credentials."[77] It was no surprise that when Howley and the group went before the Student Representative Council to request an official imprimatur for the meeting with the trustees the Council voted against it on the grounds that "publicity detrimental" to the college would result from "answers trustees might have to give to [the students'] questions" or "continued evasion" of student questions.[78] The student committee never met with the trustees.

The Alumnae Association, determined to quell any controversy at the upcoming meeting, made a final push to organize overwhelming support for Ham. The association sent a letter signed by twenty-two alumnae to all alumnae and enclosed a postcard with a pre-written statement:

> I recognize the election of Doctor Roswell Gray Ham as the next President of Mount Holyoke College is a closed issue. I feel that the recent publicity and attempt to arouse the alumnae is extremely harmful to Mount Holyoke College, and I am ready as loyal alumnae to support the College and the new administration.

Alumnae were asked to check off whether or not they endorsed the statement.[79]

When the board of trustees/Alumnae Council weekend finally arrived, tensions were high. White and allies in the Alumnae Association were prepared for confrontation but were feeling confident. The returns on the alumnae mailing were better than they had hoped for. Two thousand women replied in the short ten-day period, more than nineteen hundred of whom signed the statement supporting the board. Maguire, in her role as alumnae trustee, would be able to bring this good news to the board of trustees at the meeting on March 5. Maguire acknowledged that many of these women were probably unhappy with the trustees' decision to hire Ham. What they were "voting" for was an end to the publicity surrounding the opposition's protest.[80] They wanted "peace."[81]

Meanwhile, the Committee of 100, in anticipation of this final "showdown" weekend, had produced a second flyer, this time specifically attacking the financial management of the college during the previous five years.[82] Several trustees were mentioned by name. Rowland and Wyckoff had come to South Hadley for the weekend; Smiley stayed nearby in Holyoke. The plan was for Thompson, the sole alumna trustee who remained in opposition, to give each trustee a copy of the flyer and then read aloud the threat contained in an accompanying letter. If the trustees did not respond to the charges in the flyer by noon that day, the flyer would be released to the press. Smiley, waiting in Holyoke, was ready to hand over the flyer if she did not hear from Wyckoff soon after the board's scheduled adjournment at noon.

Things did not go according to plan. The meeting did not adjourn on time. The trustees, not about to make a quick decision, engaged in an unanticipated debate over how to respond to the Committee of 100's challenge contained in the letter. Morrison called the charges "libelous" and warned that they could ruin the career of at least one trustee. Finally, the trustees agreed to appoint a committee of three (Harvey, Cheney and Myers) to meet with Rowland, Wyckoff and Smiley later that afternoon. Smiley, meanwhile, hadn't heard from Wyckoff, and when she was approached for the second time by the *Boston Transcript* reporter, she decided to release the flyer anyway. When Wyckoff finally did contact her hours later to tell her to immediately join them at a meeting with the three trustees, Smiley told her that the flyer was already in the hands of the press. Thompson, Smiley and Wyckoff all tried to stop the story, but the *Transcript* had already published it in the afternoon paper. While the women met pointlessly with the three trustees, another three-trustee committee, composed of Morrison, Furniss and Maguire, rushed to prepare a rebuttal to the flyer. Their response went to the press before the Rowland, Smiley and Wyckoff meeting with Harvey, Cheney and Myers ended.

The rebuttal reiterated the board's absolute refusal to reconsider Ham's appointment and asserted that the charges on the flyer were completely false. Meanwhile, Rowland, Smiley and Wyckoff, defeated by the board's unanimous approval of Harvey's financial report, withdrew the charge of financial misconduct. When their meeting adjourned, the three women met with reporters at a local restaurant and gave them the revised story.[83] Although Rowland made certain that the AP reporter understood their position—"Opposition to Ham will continue"—the women had come up empty-handed. There was no clear "next step" for the opposition.

On the morning of the fifth, Rowland and Wyckoff had met with Woolley at the President's House to discuss their plans to demand both the resignation of the search committee trustees and the withdrawal of the offer to Ham. By the end of the day, they had found no opportunity to make either of these demands. Morrison's press release confirms this. "Since no question was raised regarding the action of the trustees in appointing Dr. Ham to succeed President Woolley the Board had no occasion to consider again the matter of his succession to the presidency."[84] Despite Rowland's statement to the contrary, the issue seemed altogether closed.

At the trustee/alumnae dinner that night, Cheney made a casual remark that different colleges have different relationships between boards of trustees and the various college constituencies—students, faculty, alumnae and administration. Rowland, Wyckoff and an ally, Mrs. Painter, attended the dinner, and it appears that Cheney's comments gave the women a face-saving way to surrender. They had been overwhelmed by the combined show of force of the trustees and the Alumnae Association. There was also the painful recognition that there were too few allies on the Alumnae Council. The next morning, when Painter gave the keynote address at the opening of the Alumnae Council meetings, she seized on Cheney's statement. It was the way, she said, to create a constructive program, one that would unify the alumnae. Painter proposed the creation of a committee to study the interrelationships of the various groups on campus. Rowland expressed the hope that such a committee could create lines of communication so that "similar castrophes [*sic*] can be avoided in the future."[85] White reported to Ham afterward that Painter, whom she thoroughly disliked, spoke for a unified alumnae association. As White saw it, "They were beaten, and knew it." White couldn't stop Painter's nomination to the board of trustees, complaining that "now they are trying to ensure her election as trustee by sending out the word that she saved the situation!" White warned Ham, "She'll make a great deal of *trouble* for you if she goes in as trustee unless you can win her over."

Painter's proposal was at first favorably received by the alumnae in attendance. However, it was quickly misconstrued to suggest the need for an "investigating committee," and fears of reopening the controversy began to resurface. The group eventually agreed to create a preliminary committee mandated to "consider the formation and function of a coordinating committee."[86] White was certain that there was "strength enough to pass a resolution in support of the trustees..., but it would not have been unanimous." She told Morrison, "We'd have lost a block of alumnae. I think everything worked out for the best." Wyckoff and Rowland announced that they were abandoning the fight and agreed to meet with reporters the next day. Thompson visited Woolley that Sunday morning and told her that the Council had expected the Committee of 100 to "present its case, but it had not done so." Thompson spoke positively of the Alumnae Council's resolution, but Woolley, fully aware that Thompson was reporting a complete surrender, "expressed her disappointment at the results."[87] Woolley had steadfastly resisted pressure from trustees to use her influence to stop the efforts of the Committee of 100. During and after the trustees/Alumnae Council weekend, it was the Committee of 100 itself that abandoned the struggle. Only Smiley refused to give up, insisting that she would "continue open opposition to the action of the trustees." And so what began in a hail of publicity and fierce protest in early February by the middle of March had ended with a whimper.[88]

CHAPTER 7

The Last Word

Plans for the college's centennial celebration in May of 1937 had been under way for years, since the first centennial committee meeting in May of 1934,[1] but with Ham's election the centennial itself quickly became a source of conflict and controversy. In June of 1936, Woolley told the trustees, including Furniss, who was the chair of the centennial committee, that she would not be attending. She told them

> her presence would put a great burden upon many persons, alumnae, faculty and others, as well as upon Mr. Ham and herself.
> [T]here would be a certain nervous tension and strain that would seriously mitigate against the success of the whole occasion; the alumnae, guests, and faculty would all wish not to be failing in any way in their recognition of Mr. Ham and at the same time they would feel that the retiring president had a certain claim upon them.[2]

For the majority of the college community, it was inconceivable to hold the centennial without Woolley. The trustees quickly voted to move the event from October to the previous May, shortly before Woolley's last commencement, but she still refused. In 1935, she had told the trustees that if a man were appointed to succeed her "it would be better not to celebrate the Centennial."[3] She was not persuaded to change her mind. Purington begged her to reconsider:

> Why can't you if it comes in May? I so long to know that you have decided to accept the situation as it is.... You have met so many difficult situations in a big way, why not meet this in the same way? I believe so it is still possible to make your last year a happy one, the triumphant conclusion of a wonderful service. That is what I crave for you.[4]

Just as she was persuaded to withdraw her resignation after the board's decision on June 6, Woolley now agreed to participate in the centennial celebration. Perhaps it was the knowledge that, without her involvement, Furniss as chairman of the centennial committee would have his way with all the major decisions—the theme, the speakers, the recipients of honorary degrees. There was every reason to believe that Furniss needed to be challenged. Initially, Furniss appeared cooperative, agreeing to grant honorary degrees exclusively to women and to cover expenses along with honoraria for prominent women in scholarship and public affairs who came from abroad.

It soon became evident, though, that there was a deep divide between Woolley's and Furniss' visions for the centennial. Furniss imagined a celebration of the family and of civic influence at Mount Holyoke, to "represent the rank and file of college women." Woolley rejected this proposal outright and argued for a focus on women in leadership and of outstanding accomplishment. Woolley recommended Secretary of Agriculture Henry Wallace as one of the speakers. Furniss, along with other trustees, rejected him because of his "pronounced political views." Furniss asserted that Wallace's appearance would negatively affect fund-raising. His list of proposed speakers included President Angell of Yale, President Hutchins of Chicago, President Conant of Harvard and historian Charles Beard (Mary Beard's husband).[5]

The centennial was a huge undertaking. A total of forty-one committees were created. The invitation list included close to fourteen thousand guests. Woolley encouraged subcommittee work on several centennial publications, the major one a history of the college whose purpose was "to record the development of higher education for women, not only in Mount Holyoke, but as it reflects social and educational changes from 1837 to 1937."[6] The trustees were the sponsors of the event, but by January of 1937 Woolley was fully in charge. Her roster of speakers included Corbett-Ashby, Virginia Gildersleeve, president of the International Federation of University Women and dean of Barnard College, Perkins, Mary Beard, and President Roosevelt, who promised to make every effort to attend (though, in the end, he did not). Woolley envisioned a symposium on women at work in the world. The participants would all be women accomplished in their respective fields, not Furniss' "rank and file." Furniss had been less and less involved through the fall. By January he had little to no influence over the planning. Then in February, the Broadside appeared with its accusation of a "packed" search committee and a "railroaded" election. Cheney talked to Morrison about canceling the centennial if Woolley couldn't give them full assurance that it would be "a celebration of what Mount Holyoke contributed in the past," not "a battle-ground of controversy [that] would do untold harm to the College." As if it were a simple matter of trustee decree, Cheney pronounced that if Woolley would not or could not "deliver," "then it [the centennial] should be dropped."[7] He wanted the issue addressed at the trustee/alumnae meetings in March, when everyone expected a "last ditch effort" from the opposition to reverse the Ham decision.

When the Committee of 100 failed and surrendered, the trustees abandoned the effort to stop Woolley. Cheney's suggestion of an ultimatum was forgotten. With the defeat of the opposition, the impact of the centennial became less potent to the trustees. In addition, little could have alienated larger numbers of alumnae or brought on more damaging publicity than canceling the centennial. Furniss made a move to disassociate himself from the entire event. He wrote to the executive secretary of the centennial committee two days after the March 6 meetings. He was, he said, "dismay[ed]" because his new appointment as provost of Yale required his presence at corporation meetings that were scheduled on the two centennial days. He suggested that the committee take action right away to appoint another chairman, adding that Yale president Angell was "obliged to decline the invitation for the same reason." Furniss bypassed Woolley, his co-chair, with this news, choosing instead to have the executive secretary relay the message. Only one scheduled meeting remained before the centennial. Woolley, returning her message through the secretary, told Furniss that it was "very unsatisfactory to change chairman now." As for the centennial itself, she hoped that he would at least be able to attend the Saturday morning session. Furniss agreed to remain on the committee but did not commit to attending the event. He, in fact, did not.[8]

In mid–April, Morrison, too, bypassed Woolley when he contacted Dean Cheek to inform her that he would not be attending the centennial. As president of the board of trustees, he was scheduled to speak at the luncheon honoring 246 representatives from other colleges and universities. Presidents King and Neilson from Amherst and Smith Colleges would be there. President-elect Ham would not. Morrison assured the centennial committee that while he had "no personal feeling in the matter whatever," he could not "be a party to an obvious and public slight to Dr. Ham." He wanted Ham to speak in his place, alongside King and Neilson ... the only means," he said, "left to the College of presenting a united front to the general public." Cheek had told him that the committee would not "take 'no' for an answer.... I can understand," she said, "that it may not be an easy thing for you to do, but we have every confidence that you will stand by the College on this very important occasion." Everyone "would be very much distressed ... and I am sure that it would cast a real shadow ... not to have you here." Morrison responded that the shadow his absence might cast on the events would "be so faint as compared with the dark shadow that already hangs over the Centennial." Morrison kept Ham apprised of the situation while he (Morrison) "manoeuvred" to get Ham "into the Centennial picture."[9]

"Rights Denied, Women Charge
Men Roundly Criticized at Mount Holyoke
Successor to President Woolley Unmentioned at Centennial"[10]

When the two-day centennial finally arrived, the college presented a united front but not the one that Morrison envisioned. He had not succeeded in getting Ham "into the ... picture." The program included no message from the president-elect. Morrison fulfilled his responsibility by being physically present, but he made no speech, nor did anyone officially acknowledge his presence. A reporter observed that while Morrison "grimly accepted his role of silent auditor, no man's face was so red" as that of the "distinguished-looking Harvard graduate ... chairman of the Board of Trustees." Captive beside Woolley on the dais, Morrison listened to speech after speech about women's loss of leadership opportunities, about men's sense of entitlement, about the unchallenged expectation of women's subservience to male leadership. The same reporter, observing the strangeness of the non-participation of both the college president-elect and the trustees, commented: "From all that was said and done here a stranger would assume that Mt. Holyoke has no trustees and Miss Woolley no successor."

The climate of conflict at the college made it impossible for the centennial to celebrate the transfer of power from Woolley to Ham. However, a centennial that celebrated the progress women had made but also identified the ominous present and future that threatened to erode that progress carried a potential for healing and empowerment. One of the numerous reporters at the event noted that "some of the most distinguished women in the world" were celebrating "the 100th anniversary of the higher education of women in America." The women were also there to challenge the myth that "men are giving women fair play in according them the chances for responsibility and leadership for which these 100 years of equal education have fitted them."[11] Mount Holyoke was a clear case in point.

On the first day of the centennial, Woolley and Perkins sat together on the dais, Perkins in her signature tri-cornered hat. She spoke first. After a lengthy "report" on the achievements of Mount Holyoke graduates, she shifted to women's organizations in general and the power inherent in them. Despite the many different interests of women's groups, Perkins argued, the groups shared a common purpose. They all worked for progressive change. These women's organizations accomplished their objectives with virtually no opportunity for women to hold "important public positions." It was through these women's groups, Perkins said, that women had become

one of the great present factors in developing public opinion.
Despite their diversity of interests the great majority of these organizations have some similar planks in their platforms ... such as the promotion of health,

peace, and women and child welfare, social security measures, higher educational standards, political reform, better legislation, better citizenship, cultural standards and development, to mention the most outstanding aims. Most of these organizations are nation wide in their set up, ready to be galvanized into activity for a particular cause by a dynamic appeal from the national headquarters.[12]

Perkins had no fiery words of condemnation for the trustees' and the Alumnae Association's actions.

Woolley had hoped not to speak, but she had conceded to alumnae pressure and followed Perkins with a brief address about her pride in the "international mindedness" of Mount Holyoke. "Education," she told the assemblage, "in the ordinary sense won't save us. We want something that works faster; something, if possible, that changes men.... [T]hinking men and women" understood that the "future of the world depends not only upon the cultivation of the 'things of the mind' but also the 'things of the spirit.'" She predicted that technology would not save humanity, only create "increased proficiency in the great province of human relations." Woolley's rousing final words, "If being good can save us, it is high time we tried it," brought the audience to its feet in a spontaneous, emotional tribute.[13]

Beard was scheduled to speak immediately after the alumnae luncheon attended by twelve hundred women. Woolley planned the timing "to increase the significance of the occasion."[14] Beard was a brilliant and provocative speaker who would not allow post-luncheon languor to set in. "What happens on this campus," Beard began, "...is symbolic of happenings in all women's education." For those in the audience who understood the import of Beard's message—the connections that she was making between the rise of fascism, the "lust" for warfare and the systematic replacement of women with men—was absolutely clear:

> It is prophetic of men's fate no less than women's. Any evasion of evident duties would spell cowardice. Such evasion would be a sign of intellectual and moral anaemia the inertia of life forecasting death for individuals, for institutions and for society at large. Such an inertia to the point of cowardice would be particularly tragic at this hour when all western civilization has reached a crisis in its economy, in its thought, and in its human relations. The nature of this crisis is ominous in that such prosperity as the world now enjoys synchronizes with mounting expenditures for instruments of human destruction unparalleled in the long and appalling history of mankind.[15]

In Beard's view, women had made a serious error when formal education opened to them. They "too lightly accepted as education the body of knowledge and the developing doctrines which the masters of these institutions deemed to be education in its fullness."[16] "Education," she argued, constituted a "secular, amoral, materialistic, mechanistic doctrine of each against all, sometimes described in a daintier fashion as laissez faire."[17] As young women came into college, they came under the spell of this individualistic conception of reality, one that disallowed the "feminine tradition of concern with social principles ... with the distribution of wealth as a principle of culture, and with the good life." Beard blamed the break in this tradition squarely on the opening of formal college education to women.[18] Woolley, she said, was among the great women who "revived the feminine tradition" both in her work at Mount Holyoke and in the wider world:

> For President Woolley the college was never a mere cloister for refining ancient theories or splitting hairs inordinately split in times past.... She encouraged her faculty to keep their windows open upon the wide world. She tried to remove the barriers between learning and living ... recognizing the truth that the leader in education must bear the hazardous but challenging responsibilities of a public personality.[19]

Beard's radical interpretation of the struggle at Mount Holyoke was in accord with what Woolley believed and wanted to convey. The alumnae and others were captive, and Woolley hoped that they listened.[20]

"Changing America," a dance performance inspired by a theme in Beard's talk, followed in the afternoon program. The dance depicted a society that followed a false messiah, the god Mammon. People lusted after wealth, and life became viciously competitive. Men built cities with skyscrapers to worship their god, but conflict destroyed the society, and its citizens destroyed Mammon. People returned to the simple life of an earlier America with a renewed understanding of the need for social cooperation.

Chill air and clouds persisted into the morning of the next day when Woolley introduced Corbett-Ashby. Morrison and other trustees in attendance may have believed they had suffered through the worst the previous day. If so, they were mistaken. Corbett-Ashby began her speech with an open challenge:

> [O]pportunities for responsibility and leadership, though they are increasing, are still few. It is to gain these opportunities that is the new aim of the Women's Movement. How many women are government executives? How many are heads of great educational establishments?[21]

Audible gasps were heard throughout the audience. Many glanced at Morrison, who was officiating in stony silence for the second day.[22] "Are women less capable than men when given the chance?" Corbett-Ashby asked. "The opposition is still here, but it is disguised." The audience sat stunned.

> Any one of us, however timid and soft, can be educated; the lower ranks of employment at lower rates of pay are open to us; there is social and personal freedom, *but* this has its disadvantages. Because school and college are easy, because

the young girl is welcomed for her cheapness in office, factory, and workshop, we believe we have equality and freedom, and can gain the goal of leadership or wealth equally with men. This is a delusion; we generally discover after ten years of work that we are passed over for promotion, and that the difference between men's and women's salaries and opportunities yawns more widely. We still need the loyalty and comradeship among women that won us the world of today. We must break the vicious circle which denies us posts of leadership and responsibility, because we have not had the experience which society has denied us.... Women have given, can give, precious service to the world, but the world must pay the price, if it is to benefit. The price is first education, then opportunity.

As she concluded, Corbett-Ashby called for "[l]oyalty of women to women, fair play from men," an unmistakable challenge to the alumnae who had failed to support the opposition and to the men who had engineered the hiring of Ham.

She exhorted the women not to "throw away" what "former generations have won" and urged them to determinedly face the truth: "Are your horizons expanding, or do you see insidiously creeping in an attack on women's opportunities and chance? The price of freedom is eternal vigilance." Corbett-Ashby's perspective was broad. The freedom she spoke of was threatened by "[t]he menace of fascism [that] lies dark over Europe."[23]

Gildersleeve followed Corbett-Ashby. In her introduction, Woolley spoke about how women had learned to work together in large organizations despite the "disbelief in women's ability to do this very thing." She recalled "statements that women, if given added opportunities, would not show solidarity, unity."[24] Woolley left the question of why so many alumnae, and especially alumnae trustees, had failed to show solidarity in the presidential succession fight unasked and unanswered. Gildersleeve focused her attention on the women's colleges. Women professors, she said, "have fared less well in recent years than before just because women are more open-minded and impartial" than men about the issue of "sex" balance on college faculties. Women had lost ground in the past twenty-five years with a handful of women professors in coeducational universities and "proportionately fewer in women's colleges." Based on her "casual and enjoyable visits" to coeducational institutions, Gildersleeve said she had observed that "women stay in their place.... Men are quite naturally expected to do the leading. This atmosphere of expected subservience on the part of our sex—in which I must say they seem for the most part quite happy—strikes oddly the visitor from a college for women."

She endorsed the effort made at the women's colleges to increase the number of men on the faculties because it created "a more live and varied ... community on campus." However, the price for this openness was high: "Our sex seems to be losing out on both fronts." Unless men in colleges could be persuaded to "take a view as broad-minded," the future looked dim for women scholars. In a veiled allusion to Mount Holyoke, she encouraged her audience, "[I]n spite of temporary setbacks, we shall go on advancing."[25] Beard, Corbett-Ashby and Gildersleeve each made it clear that what had just happened at Mount Holyoke was part of a disturbing national and international trend. This reality had to be acknowledged, and women needed to fight back.

President Neilson, Woolley's longtime friend, spoke last. She had asked him to speak on behalf of the "sister colleges," but Neilson's address was a personal, affectionate tribute to Woolley. "Modern Mount Holyoke *is* Miss Woolley," he said. She had brought the college "fully abreast of all the institutions of its kind throughout the world." Woolley was "fortunate" because she knew this. It was her "keen appreciation of forward movements [that] has set new standards" and her "acuteness in the selection of staff [that] has built up its distinguished faculty." Her "spirit, extraordinarily profound and broad, [has] given Mount Holyoke the quality that it has today."[26] There was no mistaking the challenge to those within the Mount Holyoke community, trustees and alumnae alike, who had repudiated Woolley's vision.

Woolley closed the two-day program with a few words of gratitude and appreciation on behalf of the college and with a simple, personal good-bye. She possessed, as always, great dignity. Those who knew Woolley best understood the toll taken by the events of the past three years. Her friend Glass told her that the centennial was wonderful, but the "best thing about it all was you. You seemed at your high level—and that is high."[27] McHale told Woolley that she knew "the price [she] paid for this disagreeable experience," but the centennial was so significant in the history of higher education for women that she was "inclined to think that [Woolley was] in a stronger position as a result of the celebration than at any time since the continuity of its great development was broken."[28]

Ada Comstock, dean of Radcliffe College, agreed with McHale. She wrote to Woolley: "Never in my experience has an audience been so deeply stirred by a conviction of the importance of giving free and wide opportunities to women." It seemed to her that "the consciousness of what had happened became a great sounding board for the ringing words which were so well spoken by Miss Gildersleeve and Mrs. Corbett-Ashby." Comstock had overheard comments by both women and men after the speeches. She told Woolley that "perhaps the events which [you] deplored will be the cause of a fresh awakening of the public mind to the necessity of keeping open the doors of equal opportunity—and perhaps of opening new doors."[29]

Before she left for home, an alumna dashed off a letter to Woolley from a nearby inn. The celebration, she said, "seemed like a crowning event" for Woolley's great work. "I shall live the rest of my life in the warm glow of that

President Mary Emma Woolley at Mount Holyoke College, c. 1930s.

Mount Holyoke College Centennial, 1937. Left to right: Mildred McAfee, Wellesley College president; Virginia Gildersleeve, dean of Barnard College; Mary Emma Woolley; Katharine Blunt, president of the Connecticut College for Women; Aurelia Reinhardt, president of Mills College; Margaret Shove Morriss, dean of Pembroke College in Brown University.

picture.... I can hardly express also the pain and sorrow I feel that some woman of strength and vision and scholarship is not to have the opportunity of future leadership at Mount Holyoke."[30]

A week later in a newspaper interview, Corbett-Ashby warned British women that the actions of Mount Holyoke's trustees were significant to the women's movement all over the world. She called the successful stalling of progress in female leadership "a tragedy due to the jealousy (or blindness) of small men and the inertia of small women."[31] When Willystine Goodsell, historian of women's education, read Corbett-Ashby's article, she wrote to her friend Woolley: "How little the trustees must have valued the long tradition of the college, how meager must have been their understanding."[32]

In Conclusion

Many years later Perkins was asked about the events that led to the hiring of Ham at Mount Holyoke. "[T]he choosing of a successor to Miss Woolley," she recalled, "was engineered by a rather high-powered group of businessmen."[33] In December of 1936, McHale had known that the ministers on the board of trustees opposed Ham's appointment while the businessmen supported it. McHale's correspondent at the college, historian Bertha Putnam, told her that the "business men were the worst of all."[34] McHale believed that this should be publicized. It was true that the three ministers on the board, Edwards, Potter and Day, all opposed Ham's appointment. Potter had moved to delay the decision at the June 6 meeting. However, it was also Potter who had changed his vote at that meeting, providing the crucial margin of victory necessary for Ham's election.[35] Trustees Pratt and White were businessmen who strongly supported Woolley throughout the controversy. Aside from Kendall, Furniss was the most aggressive in the "behind the scenes" search for a man. Continually deferred to as "the outstanding educator" on the board,[36] Furniss had the greatest incentive for hiring not just any man but a Yale man. Mount Holyoke was for Provost Furniss a new frontier for employment for Yale graduates.

The attitudes and behavior of Kendall, Cheney, Morrison, Hazen, Davis and others played important roles in how the specific struggle played itself out at Mount Holyoke, but the increasing dominance of a business-oriented model in higher education represented a broader trend. This trend reactivated the AAUW's Committee on the Economic and Legal Status of Women in 1934 and prompted the AAUW leadership to educate its membership through reports, conferences and articles published in its journal. Two years earlier, an article by Henry W. Lawrence had sounded the alarm. He wrote that the businessman "is often the outstanding obstacle which educators must surmount in order to rescue their work from futility or perversion." The "aims and methods" of a business approach (cost accounting and mass production) produce an "insistent demand" for vocational training and for quantitative standards of achievement that create pressure to increase enrollment as well as class size, and place an emphasis on "splendid grounds and buildings" rather than "the splendor of the professorial wage." Mount Holyoke's recent experience was a textbook example of all that Lawrence was describing.

"Most alarming and subversive of all," he continued, was "the perennial tendency toward coercive control, by legislator, donor, and trustee, over what is sometimes called 'academic freedom'; that is, over the teacher's right and duty to be loyal to the truth as he sees it." Lawrence gave as examples the biologist who cannot teach evolution, the sociologist who "dare not speak frankly about companionate marriage," and the economist who must limit his references to socialism. He recognized that the colleges needed the business world, but as partners, not as dictators. Otherwise, he predicted that colleges would exist in "an atmosphere of stultification and hypocrisy which is rank poison for the minds of thoughtful undergraduates."[37]

Woolley, in her long tenure as president, had been the faculty's strongest advocate in every area that affected their professional lives. In the late twenties and early thirties, she had to fight an increasing determination on the part of a growing faction of trustees to insinuate themselves into areas of academic decision making that had been the exclusive province of the faculty. Woolley always encouraged an atmosphere of self-determination. Faculty who had "nearly absolute control over the development of courses and of new appointments" held permanent chairmanship positions. At faculty meetings, "senior women dominated the debate" and "few men were rarely recognized by the chair."[38] Woolley, who presided so successfully and for so long over a faculty that exercised almost total autonomy, at the end of her tenure could no longer guarantee that power.

Her lifestyle and politics had increasingly become anathema to some trustees, undoubtedly many alumnae, and a handful of faculty. Although physics professor Rusk was among the very few faculty who openly complained about the lack of "normalcy" in Mount Holyoke's presidential life, others shared his opinion that marriage and family were inseparable from the concept of "normal" home life. The professional unmarried woman, especially one in a powerful leadership position, who was living in partnership with another woman, posed a threat to "normalcy." Woolley's unapologetic attachment to Marks had created a continual undercurrent of criticism. The succession fight released strong public hostility toward Marks. There were trustees, alumnae and faculty who blamed her for almost single-handedly creating the agitation and protest against Ham's appointment, a charge that was patently ridiculous. Woolley had become increasingly outspoken about her political views, and as her pro–Roosevelt, anti–teacher's oath, anti–death penalty statements made the news, trustees and alumnae who opposed these positions were no doubt angered by the "bad" publicity. Again, some blamed Marks for undue influence over Woolley, as if Woolley were easily manipulated. Woolley's lifelong peace activism and the red-baiting that it stimulated gave many alumnae a reason to look forward to an end to such a publicly oriented administration.[39] They wanted a president who had no interests beyond the self-limiting world of the college, and Ham seemed ideal from this perspective. One of Woolley's strongest supporters among the trustees, Holyoke businessman White, had a very different perspective. He had written to Woolley while she was in Geneva:

> I have often thought that your college presidency was restricting your field of influence, and was delighted when the opportunity came for you to enter international affairs.... I am proud to be associated in a small way with one so useful in the world in trying to solve its problems.[40]

Woolley later told White that his letter was one of the nicest she had ever received. By the 1930s, his sentiments were in the minority among the trustees.

If the first question to be asked about the defeat of female leadership at Mount Holyoke is why certain individuals in the governing structure of the college wished to change the college and therefore appointed Ham as president, a second question must be why the vast majority of alumnae failed to respond positively to the organized opposition to Ham's appointment. Sophonisba Breckinridge, a pioneer social work scholar and activist at the University of Chicago, asked exactly this in August of 1936 in a forceful letter to the Mount Holyoke alumnae on the board of trustees.[41] She severely chastised those alumnae who had voted for and supported Ham:

> I find myself so constantly filled with a sense of disloyalty ... to the causes for which so many have struggled and to which Mount Holyoke has contributed so nobly that I can no longer resist asking the Alumnae members of the Board of Trustees if there is really nothing that could be done.

She had known for several years that a member of the board was "hunting a man" while she and others had been giving him lists of women to share with the other trustees. She had been told that Ham "is related to wealth," but she couldn't believe that "the alumnae trustees would ... have sold out for thirty pieces of silver. It is the cause of women's education, of woman's scholarship, of fair play, of recognition, of liberal participation in the great issues." Breckinridge was entirely unimpressed by Ham as an individual. His qualifications were, she said, "meager and dull," and his character was lacking, as evidenced from his failure to grasp "the impossibility" of his task. Breckinridge leveled harsh criticism at the women trustees for their lack of courage at a time when courage was essential:

> If you and your fellow alumnae really acquiesced after asking three women as the papers report, you may not care for the judgment upon your loyalty to all these causes, your courage or your ability really to represent the Mount Holyoke of the past. It is a cruel situation in which you have placed those to whom these interests have seemed so precious and so well worth conserving in the days of difficulty we are now facing.

She told them that they needn't reply, that, in fact, she had no right to demand an explanation. She was writing so that she could speak to her "fellow workers in the cause of women's opportunity with some sense of self-respect." She wanted the alumnae trustees to know what many people thought of their actions. She had "only ... a great need of [their] knowing what[was] being thought and felt by many of whom [she was] only one."[42] We can only guess how Keyes, Whitman, Maguire and Bishop reacted to Breckinridge's challenge. Keyes, who yielded so completely to a position she had strenuously opposed for more than a year, appeared remorseless. She became one of Ham's most vocal advocates.

Mary Beard's analysis of the fruits of women's higher education in the first third of the twentieth century provides the basis of an answer to the alumnae trustees' choice. According to Beard, the adherence to the academic model that had been set by the men's and coeducational institutions constituted a trap for women's higher education. Women's willingness to defer to established thought had, she wrote,

> deepened the intellectual cowardice of women instead of alleviating it.... The objective of equal pay for equal work, of the mere feministic enthusiasm for sheer equalitarian effort with scholastics, has developed in women an over-respect for established thought.... On their own initiative, through more worldly experience, they might regain their poise.[43]

In April of 1933, McHale had invited Woolley to lead a discussion following a presentation by Beard at the upcoming AAUW convention. Beard wrote to McHale at the time, concerned that her message might be too radical for the AAUW, but McHale saw a useful way to begin a dialogue. Beard shared with McHale her growing conviction:

> [F]or a year or more I have been growing more convinced every week that our whole educational system will have to be revised like our general economy. I can't rid myself of the notion that the educational system and its upshot definitely reflect the economic system and have been geared to an incompetent competitive individualism.

She argued that the traditional approach by professional women "to enter the professions and operate according to the prevalent code of honor, to work merely for equality in what seemed to be a successful man's world," was no longer sufficient. "The crisis has come. The outlook will have to change.... The challenge to women is thorough." Do "your women want to face it?" she asked McHale.[44]

Beard had mildly challenged her audience at the Mount Holyoke Centennial, only implicitly criticizing the college when she emphasized Woolley's efforts "to remove the barriers between learning and living ... recognizing the truth that the leader in education must bear the hazardous but challenging responsibilities of a public personality."[45] The following year, Beard's criticism would be far harsher. In an article published in the AAUW journal, Beard asserted that when American women were given opportunities in higher education through the rise of high-quality colleges like Mount Holyoke they actually took a step back from where women had been throughout early history. She wrote:

> Much as I hate to say it, in my opinion what Oberlin and Holyoke represented was a petty bourgeois provincialism in America steeped in more sex bigotry than the old pagans knew and ... I tried to show in my address at Mount Holyoke last

spring ... that women had always partaken of the education of their time. But American men and women have been loathe to believe it because unwilling to study the history of women with free minds and industry.... And so American women of today even forget American women of the seventeenth, eighteenth and nineteenth centuries. Knowing only themselves they do not know *women*.[46]

Woolley, who had worked to broaden the experience and thinking of the students throughout her years at Mount Holyoke, in the end was confronted with proof of Beard's thesis. She had hoped that the majority of alumnae would have grasped the importance of Mount Holyoke's example, but the college had not sufficiently created the consciousness required for that understanding. Many alumnae did understand what was at stake; more did not. Woolley had achieved the highest position in educational leadership, but she could not safeguard it for future generations of women. The perception of female leadership had radically changed since 1900. Woolley still believed that women brought specific and unique characteristics "to the table" – a willingness to work constructively, collaboratively and inclusively. Woolley's work at Mount Holyoke was a very successful model of this leadership approach. But the strength that women had gained in leadership provoked fear and resentment and the urge among many to put women leaders back "in their place." Mount Holyoke historian Viola Barnes, one of a handful of faculty who championed Ham throughout the controversy, shared the sentiments of many alumnae who did not see the value of sustained political or social action. Barnes was in favor of the advancement of individual women—the collective interests of women as a larger social group were of no interest to her.

Beard's analysis explains the failure of the alumnae to support Woolley's position. By making certain that Mount Holyoke provided an education comparable to one at men's liberal arts institutions, the college had neglected to address the importance of solidarity among educated women. Young women from earlier decades knew that united struggle was an integral part of the pursuit of higher education. By the 1920s and 1930s, many young people took higher education for granted. In 1929, Woolley told an interviewer from *Ladies' Home Journal* that "[t]he college girl today is in the grip of the extreme wave of individualism that has swept the country."[47] Nevertheless, despite continual attempts to characterize Woolley as old and passé, she never lost her popularity with the students. While Mount Holyoke students in the 1930s joked semi-seriously about their "spinster" school[48] and the prospect of becoming "doctorated old maids at thirty,"[49] they still described Woolley as full of life. When one young woman waited on Woolley's table in a private dining room at the college, she found her "a riot ... [President Woolley] has a wit as keen as a knife, which she uses with as much grace as she does her knife."[50] Woolley "stood out as a star."[51] A student described one Founder's Day speech as "so perfect, so stirring,"[52] while "Ham stumbled over his words in Chapel—only thing he can do is make humorous remarks."[53] A student from the class of 1939 described all the faculty of the botany department as "queer old maids," the campus as "seething with politics," and Woolley "going stronger than ever."[54]

From Pastoral to Tragedy

Many in the press and elsewhere were quick to call the defeat of female leadership at Mount Holyoke a "tragedy." Woolley's failure to maintain the succession of female presidents was called "tragic."[55] Woolley herself said that she was "deeply ashamed" that it was Mount Holyoke that had lost the fight.[56] She was described by the press and colleagues alike as a "tragic" figure and her determination to never return to the college viewed as a "tragic" consequence of the defeat. Were there the necessary ingredients of tragedy in the story—a heroic figure with a "tragic flaw," an inexorable process with a foreordained conclusion? Or was it melodrama—happenstance, not certainty? "[Defeat], in a melodrama, is really horrible because it is never inevitable," writes playwright Jean Anouilh.[57] What if Board Chairman Hyde hadn't died so suddenly and unexpectedly? What if Cheney had successfully convinced the board to appoint Woolley to the chairmanship of the board after Hyde's death? What if Nicolson had not felt herself such a "poor fit" with Mount Holyoke and had accepted the offer in 1935? What if Keyes had held her ground and taken her Bixler versus Schenck proposal to the full board? What if Potter had not changed his mind at the last moment and followed his true instinct to vote against Ham?

"In a tragedy, nothing is in doubt and everyone's destiny is known,"[58] Anouilh tells us. Given the makeup of the board of trustees in the 1930s and given the profile of the majority of the college's alumnae, the opposition had no chance of "winning." The flaw in Woolley's greatness of vision is clear. She had achieved all that she had set out to do to create a first-rate institution of higher education for women—one of the best in the nation. What she failed to see was that the young women who benefited from this education would not naturally comprehend its uniqueness. Some did, but the majority seemed to prove Beard correct. Many educated women were beset by "intellectual cowardice" and by "an over-respect for established thought." This made them think and act against their own self-interest. When Woolley said that she had failed in the most profound way, this is what she meant.

Woolley and her allies continually asserted that the issue was much larger than Mount Holyoke. They were correct. Women in leadership from the

AAUW and from abroad reacted so strongly to the Mount Holyoke situation because they recognized an example of broader changes at work. It was these changes that led to the defeat. In the context of the Depression, women all over the world were losing out as men sought to take for themselves a larger share of shrinking opportunities. The particular way that this played itself out at Mount Holyoke was in the apparent effort to "colonize" the college for Yale University. The details of the defeat of female leadership at Mount Holyoke in 1936–1937 should not blind us to the fact that, ultimately, the balance of forces in the struggle was weighted against Woolley and her allies from the beginning.

The fact that the odds were so heavily weighted against Woolley makes her principled struggle the more heroic. Similarly, the tenacity and astuteness of Woolley's allies among the faculty, the alumnae group, the AAUW, as well as individuals such as Perkins, Breckinridge, Wilcox, and Corbett-Ashby, demonstrated heroism. One of the most respected members of Mount Holyoke's faculty, Professor Ellen Deborah Ellis, believed that, despite the odds, the struggle to resist Ham's appointment was essential. When Ellis participated in the Mount Holyoke twentieth-century oral history project, over thirty years had passed since the events described in this book. She recalled, "Mr. Ham's appointment to the presidency of Mount Holyoke College seems to me, as it seemed at the time when it was made, so unfortunate that I therefore believe the accompanying struggle among various factions to have been justified."[59]

I submit that, despite the numerous "what-ifs," the defeat of female leadership at Mount Holyoke was a tragedy by Anouilh's definition. More than forty years would pass before a woman would again be selected as president of the college. She would assume leadership of an institution very different from the one Woolley left in 1937.

Epilogue

The Mount Holyoke of 1937 was the product of Woolley's vision and extraordinary abilities.[1] In her final report as president-emeritus, Woolley cited the aspects of the college that meant the most to her. First in importance was the Mary E. Woolley Fund, earmarked to increase the salaries of the faculty. The Fund gave her "peculiar pleasure" because she had not succeeded in achieving competitive salaries. In the closing remarks of that final report, Woolley noted that "a great deal has been done [at the college] on the material side." It would be the task of her successor, she wrote, "to impersonally evaluate changes as well as record them, remembering that the material development is a means to an end, not an end in itself."[2]

Woolley in Retirement

By October of 1937, Woolley was living permanently in Marks' Westport, New York, family home. Woolley would have liked to return to South Hadley but didn't feel that she could until Marks' retirement in 1941. Marks discouraged her and Woolley agreed. "I am sure," she wrote to Marks, "that living in South Hadley, at present at least, would make it embarrassing for all concerned. 'Things' must go with as little agitation as possible, as long as you are on the faculty."[3] Woolley turned down all official invitations from the college. Those who believed that her severing of her ties with Mount Holyoke constituted a "tragic" end to her professional life misunderstood her. She had made her public statement of protest and would maintain a principled silence thereafter. Woolley had made a clear choice when, immediately after retirement, she threw her energy and the weight of her reputation behind her public work. She signed with a booking agency, accepted as many engagements as she could schedule, and agreed to accept the chairmanship of numerous organizations.[4]

In January of 1938, en route to Atlanta from Washington, D.C., where

183

Jeannette Augustus Marks with her collie at Fleur de Lys, undated.

Mary Emma Woolley with her collies at Fleur de Lys, her home in Westport, New York, late 1930s.

she visited Eleanor Roosevelt, Woolley commented on a successful People's Mandate meeting in New York: "[M]any women leaders in peace organizations were there—strengthening my feeling that women are increasingly the force with which to reckon in the Movement."[5] In February, she set off on a five-week trip that began in Toronto, where she spoke to a League of Nations group,[6] then continued on to Chicago and St. Paul, where she met with Mount Holyoke alumnae, none of whom mentioned "the college of 1938–9," and finally to San Francisco where she spoke to the National League for Women's Service.[7] She called the trip "strenuous 'pleasure exertion.'"[8] In June, she was off again to Toronto, Lake Erie College, Chicago, Beloit College, Boston and Wellesley.[9] In July, she set sail for England with her friends Glass and Gildersleeve to attend the Conference of the International Federation of Women and traveled to Paris for a second conference before returning to the States[10] to speak at an Armistice meeting in Philadelphia before two thousand people.[11] Six days later, she accepted a last-minute invitation from Dorothy Kenyon to speak in Washington, D.C., at the Conference of Lawyers Committee on American Relations with Spain. She shared the podium with her friend Neilson where they discussed "why the embargo should be lifted now."[12]

When people asked about the events at Mount Holyoke, Woolley acknowledged her unhappiness over Ham's appointment but never spoke critically of his administration. Personally, Woolley had achieved a certain serenity. When Marks complained about her troubles at the college, Woolley told her:

> I just hope that you will do what I am learning to do, acquire a "protective coating" ... of refusing to think about the persons who are disappointing ... save all [your] energy for those who "stand-by" under all circumstances—[the]less we think about the destructive and more we think about the constructive, the more we shall be able to do for the latter.[13]

By 1940, the war in Europe dominated Woolley's thinking, and the limits of her pacifism became evident:

> I am glad that the President included the word anger in characterizing the reaction of the American people to this incredible atrocity of the Nazi government, "whom the gods would destroy they first make mad," I hope may be realized in the case of Hitler and his cohorts. They should meet the fate of a poisonous viper, put out of the way for the common safety.[14]

In November, after the presidential election, Woolley sent a telegram to the White House. "Our Westport household deeply thankful for outcome. God bless you."[15] Days later, in Boston and New York, Woolley encountered the "businessman's reaction" to the election and wrote Marks, "You could have sliced the gloom with a knife."[16]

Woolley turned seventy-eight in 1941 during her fourth year of retirement. She remained extraordinarily busy, still apologizing to correspondents about her delayed responses to their queries or requests. Time, she said, was "over full."[17] In preparation for the Biennial meeting of the AAUW, Woolley urged the board of directors to consider discussion of the Equal Rights Amendment, well aware of strong opposition within the organization. She was not yet in favor of the amendment[18] and had deliberately avoided a meeting with Alice Paul, the National Woman's Party advocate for the ERA, because she did not want AAUW members to think that Paul had influenced her.[19] Despite her appeal that "time may be allowed for more thought" before rejecting the amendment,[20] the membership came out in strong opposition. "My friends were fine," Woolley said, "—but I suspect that there was quite a 'wave of criticism' with regard to my motion."[21]

As she had throughout her professional life, Woolley continued to derive much satisfaction and pleasure from her association with young college women. They embodied her hopes for a better future, and despite disappointment over her own perceived failures, she never wavered in her hopes for the young. In 1945, on a bright, warm day in November following several days of rain, Woolley went "motoring" in the countryside around Lake Champlain and returned home to dictate a letter to a young friend in China. "The war is over," she said, "and it must be a great relief to you. We have a wonderful amount to do in the new world. A much larger part than ever faced the world before this day. May we be true to it."[22]

Woolley's high level of engagement and commitment to causes[23] had ended the previous year when she suffered a disabling stroke, confining her to a wheelchair. Marks cared for her at Fleur de Lys for three years until Woolley's death on September 5, 1947. She was 84 years old. Perkins wrote to Marks four days later with a keen understanding of Marks' grief and loss.

> And let me say to you how much sympathy I have for you in a grief which I know is over and above all other and public sense of loss in her death. Your close and intimate association, your enduring friendship, and the compassion and charity with which you shared the last hard days and ministered to her physical, intellectual and spiritual needs, have left you with a unique sorrow and a vacancy of heart for which one scarcely dares to offer you comfort.[24]

A friend wrote,

> She was such a womanly woman, that in spite of the completeness of her own mind and soul, she had a yearning for, and appreciation of family and all that means—that you have given her ... We grieve with you even though your sister-in-spirit had lived her life all the way and done her work to the sword's hilt.[25]

Marion Park, President Emeritus of Bryn Mawr, wrote,

I have always admired and loved her. She helped me constantly in my job at Bryn Mawr, more especially because she had known and worked with Miss Thomas and understood some of the special problems there. And like the other college presidents at the women's colleges, I relied on her right-mindedness and honesty and intelligence which she put so simply and directly at our service.[26]

Purington, Woolley's administrative "right hand" at Mount Holyoke, wrote: "She was a wonderful woman. The world seems empty without her. I have only a few years left at best and I hope they may be spent in worthwhile work in her memory."[27] Dean Cheek, president of Rockford College, wrote, "There is no loss except that of my own mother that I could feel more keenly. [It was] a rare privilege to be one of the inner circle under her leadership."[28] An alumna said: "I think of Emerson 'To be great is to be misunderstood—For non-conformity the world whips you with its displeasure.'"[29] A second alumna wrote, "I loved Miss Woolley, and there is no one who had or has had more influence over me. I suppose I never told her so."[30]

Changes at Mount Holyoke

In early February of 1937, in response to the Broadside, the *Boston Globe* ran a comprehensive story of Ham's succession to the presidency of Mount Holyoke. The reporter's sources convinced him that the heart of the matter for the search committee was the necessity to remake Mount Holyoke—to eliminate "spinster management" and a hundred years of "petticoat government." It was a job only a man could accomplish, and Roswell Gray Ham was the man for the job. The women on the committee who had expressed preference for a woman were persuaded that Ham "could manage women." The reporter offered his evidence. "[T]he big, amiable, studious, personable son of California ... physically ... looked like a leader.... [H]is two marriages, his great personal charm, his rich, cultivated voice, his easy platform manner." The photograph in the article was not of Ham but rather of his new wife, and the caption read, "Her marriage won her husband a job! Mount Holyoke turned him down as a widower, turned back to him when he remarried last spring." It was true that Ham's candidacy had been held in limbo until he remarried. The multi-year search for a suitable woman candidate to succeed Woolley had devolved into a search for a suitable wife.

The reporter identified the "sex balance in the college staff" as the major problem facing both the new president and the college's "men of affairs." "In the next five or ten years," the reporter predicted, "the new president can largely remake Mt. Holyoke."[31] How far did Ham go in that effort?

The college that Woolley left in 1937 was dominated by women.[32] Eighty-

Alva Morrison, chairman of board of trustees, left, with Mount Holyoke President Roswell Gray Ham, right, at Mount Holyoke College Founder's Day, 1937.

three percent of the ranked faculty were women (90 out of 108). Woolley had built a dynamic and accomplished faculty from her earliest years as president. It is not surprising that the largest number, 29, were ranked as full professors. In 1937, women accounted for 78 percent of full professors, 94 percent of associate professors, 83 percent of assistant professors and instructors. In 1950, after twelve years of Ham's presidency, these percentages had changed significantly. The ranked faculty had increased from 108 to 136, but the number of women had only risen to 93. Men made their greatest gains within the ranks of full and associate professors. In 1950, the percentage of men at the full professor level was 34 percent, an increase of over 50 percent. At the associate level, it was 50 percent, a more than eight-fold increase. At the assistant level, the percentage of men climbed moderately to 19 percent from 17 percent while, at the instructor level, the percentage remained near 17 percent.

Ham had clearly made some headway in an effort to transform Mount Holyoke's faculty from one with a large numerical majority for women, which included a high percentage of women at the highest ranks, to a faculty where men had advantages in hiring and promotion. How well did Ham meet the trustees' expectations that he was capable of "a sense of ruthlessness" even if it required "giving pain?"[33] During his interview with Price, Ham had told her somewhat testily that he was definitely not "the trustees' man,"[34] despite the manner in which he was selected.

The recollections of his secretary offer useful insight into Ham's leadership and priorities. Olive Copeland was Ham's secretary throughout his twenty-year presidency. (Copeland had been Woolley's secretary. She continued in that role under Richard Gettell, Ham's successor.) It was her opinion that Ham left most administrative offices to work things out for themselves. "I think the head of every office would agree that we pretty much ran our own 'show' ... I am sure he assumed each one was capable and experienced and I do not recall any interference." She summed up Ham's leadership. He "had [no] interest in, or ability as an administrator. Mr. Ham loved his teaching."[35]

It is revealing to briefly look at some of the issues and changes experienced within departments during Ham's administration. The English, history and physics departments represent the division of a typical liberal arts college— the humanities, social sciences and physical sciences. The faculty members discussed here each taught under Woolley's administration for many years and remained at the college for many more under Ham's leadership. They are Sydney Robinson McLean of the English department, Mildred Allen of the physics department and Viola Barnes of the history department.

The English Department

Sydney Robinson McLean was a 1922 graduate of Mount Holyoke and, in 1937, was the only Yale Ph.D. in the English Department.[36] Just seven days after the June 6 decision, McLean wrote a lengthy, thoughtful letter to Ham,[37] her tone cordial as she reassured Ham that what she was about to say in no way indicated disapproval of him as a person. Mount Holyoke, she told him, had a tradition of "widening of opportunities for women ... so long as the men's colleges maintain a closed door against women on their faculties, so long as opportunities for women are limited," women must continue to have those opportunities at Mount Holyoke as well as at the other women's colleges. The controversy over his hiring was founded, she said, on "very real and true principles." No man was acceptable at Mount Holyoke, just as no woman was acceptable at Yale.

Woolley had hired McLean as an assistant professor in 1933, the year McLean completed her Ph.D. She was promoted to associate professor in 1943, six years into Ham's presidency, joining four other women, three of whom had Ph.D.s. There were no male associate professors in 1943. That same year, Ham hired Alan McGee, a Yale Ph.D., as an assistant professor. In three years, McGee would be promoted to the associate level, joining the five women, four with Ph.D.s. Two years later, in 1948, Ham appointed McGee chair of the department without a promotion. McLean was promoted to full professor. The department now had six full professors, five of whom were women. Two years later, in 1950, Leslie Gale Burgevin, the sole male full professor, was appointed chair of the department.

With the retirement in 1949 of Shakespearean scholar Dorothy Foster, Ham and McGee enthusiastically took over the course offerings in Shakespeare, teaching both the early and late plays. (Ham had already created a regular position for himself as lecturer within the department when, in 1940, he took over a course from a popular professor who was on sabbatical leave.) According to historian Viola Barnes, Ham pressured Foster to retire early, claiming that she was a poor teacher and under-qualified without a Ph.D. Barnes disagreed. Foster, she said, "had built up a reputation as a very fine teacher of Shakespeare."[38]

By all accounts, McLean would have been an excellent choice for the chairmanship. Within the department, she served as chair of the Committee on Graduate Work, and in the college as a whole, she was a member of the standing Committee of the Faculty on Graduate Work. Inspired by Woolley's leadership and vision, in 1933, she also volunteered to teach in a new unique program in Hartford, Connecticut, during her first year at Mount Holyoke.[39] Mt. Holyoke-in-Hartford was a freshman year experiment for Hartford girls who could not afford tuition at private colleges. Woolley, Dean Harriett Allyn and Harriett Newhall were fully in charge of the program. Classes were taught by Mount Holyoke faculty at the YWCA with tuition cost half of what Mount Holyoke students paid. Individuals in the Hartford community sponsored the young women who were carefully selected by Newhall. The program was instantly popular and highly successful. The first class of twenty-two students sent fifteen on to four-year colleges. Nine went to Mount Holyoke, six of the nine winning scholarships, and six of the original twenty-two pursued graduate work. Woolley enlisted Smith and Wellesley among other colleges in accepting the students as sophomores upon successful completion of their freshman year. By Woolley's retirement, in 1937, the program had educated ninety-one young women in four years, sixty-seven of whom went on to four-year colleges, thirty-five to Mount Holyoke.

Mount Holyoke-in-Hartford students visiting the campus of Mount Holyoke College as the guests of the class of 1935. Front row, left to right: Evelyn Mag, Jean Milliken, Jean Sapp, Kathleen Hope, Louise Jones, Jane Flannery, Bernice Wheeler and Frances Carroll. Second row, left to right: Helen Stoelzel, Susan Hubert, Carol Reynolds, Evelyn Hutchinson, Margaret Dyer and Evelyn Kassabian. Back row, left to right: Margaret Prior, Marjorie Manning, Helen Lahey, Annette Marzano and Octavia Scalera.

In 1938, during his first year in office, Ham decided to eliminate the program. He gave as the reasons a decline in "intellectual qualifications" of the students, the burden on Mount Holyoke instructors, the financial burden on the college, and the fact that many of the students were enrolled simply because they preferred to live at home. There was no true financial necessity.[40] Hartford would have to create its own junior college if the community wanted it. Under pressure from those committed to the program, Ham agreed to delay the closing for one year. Hartford Junior College was incorporated in 1939, and all institutional resources were withdrawn as Mount Holyoke dismantled a unique program that had provided opportunity to talented young women with limited financial means.

The Physics Department

During Woolley's administration, the sciences grew rapidly as outstanding women scientists took charge of independent departments that emphasized cutting edge research and scholarship. Woolley granted leaves and provided financial support for faculty to pursue post-doctoral interests at universities. In 1938, Mount Holyoke was the third largest employer of women faculty members in science in the country with twenty-five women at the associate and full professor level.[41] Ann Haven Morgan headed the zoology department until A. Elizabeth Adams took over in 1950. In 1937, the department consisted of three women professors with Ph.D.s, one woman assistant professor with a Ph.D. and three women instructors, one with a Ph.D. In 1950, the only changes were the addition of a woman associate professor with a Ph.D. and the loss of two instructors. Emma Perry Carr was the chair of the chemistry department in 1937. The department consisted of four women professors all with Ph.D.s, one woman assistant professor with a Ph.D. and one woman instructor with a Ph.D. By 1950, the department had lost two women professors, gained a woman associate professor with a Ph.D. and a male assistant professor with a Ph.D., lost a woman assistant professor and gained three women instructors, two with Ph.D.s and one lab instructor. Ham's administration had little impact on the quality or composition of either of these departments. The history of the physics department tells a different story.

In 1937, the department had three members, all with Ph.D.s. Professor Elizabeth R. Laird, who had been at the college since 1901, had also been the chair since 1904. She was a highly regarded research physicist who, in her years at Mount Holyoke, had helped train many women scientists.[42] Associate Professor Rogers Rusk had arrived at the college in 1928. Rusk was one of a handful of faculty who had expressed a strong preference for a male president in

1935 when the Faculty Conference Committee solicited faculty opinion. Associate Professor Mildred Allen received her Ph.D. from Clark University in 1922 and had done post-graduate research at Yale and the University of Chicago before accepting a permanent position at Mount Holyoke in 1933.

As soon as Ham took office, Rusk began to work toward two goals—Laird's early retirement from the department and his ascension to the chairmanship. Laird strongly recommended Allen to succeed her when she retired in 1940, but Ham appointed Rusk. During Woolley's administration, there had been no formal procedure for hiring, promotion or appointment of chairs. For the most part, Woolley appointed chairs and gave them autonomy. Soon after Ham's arrival, there were rules in place that required consultation with members of the department about the selection of chairmen.[43] In advance of a meeting between Allen and Ham, ostensibly to discuss who should succeed Laird as chair, Laird had informed Allen that Ham had already made up his mind. The meeting thus became a charade. Allen described what Ham told her after his meeting with Rusk:

> Mr. Rusk was violently opposed to my having it [the chairmanship] and that he [Ham] did not think Mr. Rusk would do any work under me.... Apparently also he [Rusk] has been using influence on Mr. Ham for two years to get Mr. Ham to retire Miss Laird immediately.... I did ask whether he thought I could work under Mr. Rusk and he said he would stand behind me.... I also asked whether the President thought I was any more use to Mt. Holyoke and he seemed to think so.[44]

Rusk's lax leadership and arbitrary behavior during the three years of his chairmanship made the work lives of Allen and her colleagues difficult. Rusk simultaneously neglected department work and interfered in Allen's coursework without consulting her. When she appealed to Ham, he did nothing. When Rusk's three-year term ended in 1943, Ham reappointed him. A colleague told Allen, "Mr. Rusk merely told the president that he was

Physics professor Mildred Allen working in the physics lab at Mount Holyoke with two students, undated.

unwilling to work under anybody, and with the difficulty of getting physicists there was not much to do about it except to reappoint him."[45]

In 1945, Allen was denied promotion to full professor on the basis of insufficient scholarship. A colleague spoke to Ham on Allen's behalf to explain that because she was teaching sixteen hours a week, research was impossible.[46] By 1946, Ham had apparently had enough of Rusk.[47] He appointed Allen to the chairmanship but not until he first offered it to visiting lecturer Frederick Saunders, the colleague who had contacted Ham on Allen's behalf. Saunders had been teaching at the college since 1943, had no interest in the chairmanship and believed Allen should have it. Allen was finally promoted to full professor in 1948. According to the committee that had denied her promotion just two years earlier, the basis for this

Rogers Rusk, Mount Holyoke College professor of physics, undated.

positive decision was good teaching and "some weight attached to a philosophic attitude in dealing with the problems of the Department."[48] Scholarship apparently held less weight when Ham had run out of options. Two years into her first term as chair in 1948, Allen had harsh criticism of Ham's leadership. Rusk had spent ninety minutes with Ham complaining about how badly Allen was running the department. According to Allen,

> Ham had no solution to offer ... things are complicated by the fact that Mr. Ham has nothing which even slightly resembles back-bone or common sense. For instance, he told Mr. Rusk that Mr. Clancy would not consider working under Mr. Rusk! So Mr. Rusk suggests that Mr. Clancy be given a year by year appointment and be asked to look for another job.[49]

Allen had hired Edward Clancy in 1947, during the first year of her chairmanship, and she worried that Rusk would drive him away. Ham got sufficiently involved to assure Clancy of an early promotion to associate professor and to promise that "Mr. Rusk will never be chairman again."[50] Allen and Clancy would rotate in the chairmanship until Allen's retirement in 1960. Interestingly, Allen had attractive opportunities over the years to leave Mount Holyoke and pursue teaching and research elsewhere, but her loyalty to Mount Holyoke and its students prevailed. Despite Ham and Rusk, Allen was able to work cooperatively with her other male colleagues, to enjoy their company, and ultimately, to pursue her research interests for many years after retirement.

The History Department

In 1941, Allen heard a rumor at the college that she shared with her mother.

> Mr. Ham told one department chairman to look around and find a person to fill the coming vacancy although he suggested that she wait until after the Christmas meetings in case she found some one more to her liking. She already had some one (a woman) in mind that seemed just right for the job, right part of the field, etc. When she reported to him after Christmas, he said that the appointment had already been made. Apparently he himself went to New York, registered in a different hotel from where the association was meeting, interviewed candidates and appointed one without consulting her in any way. The appointee is a man, is in a part of the field already well covered here, is being paid by Harvard this year but is not actually teaching there, which sounds very fishy.... I did not think him [Ham] capable of this kind of a manoeuvre.[51]

The department in question was history and the chair Viola Barnes, the historian who had helped the trustees make the case for appointing Ham by informing them of the offer of Mount Holyoke's presidency to a man in 1852. Though Allen reported this story as a rumor, it was completely accurate.[52]

Barnes had earned a Ph.D. in colonial history from Yale University and began her career at Mount Holyoke in 1919. By 1937, she was one of three women professors in the department. Nettie Neilson, the chair, was soon to retire. When news of the Broadside hit the newspapers in February, Barnes wrote to Ham:

> After reading the newspaper this morning, I thought I would drop you a note wishing you good cheer in the latest onslaught of the die-hards, of which the only item of interest was that Miss Woolley had openly joined their ranks. I wish one could see inside her mind to find out how she reconciles a feminist war with world peace. Whenever one hears opinion expressed by the students and younger alumnae it shows increasing disapproval of the cheap publicity given the whole affair, and the hope that your coming will mean the dawn of a new era....
>
> The pleasant anticipation of your coming is not however by any means limited to the young. Someone was telling us that when the news of your election reached the fifty-year class reuning [*sic*] here at Commencement last June, they broke into cheers and said, "Now perhaps Mount Holyoke can lose its reputation of being an Old Maids' college!"
>
> It is still my belief that the opposition movement is primarily one led by selfish faculty interest backed by a few fanatics among the alumnae. One of the faculty-administrative leaders, when asked what woman she wanted, said it did not mat-

ter who it was, just so it was a woman, for then they could do as they pleased. The whole affair therefore appears to be just another bit of evidence as to what has been wrong with the college for some time.[53]

Barnes and Neilson had a history of conflict. Barnes welcomed Ham as an ally and sought his support in replacing Neilson in the chairmanship. In 1938, Ham agreed to appoint Barnes for one year, telling her, "For the time being, I can't do anything else."[54] Barnes was unpopular in the department and could never have won an election. According to Barnes herself, Neilson threatened to make trouble for her if she stayed in office any longer than the year. During that year, Barnes searched for Neilson's replacement, anxious to find a woman candidate to prevent a male majority within the department. Ham had other plans. He pressured her, instead, to hire Henry Grattan, an English intellectual historian from Yale.[55] In 1940, Ham extended Barnes' chairmanship for two more years. It was during this period that she found herself in constant conflict with Ham as she made "every effort to see to it that the next addition to the department is a woman." She made lists of women candidates, appealed to contacts for suggestions and recommendations, and found an excellent candidate, Norma Adams with a Ph.D. from the University of Minnesota. It was at this point that Ham engaged in what Allen referred to as the "manoeuver." Without consulting Barnes, he hired a medieval historian, Dana Durand, from Harvard University. Barnes confided to a friend, "Needless to say, I am beside myself with rage. But what can one do?"[56]

When a second position opened after a male assistant professor left for military service, Barnes was able to hire Adams. In 1943, Ham did not reappoint Barnes and, in a decision that must have been galling to Barnes as the senior member of the department, appointed Adams, who had been at Mount Holyoke for one year, to succeed her as chair. When Adams' term ended in 1946, Ham appointed Frederick Cramer, an assistant professor who was promoted the following year. In 1972, twenty years after her retirement, Barnes summed up her feelings about Ham and his leadership. "He did deal with the business men and he was very well liked by the men everywhere. But I think he was just time wasted for Mount Holyoke. I don't think I'm bitter about it. I suffered an awful lot under him, I know."[57] This recognition must have been painful for Barnes. She also recalled how fond she had always been of Woolley, grateful for Woolley's support and kindness when Barnes, as a junior faculty member, felt mistreated by the senior members of her department. She certainly regretted her early support for Ham. She gave no hint of how enthusiastically she had welcomed Ham's appointment.

Woolley's Thoughts

In 1942, Woolley had been away from the campus for over four years, but she continued to follow events there. After reading of eight new appointments at the college, four women and four men, she wrote to her cousin, "The posts given to the men were of the professional rank; the posts given to the women were of instructors rank.... I could say much more; perhaps, however, it is sufficient to convince you that I cannot give up my protest." She explained her refusal to go back to Mount Holyoke. "The policy that I am following ... is my protest against what was done. You know me well enough that I never say a word against the present administration. The question is something bigger than the personal."[58]

These stories of faculty experiences under Ham's administration reveal several aspects of his leadership qualities and priorities. For one, Ham was not the hard-driving, ruthless leader that the committee trustees claimed the college needed. Rather, he combined a laissez-faire style toward certain individuals with a bullying approach toward others.[59] His failure to take decisive action in the case of the physics department interfered with the department's ability to develop. His detached approach benefited other departments such as chemistry and zoology where strong female leadership remained in place throughout his tenure.

Those critics who had been unhappy with Woolley's public life outside of the college approved of Ham's exclusive commitment to the college and its affairs. Copeland recalled, "With the exception of meetings with the Alumnae, I do not remember that ... Mr. Ham ... had many off-campus activities."[60] He escaped publicity about some liberal political views that would have shocked the conservative majority on the board of trustees, especially those on the search committee. When Woolley shared a stage with Smith College's Neilson at a rally in support of lifting the embargo against Republican Spain, Ham lent his name to the same effort. Over the years, while President of Mount Holyoke, Ham publicly supported a number of organizations that brought him to the attention of the FBI in the context of Cold War America. In 1952, the FBI listed ten so-called Communist Front organizations with which Ham had been affiliated.[61] This affiliation meant that he had simply signed his name to petitions. Nevertheless, his politics and his idiosyncratic behavior as an administrator indicate that he was less the man the trustees claimed was needed to cure the ills of Woolley's college.

Ham, in one of his last presidential reports, declared 1930s-style feminism "false." He was glad it was gone. He also criticized the college's 1937 centennial, an event that, after almost twenty years, still apparently irritated him. The celebration of women's accomplishments was, he said, a kind of idolatry.[62]

In the end, the Mount Holyoke community can consider itself fortunate that Ham had an uneven impact on the college. The *Boston Globe* reporter predicted that Ham was given the opportunity to "largely remake Mt. Holyoke." How far did Ham go? The evidence shows that he did not go very far.

Appendix: Cast of Characters

Committee on the Succession to the Presidency
(aka the Committee of Nine)

Original Committee of Five

Alva Morrison, chairman of the board of trustees, stockbroker, Boston

Howell Cheney, industrialist, Connecticut

Henry Kendall, industrialist, Boston

Rowena Keith Keyes, alumna trustee, Ph.D. New York University, principal of Girls' High School, New York City.

Mary Hume Maguire, alumna trustee, Ph.D. Radcliffe College, tutor in history at Radcliffe College

Four Members Added in Early 1936

Edgar S. Furniss, chairman of the committee, dean of the Graduate School at Yale University

Lottie Bishop, alumna trustee, executive secretary at Yale University

Paul Davis, stockbroker, Chicago

Helen Pope Whitman, alumna trustee, former president of the Alumnae Association

The Mount Holyoke Board of Trustees (absent the Committee of Nine)

Horace Day, minister, Connecticut

Boyd Edwards, headmaster, Mercersburg Academy

William James Davidson, businessman, Boston

Elbert Harvey (College Treasurer), financier, Boston

Maynard Hazen, banker, Connecticut

Richard Hoe, New York City

Frank Clayton Myers, attorney, New York and Washington, D.C.

Frances Perkins (MH alumna), secretary of labor

Rockwell Harmon Potter, minister, Connecticut

George Dwight Pratt, businessman, Springfield, Massachusetts

Florence Purington (MH alumna), dean at Mount Holyoke

F. Charles Schwedtman, financier, New York City
James M. Speers, businessman, New York City
Philip Warren, investment banker, Waban, Massachusetts
Edward White, businessman, Holyoke, Massachusetts
Rohl Wiggin, banker and businessman, Boston
Harriet Love Thompson (alumna trustee), full-time homemaker

Five Candidates for the Presidency

Meta Glass, Ph.D. Columbia University, president of Sweet Briar College, president
     of the AAUW
Marjorie Hope Nicolson, Ph.D. Yale University, academic dean, Smith College
Millicent Carey McIntosh, Ph.D. Johns Hopkins University, formerly acting dean of
     Bryn Mawr, head of Brearley School in New York City
Julius Seelye Bixler, Ph.D. Yale University, professor of theology at Harvard
Eunich Schenck, Ph.D. Bryn Mawr College, professor of French and director of the
     graduate programs at Bryn Mawr

The Alumnae Committee of Investigation (aka the Committee of 100)

Amy Rowland, alumna trustee, 1928–1935, retired head of Editorial Department of
     the Cleveland Clinic
Carolyn Smiley, alumna, business editor of *World Youth*

American Association of University Women

Kathryn McHale, general director
Esther Caukin Brunauer, associate in international education
Esther L. Richards, (MH alumna), associate professor of psychiatry at Johns Hopkins
     Medical School

Mount Holyoke Administrators

Harriet Allyn, academic dean
Mary Ashby Cheek, dean of residence
Harriet Newhall, secretary of the board of trustees, director of admissions
Florence Clement, editor of the *Alumnae Quarterly*
Maude Titus White, president of the Alumnae Association

Chapter Notes

ABBREVIATIONS: AAUW—American Association of University Women; AAUWA—American Association of University Women Archives; AEA—A. Elizabeth Adams; CON—Committee of Nine (papers related to the internal activities of the presidential search committee); FCC—Faculty Conference Committee (Mount Holyoke College Faculty); JM—Jeannette Marks; MEW—Mary Emma Woolley; MHA—Mount Holyoke Archives; MHTC—*Mount Holyoke in the Twentieth Century,* Elizabeth Green: Oral History Interviews, 1971–1972; NONA—*Notes on "Autobiography"* ms.; RGH—Roswell Gray Ham; TMH—*The Mount Holyoke*; WCSC—Wellesley College Special Collection

Foreword

1. Patricia Ann Palmieri, *In Adamless Eden: The Community of Women Faculty at Wellesley* (New Haven, CT: Yale University Press, 1985), 232–235; Helen Lefkowitz Horowitz, *The Power and Passion of M. Carey Thomas* (New York: Alfred A. Knopf, 1994), 436–437.

2. See, for example, Ellen Carol Dubois and Lynn Dumenil, *Through Women's Eyes: An American History*, 3rd edition (Boston and New York: Bedford/St. Martin's, 2012), and Nancy Woloch, *Women and the American Experience*, 5th edition, (New York: McGraw-Hill, 2011).

3. Lois Scharf and Joan M. Jensen, eds., *Decades of Discontent: The Women's Movement, 1920–1940* (Westport, CT: Greenwood Press, 1983).

4. Barbara Miller Solomon, *In the Company of Educated Women: A History of Women and Higher Education in America* (New Haven, CT: Yale University Press, 1985).

5. Lynn D. Gordon, "Education and the Professions" in *A Companion to American Women's History,* edited by Nancy A. Hewitt (Oxford: Blackwell Publishing, 2002), 239.

6. Penina Migdal Glazer and Miriam Slater, *Unequal Colleagues: The Entrance of Women into the Professions, 1890–1940* (New Brunswick, NJ: Rutgers University Press, 1987), 64.

7. Linda Eisenmann, *Higher Education for Women in Postwar America, 1945–1965* (Baltimore: Johns Hopkins Press, 2007).

8. Susan Levine, *Degrees of Equality: The AAUW and the Challenge of Twentieth-Century Feminism* (Philadelphia: Temple University Press, 1995), 44.

9. Ibid., 45.

10. Palmieri, 262.

11. Kristin Downey, *The Woman Behind the New Deal* (New York: Anchor Books, Random House, 2010), 167.

12. William H. Chafe, *The American Woman: Her Changing Social, Economic, and Political Role, 1920–1970* (Oxford: Oxford University Press, 1974), 101.

13. Ibid., 132.

14. Susan Becker, "International Feminism Between the Wars," chapter 10 in Scharf and Jensen, *Decades*, 238.

15. Scharf and Jensen, "Introduction," in *Decades*, 8–9.

16. Gordon, 239.

17. Susan Ware, *Holding Their Own: American Women in the 1930s* (Boston: Twayne, 1982), 105.

18. Ware, *Holding*, 81.

19. Estelle Freedman, "Separatism as Strategy: Female Institution Building and American Feminism, 1870–1930," *Feminist Studies* 5 (Fall 1979): 512–552.

20. Ware, *Holding*, 64.

21. Helen Lefkowitz Horowitz, *Alma Mater: Design and Experience in the Women's Colleges from Their Nineteenth-Century Beginnings to the 1930s* (New York: Alfred A. Knopf, 1984), 287, 293.

22. Alice Kessler-Harris, *In Pursuit of Equity: Women, Men, and the Quest for Economic Citizenship in 20th-Century America* (Oxford: Oxford University Press, 2001), 57.

23. Ibid., 84.

24. Nancy F. Cott, *The Grounding of Modern Feminism* (New Haven, CT: Yale University Press, 1987), 279.

25. Ibid., 229–231.

26. Susan Ware, *Beyond Suffrage: Women and the New Deal* (Cambridge: Harvard University Press, 1981), 3, 16.

27. Ibid., 116–117.

28. Ibid., 124, and also in Susan Ware, *Letter to the World: Seven Women Who Shaped the American Century* (New York: Norton, 1998), xxiii.

29. Ware, *Holding*, 94, 104.

30. Sandra F. VanBurkleo, *"Belonging to the World": Women's Rights and American Constitutional Culture* (Oxford: Oxford University Press, 2001), 233–234.

31. Nancy Woloch, *Women and the American Experience*, 5th edition (New York: McGraw-Hill, 2011), 430.

32. Stephanie Coontz, *A Strange Stirring: The Feminine Mystique and American Women at the Dawn of the 1960s* (New York: Basic Books, 2011), 46–47.

33. Ware, *Holding*, 71–81.

34. Ibid., 105.

35. Ibid., 112.

36. Ibid., 88.

37. Ware, *Beyond*, 4.

38. Sherna Berger Gluck, "Socialist Feminism between the Two World Wars: Insights from Oral History," chapter 10 in Scharf and Jensen, *Decades*, 280.

39. Estelle B. Freedman, "Separatism Revisited: Women's Institutions, Social Reform, and the Career of Miriam Van Waters," chapter 8 in *U.S. History and Women's History: New Feminist Essays*, edited by Linda K. Kerber, Alice Kessler-Harris, and Kathryn Kish Sklar (Chapel Hill: University of North Carolina Press, 1995), 173–175.

40. Ibid., 173.

41. Kristin Celello, "A New Century of Struggle: Feminism and Antifeminism in the United States, 1920–Present," in *The Practice of U.S. Women's History: Narratives, Intersections, and Dialogues*, edited by S. Jay Kleinberg, Eileen Boris and Vicki L. Ruiz (New Brunswick, NJ: Rutgers University Press, 2007), 333–334.

42. Cott, 239.

Introduction

1. Anne Carey Edmonds, *A Memory Book: Mount Holyoke College 1837–1987* (South Hadley, MA: Mount Holyoke College, 1988), 121.

2. See "Dr. Mary Woolley, Educator, 84, Dead," *New York Times*, 6 Sept. 1947, 16.

3. Perkins, letter to JM, 9 Sept. 1947, JM Papers, Series 8, Box 32, MHA.

4. The official name for the search committee was the Committee on the Succession to the Presidency. It will be referred to in this book as the search committee. The archival records refer to the search committee as the Committee of Nine. All notes to those records will be abbreviated CON. These documents have been digitized and are available as part of the Mount Holyoke College Archives and Special Collections' digital collections: https://www.mtholyoke.edu/archives/collections/digital.

5. Anna Mary Wells, the author of *Miss Marks and Miss Woolley* (Boston: Houghton Mifflin, 1978), assumed that the mysterious package of material had been given to Mount Holyoke College by Jeannette Marks, Mary Woolley's partner, and that the contents would probably reveal more about their relationship. She was mistaken.

6. Maude Meagher to (Board Chairman) Alva Morrison, 29 Oct. 1936, RGH Papers, Series A, Sub-Series 1, Folder 11, MHA. (All subsequent notes to the RGH files will drop the reference to the Mount Holyoke Archives.)

Chapter 1

1. MEW, "Miscellaneous Notes" typed ms., Autobiographical Materials, Box 1, MEW Papers, MHA; Woolley's handwritten *Notes on "Autobiography"* (NONA) is located in the same box.

2. MEW, letter to JM, 31 Dec. 1900, MEW Papers, Marks-Woolley Correspondence, MHA. All letters between MEW and JM referenced in this book exist in this special section of the MEW papers in the Mount Holyoke Archives and all subsequent endnotes will omit that fact.

3. Woolley used the term herself in NONA, 44.

4. "Miss Mary E. Woolley Is Elected President of Mt. Holyoke College," Pawtucket *Gazette and Chronicle*, 18 Jan. 1900, MEW Papers, Oversize Materials, Box 46, MHA, n.p. [3].

5. Arthur Cole, A *Hundred Years of Mount Holyoke College* (New Haven, CT: Yale University Press, 1940), 201. Until 1887, only three members of the staff had not been educated at Mount Holyoke.

6. Faculty and administration, by tradition, continued to live among the students both for cost efficiency and for the edifying influence on students.

7. MEW, letter to JM, 6 Jan. 1901.

8. Marks had grave misgivings about her life with Woolley at Mount Holyoke, fearing that their relationship would meet with disapproval and she would suffer the most. She also preferred writing to teaching, but this position offered income and security.

9. Student bed makers found letters and notes that Woolley and Marks regularly wrote to each other and joked about what they discovered. A group of girls named a doll "Jamew," combining the three initials of Woolley's and Marks' names, and the doll became a dorm mascot. See MHTC 10 (Susan R. Stifler), 2–3. On one occasion Woolley admonished Marks: "Do not leave my letters around! ... lock them up as soon as received" (MEW to JM, 17 Sept. 1901).

10. See draft Viola Barnes interview with Elizabeth Green for MHTC (9 and 10 March 1972), Box 16, Series V, Mount Holyoke, Folder 17, Viola Barnes Papers, MHA.

11. *Springfield Republican*, 16 May 1901.

12. MEW, "Inaugural Address," TMH 11 Inauguration Number (1901), 9 (hereinafter Inauguration).

13. Ibid., 12.

14. Ibid., 13–14.

15. George Harris, "Address by President Harris of Amherst," Inauguration, 21.

16. William Faunce, "Address by President Faunce of Brown University," Inauguration, 26.

17. Ibid., 27.

18. Hall had been trained in psychology. He had studied under William James at Harvard University.

19. All direct quotes from G. Stanley Hall, "The Kind of Women Colleges Produce," *Appleton's Magazine,* n.d., filed with MEW, "College Woman's Place in the World," Speech 44 (Staten Island [NY] Woman's Club), 9 Dec. 1910. (All references to speeches by MEW unless otherwise indicated are available by speech number in MHA.)

20. See MEW, "Education of Women" Speech 28 published in *Encyclopedia Americana* (1905).

21. NT, Rom. 11.33.

22. *French American*, 1 June 1901, in MEW Papers, Oversize Material, Box 45, MHA, n.p. [17].

23. NONA, 6.

24. MEW, "What I Owe to My Father," in *What I Owe to My Father,* edited by Sydney Strong (New York: Henry Holt, 1931), 3.

25. Quoted in JM, *The Life and Letters of Mary Emma Woolley* (Washington, DC: Public Affairs Press, 1955), 17.

26. George L. Rockwell, *The History of Ridgefield, Connecticut* (Ridgefield: Privately Printed by the author, 1927), 261. See also Daniel W. Teller, *History of Ridgefield* (Danbury, CT: 1878).

27. After several months, he contracted a serious infection and the army sent him home to recuperate.

28. J. J. Woolley to Center Congregational Church, 30 Sept. 1862, Meriden Center Congregational Church Records 1846–1915, Meriden, CT.

29. "Resolved ... That We Extend the Hand of Christian Fellowship to All Other Evangelical Churches ...," Center Congregational Church, "Church Resolutions," 13 June 1867, Meriden Center Congregational Church Records 1846–1915, Meriden, CT. Prior to 1864, the pastoral term in the Methodist Episcopal Church was limited by design to two years. Woolley was beginning to raise a family and the desire for a permanent position for economic stability probably also contributed to his willingness to change denominations.

30. Martha Kunhardt, letter to MEW, 9 June 1936, MEW Papers, Series 1 Correspondence, MHA.

31. NONA, 5. Later, Woolley quoted her mother saying, "I believe that there is nothing in the world of which your father is afraid" (NONA, 7).

32. MEW, "What I Owe to My Father," 3.

33. NONA, 9.

34. See, for example, MEW, letter to "Cousin Nancy," 24 Jan. 1875: "I had a splendid Christmas. We had a Christmas tree here in the Hotel for the children.... Mama gave me a photograph album. Papa gave three handkerchiefs. Grandma gave me a writing desk. Ervie [her brother] gave me a handkerchief and a pair of cuffs. Mr. Shipple [one of the boarders] gave me a bottle of cologne. Mr. Crawford [another boarder] gave me a work box. Mr. Ingraham gave me a bottle of cologne. Mrs. Leonard gave me a roman necktie" (quoted in Jeannette Marks, *The Life and Letters of Mary Emma Woolley* [Washington, DC: Public Affairs Press, 1955], 27).

35. Quoted in Marks, 31.

36. MEW, "What I Owe to My Father," 3.

37. See Annual Meeting Records, 25 Jan. 1881, 1 Feb, 1881, 8 Feb. 1881, Pawtucket Congregational Church Archives, 294–299.

38. J. J. Woolley, letter to Pawtucket Congregational Church, 11 Sept. 1881, 9 Oct. 1881, Pawtucket Congregational Church Archives.

39. Quoted in Marks, 31.

40. See J. J. Woolley, letter to Pawtucket Congregational Church, 31 Jan. 1882, Annual Meeting Records, 3 Jan. 1882, Pawtucket Congregational Church Archives, 308.

41. See "Report of the Committee," 7 March 1882, Pawtucket Congregational Church Archives.

42. See Robert Morgan Mitchell, *This Branch of His Planting* (Pawtucket, RI: Park Place Congregational Church, 1982), 4.

43. See Marks, 31.

44. Ibid., 32.

45. *Park Place Congregational Church, a Record of 50 Years* (Pawtucket, RI: Park Place Congregational Church, 1932), 6.

46. She would complete the seminary course in two years rather than the more typical four, but the certification was for just two years post–high school work. For a more detailed description of both Wheaton Seminary and Woolley's years there—as both student and teacher, see Ann Karus Meeropol, *A Practical Visionary: Mary Emma Woolley and the Education of Women,* diss. University of Massachusetts, 1992 (Ann Arbor: UMI, 1992), chapter 3.

47. Vassar had opened in 1865, Smith and Wellesley in 1875.

48. J.J. was not alone in his preference. During the 1880s and early 1890s, Wheaton's enrollment grew steadily, in part because the colleges did not guarantee the spiritually focused life of the seminary. Finances were likely an issue, too. Daughters of clergy had fees waived or adjusted downward.

49. See Ann Augur, letter to her father, 9 Sept. 1888, excerpted and enclosed in Belle Ferris Briggs (cousin of MEW), letter to JM, 2 Feb. 1952, JM Papers, Box 113, Folder 2, WCSC.

50. NONA, 22.

51. There were forty-three such "exiles" in 1891 and more than one hundred were then preparing for college. See Grace E. Hawk, *Pembroke College in Brown University: The First Seventy-Five Years, 1891–1966* (Providence, RI: Brown University Press, 1967), 19.

52. For a detailed discussion of Woolley's years at Brown see Meeropol, 110–127. For specific references to Andrews' efforts to bring coeducation to Brown, see ibid., 109–110.

53. Quoted in Anna Mary Wells, *Miss Marks*

and Miss Woolley (Boston: Houghton Mifflin: 1978), 36.

54. Lucy Larcom, *Wheaton Seminary: A Semi-Centennial Sketch* (Cambridge: 1885), 92.

55. Ibid., 70.

56. Quoted in Wells, 37.

57. Quoted in Frances L. Warner, *On a New England Campus* (Cambridge: Riverside-Houghton, 1937), 47.

58. Quoted in Marks, 42.

59. Quoted in ibid., 39.

60. See Mary Louise Record, "Half a Century Ago Brown Said It Was an Experiment," *Providence Sunday Journal,* 21 Sept. 1941, section 6, 3.

61. Quoted in Wells, 37.

62. Quoted in Record.

63. In addition to Jameson, she studied Hebrew with Professor James Jewett and moral philosophy with President Andrews. She would ultimately work with Jameson on several research projects in history, three of which were published. They were MEW, "The Passover Scandal," *The Brown Magazine* 4 (1892–1893): 189–196; MEW, "Early History of the Colonial Post Office," *Publications of the Rhode Island Historical Society,* New Series 1 (1893–1894): 270–291; MEW, "The Development of the Love of Romantic Scenery in America," *American Historical Review* 3 (1897): 56–66.

64. E. Benjamin Andrews, *Annual Report of the President to the Corporation of Brown University,* 21 June 1894, quoted in Hawk, 15.

65. Hawk, 37.

66. MEW, "The Passover Scandal."

67. The first set of "Etchings" in *The Brown Magazine* appeared in volume 5 (1893–1894). For Woolley's contributions: 26–28, 63–65. The university yearbook, *Liber Brunensis,* excluded Woolley from the group photograph of the editorial staff, and subsequent volumes excluded her successors, all female, until 1898. (See Hawk, 40.) For an example in the bound volume of *The Brown Magazine* when Woolley first joined the editorial board, compare the title page or page 5 (1893–1894), where she is listed on the board with the facing photograph, which includes all the male members of the board but not her.

68. Hawk, 35.

69. Walter C. Bronson, *The History of Brown University, 1764–1914* (New York: Arno, 1914, and New York Times, 1971), 463. The story of Andrews' resignation and subsequent reconciliation with the Brown Corporation can be followed in Bronson, 462–466. All direct quotes in the next paragraph are from Bronson.

70. This is a direct quote from the Brown Corporation's conciliatory statement on the Andrews affair. The corporation stated that they were not

attempting to "prescribe the path in which you [Andrews] would tread .... but simply to intimate that it would be the part of wisdom for you to take a less active part in exciting partisan discussions and apply your energies more exclusively to the affairs of the college" (quoted in Bronson, 466).

71. Quoted in Record.

72. Between 1894 and 1896, forty-seven teachers left Wellesley—through either retirement or dismissal.

73. See George Herbert Palmer, *The Life of Alice Freeman Palmer* (Boston: Houghton, 1908), 230–231, 234. See also Patricia Palmieri, *In Adamless Eden: A Social Portrait of the Academic Community at Wellesley College 1875–1920*, diss., Harvard University, 1981 (Ann Arbor: UMI, 1981), 96–101, 106–136.

74. This reference is one used by Woolley in a speech she gave eight times between 1905 and 1907. Titled "Idealism in Education," it is Speech 36. In it, she spoke about Herbert Spencer's idea that a teacher must try to produce "a pleasurable excitement" in his or her students. At Wellesley College, Woolley would join a community of academic women who made this a goal of their teaching.

75. Woolley, like Palmer, had large ambitions for women's education. In the previous year, Woolley had written an eloquent rationale for the support of women's equal education at Brown: "Surely, the Women's College is very much alive; all that it needs and asks is room in which to expand and develop to its fullest capacity. That it has the elements of power, no one who has watched its progress can doubt. It has already established its reputation for scholarship, a reputation which the coming year of opportunity cannot but see increased rather than diminished. That there is a demand for it, the very numbers alone prove.... The Women's College, in its fourth year, already numbers one hundred, and that without any inducements in the way of accommodations" (MEW, "The Women's College," *The Brown Magazine* 6 [1894–1895]: 379).

76. Quoted in Florence Converse, *The Story of Wellesley* (Boston: Little, 1915), 177.

77. See Palmieri (diss.), 108.

78. Converse, 90.

79. MHTC, Viola Barnes, 4.

80. Alice Freeman had rejected both Mount Holyoke Seminary and Vassar College for her own undergraduate studies because of their academic weaknesses and their intrusive social control, choosing instead to attend the newly coeducational University of Michigan. (See Converse, 59.) The faculty whom Freeman hired after assuming the presidency of Wellesley in 1881

were, for the most part, opposed to required participation in organized religion. Freeman warned the board of trustees that Wellesley was in danger of losing its best faculty if the religious requirements, including a religious oath, were not modified. The board ultimately accepted her view and the oath was dropped from the statutes. Freeman also sympathized with the students as they became increasingly unhappy and outspoken about repressive conditions that included the closing of the library on Sundays, the use of chaperones, and required Bible classes and she would eventually see all of these regulations modified. See Palmieri (diss.), 154–155.

81. Marks quoted Woolley: "As I look back upon my blithe acceptance of that post, I am reminded of a remark of General Howard, a guest in our Pawtucket home during my childhood. 'I have often wondered,' said the General, 'how I dared assume such grave responsibilities during the Civil War. I never would have dared had I not been so young.' Blessed be the confidence of youth!" (Marks, 43.)

82. MEW, "Some College Tendencies," *The Wellesley Magazine* 6 (1897): 6.

83. Within one year, by 1896, the department expanded into the Department of Biblical History, Literature and Interpretation. In 1897, Woolley taught a course in Hebrew, two Old Testament courses and two New Testament courses. She introduced new courses in the study of church history and hired male religious scholars to teach part-time. She encouraged diversity and discussion by inviting lecturers including Lyman Abbott and Dwight L. Moody. For details on Woolley's work in the new department, see Meeropol, 142–147.

84. See "Christian Association Notes," *The Wellesley Magazine* 4 (1896): 283.

85. Claire Godwin Swift, letter to JM, 25 March 1950, Jeannette Marks Collection, Box 112, Folder 7 (typed), Folder 6 (original), WCSC.

86. Anna E. Wolfson, letter to JM, 18 Feb. 1950, Jeannette Marks Collection, Box 112, Folder 6, WCSC.

87. On the offer from Wheaton, see Paul C. Helmreich, *Wheaton College, 1834–1912: The Seminary Years* (Norton, MA: Class of 1949, Wheaton College, 1985), 69. On the offer from Smith, see "The New President of Mount Holyoke," unidentified newspaper clipping, MEW Papers, Scrapbook 45, MHA, n.p. [4].

88. See Palmieri (diss.), 332–356. Mary Whiton Calkins, a socialist and pacifist, was a Smith College graduate who earned an unofficial doctorate from Harvard University and taught Greek, philosophy, and psychology at Wellesley. A colleague described her as "the most perfectly

integrated personality I have known" (quoted in "Calkins, Mary Whiton," *Notable American Women 1607–1950* (1971). See also Converse, 94.) Vida Scudder, also a Smith graduate, attended John Ruskin's lectures at Oxford University and was struck by a painful awareness of the "plethora of privilege" in her own life. She taught English literature at Wellesley, but the desire to work toward the improvement of society became paramount in her life. She could never forget "the debt that had to be paid back, the debt owed by the privileged to the dispossessed" ("Scudder, Vida," *Notable American Women: The Modern Period* (Cambridge, MA: Belknap Press of Harvard University Press, 1980). Uneasy about the elite status of America's colleges, Scudder organized the College Settlement Association at Wellesley because she believed that the settlement movement in England and America represented true democracy. Two years before Woolley's arrival, Scudder took a year's leave from the college to open Denison House, a settlement in Boston. She was in open conflict with the Wellesley trustees over her political activities and President Irvine called her "a thorn in the side of the institution" (quoted in Palmieri [diss.], 175), but Scudder was one of the most popular teachers at the college. (See Maynard Force Thayer, letter to JM, 5 March 1950, Jeannette Marks Collection, Box 112, Folder 7 (typed), Folder 6 (original), WCSC.) Katherine Coman earned a B.A. and a Ph.D. from the University of Michigan before she followed her friend Alice Freeman to Wellesley to teach political economy and history. She, along with Scudder, was a founder of the CSA and a principal fund-raiser for the association. When Denison House opened, she became the chair of the Boston Settlement Committee and served on the executive committee of the Consumers' League, one of the first political organizations that Woolley joined. The National Consumers' League (Woolley dropped the word "National" from its title when she referred to it) was formed in 1892. "[It] agitated for seats for salesmen in department stores, promoted clean ventilated lunch rooms, published white lists of stores that treated employees well, and issued labels to be attached to items made under sanitary and healthful conditions" (Alice Kessler-Harris, *Out to Work: A History of Wage-Earning Women in the United States* [New York: Oxford University Press, 1982], 166). As chair of the committee on grievances of the Women's Trade Union League, Coman publicized a seamstresses' strike and helped them to win union recognition. She was trained in the best of graduate programs and published several books on U.S. industrial history, conducting her research directly in the field. (See

"Coman, Katherine," *Notable American Women 1607–1950,* 1971. See also Converse, 143–145.) Emily Green Balch, "the plainest of gaunt New Englanders, ... possessed of an inner radiance," graduated from Bryn Mawr in economics and studied at the Sorbonne. In 1892, she attended Felix Adler's Summer School of Applied Ethics, where she met Jane Addams, Scudder and Coman, and joined Coman at Wellesley in 1896 as her assistant. Balch was convinced that economics had a "direct relation to the social question" and wanted to teach in order to awaken "the desire of women to work for social betterment." (See "Balch, Emily Greene," *Notable American Women 1607–1950.*) Katherine Lee Bates earned a B.A. from Wellesley in 1880, spent a year at Oxford and returned to earn an M.A. at Wellesley, where she joined the Department of English Literature. Bates' mother was a graduate of Mount Holyoke Seminary and her father a Congregationalist minister. She and Woolley had much in common and became good friends in spite of Bates' spirited rejection of organized religion. When the board offered her the chairmanship of the English department, she refused the position as long as she was required to take the religious oath. Bates wrote prolifically and supported the social reform activities of her colleagues. She and Coman lived together and both lavished attention on a collie named Sigurd, whose son, Lord Wellesley, Bates would give to Woolley. Lord Wellesley was the first of many collies to become Woolley's beloved pets. (See Wells, 178n, 183.) Coman and Bates co edited a major book on English history, and when Coman retired in 1913 Bates assisted her in volunteer work for the Progressive Party on a comprehensive study of European social insurance programs ("Bates, Katharine," *Notable American Women 1607–1950*). Ellen Hayes came to Wellesley from Oberlin in 1879. Durant, recognizing her extraordinary talents, favored her for leadership along with Freeman, but her views soon became too radical for the administration of the college. She remained in the mathematics department and kept the Wellesley community aware of feminist activity in the "outside world." She was active in both the National Woman's Suffrage Association and the American Woman's Suffrage Association, continuously investigating and reporting on the professional and occupational status of women. She believed that socialization was responsible for the attitudes of both men and women. Hayes objected to the discomfort of women's clothing and dressed in handmade outfits of loose fitting pants and jackets that resembled men's clothing. (See Palmieri [diss.], 151–152.)

89. Quoted in Nan Beaver Maglin, "Female

Friendship: Vida D. Scudder and Florence Converse," ms., 27.

90. Ibid., 34. Scudder found an intimate friend in one of her students, Florence Converse, who was ten years younger and whose talents in creative writing complemented Scudder's. After graduation, Converse became an editor for the *Atlantic Monthly* and she and Scudder lived together, sharing, in Scudder's words, "both jokes and prayers" (quoted in "Scudder, Vida," *Notable American Women: The Modern Period*) for the rest of their long lives.

91. Nettie I. H. (Mrs. Hill) Brougham, letter to JM, 31 Mar 1950, Jeannette Marks Collection, Box 112, Folder 7 (typed), Folder 6 (original), WCSC.

92. Swift.

93. Harriet Albertson Buckhout, letter to JM, 1 July 1950, Jeannette Marks Collection, Box 112, Folder 6, WCSC.

94. The full context of this self-admonition can be seen in the following passage from a speech Woolley gave that she published in 1909: "In the rush of the modern world, we should add to, 'I strive to keep my body under,' 'I strive to keep my nerves under!'" (MEW, "Some Results of Higher Education for Women," *Harper's Bazar* 43 (1909): 587.

95. Quoted in MHTC 11 (Olive Copeland), 10.

96. Mrs. Cyrus (Grace Frazee) Brewster, Sr., letter to JM, 24 July 1950, Jeannette Marks Collection, Box 112, Folder 7 (typed) , Folder 6 (original), WCSC. Woolley's tweed suits and shirtwaists, immaculate with ascots pinned perfectly in place, prompted another to observe that "she might have stepped out of a bandbox" (Mary Hewett Hildreth, letter to JM, 28 July 1950, Jeannette Marks Collection, Box 112, Folder 7 [typed], Folder 6 [original], WCSC; see also Lucile Reynolds Hall [Mrs. Walter A. Hall], letter to JM, 3 April 1950, JM Collection, Box 112, Folder 7 [typed], Folder 6 [original], WCSC).

97. Katharine Jones Rew, letter to JM, 31 March 1950, JM Collection, Box 112, Folder 7 (typed) , Folder 6 (original), WCSC.

98. Grace Phemister, letter to JM, 17 Feb. 1950, JM Collection, Box 112, Folder 7 (typed), Folder 6 (original), WCSC.

99. For details about Marks' early years and her relationship with her family, see Wells, 42–45.

100. At Wellesley, she immediately threw herself into academic and creative work, finding a source of support in Bates, who was always interested in students with literary talents. Marks submitted poems and stories to college and outside publications and quickly began to see her work published. Her stories were often tales of the needless deaths of pathetic victims, her poems about the search for love and the beauty of nature. Marks studied literature with Bates and Scudder in seminars that inspired her, and she enthusiastically accompanied Coman and other faculty members to meetings on labor and reform issues. She joined the College Settlement Association and gave monthly readings at Wellesley of her own and other writers' works. In her first publication in a national magazine, she wrote about Wellesley College with great affection. Buried in the glowing descriptions of the college is a revealing sentence: "Since man is as rare and as hard to find as a needle in a haystack, nothing is present to revile" (quoted in Wells, 51–52).

101. Pauline Durant, the widow of the founder of Wellesley, was still alive and was determined to fight for her husband's vision. "If we get a man now," she said, "we will never again have the place for a woman" (quoted in Wells, 54). For the beginnings of Wellesley College, particularly the role of Henry Durant in its creation, see Meeropol, 133–137.

102. Hazard came from an established Rhode Island family that counted among its members abolitionists, suffragists, and fighters for women's education. Her grandfather was a founder of Brown University, and her father was a member of the Brown Corporation. Hazard was in her mid forties, a large, vigorous woman who despite a lack of formal education had become a published expert in Rhode Island history as well as an accomplished poet. (See "Caroline Hazard," *Notable American Women, 1906–1950* (Cambridge, MA: Belknap Press, 1971), edited by Edward T. James, Janet Wilson James, and Paul S. Boyer.)

She had traveled extensively, was an effective public speaker and spent much of her time administering the affairs of Peace Dale, the town based on progressive principles of social welfare that her father had created for the workers in his factories. Hazard accepted Wellesley's offer of the presidency "only with great reluctance and after much hesitation" (quoted in "Editorials," *The Wellesley Magazine* 7 [1899]: 367) both because she doubted how successful she would be in fundraising and because she believed that her lack of academic training would be a handicap. She was persuaded by a promise of help with fund-raising, by the appointment of a dean for administrative assistance and by the appointment of her brother, an astute businessman, to the board of trustees. She accepted in March 1899 with the comment "A man's reach should exceed his grasp" (quoted in Palmieri [diss.]: 179).

103. MEW to Caroline Hazard, 13 March 1899, Wellesley College Archives.

104. See Wells, 53.

105. MEW, "Free Press," *The Wellesley Magazine* 8 (1900): 331–333.

106. Caroline Hazard, "President's Annual Report," *Annual Reports of the President and Treasurer of Wellesley College, 1900* (Boston: Wellesley College, 1901), 4.

107. Brougham.

108. See Thayer.

109. Hazard, 9.

110. Converse, 131.

111. Quoted in Marks, 52.

112. Hazard, 6.

113. The question of what lay ahead after college was a disturbing one for many women graduates. After four years of intense and rigorous liberal arts education, the vast majority of young women faced limited work opportunities and expected heavy family responsibilities. Many experienced post-college depressions. In an article titled "After College, What?" historian Joyce Antler documents the frequent incidence of depression after graduation among members of the Wellesley class of 1897 (*American Quarterly* 32 [1980]: 409–434). Marks received her B.A. in 1900.

114. MEW to JM, 9 July 1900.

115. MEW to JM, quoted in Wells, 57.

116. MEW letters to JM, quoted in Wells, 58–59.

117. Lady Margaret Somerville, St. Hugh's, Newnham, Girton, Bedford in London, and Royal Holloway in Surrey

118. MEW to JM, 10 Oct. 1900.

119. MEW to JM, 14 Oct. 1900.

120. See Hawk, 66.

121. MEW to JM, 6 Oct. 1900.

Chapter 2

1. Carolyn Hazard, "Address by President Hazard of Wellesley," Inauguration, 17.

2. Formerly the chair of ecclesiastical history at the Oberlin Theological Seminary.

3. Smith referred to the college's $500,000 endowment, the value of the physical plant estimated at $500,000, the twelve building on campus, ten of which had been built in the previous five years, the growing student body currently at five hundred, and the growing faculty, already at forty full-time members (Judson Smith, "Address and Presentation of the Keys," Inauguration, 6).

4. See A. L. Williston, letter to M. Carey Thomas, [11] Oct. 1900. Thomas' reply is in a letter to Williston, 15 Oct. 1900. Both letters and the original newspaper article that prompted Williston's initial letter are in Trustees Correspondence, MHA. They are both quoted and discussed in Meeropol, 185–186.

5. Editorial, TMH 16 (1906–1907): 306.

6. "Public Opinion," TMH 20 (1910–1911): 212.

7. Mary Lyon, *The Inception of Mount Holyoke College* (Springfield, MA: 1887), 17.

8. See [anonymous student class of]1914, "Our Honor," TMH 23 (1913–1914): 47–48.

9. See MHTC 10 (Susan R. Stifler): 1–2.

10. B. M. Marvel ('38), letter to Mount Holyoke College, 3 March 1981, MEW Papers, Series 1 Correspondence, MHA. (All subsequent references to MEW's correspondence will omit the designation MHA.)

11. Quoted in Marks, 66.

12. MEW, "Education for Life" Speech 49 (Civitas Club, Brooklyn, New York), 8 Feb. 1911. The quote is from the version delivered at the Nurses Training School in Holyoke, Massachusetts, 6 June 1911, 1.

13. See "Alumnae Notes," TMH 18 (1907–1908): 355.

14. See Judson Smith, "Mount Holyoke College and Its Alumnae," TMH 17 (1907–1908): 2.

15. MEW, quoted in "Alumnae Notes," TMH 19 (1909–1910): 365.

16. MEW, letter to JM, 10 Dec. 1909.

17. MEW, "What the Alumnae May Mean to the College" Speech 47 (Springfield [Massachusetts] Alumnae Club), 4 Dec. 1909.

18. MEW, *Annual Report of the President, 1906–1907* (South Hadley, MA: Mount Holyoke College, 1907), 20.

19. See, for example, MEW, "The Significance of Changes in Education for Women" Speech No. 43 (Western Reserve University), 14 June 1905, 5–6.

20. See, for example, MEW, Speech 35 "Some Result of Higher Education for Women," MEW, "The College Woman as a Home-Maker," *Ladies' Home Journal* 1 Oct. 1909. (She published frequently in *Harper's Bazar* as well.)

21. Between 1850 and 1859, 75 percent of Mount Holyoke students married. Between 1905 and 1908, 59.4 percent married. The percentage who would never marry increased from 24.5 to 40.6 over that fifty-year period. The average number of children per Mount Holyoke mother (1850–1908) was 2.5. In the 1880s, 33.6 percent of Mount Holyoke marriages were childless, with that percentage falling to 23.6 in the period 1900–1908. See Tiziana Rota, *Between "True Woman" and "New Woman"*: *Mount Holyoke Students, 1837 to 1908*, diss., University of Massachusetts, 1983, 317–319.

22. MEW, "Commencement Address" Speech 79 (Western College, Oxford, Ohio), 14 June 1905, 8.

23. Ibid., 14.

24. MEW, "What Should College Training Accomplish?" Speech 3 (Woman's Club, Milwaukee, Wisconsin), 28 April 1910, 17.

25. MEW, "The College Woman as Home-Maker."

26. MEW, "What Should College Training Accomplish?" 12.

27. MEW, "Bryn Mawr College, Twenty-Fifth Anniversary" Speech 45 (Bryn Mawr, Pennsylvania), 22 Oct. 1910, 2.

28. MEW, letter to JM, 17 Dec. 1900.

29. MEW, letter to JM, 6 Jan, 1901.

30. See, for example, the manager of *The Worthy* (Springfield, Massachusetts), letter to Miss Henrietta A Marks [sic], 7 May 1902, which states they are "pleased to reserve a room for Miss Woolley and yourself for Saturday and Sunday night, in a quiet part of our house" (quoted in Meeropol, 438).

31. JM, letter to MEW, 7 April 1905.

32. MEW, "Some Results of Higher Education for Women," 588.

33. MEW, "College Woman's Place in the World," 2–3.

34. Ibid., 6.

35. Woolley, along with many of her colleagues, advocated alternatives to traditional health care. "The physician no longer has the field entirely to himself," she said. "[H]e must share it with the physical culturist, the Fletcherite, the advocate of health foods, the psycho therapeutist" (MEW, "College Woman's Place in the World," 5a.) She herself incorporated some of these habits into her daily life. She argued that every college woman should practice deep breathing in fresh air, take cold-water baths, and drink pure water throughout the day (MEW, "What Should College Training Accomplish?" 14). Woolley valiantly tried to avoid meat and rich foods and took brisk walks when she had time. Marks, who was more committed to regimens than Woolley, became her conscience in these practices.

36. MEW, "Some Phases of a Girl's Education," 2.

37. See Mount Holyoke in 20th Century as told by Viola F. Barnes to Elizabeth Green—Draft (tape-recorded conversation for archives by Elizabeth Green March 9 and 10, 1972, 4). See Chapter 1 Note 79.

38. MEW, *Annual Report of the President, 1904–05* (South Hadley, MA: Mount Holyoke College, 1905), 6–7. Woolley would petition for this every year, but the trustees would not vote to create sabbaticals until 1925. (See Cole, 253.) By 1910–1911, the staff had increased from 69 to 130. (See MEW, *Annual Report of the President, 1910–11* [South Hadley, MA: Mount Holyoke College,

1911], 5–6.) Ninety of the 130 staff at Mount Holyoke were members of the faculty, and 34 of the 90 had earned Ph.D.'s from fourteen different institutions. (See MEW, *Report of the President, 1901–11*, 8–9.) In 1912 in *The Mount Holyoke*, an alumna Marion F. Lansing ('03) stated that Mount Holyoke College had 108 faculty, thus sharing with Bryn Mawr the lowest ratio of students to faculty among the women's colleges, one to seven ("The Curriculum Today," TMH 22 [1912–1913]: 81). The contradiction between her number and Woolley's is because of her inclusion of assistants as faculty. Woolley identified 90 members of the "Faculty proper" in the 1913–1914 academic year. (See MEW, *Report of the President, 1913–1916* [South Hadley, MA: Mount Holyoke College, 1916], 6.) Woolley's figure creates a ratio of one to eight and a half, a lower ratio than Wellesley, Vassar and Smith. Twelve faculty members were able to complete their degrees by 1911, taking advantage of Woolley's generous leave policy despite the absence (till 1925) of an official sabbatical policy.

39. Within the group that stayed on, there was a higher percentage of master's over bachelor's degrees. The ratio was four to one as compared to less than two to one for the group that left the college. Of the 133 faculty members hired during this period from 1901 to 1911, only 24 were Mount Holyoke graduates. Recent graduates continued to fill the position of assistant, especially in the sciences and typically for one year (Alumnae Association of Mount Holyoke College 1937, *One Hundred Year Biographical Directory of Mount Holyoke College 1837–1937*, Bulletin Series 30, No. 5 [South Hadley, MA: Mount Holyoke College, 1937], 11–37). All faculty (exclusive of administrators and assistants) hired between the years 1901 and 1911 were counted. The number of years that they remained at Mount Holyoke placed them into two different categories, those who left before 1912 and those who stayed past that benchmark year. The group of 50 faculty that stayed past 1912 had earned twenty-two doctorates, twelve master's, and three bachelor's degrees. The group of 83 who left before 1912 included thirty-one doctorates, twenty-four master's and fifteen bachelor's degrees. Faculty with earned doctorates represented 44 percent of those who remained at the college, while faculty with earned doctorates who left the college represented 37 percent of the total. There were appointees who did not have a degree or whose degree was not furnished in the directory.

40. By 1915, the faculty would consist of sixteen professors, twenty-nine associate professors, four lecturers and thirty-eight instructors. Salaries ranged from $3,000 for a male full professor to

$600 for a female instructor. The averages of salaries for full professors were $2,500 for the (three) men and $1,900 for the (fourteen) women. For associate professors, the averages were $1,866 for (four) men and $1,361 for (twenty-five) women. The averages for lecturers showed the women receiving higher salaries, $1,425 as opposed to $1,150 for the men. Instructors' salaries were on average very close, $1,100 for the (five) men and $1,016 for the (thirty-three) women. (This information is contained in the answer prepared by Woolley to a questionnaire sent by the Department of the Interior's Bureau of Education collecting Statistics of Colleges and Universities, 1915–1916, MEW Papers, Official Documents, Folder 14, MHA.)

41. "Alumnae Notes," TMH 20 (1910–1911): 438. By July 1, 1911, endowment had reached $861,823. See MEW, *Report of the President, 1901–1911*, 21.

42. Editorial, TMH 20 (1910–1911): 452.

43. In 1906, students debated the idea that courses in domestic science should be offered in the curriculum and the affirmative won. See "College Notes," TMH 15 (1905–1906): 281.

44. MEW, quoted in Wells, 155.

45. MEW, "The Vocational Power of the Women's College," TMH 19 (1909–1910): 172.

46. MEW, "Address at the Inauguration of President Burton" Speech 44 (Smith College, Northampton, Massachusetts), 5 Oct. 1910, 4–6.

47. MHTC 11 (Olive Copeland), 2, 6, 1–2.

48. See MEW, *Annual Report of the President, 1903–1904*, 8.

49. See Warner, 36.

50. See "Report of the Board of Examiners from June 12, 1918, to April 7, 1919," 3, Mount Holyoke College Faculty Committees, Board of Examiners, MHA.

51. Ellen C. Hinsdale, "The New Plan of Admission," *Mount Holyoke Alumnae Quarterly* 1 (1917–1918): 4.

52. That year, Woolley became President of a Phi Beta Kappa charter group that included eleven faculty members, ten members of the class of 1905 and four of the class of 1906. (See "College Notes," TMH 14 (1904–05): 303–5.)

53. See "Woolley, Mary Emma," *Notable American Women: The Modern Period*, 662.

54. MEW, *Report of the President, 1901–1911*, 12.

55. Nineteen were faculty members at colleges (ten at Mount Holyoke), five were high school teachers, seven were still studying, three were married, two still lived at home, and one was doing settlement work. (See Elisabeth S. Williams, "Historical Sketch of the Fellowships," TMH 22 [1912–1913]: 478.)

56. See Editorial, TMH 15 (1905–1906): 234–235. See also "The 'BlackBook,'" TMH 15 (1905–1906): 316–317.

57. Editorial, TMH 12 (1902–1903): 378.

58. See "College Notes," TMH 14 (1904–1905): 221. See also Cole, 275, and Hazel Sanford, "The Students' League—a Sketch of its History," TMH 24 (1914–1915): 469.

59. "Rules, Regulations and Revolution," TMH 30 (1920–1921): 164–165.

60. See "Domestic Work: Students' Opinions, 1900–1901," MHC Student Life, General Folder 3, MHA. Other positive sentiments supporting the system noted that it "gives the girls a chance to meet in an altogether different way," "promotes a democratic spirit," "makes me feel more at home," "gives a girl a personal interest in her college," "allows no class distinctions," "enables girls who otherwise could not afford it to go to college," "teaches a certain class of girls that no one is too good to work," and "gives a foretaste of the cooperative system which seems destined to become prominent in the twentieth century."

61. See "Domestic Work—Faculty Opinions," c. 1901, Mount Holyoke College Student Life, General Folder 2, MHA.

62. Woolley's report emphasized the impracticality of the system and characterized the issue as one of "scientific management" because of the rapid growth of the college. Woolley expressed her view on the academic impact of domestic responsibilities: "I am confident that the large majority of the Faculty feel that the domestic system is responsible for the added pressure." She reported that the work was often "poorly done, with a consequent injurious influence upon the student," arguing that lack of time forced the student to choose academic work over the domestic. Her report included the financial cost of the system and comparative estimates of the differences in cost if women workers were employed to replace students. By 1913, 547 students had domestic duties involving aspects of cleaning and all were under the supervision of one woman. (Duties in academic departments and the library were not included.) Woolley proposed a $50 per student increase in board fees, which would generate $38,500 in added revenue from the 770 students currently enrolled. Even with maximum estimates of the cost for paid maid service as well as paid assistants in the library and laboratories, substantial monies would remain for other college needs. See MEW, "Arguments in Favor of Discontinuance of Domestic work" (c. 1913), MHC Student Life, General Domestic Work Folder 3, MHA, 1.

63. A survey taken in 1916 of the 170 seniors (135 responded) revealed that 94 (70 percent)

had neither earned nor borrowed money to finance their college educations. Twenty-seven students had earned $100 or more and nineteen had borrowed (some both worked and borrowed). Three students had to pay all of their own expenses, receiving no financial support from their families. (See Harriet Pease, "Report of the Second Annual Meeting of the Graduate Council of Mount Holyoke College," TMH 25 [1915–1916]: 437.)

64. See [anonymous student, class of] 1918, "Is College Different?" TMH 27 (1917–1918): 111.

65. See Pease, 438.

66. See "College Provision for Living," 8 March 1916, MEW Papers, Series A, Sub-Series 2, Folder 11, MHA.

67. See, for example, an exchange article from Vassar: Anne Thorpe [Vassar], "The Social Side of Domestic Service at Vassar College," TMH 25 (1916–1917): 364–370. This article describes the organization of the Good Fellowship Club House at Vassar, a place for the housekeeping force, almost all of them young women, to gather socially. The goal of the house was to give "more power" and "opportunity to employees of the college."

68. See note 63 above.

69. Mills was in California, Western and Lake Erie in Ohio and Rockford in Illinois.

70. M. Carey Thomas, letter to MEW, 28 June 1913, MEW Papers, Series 1, Correspondence, Box 1, MHA.

71. Cole, 320.

72. Woolley utilized her presidential report in 1923 to air her frustrations over the never-ending requirements for raising money. The college had just completed a $3 million campaign, the largest in the college's history, and Woolley had been personally involved in an extraordinary amount of fund-raising throughout the country. The efforts were successful, but Woolley argued that a campaign was a waste of the time and energy: "I question whether it is good for a college to have its representative, president or other members of its faculty, subjected to some of the experiences in a campaign" (MEW, *Report of the President, 1920–23* [South Hadley, MA: Mount Holyoke College, 1923], 4.

73. MEW, "The College Woman in This World Leadership" Speech 330 (Association of American Colleges, Chicago, 8 Jan. 1920), 24.

74. MEW, letter to JM, 25 Sept. 1919.

75. MEW, "The College Woman in This World Leadership," 16.

76. MEW, letter to JM, 25 Sept. 1919.

77. MEW, letter to JM, 13 April 1920.

78. MEW, letter to JM, 4 May 1921.

79. MEW, letter to JM, 18 July 1920.

80. MEW, letter to JM, 16 April 1921.

81. MEW, letter to JM, 2 May 1921.

82. MEW, *Report of the President, 1920–23*, 5.

83. MEW, letter to JM, 15 June 1921.

84. MEW, letter to JM, 17 June 1921.

85. MEW, *Report of the President, 1920–23*, 8. For a detailed itinerary of the trip see Edward Burton (Chairman, The China Educational Commission) letter to All Friends of the Commission, 29 July 1921, MEW Papers, Series 1, Correspondence, Box 1, Folder 10.

86. MEW, letter to JM, 6 Nov. 1921.

87. For a classic statement of this alternative analysis of Wilsonian foreign policy, see William A. Williams, *The Tragedy of American Diplomacy* (1959; New York: Dell, 1972), 59–107.

88. MEW, letter to JM, 19 Jan. 1922.

89. See J. Merle Davis, letter to MEW, 13 Nov. 1925, MEW Papers, Series 1, Correspondence, Box 1, Folder 14.

90. J. B. Condliffe, ed., *Problems of the Pacific, Proceedings of the Second Conference of the Institute of Pacific Relations, Honolulu, Hawaii, July 15 to 29, 1927* (Chicago: University of Chicago Press, 1928), v.

91. See J. Merle Davis, "The Institute of Pacific Relations," *International Conciliation*, no. 218 (March 1926): 131–132 (13–14 in pamphlet form) in MEW Papers, Series 1, Correspondence, Box 1, Folder 16.

92. Carter was secretary of the organization from 1926 to 1933. Prior to that, in 1922, he joined the staff of *Inquiry*, a journal focusing on world affairs. He became chairman of that publication, remaining with it for eleven years. He was secretary general of the IPR from 1933 to 1946 and executive vice chairman from 1946 to 1948. In 1948, he became provost of the New School for Social Research, and in 1950 he became director of the New School's division of international studies. (See Edward C. Carter, 1916–1954 Biography, http://cdi.uvm.edu/findingaids/collection/carter.ead.xml#Biography.)

93. See Carter, letter to (Stanford president) Wilbur, 26 April 1926, MEW Papers, Series 1, Correspondence, Box 1, Folder 16.

94. Blakeslee to Carter, 3 May 1926 MEW Papers, Series 1, Correspondence, Box 1, Folder 16.

95. Woolley's recommendations were Grace Abbott, Carrie Chapman Catt, Ada Comstock, Mrs. William Hibbard and Ellen Pendleton. See MEW, letter to Carter, 1 June 1926, MEW Papers, Series 1, Correspondence, Box 1, Folder 16.

96. See MEW, letter to Carter, 23 Nov. 1927, MEW Papers, Series 1, Correspondence, Box 1, Folder 18 (on reverse from Carter to Woolley, 16 Nov. 1927). She would miss the 1929 meeting at

---

Kyoto and the second Pan Pacific Women's Conference in Honolulu in 1930.

97. MEW, "Greetings from Our New President," *Journal of the American Association of University Women* 20 (1926–1927): 99.

98. MEW, letter to Dean Florence Root (Wooster College), 30 March 1929, Reel 48, C-12 AAUWA. See also MHTC, Olive Copeland, 3.

99. See Susan Levine, *Degrees of Equality: The American Association of University Women and the Challenge of Twentieth-Century Feminism* (Philadelphia: Temple University Press, 1995), 19.

100. Kathryn McHale earned a Ph.D. in psychology at Columbia University in 1926 and joined the faculty of Goucher College in Maryland. When she was offered the AAUW position in 1929, she decided to leave the academic world and its restricted opportunities for women. During her twenty-year tenure, McHale unified and strengthened the national organization. (See Levine, 21–22.)

101. Ibid., 27 (quoting Woolley).

102. Ibid., 28.

103. MEW, "Achievement versus Possibility," *Journal of the American Association of University Women* 22 (1928–1929): 172–173.

104. See, for example, Elizabeth Eastman letter to MEW undated [1928], describing the effort of a member of the AAUW to have a pacifist removed from the Women's Joint Congressional Committee. Woolley's responses are contained in MEW, letter to Eastman, 11 Jan. 1928, and MEW, letter to Belle Rankin, Executive Secretary of the Board of Directors of the AAUW, 11 Jan. 1928. By return mail, Rankin advised that the woman in question would be appointed as a "special representative" on the Women's Joint Congressional Committee, a compromise of sorts (Rankin, letter to MEW, 15 Jan. 1928, Reel 48, C-12, AAUWA). For indication that the leadership was strongly anti-militarist, see Rankin, letter to MEW, 29 March 1929: "I personally, am very much opposed to our Association being implicated in, what I firmly believe, a scheme of the War Department to boost military training. What they want to do is to get women enlisted so that they will be willing to wave the flag and boost enlistments and back the War Department and war propaganda, should the possibility of conflict arise" (Reel 48, C-12, AAUWA).

105. Quoted in Wells, 200.

106. Elizabeth Dilling, *Red Revolution: Do We Want It Here?* (Chicago: Published by the Author, 1932). Dilling's major work, *The Red Network* (Chicago: Published by the Author, 1934), was a 350-page book that purported to expose subversive supporters of Communism in America.

Woolley's entry reads: "Woolley, Miss Mary E.: pres. Mt. Holyoke Coll.; Russ.Reconst.Rams, 1925; A.C.L.U. Mass.Com.; nat.advis.com. Sacco-V. Nat. Lg.; Nat.Citiz.Com.Rel. Lat. Am. 1927; vice pres. Nat.Cons. Lg.; Nat. World Ct. Com. 1931; dir.Lg. of Nations ssn. And vice chmn. Of its Mass. Br.; endors. Com. World Peaceways; celg. Disarm. Conf. 1932; Griffen Bill sponsor; nat. bd. Y.W.C.A.; advis. Com. Am . Assn. Lab. Legis.; advis. Com. Open Road (affiliate of Intourist of Soviet Govt.); Nat. Coun. Congl. Chs. in U.S.; signer Fell. Recon. Pet. Tuss. Recog. 1932; Lg. Women Voters; nat. coun. C.M.E.; Peace Patriots; vic pres. Fell. Faiths nat. com. 300, 1933; Nat. Save Our Schs. Com.; endors. Lane Pamphlet" (335). Dillings notes that all individuals listed in her book through their membership in "Communist, Anarchist, Socialist, I.W.W. or Pacifist-controlled organizations ... knowingly or unknowingly, have contributed in some measure to one or more phases of the Red movement in the United States" (258–259). A quick glance at the book shows that Jane Addams, Eleanor Roosevelt, Senator William Borah of Idaho and Woolley's friend Smith College president William Neilson are part of Dillings' fantasy world of the "red network."

107. See "Miss Woolley Chapter Won't Recognize Ban," *Springfield Republican,* 4 April 1928, MEW Papers, Biographical Information, 1895–1947, Box 75 Folder 3 (Articles 1913–1929). In 1937, the Pawtucket Chapter sent Woolley a greeting restating their pleasure that she had "always remained a member" (Pawtucket Daughters of the American Revolution, letter to MEW, 26 May 1937, MEW Papers, Correspondence. MHA).

108. The *Springfield Republican* article is in MEW Papers, Series 14, Box 75, Folder 3.

109. See "Women Leaders Join in Peace Parade," *Christian Science Monitor,* 19 Jan. 1931, MEW Papers, Series 14, Box 75, MHA.

110. Alice Booth, "America's Twelve Greatest Women: Mary E. Woolley," *Good Housekeeping,* March 1931, 200–2004. See also "The Complete Roster of America's Greatest Women," *Good Housekeeping,* March 1931, 342. The women were selected by the readers of *Good Housekeeping* and a panel of five men: Newton Baker, Bruce Barton, Booth Tarkington, Henry Van Dyke and Otto H. Kahn. The women in addition to Woolley were Grace Abbott, Jane Addams, Cecilia Beaux, Martha Berry, Willa Cather, Carrie Chapman Cott, Grace Coolidge, Minnie Maddern Fiske, Helen Keller, Florence Rena Sabin, and Ernestine Schumann-Heink.

111. MEW, letter to Cheney, 15 June 1931, MEW Papers, Series 1, Correspondence, MHA. In this letter, Woolley noted the board's request

that she stay on until 1934 rather than retire upon reaching the age of seventy.

112. Boyd Edwards joined the Mount Holyoke Board of Trustees in 1920 and resigned in 1937.

113. The board consisted of twenty-five members plus the president ex officio. Twenty trustees elected by a two-thirds vote of all trustees present served ten-year terms while five alumnae trustees (elected by the alumnae) served five-year terms.

114. George W. Pierson, *Yale College and University, 1871–1937*, vol. 2: *Yale—the University College* (New Haven, CT: Yale University Press, 1955), 507.

115. See Edwards, letter to MEW, 20 Oct. 1930, Folder 1, Boyd Edwards Papers, MHA.

116. See MEW, letter to Edwards, 25 Oct. 1930, Folder 1, Boyd Edwards Papers, MHA.

117. Edwards, letter to MEW, 13 Nov. 1930, Folder 1, Boyd Edwards Papers, MHA.

118. See Edwards to Cheney, 13 April 1931, Folder 2, Boyd Edwards Papers, MHA.

119. See MEW, letter to Edwards, 2 April 1931, Folder 2, Boyd Edwards Papers, MHA.

120. See MHTC 11 (Olive Copeland), 2.

121. White was a Holyoke businessman who had been on the board since 1920. He was director of the Holyoke Public Library, director of the YMCA, and chairman of the City Planning Board and served on both the Holyoke School Board and City Council.

122. See Edwards, letter to White, 15 April 1931, Folder 2, Boyd Edwards Papers, MHA.

123. Frederick Winslow Taylor was a mechanical engineer who proposed what he called "scientific management," which was a way that business owners could get the maximum amount of effort out of their employees. See Taylor, *Principles of Scientific Management* (New York and London: Harper & Brothers, 1911).

124. Wells, 228. Woolley realized this as early as 1931. In a letter to Marks she noted that trustee White believed that "Mr. Kendall is the 'opposition' " (MEW, letter to JM, 13 June 1931).

125. On this decision, see MEW, letter to Cheney, 15 June 1931. See also Edwards, letter to MEW, 16 June 1931, Folder 2, Boyd Edwards Papers, MHA.

126. "Selection of Miss Woolley Is Criticized," *Springfield Evening Union*, 24 Dec. 1931, Seri-Container 48 (Folio), n.p. [13], MEW Scrapbook, 1932–1945, MHA.

127. See "Picks Miss Woolley as Arms Delegate," *New York Times*, 24 Dec. 1931, 1, 6.

128. See Kendall, letter to MEW, 28 Dec. 1931, MEW Papers, Series 1, Correspondence Box 3, Folder 2. (A letter from Furniss—27 Dec. 1931—is in Folder 1.) Woolley's note to the

trustees as well as the many responses and congratulations she received are in numerous folders from Box 3 and two folders from Box 2 as well—see MEW Papers, Series 1 Correspondence 1, Box 2, Folders 12 and 13.

129. Carrie Chapman Catt, letter to MEW, 21 Dec. 1931, MEW Papers, Series 1, Correspondence, Box 3, Folder 4. The details of the discussions with Hoover over Judge Florence Allen and his quoted statement are all contained in this letter.

130. See confidential telegram, Dorothy Detzer to MEW, 18 Dec. 1931. See Woolley's responses, telegrams, MEW to Detzer, 18 Dec. 1931 and 21 Dec. 1931, MEW Papers, Series 1, Correspondence Box 3, Folder 6.

131. See MEW to Catt, 23 Dec. 1931, MEW Papers, Series 1, Correspondence, Box 3.

132. "Hoover Names Dr. Woolley," *Boston Globe*, 24 Dec. 1931, 1.

133. *Springfield Evening Union*, 24 Dec. 31, MEW Papers, Series B, Container 48 (Folio), n.p. [13].

134. The statement is included in Nellie Neilson, letter to MEW, 30 Dec. 1931, MEW Papers, Series 1, Correspondence 1931, Box 3, MHA.

135. Ellen and Mignon Talbot, letter to MEW, 28 Dec. 1931, MEW Papers, Series 1, Correspondence Box 3, Folder 6, MHA.

136. Barnes, letter to MEW, 31 Dec. 1931, MEW Papers, Series 1, Correspondence Box 3, MHA.

137. "Hoover Names Dr. Woolley."

138. "Selection of Miss Woolley is Criticized"

139. She was a writer, educator, anti-suffragist and founder of Barnard College

140. *Weekly News* 9, no. 1 (1 Jan. 1932), New York League of Women Voters. The article concluded: "We believe that Miss Woolley's presence will help to keep to the fore what seems easily to slip of mind, the deep conviction of the rank and file of thoughtful men and women who now know beyond misunderstanding what war is and now that to win peace, sacrifices must be made, even danger faced. But at the moment the picture that rises clearest in our minds is that of the solitary grave on the Mount Holyoke campus of a devout and dauntless woman who builded better than she knew." The article is enclosed in Meyer, letter to MEW, 7 Jan. 1932, MEW Papers, Series 1, Correspondence Box 4, Folder 7.

141. Matthew Woll, open letter (addressed "Dear Sir or Madam"), 19 Oct. 1931, attached to Woll, letter to MEW, 12 Jan. 1932, MEW Papers, Series 1, Correspondence Box 4, Folder 9.

142. MEW, letter to Mary Augusta Clark, 18 Jan. 1932, MEW Papers, Series 1, Correspondence Box 4, Folder 1. Woolley was responding to a let-

ter Clark had received from Mrs. Lillian Burr Whitman dated 1/12/32, which Clark had sent to Woolley's secretary, Olive Copeland. In this letter, Whitman reported criticisms of Woolley that were no doubt found in the Dillings pamphlet *Red Revolution*. A speaker from the Massachusetts DAR had addressed the Bronxville Chapter "reading from the literature compiled by these red groups." Whitman reported: "Miss Woolley's name was on the boards, or a member, of a dozen or more societies which were distinctly socialistic in their tendencies, yes red at the foundation, such as the Sacco-Vanzetti affair." She closed with a warning that: "It would be humiliating to Mount Holyoke and all of her friends if Miss Woolley should be recalled and yet there are people working, I am certain, towards such an end."

143. Allyn was a graduate of Mount Holyoke who had earned a master's and Ph.D. from the University of Chicago. She was a professor of anthropology at Mount Holyoke until she became the academic dean in 1929.

144. MEW, Draft ms., *Introduction to my Career as a Diplomat*, MEW Papers, Autobiographical Materials, Box 1, 1.

145. Will Rogers, letter to *New York Times*, 2 Feb. 1932, MEW Papers, Scrapbooks Geneva, 47 MHA, n.p. [1].

146. The statement by the National Council for Prevention of War is included in Neilson, letter to MEW, 30 Dec. 1931.

147. Letter, (Mrs. Edwin) Johnson to MEW, 18 Jan 1932, MEW Papers, Series 1, Correspondence Box 5, Folder 5.

148. Balch, letter to MEW, 29 Dec. 1931, MEW Papers, Series 1, Correspondence Box 3, Folder 6.

149. Balch in ibid. expressed such concerns.

150. Catt, letter to MEW, 1 March 1931, MEW Papers, Series 1, Correspondence Box 4, Folder 9.

151. Catt, letter to MEW, 6 Feb. 1932, MEW Papers, Series 1, Correspondence Box 4, Folder 9.

152. Quoted in Wells, 221.

153. MEW to JM, 21 Feb. 1932.

154. "That Woman, Woolley!" quoted in Editorials, *Journal of the American Association of University Women* 27 (1933–1934): 171.

155. MEW, *Introduction to My Career as a Diplomat*, 6–7.

156. Ibid., 1.

157. MEW, letter to "Mr. Ambassador" [Gibson], 2 July 1932, MEW Papers, Series C, Box 28, 2. Quoted in Meeropol, 325.

158. MEW, letter to JM, 19 March 1932.

159. MEW, letter to JM, 22 April 1932.

160. MEW, letter to JM, 21 Feb. 1932.

161. MEW, letter to JM, 28 May 1932.

162. MEW, letter to JM, 2 June 1932.

163. MEW, letter to Gibson, 15 June 1932, MEW Papers, Series C, Box 28. Quoted in Meeropol, 325.

164. MEW, letter to JM, 20 May 1932.

165. Quoted in MEW, *Introduction to My Career as a Diplomat*, 31.

166. MEW, letter to JM, 7 July 1932.

167. MEW, "What Happened at Geneva?" *Journal of the American Association of University Women* 26 (1932–1933): 70.

168. MEW, letters to the Trustees and to the Class of 1932 enclosed in MEW to Olive Copeland, 1 June 1932, MEW Papers, Series 1 Correspondence Box 3, Folder 8.

169. Allyn, letter to MEW, 10 April 1932, Box 3, Folder 7. She was referring to financial difficulties and efforts to cut teacher salaries, among other pressing issues.

170. See MEW, letter to President Herbert Hoover, 9 Aug. 1932. See also Herbert Hoover, letter to MEW, 19 Aug. 1932, Jeannette Marks Collection, Box 112, Folder 2, WCSC, also available in MEW Papers, Series 1 Correspondence Box 3.

171. See MEW, letter to Morgan, 24 Oct. 1932, MEW Papers, Series 1, Correspondence Box 4, Folder 9. This folder contains many letters back and forth between Woolley and Morgan.

172. MEW, letter to Gibson, 8 March 1933, MEW Papers, Series 1, Correspondence Box 4.

173. See President Franklin D. Roosevelt, letter to MEW, 19 Sept. 1933, MEW Papers, Series 1, Correspondence Box 5.

174. Corbett-Ashby, letter to MEW, 19 Jan. 1934. MEW Papers, series 1, Correspondence Box 5, Folder 10.

175. See MEW, letter to Morgan, 21 March 1934, MEW Papers, Series 1, Correspondence Box 5.

176. Kathleen Courtney, WILPFUK, Laura Puffer Morgan National Committee on Cause and Cure of War and AUW, Emilie Gourd, Swiss feminist leader, letter to twenty heads of delegations, 31 May 1934. MEW Papers, Series 1, Correspondence Box 5.

177. See McHale, letter to MEW, 20 April 1935, Reel 89, H-34, AAUWA. (This is the same letter referenced in the prologue.)

Chapter 3

1. See Harvey to Edwards, 25 March 1931, Folder 2, Boyd Edwards Papers, MHA.

2. See Harvey to Edwards, 31 March 1931, Folder 2, Boyd Edwards Papers, MHA.

3. Edwards to Harvey, 27 March 1931, Folder 2, Boyd Edwards Papers, MHA.

4. Harvey to Edwards, 31 March 1931.

5. Edwards to Harvey, 6 April 1931, Folder 2, Boyd Edwards Papers, MHA.

6. Cole, 337.

7. See President of the Board of Trustees, letter to the Mount Holyoke Alumnae Association of _____, 9 June 1931. It was proposed to send this to all associations "Who have specifically addressed the Board of Trustees on the subject of [Woolley's] retirement" (Cheney to MEW, 10 June 1931). See Woolley's reply to Cheney, 15 June 1931, MEW Papers, Series 1, Correspondence.

8. MEW, letter to JM, 13 June 1931.

9. See Speers to Edwards, 2 April 1931, Folder 2, Boyd Edwards Papers, MHA.

10. See Edwards to MEW, 6 April 1931, Folder 2, Boyd Edwards Papers, MHA.

11. This is a letter to board member F. B. Towne, 14 April 1931, Folder 2, Boyd Edwards Papers, MHA.

12. Edwards to White, 15 April 1931, Folder 2, Boyd Edwards Papers, MHA.

13. See Susan D. Arnold to Edwards, 20 Oct. 1931, Folder 2, Boyd Edwards Papers, MHA.

14. Edwards to Newhall, 14 Nov. 1931, Folder 2, Boyd Edwards Papers, MHA.

15. The well-known George Washington Plunkitt of Tammany Hall who died in 1924 was known for having said. "I seen my opportunities and I took 'em." See "Old-Time Tammany Leader Saw His Opportunities and Took Them," *New York Times*, 23 Nov. 1924.

16. Brotherton to Edwards, 18 Feb. 1932, Folder 2, Boyd Edwards Papers, MHA.

17. MEW to Edwards, 22 Sept. 1932, Folder 2, Boyd Edwards Papers, MHA.

18. See Marks, 155.

19. See Laura Wild (Professor Department of History and the Literature of Religion) to Edwards, 1 Sept. 1933. See also Edwards to Hyde, 15 Sept. 1933, Hyde to Edwards, 22 Sept. 1933, and Wild to Edwards, 1 Nov. 1933. All in Folder 4, Boyd Edwards Papers, MHA.

20. MEW to Edwards, 21 Nov. 1933, Folder 4, Boyd Edwards Papers, MHA.

21. Edwards to MEW, 22 Nov. 1933, Boyd Edwards Papers, Folder 4. MHA.

22. See Edwards to Arnold, 28 Feb. 1934, Boyd Edwards Papers, Folder 5, MHA.

23. See Arnold to Edwards, Feb. 1934, Folder 5, Boyd Edwards Papers, MHA. For the Board of Trustees in 1936 see Appendix. For the dates of when all trustees joined and left the board see www.mtholyoke.edu/archives/history/trustees18 36.

24. The percentage of women serving on the Mount Holyoke board was significantly lower (even including the provision for five alumnae trustees) than at Wellesley and Bryn Mawr.

25. Carlisle Bergeron, "A Person Named Perkins: After Five Years in Office, the Secretary of Labor Is Still Public Puzzle Number One." *The Commentator*, Feb. 1938, 106. This article is available in the Frances Perkins Press Clippings Compilation, MHA. It is quoted in a student paper: Gayle Higgins, "An Analysis of Topics Covered by the Press Regarding Frances Perkins," 14 April 1992, MHA.

26. See George W. Martin, *Madam Secretary, Frances Perkins* (Boston: Houghton Mifflin, 1976), 49–51.

27. Frances Perkins, memorandum enclosed in letter to Hugh Hawkins, 21 Sept. 1961, Frances Perkins Papers, Correspondence Folder 10, MHA, 3.

28. In this regard, consider the following letter of recommendation for the ultimately successful candidate, Roswell Gray Ham, written by Charles Seymour, then provost of Yale: "If [Ham] were made head of Mount Holyoke College, I should see him go with the same sort of regret that I saw Valentine go to Rochester, but with the feeling that Yale was fulfilling a duty to American education which has become traditional with us: That of preparing first-rate young men for our educational responsibilities and giving other educational institutions the benefit. After all, Yale as a great educational institution of America will in the long run profit thereby" (enclosed Cheney to Morrison, 27 May 1935. Records of the Committee of Nine [hereinafter CON] Box 2, Folder 6). Part of this quote is included in the prologue.

29. See "Report Dr. Merrill Will Be Miss Woolley's Successor" in CON, Box 3, Folder 1.

30. See Morrison to W.G. Dwight (editor of the *Holyoke Transcript and Telegram*), 26 July 1934, CON Box 3, Folder 1.

31. Keyes, letter to Morrison, 6 July 1934, CON Box 3, Folder 1.

32. See Keyes to Morrison, 12 July 1934, CON Box 3, Folder 1.

33. Keyes to Morrison, 18 July 1934, CON Box 3, Folder 1.

34. See "Mount Holyoke Students Resent Statements in Magazine Article," *Springfield Republican*, 29 Sept. 1934 (*Time* quotes included in this article; see *Time*, 28 Sept. 1934).

35. See Keyes to Morrison, 18 July 1934.

36. See *Notable American Women*, 661.

37. See "Mount Holyoke Students Resent Statements in Magazine Article."

38. At the time, Cheney was sixty-four,

Kendall fifty-seven, and Keyes fifty-four. Maguire was thirty-seven and married to a Harvard law professor, had two children, and had earned a Ph.D. from Radcliffe College.

39. The letters from Morrison to the four board members (Kendall, Bishop, Maguire, Cheney) is from 8 Oct. 1934. Bishop's response is from 11 Oct. 1934. CON Box 3, Folder 1.

40. Quoted in *One Hundred Year Biographical Directory of Mount Holyoke College 1837–1937*, Bulletin Series 30, no. 5 (South Hadley, MA: Alumnae Association of Mount Holyoke College, 1937), 112.

41. See Cheney to Morrison, 27 Dec. 1934 CON Box 1, Folder 3.

42. See "Copy of Mr. Morrison's Reply to Mrs. Cooper's Letter of Inquiry," 19 Feb. 1937, "Copy of Letter of Inquiry from Mrs. Cooper to Mr. Morrison," 5 Feb 1937, "Memorandum by Mrs. Mary Hume Maguire," all available in RGH Papers, Series A, Sub-Series 1, Folder 13.

43. See Woolley to Morrison, 28 Nov. 1934, CON Box 2, Folder 6.

44. Edward W. Tayler, "In Memoriam: Marjorie Hope Nicolson (1894–1981)," *Journal of the History of Ideas* 42, no. 4, 665.

45. Nicolson, speech to Smith student body, 5 Oct. 1938, Faculty Nicolson, Marjorie Hope Box 3. Smith College Archives.

46. See Tayler, 666.

47. Marjorie Hope Nicolson, "The Rights and Privileges Pertaining Thereof," Address (condensed) delivered at the celebration of the centennial of the establishment of the University of Michigan, 14–17 June 1937, *Journal of the American Association of University Women* 31 (April 1938): 139–141.

48. From a *New York Times Magazine* article 17 March 1940.

49. See Woolley to Morrison, 28 Nov. 1934.

50. The Kendall Questionnaire is in CON, Box 3 Folder 1 (attached to Logan to Morrison, 1/3/35 and Morrison to Logan 1/7/35).

51. See Cheney to Morrison, 14 Jan. 1935, CON Box 3, Folder 1.

52. The statement was organized into five sections: "Introduction," "My Proposition—Young Woman," "Answer to Arguments for Man President," "Positive Arguments in Favor of Selecting a Woman" and "Conclusion." It is enclosed with Keyes to Morrison, 18 July 1934 CON Box 3 Folder 1. For Keyes' desire to send it to other members of the committee, see Keyes to Morrison, 1/2/35 CON Box 3 Folder 1 (Keyes misdated it 1/2/34 but the correct date is clear from context).

53. Morrison to Keyes, 11 Jan. 1935, CON Box 3, Folder 1.

54. Keyes, letter to Perkins, 18 Jan. 1935, quoted in Martin, 369–370. Keyes continued: "Mr. Kendall's arguments emphasize the following ideas: 1. We need some strong professor to replace the many soon to retire, and a man can get better ones, especially men. 2. A man with a nice wife would give social tone which the faculty has lacked. 3. A man can be a good pal with men outside (raising money, I suppose). Some of these seem to me to have some force, but I contend that the answer is always that for the essential ones, a really *good* woman would be as efficient."

55. Perkins, letter to Keyes, 23 Jan. 1935, quoted in Martin, 370.

56. See Newhall to Morrison, 9 March 1935, CON Box 3, Folder 1.

57. See Morrison to MEW, 4 Dec. 1935; MEW to Morrison, 8 Dec. 1935, CON Box 2, Folder 6.

58. Keyes to Morrison, 9 March 1935, CON Box 3, Folder 1.

59. All quotes from (David) Adams to Morrison, 3/23/35 CON Box 3 Folder 1. This was a follow-up to (David) Adams (for the Faculty Conference Committee) to Morrison, 18 March 1935, FCC Box 2, Folder 7, MHA. This letter attached extracts from the Minutes of the FCC meeting of 4 Feb. 1932 reporting a request from the board of trustees for the appointment of two faculty members to serve as non-voting members of a committee to be appointed by the board to consider the choice of Woolley's successor. The committee had consulted acting president (dean) Harriet Allyn, who argued that because Woolley was in Geneva it would be an "unfortunate time to discuss the matter of [Woolley's] successor." Allyn had persuaded the FCC to defer choosing the two members at that time.

60. See Helen E. Patch, Secretary to the FCC, to Heads of Departments, 20 Feb. 1935, CON Box 1, Folder 1.

61. See Ann Haven Morgan to Morrison, 4 Feb. 1935, CON Box 1, Folder 1.

62. Ellen B. Talbot to David Adams, Chair of the FCC, 21 March 1935, FCC Papers, MHA.

63. Rogers Rusk to FCC, 18 March 1935, CON Box 1, Folder 1.

64. John M. Warbeke to the Board of Trustees FCC, 3 April 1935, CON Box 1, Folder 1.

65. "Memorandum by Mary Hume Maguire," RGH Papers, Series A, Sub-series 1, Folder 13, 1–2.

66. The list is included in Maguire to A. Elizabeth Adams, 8 May 1935, AEA Papers, Box 1, Folder 1, MHA.

67. David Adams to Morrison, 18 March 1935, CON Box 2, Folder 7.

68. Morrison to David Adams, 3 April 1935, CON, Box 1, Folder 1.

69. See Alzada Comstock to Morrison, 7 April 1935 CON Box 3, Folder 3. This letter was in response to Morrison to Comstock, 2 April 1935.

70. See Morgan to Mount Holyoke College Faculty, 25 April 1935 and 30 April 1935 CON Box 3 Folder 1.

71. Ann Haven Morgan, "Mount Holyoke's Next President, Comments and Discussion," *Mount Holyoke Alumnae Quarterly* 19, no. 1 (May 1935): 28–29.

72. Morrison to Morgan, 29 April 1935, CON Box 2, Folder 6.

73. Telegram, Frances Perkins to A. Elizabeth Adams, 30 April 1935, AEA Papers, Box 1 Folder 7, MHA.

74. See Kendall to Glass, Kendall to Wriston, Kendall to Keyes all 29 April 1935 in CON, Box 2 Folder 7.

75. Maguire to Professor Mary Sherrill [Mount Holyoke College], 10 May 1935, CON Box 3, Folder 1.

76. See, for example, Corinne Loomis, '11, to Morrison, 8 May 1935, CON Box 2, Folder 6.

77. Maybe Louise Dunbar '16 to Morrison, 18 May 1935, CON Box 2, Folder 6.

78. Eunice Goddard '03 to Morrison, 16 May 1935, CON Box 2, Folder 6.

79. Mary Ely Lyman to Morgan, 1 May 1935, CON Box 2, Folder 8.

80. Ursula Hubbard '26 to Morrison, 4 May 1935, CON Box 2, Folder 7. Hubbard at the time was working for the Carnegie Endowment for International Peace.

81. Former faculty member at MHC Eleanor Wembridge to Morrison, 4 May 1935. CON Box 2 Folder 7.

82. A graduate student in zoology at Johns Hopkins University, Elizabeth Kirkwood.

83. Telegram, Marion Park to Morgan, 26 April 1935. CON Box 2 Folder 7. Park as president of Bryn Mawr College noted that she hesitated "to express myself on plans of another college" and so confined her telegram to the general statement quoted.

84. Ellen Deborah Ellis (History Dept. MHC) to Morrison, 2 May 1935, CON Box 2, Folder 7.

85. See Chapter 2.

86. McHale to MEW, 20 April 1935, Reel 89, H-34, AAUWA.

87. MEW to McHale, 23 May 1935, Reel 89, H-34, AAUWA.

88. AAUW general director's letter, *Journal of the American Association of University Women* 2–3, no. 5 (October 1934–June 1936): 13–15. In 1934, the Committee on the Economic and Legal Status of Women met in New York City and their activities were summarized in the June, 1935 issue. They wanted more intensive studies on how the depression had affected women and warned: "It is hoped that university women will recognize their responsibility in helping to shape developments in this country, so that they will be in no danger of being caught unawares by a movement which threatens all their hard-won gains, as has happened in more than one European country." Among the members were the lawyer-activist Dorothy Kenyon, the management expert Dr. Lillian Gilbreth and Susan Kingbury. (See *Journal of the American Association of University Women* [June 1935]: 239.)

89. Like Woolley, she was committed to fostering scholarly research among the faculty and students and she was achieving this through the aggressive hiring of scholars particularly in the social sciences, where the carryover into social service opportunities was possible (Dzuback, 188, HofEQ).

90. See MEW to Morrison, 26 April 1935, CON Box 3, Folder 1.

91. See A. Elizabeth Adams to Morrison, 28 April 1935, CON Box 1, Folder 1.

92. Morrison to Adams, 1 May 1935, CON Box 1. This could hardly have been reassuring to Adams, who, along with many of her colleagues on the faculty, believed that the best approach was to find a young, outstanding woman scholar and let her grow into the administrative aspects of the job—as had Woolley.

93. Keyes to Adams, 28 April 1935, AEA Papers, Box 1, Folder 7, MHA.

94. Adams to Keyes, 1 May 1935, AEA Papers, Box 1, Folder 7, MHA.

95. Maguire prepared the list and sent it to Adams on May 8. See Maguire to Adams, 8 May 1935, AEA Papers, Box 1, Folder 7, MHA.

96. Morrison to Cheney, 3 May 1935, CON Box 2, Folder 7.

97. Cheney to Morrison, 11 May 1935, CON Box 3, Folder 1.

98. See Cheney to Morrison, 7 May 1935, CON Box 3, Folder 1.

99. Cheney to Morrison, 15 May 1935, CON Box 3, Folder 1, (Morrison wrote in the margin: "I wonder why?").

100. Cheney to Morrison, 7 May 1935, CON Box 3, Folder 1.

101. See Morrison to Keyes, 3 June 35, CON Box 2, Folder 7.

102. See Cheney to Morrison, 27 May 1935, CON Box 2, Folder 7.

103. Morrison to Cheney, 29 May 1935, CON Box 2, Folder 7.

104. See Nicolson to Morrison, 4 June 1935, CON Box 2, Folder 8.

105. Nicolson to Neilson, n.d. [June 1935], Neilson Presidential Records, Box 19, Folder 3, Smith College Archive. In describing the offer, Nicolson called the college Holy Oak to emphasis the traditional religious focus of the college and perhaps to also emphasize her religious unconventionality.

106. See Maguire to Florence Clement (editor of the *Alumnae Quarterly*), 21 June 1935, CON Box 2, Folder 7.

107. See quote in the Prologue. MEW to the Rev. Rockwell Harmon Potter, 1 July 1935. CON Box 3 Folder 3.

108. MEW to Maguire, 1 July 1935, CON Box 3, Folder 3. Woolley felt it necessary to give all these details to give an impression in Maguire's letter there was a clear tone suggesting that Woolley was not focusing fully on college issues.

109. Pratt to Morrison, 27 July 1935, CON Box 2, Folder 7.

110. Tom Mooney and Warren Billings were labor leaders in San Francisco who had been convicted of a 1916 bombing of a pro-war march. Mooney was sentenced to death, Billings to life imprisonment. Because of the intervention of President Woodrow Wilson, Mooney's death penalty had been commuted to life imprisonment. By the early 1920s the case against Mooney had been exposed as a frame-up, as many of the people who conspired in that effort recanted their testimony. Yet for over twenty years Republican governors of California refused to pardon Mooney and Billings. Their case became a national and international cause celebre, and when a Democratic governor was elected in 1938, he immediately pardoned both men. See http://www.spartacus.schoolnet.co.uk/USAmooney case.htm.

111. Morrison to Bishop, 7 Aug. 1935, CON Box 2, Folder 7.

112. Maguire to Morrison, 19 Aug. 1935, CON Box 2, Folder 7. Morriss had been a professor of history and an administrator at Mount Holyoke College. Woolley had given Morriss support and guidance in a professional life that closely paralleled her own. See "AAUW News and Notes," *Journal of the American Association of University Women* 30 (1936–1937): 229.

113. Henry Gideonse to Kendall, 20 Aug. 1935, CON Folder 2, Box 8. This was in response to a letter sent by Kendall to Gideonse 14 Aug. 1935, CON Box 2, Folder 8.

Chapter 4

1. Morrison to Thompson, 30 Sept. 1935, CON Box 2, Folder 7.

2. See MEW to Morrison, 28 Oct. 1935, CON Box 2, Folder 7. She enclosed the recommendation from President Wilbur of Stanford that had been sent a week earlier.

3. Morrison to MEW, 29 Oct. 1935, CON Box 2, Folder 7.

4. See telegram, Morrison to Cheney, 1 Nov. 1935, CON Box 2, Folder 7. It is likely that between May and the fall someone who had access to the list would have shared it with Woolley, but there is no direct evidence of that.

5. For biographical and professional information on Bixler, see the Finding Aid to the Julius Seelye Bixler Papers, 1926–1969, in the Smith College Archives.

6. Kendall to Morrison, 29 Oct. 1935, CON Box 2, Folder 8.

7. Telegram, Morrison to Cheney, 1 Nov. 1935, CON Box 2, Folder 8.

8. Cheney to Morrison, 5 Nov. 1935, CON Box 2, Folder 8.

9. Adams to Morrison, 5 Nov. 1935, AEA Papers. Box 1, Folder 7, MHA.

10. Keyes to Adams, 11/14/35. AEA Papers, Box 1, Folder 7, MHA.

11. Kendall to Adams, 15 Nov. 1935, AEA Papers, 15 Nov. 1935, Box 1, Folder 7, MHA.

12. Enclosed with Morgan to Morrison, 7 Nov. 1935, CON Box 2, Folder 6. The typed copy of the letter has no salutation but begins: "I am sending this letter to each member of the Board of Trustees" (6 Nov. 1935). Cheney's response to Morgan is dated 11/16/35 and is enclosed with Cheney to Morrison of the same date (CON Box 2, Folder 6).

13. Cheney to Morrison, 16 Nov. 1935.

14. Morrison to Cheney, 19 Nov. 1935, CON Box 2, Folder 6.

15. See Arthur Bradford to Cheney, 7 Nov. 1935, and Diocesan House, Boston to Cheney, 12 Nov. 1935, CON, Box 2 Folder 6. Cheney also received a note from Professor Ernest Hocking of Harvard who stated "Bixler strikes me as a man of executive quality ..." 8 Nov. 1935, CON, Box 2, Folder 6.

16. Memo from Morrison, 29 Nov. 1935, CON Box 2, Folder 6, MHA, referencing a telephone call with Nicolson.

17. Brinton visited Boston from California at Mount Holyoke's expense and finally met with Morrison. Among the suggested candidates, fifty-three-year-old Sarah Wambaugh, an eminent American political scientist and one of the world's leading experts on plebiscites, a new field of study, emerged. She had spent ten years working with the Women's Educational and Industrial Union of Boston. It was unlikely that Wambaugh was interested in the presidency of Mount Holyoke,

but whether she was interested or not, what is significant is that the faculty recommendations included the most outstanding women of the era, those who combined intellectual accomplishment with social activism that took many and varied forms. For one recommendation of Wambaugh, see Ellen Deborah Ellis to Morrison, 28 Nov. 1935, CON Box 1.

18. For one recommendation of Schenck, see Ellis to Morrison, op cit. The quote from Park as well as Keyes' responses to Maguire and to the negative views of M. Carey Thomas, the former president of Bryn Mawr, and Millicent Carey McIntosh, her niece and headmistress of the Brearly School, are contained in Keyes to Morrison, 24 Nov. 1935, CON, Box 2, Folder 6. Thomas had made disparaging comments about Schenck that President Park told Keyes to disregard. Thomas apparently did not want Schenck to create the graduate program at Bryn Mawr.

19. Keyes to Morrison, 29 Nov. 1935, CON Box 2, Folder 6.

20. Morrison to Keyes, 2 Dec. 1935, CON Box 2, Folder 6.

21. Cheney to Morrison, 6 Dec. 1935, CON Box 2, Folder 6.

22. Woolley and Morrison had had a conversation on the matter on December 3, 1935. See MEW to Morrison, 8 Dec. 1935, CON Box 2, Folder 6.

23. Cheney's document was titled "Memorandum on the Problems Involved in the Selection of a President of Mount Holyoke College." It is typed and dated Dec. 7, 1935 (CON Box 2, Folder 6). All subsequent quotes are from this document.

24. Keyes' document was titled "A Statement of Consideration Indicating the Advisability of Choosing a Woman as President to Succeed President Woolley upon Her Retirement" (CON Box 3, Folder 1). See Chapter 3.

25. Morrison to Cheney, 9 Dec. 1935, CON Box 2, Folder 6.

26. On this issue, see Miriam R. Levin, *Defining Women's Scientific Enterprise: Mount Holyoke College and the Rise of American Science* (Hanover, NH, and London: University Press of New England, 2005), especially chapter 5.

27. Morrison to Cheney, 9 Dec. 1935.

28. Keyes to Morrison, 15 Dec. 1935, CON Box 2, Folder 6.

29. Keyes to Morrison, 11 Jan. 1936, CON Box 2, Folder 6.

30. Furniss to RGH [n.d.], RGH Papers, Series A, Sub-Series 1, Folder 9. (The information about the offer of the principalship to Professor Hopkins is in an enclosure from Viola Barnes.)

31. Though Meta Glass had a Ph.D., Morrison pursued the arguably insulting habit (which he

and other board members used with Woolley despite her numerous honorary doctorates) of not describing Glass with the title "Dr." but instead using "Miss."

32. The implication of this quote (and the earlier reference to Bixler's inability to understand Elliot's point) is that one of Woolley's failings was her unwillingness to "give pain" to the faculty. Certainly, those on the board who hoped Glass would not take the job felt one of the strikes against her was that she was too much like Woolley (single, older, involved with outside activities). However, the implication that Woolley could not or would not "give pain" is totally false. Woolley was a supporter of faculty self-government, but according to the short biography in *Notable American Women* she "presided deftly at monthly faculty meetings, using humor to ease tension. Sometimes she allayed clashes by reorganizing departments. When necessary, however, she did not shrink from causing pain" (661). The author quoted a letter Woolley wrote to a disappointed would-be department chair: "It is not fair to save the feelings of one or two people at the expense of the students, other members of the staff and the college ...[T]he question must be considered impersonally and 'in the large.'" (quoted from Marks, 67).

33. See Morrison, letter to Furniss, 19 March 1936, CON Box 2, Folder 5.

34. See Furniss to Morrison, 1 April 1936, CON Box 2, Folder 5.

35. MHTC (Olive Copeland), 6.

36. For more details on the McIntosh "offer" See Chapter 6.

37. How would Copeland know the salary offer was "so low?" Perhaps she heard it from Woolley, who was a close colleague of Glass' and who therefore might have learned it directly from Glass. This, of course, conflicts with Glass' public reason for declining the offer. If Copeland is right, Glass must have privately shared the information about the low salary offer but adopted a very different public posture.

38. See Morrison to Bishop, et al., 28 May 1936. Quote from Morrison to Cheney, 28 May 1936, CON Box 2, Folder 5.

39. Bishop, letter to AEA, 25 Jan. 1936, AEA Papers, Box 1, Folder 8, MHA.

40. Morrison to Keyes, 28 April, quoting Keyes to Morrison, 23 April, CON Box 2, Folder 5

41. The term "over-feminized" was used by Morrison to describe the situation at Mount Holyoke where there were very few male faculty and the administration was totally dominated by women. (In 1937, Mount Holyoke had only four male full professors and forty-six women. Wellesley and Vassar had a majority of women profes-

sors, but the ratio of men was higher. Smith, Bryn Mawr and Barnard had more male full professors than women.) While many would have seen this as a strength for Mount Holyoke, Morrison was arguing (and would argue at the board meeting that hired Ham) that this was a great danger to Mount Holyoke's future. (For the ratios of men to women on the faculties, see Dorothy Kenyon, "The Presidency of Mount Holyoke College," *Journal of the American Association of University Women* 30, no. 1 [October 1936]: 16, quoting a *New York Times* editorial.)

42. This last assertion was not true. Nicolson by her own admission believed she would have been a most effective president. She just did not want the job. For McIntosh, See Chapter 6.

43. Morrison, letter to Whitman, 7 May 1936, CON Box 2, Folder 5, filed with a copy of Whitman, letter to Morrison, 2 May 1936.

44. It is interesting to note that the meeting at which Ham was agreed upon was held in Furniss' apartment at Yale University. (Bishop, letter to Russell, 19 July 1972. This initially was in the folder for Edgar Furniss, Trustee 1930–1940, Trustees Biographical Files, MHA.)

45. Telegram, Morrison to Prof David E. Adams, sec'y Conference Committee MTHOL-YOKE College SO HADley Mass, 22 May 1936, FCC Folder, also available in Meeropol Research Findings, Folder 1, MHA.

46. See FCC to Morrison, 23 May 1936. Morrison to FCC 29 May 1936 in Meeropol Research Findings, Folder 1, MHA.

47. Keyes to AEA, 29 May 1936, AEA Papers, Box 21, Folder 8, MHA. For Keyes' letters to Woolley see Meeropol Research Findings, Folder 1, MHA.

48. In May of 1937 Perkins wrote to a classmate: "[Rowena] behaved like quite a rotter on the matter of the President and I don't think she is entitled to the hearty and earnest support of her old associates" (Perkins, letter to L. R. Rounds, 1 May 1937, quoted in Martin, 375).

49. Pratt to Furniss, 4 June 1936, CON, available in Meeropol Research Findings, Folder 1, MHA.

50. See Martin, 370.

51. Richards to Ball, 12 June 1936, Margaret Ball Papers, Box 9, Series 3, MHA.

Chapter 5

1. Henry A. Stimson, "Is Woman's Suffrage an Enlightened and Justifiable Policy for the State" *Biblioteca Sacra* 67 (April 1910): 335–346.

2. See MEW to Morrison, 5 June 1936, CON Box 2, Folder 5.

3. This board of trustees meeting was in executive session and the minutes were not made public until 1999. All quotations and paraphrases to what occurred at the meeting are in "Minutes of the Meeting of the Board of Trustees Mount Holyoke College in Executive Session, June 6, 1936," CON Box 2, Folder 6. (This document has nine pages.) Interestingly, the list of members present does not include Harvey, yet in the document he is recorded as having participated in the discussion. It does include the Rev. William Horace Day, but there is no record of him having participated in the discussion. If Day had been present, there would have only been five absent trustees, yet the record clearly shows that six absentee votes were recorded. The conclusion that he was not present, despite the note on the minutes, is buttressed by the fact that Day telegrammed Morrison just before the meeting urging a delay and referral back to the search committee. (See Day, telegram to Morrison, n.d., CON Box 2, Folder 5). Harvey was clearly present and voted at the meeting.

4. Alva Morrison, "The Succession to the Presidency," *Mount Holyoke Alumnae Quarterly* 20 (August 1936): 69.

5. These recollections of Carr are in the FCC papers. Also available in Meeropol Research Findings, Folder 1, MHA.

6. In a letter to Marks describing a trustee meeting that occurred less than two weeks after the June 6 meeting, Woolley had specifically used this phrase to describe how she felt. See note 21.

7. In addition to Glass and Nicolson, to whom formal offers had been made, Maguire was referring to McIntosh, who Morrison had determined would not accept an offer even though (as he told Whitman) the committee could have agreed upon her. The question of whether McIntosh was actually made an offer became a matter of dispute later on. See Chapter 6.

8. They had to reach the decision that day because it appears that Ham had been in touch by telephone with at least one member of the search committee (probably Furniss) during the debate and was asked about the proposed delay. "I responded that it was the board's decision but I would not allow my name to be advanced. The time proposed was six months. I did not care to be debated over for that time. One of my better decisions and with no hesitancy" (handwritten comments on a copy of a flyer in Folio Scrapbook: Material Relating to Mr. Ham's Succession to the Presidency of Mount Holyoke College Following Miss Woolley, RGH Papers, n.p. [1]. (That the comments were written by Ham is obvious from the context.)

9. Trustees who were absent had been given the opportunity to cast their votes for or against

Ham in advance. They voted four to two against Ham.

10. MEW to Dorothy Foster, 22 June 1936, MEW Papers, Series 1, Correspondence Box 6, Folder 3.

11. Marion Nash Groves '17 to Morrison, 7 June 1936, CON Box 1, Folder 5.

12. Morrison, letter to Groves, 11 June 1936, CON Box 1, Folder 5.

13. "Mt. Holyoke Board Puts Faith in Man," *Boston Post*, 14 June 1936, RGH Papers, Box 4, Folder 9.

14. A. Elizabeth Adams, "An Open Letter to the Trustees of Mount Holyoke College," 10 June 1936, RGH Papers, Box 4, Folder 9.

15. *Boston Post*, 14 June 1936, RGH Papers, Box 4, Folder 9.

16. Bishop, letter to Russell, 19 July 1972. This initially was in the folder for Edgar Furniss, Trustee 1930–1940, Trustees Biographical Files, MHA.

17. Groves to Morrison, 21 June 1936, CON Box 1, Folder 5.

18. Marion Sayward '13 (Radcliffe MA) to Morrison, 26 June 1936 CON Box 1, Folder 5.

19. (Mrs.) Francis J. Sill ('08) letter to AEA, 17 June 1936, CON Box 1, Folder 4 (copy of letter sent to Morrison).

20. Mary Elizabeth Baker, '29 to AEA, 16 June 1936, AEA Papers, MHA.

21. MEW, letter to JM, 14 June 1936.

22. Marian P. Whitney to MEW, 20 July 1936, MEW correspondence. Series 1, Box 6, Folder 4.

23. MEW, letter to JM, 17 June 1936.

24. MEW, letter to Esther Caukin Brunauer, 24 June 1936, Reel 89, H-34, AAUWA.

25. Brunauer, letter to JM, 27 June 1936, Reel 89, H-34, AAUWA.

26. Brunauer, letter to Edgar Furniss, 27 June 1936, Reel 89, H-34, AAUWA.

27. Maude Meagher to MEW, 19 Aug. 1936, MEW Papers, Series 1, Correspondence Box 6, Folder 4.

28. Rowland was sixty-four years old in 1936. She had been an ambulance driver in Europe during World War I and had worked for years in the Editorial Department at the Cleveland Clinic. See Alumnae Notes, Class of 1893. Rowland lived with her life partner, Nellie White, for thirty-five years up till White's death in 1948.

29. Wilcox to Woolley, 22 Aug. 1936, MEW Correspondence. Series 1, Box 6, Folder 4.

30. "Dr. Mary Woolley Backs Roosevelt," *New York Times*, 6 Sept. 1936.

31. See Nancy Elizabeth Hoffman, class of '39, 21 Oct. 1936, Student Records, Summaries of Manuscript Collections, Notebook Four, Classes of 1930 (onwards) [selected by Clara R. Ludwig, '37, Director Emeritus of Admissions], MHA.

32. See Chapter 2.

33. Allen to Morrison, 31 Aug. 1936. CON, Box 1, Folder 5 attached to Allen to the Trustees 24 June 1936.

34. Kendall to Allen, 9 Sept. 1936, CON, Box 1, Folder 3.

35. See Bishop to Morrison, 31 Oct. 1936, and Morrison to Bishop, 3 Nov. 1936, CON Box 2, Folder 4.

36. Clement to Morrison, quote. in Morrison to Ham, 6 July 1936, RGH Papers, Box 2, Series A, Folder 13.

37. The full text of Clement's introduction to Woolley's statement reads: "In order that the alumnae may understand the position which Miss Woolley holds on the question of the presidency of Mount Holyoke College, the *Quarterly* is printing at her request the following statement which she made to the Board of Trustees on June 6, 1936 and repeated at the Alumnae College on June 13[qm] ("Comments and Discussion": 102).

38. Theater had been Price's first love, but in her words, "violent family opposition thwarted this, and so I turned to journalism." Married for the first time at age fifty-two, Price would marry two more times. Price was active in the Republican Party throughout her life, ran a sheep ranch in Montana for several years, traveled extensively and studied painting. Price died one month after her hundredth birthday on August 17, 1992.

39. Price to Ham, n.d. [1936], RGH Papers, Series A, Sub-Series 1, Folder 6, 1–2. The reference to Woolley indicates that Price knew little about her. Woolley had a lifelong loving and close relationship with her father, her brothers and their families.

40. Ibid., 4.

41. Price to Ham, Oct. 1936, RGH Papers. Series A, Sub-Series 1.

42. This statement is from the record of the official minutes of that November 5 meeting ("Minutes of Meeting of Board of Trustees of Mount Holyoke College," November 5, 1936, MHA).

43. Sixty letters of disapproval representing eighty alumnae and five non-alumnae and seventy letters of approval from eighty-six alumnae.

44. Amy Rowland, letter to Morrison, 4 Nov. 1936, RGH Papers, Series A, Sub-Series 3, Box 3.

45. All direct quotes and paraphrases of statements that follow are from a document titled "Rough Memorandum of Discussion Which Took Place in the Meeting of the Board of Trustees of Mount Holyoke College, November 5, 1936, When the Trustees Resolved Themselves into a Committee of the Whole for the Discussion of the Succession to the Presidency," CON Box 3, Folder 2 (this document has twelve pages).

See above for an explanation of how these statements were excluded from the official record.

46. Interestingly, the word "consider" from Perkins' motion in the official minutes was changed to "reconsider" in the minutes of the executive session of the Committee of the Whole.

47. This motion appears three pages into the minutes of the Committee of the Whole (see note 28). In the official minutes, Furniss' motion appears right after Perkins' motion to "receive and accept" the petition as read. After the fact, the trustees moved the on-the-record discussion that preceded Furniss' motion to the off-the-record minutes that were then sequestered until 1999.

48. In Rowland's cover letter to Morrison, she explicitly stated that Woolley, the faculty and Harriet Newhall (who had handed the petitions to Morrison) had had no knowledge of the petition. See Rowland to Morrison.

49. See Chapter 4.

50. Memorandum of Mrs. Mary Hume Maguire, 3.

51. Comfortable in traditional Indian clothing, she acquired a broad understanding of the world's diversity of culture and religion. In 1930 after an extensive world trip that included visiting a mission in the Philippines (then an American colony) she wrote for the *Mount Holyoke Quarterly* with sympathy for members of religious groups who "had a great hatred and distrust for anything bearing the name of Christian. They have had reason to feel this way when one recalls the past history of the Philippines" See Mount Holyoke Alumnae Directory, Class of 1912, MHA.

52. About Meagher, See Chapter 6. "*World Youth* was established for education under Mass Charter in 1936. Its sole aim is to encourage a friendly and informed interest in the people of other countries—*World Youth* carries no propaganda whether religious or political. (*World Youth* is not connected with any organization or movement.) The magazine was published between 1936 and the late 1950s (with a wartime hiatus). The magazine's correspondents were youngsters from 47 different countries." (See Mary Ann Cook, "Saratoga's Cassa Tierra: At One with the Earth," *Saratoga News*, 23 Oct. 2002, www.community-newspapers.com/archives/sratoganews/2002.

53. See "Report of the Meeting of Alumnae Association, 6 Nov. 1936," in JM, report to AAUW "Chronological Outline of Events Bearing on the Succession to the Presidency of Mount Holyoke College," 14 Jan. 1937, Reel 89, H-34, AAUWA.

54. See Ham, letter to Morrison, 14 Sept. 1936, RGH Papers, Series A, Sub-Series 1.

55. *Alumnae Quarterly* 19–20 (1935–1937): 131–134.

56. Price, letter to Morrison, RGH Papers, Series A, Sub-Series 1, Box 2 Folder 4, Nov. 1936.

57. See Bernice L. Maclean '26, letter to MEW, 12 Dec. 1936, MEW Papers, Series 1, Correspondence Box 6, Folder 5. Maclean enclosed the text of a petition she was circulating among the alumnae.

58. See Maclean, letter to MEW, 17 Dec. 1936, attached to 12 Dec. 1936 letter, both attached to MEW to Kingsbury 19 Jan. 1937 MEW Papers, Series 1. Box 6 Folder 8. The two Maclean letters and the enclosed petition are all included in Meeropol Research Findings, Folder 1, MHA.

59. Perkins' suggestion is related in McHale to MEW, 8 Dec. 1936. Reel 89, H-34, AAUWA. Wells erroneously attributes the suggestion of "scratching" to Marks (see Wells, 235) in support of her blanket statement "The opposition to the appointment [of Ham] was masterminded by Miss Marks" (232). Jeannette Marks certainly provoked a good deal of negative sentiment at the college, but though she strongly supported Woolly and did what she could, she was certainly no "mastermind"—in fact, there was no mastermind but efforts by many different individuals. Marks had none of the leadership capacity or popularity among the faculty that, for example, Morgan and (Elizabeth) Adams had.

60. McHale to MEW, 8 Dec. 1936.

Chapter 6

1. There are two versions of the Broadside available for scrutiny. One is in the AAUW archives (the AAUW in its writings referred to this document as "the Broadside") identified as Alumnae Committee of Investigation, "The Case of Mount Holyoke vs. the Committee of Nine, 6 June 1936," Reel 89, H-34. Another version is called "1837—the Case of Mary Lyon vs. the Committee of Nine—1937" and is available in Folio Scrapbook: Material Relating to Mr. Ham's Succession to the Presidency of Mount Holyoke College Following Miss Woolley, RGH Papers, n.p. [1] (hereinafter: Folio Scrapbook). It is this version that has Ham's handwritten note referenced in note 8 to Chapter 5.

2. Dean Harriet Allyn had successfully served as interim president while Woolley was away in Geneva.

3. Since this trustee was identified as one who had voted for Ham in June, it must have been Potter who had initially asked for a delay and later revealed himself in November as the deciding vote

for Ham while still believing that it was a bad decision.

4. (Maude) White, letter to Morrison, 11 Nov. 1936, CON Box 2, Folder 4.

5. Reference to advisors being "red."

6. See Purington, letter to Morrison, 8 Nov. 1936. CON Box 2, Folder 4.

7. See Morrison, letter to White, 13 Nov. 1936, CON Box 2, Folder 4. See also Morrison, letter to Cheney, 12 Nov. 1936, CON Box 2, Folder 4.

8. *Sunday Union and Republican*, 30 Jan. 1937.

9. See Folio Scrapbook: n.p. [14] [16] [17] [18] [24].

10. Ruth Alden (Mrs. Chauncey W.) Waldron '13 to MEW, 27 Jan. 1937 MEW Papers, Series 1, Correspondence. Box 6, Folder 4.

11. MEW to Mrs. Chauncey W. Waldron, Feb 1, 1937, MEW papers, Series 1, Correspondence. Box 6, Folder 4.

12. Waldron to MEW, 3 Feb. 1937, MEW Papers, Series 1, Correspondence. Box 6, Folder 4. This letter and the previous letters are attached together and available in Meeropol Research Findings, Folder 1, MHA.

13. It had the same text as Woolley's letter to Waldron.

14. "Dr. Woolley Joins Attack on Dr. Ham," *New York Times*, 5 Feb. 1937.

15. "Dr. Woolley Leading Rebellion against Dr. Ham at Mt. Holyoke. Retiring President Asserts a 'Packed' Committee of Trustees Selected Him as First Male to Head the College in Its 100 Years," *New York Herald Tribune*, 5 Feb. 1937.

16. *Springfield Republican* 5 Feb 1937. This was certainly true. On 10 June 1936, just four days after the Board's decision to hire Ham, Woolley wrote him a most cordial letter making it clear that her opposition to him had nothing to do with him personally. See MEW to Ham, CON, Box 2, Folder 5.

17. MEW, telegram to Board of Trustees, 5 Feb. 1937, CON Box 2, Folder 1.

18. Telegram, White to United Press, Boston, 7 Feb. 1937, RGH Series A, Sub-Series 1, Folder 7.

19. See Morrison, letter to White, 9 Feb. 1937, CON Box 2, Folder 1.

20. "Dr. Ham Sees Critics More Interested in Feminism than Good of Mt. Holyoke," *Holyoke Transcript-Telegram*, 8 Feb 1937, Folio Scrapbook, MHA, n.p. [8].

21. "Many Letters Support Him, Dr. Ham Says," *Boston Transcript*, 5 Feb. 27, n.p. [1], Folio Scrapbook, n.p. [34]. The same quote appeared in an AP dispatch from New Haven in the *New York Times*, 6 Feb. 1937, n.p., Folio Scrapbook, MHA, n.p. [20].

22. Sydney R. McLean, letter to RGH, 13 June 1936, RGH Papers, Series A, Sub-Series 1, Folder 11.

23. Meagher and Smiley were co-publishers of *World Youth* from 1936 to the late 1950s, with a wartime break during which the two women hand-built a seven-thousand-square-foot home (Casa Tierra) with, according to Smiley, "a minimum of assistance from the sterner sex" (Alumnae Directory, class of 1912, MHA).

24. Meagher, letter to Morrison, 29 Oct. 1936, enclosed in Meagher, letter to RGH, 30 Oct. 1936, RGH Papers, Series A, Sub-Series 1, Folder 11.

25. "What Would Mary Lyon Say?" *Boston Sunday Globe*, 7 Feb. 1937, 1.

26. McHale to Smiley, 10 Feb. 1937, Reel 89, H-34, AAUWA.

27. Warbeke to Ham, 7 Feb. 1936, RGH Papers, Folder 16, Box 2.

28. Whitman, letter to Morrison, 8 Feb. 1937, RGH Papers, Series A, Sub-Series 1, Box 1, Folder 1.

29. Price, letter to Morrison, 17 Feb 1937, RGH Papers, Series A, Sub-Series 1, Box 1, Folder 1.

30. Smiley was in partnership with Meagher. Rowland's life partner at the time was one Nellie White.

31. Maguire, letter to Ham, 12 Feb. 1937, RGH Papers, Series A, Sub-Series 1, Box 1. Folder 1.

32. There are two versions of the meeting, one prepared by Morrison and enclosed in Morrison to MEW, 18 Feb. 1937. CON, Box 2, Folder 1 and Woolley's alternative version enclosed in MEW to Morrison, 25 Feb. 1937. CON, Box 2, Folder 1. In the following paragraphs all references to what was said at the meeting can be found in one or both of the memos.

33. Hazen to Morrison, 19 Feb. 1937. CON, Box 2, Folder 1.

34. Morrison to Hazen, 20 Feb. 1937. CON, Fox 2, Folder 1.

35. This exchange is noted in Woolley's memo on the meeting, enclosed in MEW to Morrison, 25 Feb. 1937.

36. Furniss to Morrison, 2 Feb. 1937. CON, Box 1, Folder 9.

37. See Morrison to Newhall, 1 March 1937. CON, Box 1, Folder 9.

38. Newhall to Morrison, 3 March 1937. CON, Box 1, Folder 9.

39. Morrison to Newhall, 4 March 1937. CON, Box 1, Folder 9.

40. Wyckoff, letter to *New York Herald Tribune*, 11 Feb. 1937.

41. Nicolson, letter to Morrison, 30 Jan. 1937, CON Box 1, Folder 9.

42. Nicolson, letter to Smiley, 30 Jan. 1937, CON Box 1, Folder 9.

43. Nicolson to Morrison.

44. Ibid.

45. See Chapter 3, note 47.

46. See Chapter 4, for Woolley's reference to "fraternal decisions to replace women by men."

47. Kingsbury was director of the Carola Woerishoffer Graduate Department of Social Economy and Social Research at Bryn Mawr College

48. Woolley had given her the names of prominent alumnae (Perkins, Rowland, Smiley), a copy of a protest with names listed and an invitation to the college to speak with her and several faculty members. Kingsbury's activities provoked Maguire to send a letter to Glass (who was then president of the AAUW as well as Sweet Briar College) complaining that the interests of "outside organizations" were "not at all in the welfare of the college or, indeed, connected with the higher education of women but rather with the general advancement of a principle of feminism" (Maguire to Glass, 25 Feb. 1937, CON Box 1, Folder 9). The claim that the AAUW—one of those "outside organizations"—was not interested in issues related to the higher education of women had to have struck Glass as ludicrous.

49. See Morrison, letter to McIntosh, 19 Feb. 1937. CON, Box 1 Folder 9. Available together with McIntosh's responses and Woolley's and Kingsbury's letters in Meeropol Research Findings, Folder 1, MHA.

50. Morrison to McIntosh, 19 Feb. 1937.

51. A lot of the details of the board's official responses to the charges in the Broadside are collected in the following two documents: "Copy of Mr. Morrison's Reply to Mrs. Cooper's Letter of Inquiry," 19 Feb. 1937 (responding to "Copy of Letter of Inquiry from Mrs. Cooper to Mr. Morrison," 15 Feb. 1937) and "Memorandum by Mrs. Mary Hume Maguire," RGH Papers, Series A, Sub-Series 1, Folder 13.

52. The *News-Week* article appeared in the "Education" section of the February 13 (1937) edition. It is available in Meeropol Research Findings, Folder 1, MHA.

53. Price to Mr. and Mrs. Ham, February 1937, available in Meeropol Research Findings, Folder 1, MHA.

54. See Chapter 5.

55. Price to Mr. and Mrs. Ham, n.d. [1937], RGH Papers, Series A, Sub-Series 1, Folder 6, MHA.

56. Philena Young to Adams, 28 Feb. 1937, AEA Papers. Box 1, Folder 8, MHA.

57. Marjorie Harris to Morrison, 26 July 1937. CON, Box 1, Folder 8.

58. Alice D. Brooks, 1912, letter to RGH, 9 Feb. 1937, RGH Papers, Series A, Sub-Series 1, Folder 1, 2–3.

59. Bernice Maclean, letter to RGH, 11 Feb. 1937, RGH Papers, Series A, Sub-Series 1, Folder 11.

60. Janet Wilder, letter to RGH, 1 March 1937, RGH Papers, Series A, Sub-Series 1, Folder 2, MRA. The reference is to the fact that Ham had taught at Albertus Magnus College, a Catholic women's college.

61. Gertha Williams, 1910, letter to RGH, 2 March 1937, RGH Papers, Series A, Sub-Series 1, Folder 2.

62. Elizabeth Bailey Willis, letter to RGH, 27 Feb. 1937, RGH Papers, Series A, Sub-Series 1, Folder 3.

63. Isabel Steele Blish, letter to RGH, 5 Feb. 1937, RGH Papers, Series A, Sub-Series 1, folder 6: 1.

64. Florence Pok Holding, letter to RGH, 9 Feb 1937, RGH. Papers, Series A, Sub-Series 1, Folder 6.

65. Helen Powell Schaufller, 1913, letter to RGH, 7 Feb. 1937, RGH papers, Series A, Sub-Series 1, Folder 6.

66. Mildred Auger, 1921, letter to RGH, 29 March 1937, RGH Papers, Series A, Sub-Series 1, Folder 3.

67. Miriam Best Blake, letter to RCH, 9 Feb. 1937, RGH Papers, Series A, Sub-Series 1, Folder 3.

68. Florence H. Jones to RGH, 7 Feb. 1937, RGH Papers, Series A, Sub-Series 1, Folder 4.

69. This woman was a descendant of one of Mary Lyon's original students

70. Marion E,. Dwight to MEW, 15 Feb. 1937, MEW papers, Series 1, Correspondence Box 6, Folder 7.

71. Purington to Morrison, 27 Feb. 1937, CON Box 1, Folder 7. A similar statement was expressed in a letter to Woolley on 14 Feb. 1937, by Jane Louise Mesick, a new alumnae trustee. She noted that had she been on the board the previous June she would have voted against Ham's appointment but now wanted Woolley to attempt to "put a quietus" on the activity of Rowland and Smiley and their committee. Woolley answered three days later stating that "the question of the principle at stake concerns a much larger group than the Mount Holyoke alumnae" (Mesick to Woolley, 14 Feb. 1937, and Woolley to Mesick, 17 Feb. 1937, Box 6 Folder 8, MEW Papers, Series 1, Correspondence.

72. See *Mount Holyoke News*, 12 Feb. 1937.

This editorial was reported in the *New York Times*.

73. *Holyoke Transcript*, 17 Feb. 1937.

74. Both the "Appeal from Facts" and the letter are in Meeropol Research Findings, Folder 1, MHA.

75. White to Morrison, and Morrison to White, 27 Feb. 1937, CON Box 1, Folder 9.

76. At least two of Marks' students (Ann Hebb and Ciel Jablonower) were signers of the student protest. (See *The Centenary of Mount Holyoke College, Friday and Saturday May Seventh and Eight Nineteen Hundred and Thirty-Seven* [henceforth *Centenary*] [South Hadley, MA: Mount Holyoke College, 1937], 170–171.)

77. Morrison to White, 27 Feb. 1937.

78. Telegram, Howley to Morrison, 3 March 1937, CON Box 1, Folder 9.

79. Florence Gorse Smith to Alumnae, 22 Feb. 1937, RGH Papers, Box 4, Folder 9. The cover letter read: "We feel that it is essential to the best interest of Mount Holyoke College that large numbers of loyal alumnae take a definite position against the recent harmful publicity on the election of our new President. After study of all the facts, we are convinced that a careful investigation was made by the Committee of the Trustees, and that no considerations except the best interest of the College entered into their decision when they unanimously recommended Dr. Ham. He has been elected President by the Trustees who are the only body authorized to act upon the matter. If you feel as we do that the issue is closed and that we should do all we can to stop the controversy at this time ... sign and return immediately."

80. Report of the meeting of the board of trustees, 5 March 1937.

81. Soon after that weekend, alumna Margaret Conrad wrote to Morrison that "I am sure that ... Mrs. Smith has kept you informed of the enormous majority in favor of peace as indicated by her very complete poll of alumnae opinion" (Conrad to Morrison, 10 March 1937, CON Box 1, Folder 9).

82. The events of the weekend of March 5, 6, and 7 can be followed from four separate sources. One is a detailed typed three-page report prepared after the fact (probably by Smiley) titled "Comment on Trustee Meetings and Alumnae Council Meetings, March 5, 6, 7, 1937, Mount Holyoke College, South Hadley." The second is the detailed minutes of the discussion at the Alumnae Council on March 6, "Excerpt from the Minutes of Alumnae Council, March 6, 1937." CON, Box 3, Folder 2. The third is the minutes of the board of trustees meeting on March 5. Finally, there is a detailed letter written by White to Ham on March 10, 1937 (CON Box 1, Folder

9). In the following narrative only direct quotes will be noted separately.

83. The initial version of the flyer had charged that the Comptroller's Report for June 30, 1934, 1935 and 1936 showed a total loss of close to $1 million. The newer version, in effect, acknowledged that the cumulative loss for the three years was $366,000 (p. 4 of the "Comment on Trustee Meetings ...").

84. Minutes of the board of trustees meeting, 5 March 1937.

85. This hope was expressed in a letter Rowland wrote to trustee (Edward) White on March 24, 1937 (CON Box 1 Folder 9). She noted that "nothing can be done about it at this time, but I think that it is most unfortunate for the College that such is the case."

86. This was reported in a special mailing from (Maude) White to the Alumnae, 29 March 1937.

87. "Comment on Trustee Meetings and Alumnae Council Meetings, March 5, 6, 7, 1937, Mount Holyoke College, South Hadley."

88. See "Mt. Holyoke Fight Ended by Alumnae; Council Rules 'Nothing Can Be Accomplished' by Further Opposition to Dr. Ham," *New York Times*, 7 March 1937.

Chapter 7

1. See Minutes of Meeting of Centennial Committee, 23 May 1934, MHC Centenary, Box 3, Folder 23, MHA. The centennial celebration was called the "Centenary" in the book published as *The Centenary of Mount Holyoke College, Friday and Saturday May Seventh and Eighth Nineteen Hundred and Thirty-Seven*. In the Mount Holyoke Archives, the centennial materials are listed as MHC Centenary. In the text, the events will be consistently referred to as the centennial.

2. Memorandum from Conference re Centennial Celebration, 20 June 1936, MHC Centenary Records, Box 2, Folder 21, MHA. Note that Woolley showed sensitivity to Ham's situation, making it clear that when she said that the issue was one of principle, not personal grievance, she was telling the truth.

3. See Prologue.

4. Purington, letter to MEW, 17 Sept. 1936, MEW Papers, Series 1, Correspondence Box 7.

5. Minutes of Meeting of Centennial Committee, 9 July 1936, Mount Holyoke College Centenary Records, Minutes of Central Centennial Committee, Minutes, May 1934–3 June 1937, Folder 23, MHA. See also MEW, letter to Furniss, 13 March 1937, MEW Papers, Series 1, Correspondence Box 7, MHA.

6. See Minutes of Meeting of Centennial

Committee, 3 Dec. 1935, MHC Centenary Records, Minutes of Central Centennial Committee, Minutes, May 1934—June 1937, Folder 23, 7, MHA. Mary Beard declined an offer to write the college history, and ultimately the task fell to historian Arthur Cole, dean of the Graduate School of Western Reserve University. The book was published in 1940 (*A Hundred Years of Mount Holyoke College* [New Haven, CT: Yale University Press].

7. Cheney, letter to Morrison, 5 Feb. 1937, CON Box 3, Folder 1.

8. See Furniss, letter to Marion Barbour, 8 March 1937, Barbour to Furniss, 13 March 1937, Mount Holyoke College Centenary Records, Central Centennial Office, Barbour, Marion H., Correspondence (official), Folder 28, MHA.

9. For the full correspondence see Morrison, letter to RGH, 16 April 1937, which encloses Cheek, letter to Morrison, 15 April 1937, and Morrison, letter to Cheek, 16 April 1937, RGH Papers, Series 1, Sub-Series A, Folder 13.

10. "Rights Denied, Women Charge," *Boston Sunday Globe*, 9 May 1937, 1. This article is also available in Mount Holyoke College Centenary Records, Clippings Folder 81, MHA.

11. See ibid., 1, 8.

12. *Centenary*, 27–28.

13. Ibid., 40.

14. Minutes of the Centennial Committee, 9 July 1936, Mount Holyoke College Centenary Records, Minutes of Central Centennial Committee, May 1934–June 1937, Folder 23, MHA, 3.

15. *Centenary*, 61.

16. Ibid., 53.

17. Ibid., 55.

18. Ibid., 54.

19. Ibid., 58.

20. Wyckoff had written to Woolley in late March to say how delighted she was that Beard would be speaking to the alumnae at the centennial. Given her experience with the alumnae council, Wyckoff wondered if the alumnae in attendance would listen, but Beard, she said, "will have something to say" (Wyckoff, letter to MEW, 20 March 1937, MEW Papers, Series 1, Correspondence Box 7).

21. *Centenary*, 82.

22. *Boston Sunday Globe*, 9 May 1937.

23. *Centenary*, 85.

24. Ibid., 86.

25. Ibid., 91–92.

26. Ibid., 126–127.

27. Glass to MEW, 13 May 1937 MHC Centenary, Records, MHA.

28. McHale to MEW, 10 May 1937, MHC Centenary, Records, MHA.

29. Comstock to MEW, 12 May 1937, MHC Centenary, Records, MHA.

30. Lydia S. Capen to MEW, 9 May 1937, MHC Centenary, Records, MHA.

31. See "Feminist Calls Naming Man as Head a Blow to All Women's Prestige; Stirs London by Address; Freedom League Speech, Read for Her, Denounces 'Vanity of Men, Laziness of Women,'" *New York Times*, 9 May 1937.

32. Goodsell to MEW, 18 May 1937, MHC Centenary, Records, MHA.

33. Perkins to Hugh Hawkins, 21 September 1961, Perkins Papers, Correspondence Folder 10, MHA.

34. See McHale letter to Putnam, 12 Dec. 1936, AAUWA, and Putnam, letter to McHale, 16 Dec. 1936, AAUWA.

35. See Chapter 5.

36. See Chapter 2.

37. See Henry W. Lawrence, "The Business Man and the Liberal College," *Journal of the American Association of University Women* 25 (June 1932): 214.

38. See Ellis, MHTC, 3.

39. See Chapters 2 and 3.

40. (Edward) White to MEW, 20 May 1932, MEW Papers, Series 1, Correspondence Box 2. Quoted in Meeropol, 330.

41. There were seven in all, five alumnae trustees and two, Perkins and Purington, who were serving full ten-year terms.

42. Breckenridge to Whitman, et al., 3 August 1936, CON Box 1, Folder 5.

43. Mary R. Beard, "University Discipline for Women—Asset or Handicap?" *Journal of the American Association of University Women* 25 (1931–1932): 130–131.

44. Quoted in McHale to MEW, 25 April 1933, MEW Papers, Series 1, Correspondence Box 2, Folder 4, MHA.

45. See above notes 15–19.

46. Mary R. Beard, "The Second Century Faces the First. Is It Time to Choose New Goals in Higher Education of Women?" "Some Answers to These Questions," *Journal of the American Association of University Women* 31, no. 4 (June 1938): 213–214.

47. Rebecca H. Eastman, "Seven Presidents at Home," *Ladies' Home Journal*, December 1929, 60.

48. See Eleanor Sayer, class of '39, reporting on a debate with Amherst College from 26 April 1936, Student Records, Summaries of Manuscript Collections, Notebook Four, Classes of 1930 (onwards) [Selected by Clara R. Ludwig, '37, Director Emeritus of Admissions], MHA.

49. See Louis M. Ireland, (MA) class of 1936, 23 Feb. 1935, Student Records, Notebook Four, Classes of 1930 (onwards), MHA.

50. See Annette Mowatt, class of 1936, 6 Nov. 1934, Student Records, Notebook Four, Classes of 1930 (onwards), MHA.

51. See Barbara Johnson, class of 1939. [n.d.], Student Records, Notebook Four, Classes of 1930 (onwards), MHA.

52. See Barbara Johnson, 7 Nov. 1936. Note that Woolley delivered this speech just two days after the board had refused to reconsider the hiring of Ham. See Chapter 5.

53. Barbara Johnson, 28 Sept. 1938.

54. See Mary Elizabeth Hoffman, class of 1939, 12 and 21 Oct. 1936 and 10 Nov. 1936, Student Records, Notebook Four, Classes of 1930 (onwards), MHA.

55. See, for example, MHTC 9 (Ellen Deborah Ellis), who referred to the end of Woolley's presidency as "a tragic ending to a long and distinguished career" (3).

56. In June of 1936, after the board's decision to hire Ham, Woolley confided to a faculty member, Dorothy Foster: "I feel so ashamed that it should be Mount Holyoke" (MEW to Dorothy Foster, 22 June 1936, MEW Papers, Series 1, Correspondence, Box 5, Folder 4, MHA).

57. Jean Anouilh, *Antigone* (London: Methuen, 1985), 35. Anouilh's reference is to "death" rather than defeat, but the principle of certainty for tragedy and happenstance for melodrama remains.

58. Ibid.

59. MHTC 9, 3.

Epilogue

1. In 1937, the college employed 128 faculty members and 66 assistants who had earned degrees from more than fifty institutions. There were twenty-three departments and the college plant included thirty-four buildings on 270 acres. The endowment had grown to $5 million and the library contained 150,000 volumes. See Cole, 335.

2. MEW, *Report of Mary Emma Woolley President Emeritus of Mount Holyoke College* (South Hadley, MA: Mount Holyoke College, 1937), 23.

3. MEW to JM, 12 Oct. 1937.

4. See MEW to JM, 15 Jan. 1940 and 16 Dec. 1940. She chaired the People's Mandate to Governments to End War and the Committee on International Relations of the AAUW. She was a member of the Commission on International Justice and Good Will and chair of the Cooperating Commission of Women in the Federal Council of Churches.

5. MEW, letter to JM, 12 Jan. 1938.

6. See MEW, letter to JM, 24 Feb. 1938.

7. See MEW, letter to JM, 11 May 1938.

8. MEW, letter to JM, 24 Feb. 1938.

9. See MEW, letter to JM, 5 June 1938.

10. See Marks, LAL, 222.

11. MEW to JM, 12 Nov. 1938.

12. MEW to JM, 18 Nov. 1938. "The embargo" referred to the embargo of arms to both sides in the Spanish Civil War, which was being violated by Italy and Germany but observed by Britain, the United States and France.

13. MEW, letter to JM, 8 Jan. 1940.

14. MEW to JM, 12 May 1940.

15. MEW, telegram to President and Mme. Roosevelt, 6 Nov. 1940, MEW Papers, Series A, MHA.

16. MEW to JM, 12 Nov. 1940.

17. See MEW, letter to Weston, 20 Oct. 1940, Series 1, Correspondence Box 16, Folder 2. In March, she had agreed to attend the first meeting of the Commission of the Federal Council "To Study the Bases of a Just and Durable Peace" because she was one of only two women on the commission "for the sake of our sex as well as for other reasons." (See MEW, letter to JM, 9 March 1941.)

18. MEW, letter to JM, 17 April 1941.

19. MEW, letter to JM, 3 May 1941.

20. MEW, letter to Board of Directors of AAUW, 1 May 1941, Reel 48, C-12, AAUWA.

21. MEW, letter to JM, 12 May 1941.

22. MEW, letter to Downer, 7 Nov 1945. MEW Papers, Series 1, Correspondence, Box 8, Folder 14.

23. For example, Woolley supported the Phelps-Stokes Fund in demanding an end to discrimination against African American skilled workers within companies with defense contracts. See MEW, signed statement, Series 1, Correspondence Box 16, Folder 1.

24. Perkins, letter to JM, 9 Sep 1947. JM Papers, Series 8, Folder 32, MHA.

25. Mrs. Wm. C. Dwight, letter in JM in "Confidential Last Bulletin" dedicated to MEW by JM, 1947. See JM Papers, Series 8, Folder 55, MHA.

26. Marion Park, letter to JM, Sept. 1947, JM Papers, Series 8, Folder 32, MHA.

27. Purington, letter to JM, Sept. 1947, JM Papers, Series 8, Folder 32, MHA.

28. Cheek, letter to JM, Sept. 1947, JM Papers, Series 8, Folder 32, MHA.

29. Julia Abbe Garst Goodwin, letter to JM, Sept. 1947, JM Papers, Series 8, Folder 57, MHA.

30. Mount Holyoke Alumna, letter to JM, 15 Oct. 1947, JM Papers, Series 8, Folder 51, MHA.

31. All quotes from "The Case of Mary Lyon against Trustees of Mt. Holyoke College" *Boston Sunday Globe*, "Editorial and News Feature" section, 7 Feb. 1937.

32. In the following pages, all references to the numbers of faculty at Mount Holyoke in different ranks at different times and to the dates at which faculty were hired or left Mount Holyoke unless specifically identified elsewhere come from various years of the Mount Holyoke College Catalogues. Much of the numerical data is from the 1937–1938 and 1950 catalogues.

33. The reference to "ruthlessness" is from Keyes. The reference to "giving pain" is from Cheney's letter to Morrison where he refers to President Elliot of Harvard and his belief that good administrators have to be about to "give pain."

34. See Chapter 6.

35. MHTC (Olive Copeland), 2.

36. McLean's professional career including details of her years at Mount Holyoke can be found in McLean, Sydney R. English 1927–1965 Faculty, Biographical File, MHA. She did not join the faculty on a full-time basis until 1933.

37. The letter is quoted in Chapter 6.

38. MHTC (Viola Barnes), 33. Also available in Viola Barnes Papers Box 16, Folder 17, MHA.

39. Information on Mount Holyoke-in-Hartford is available in Hartford College for Women, Hartford, Ct. Descriptive Material, MHA. Aside from annual brochures describing the courses offered, the faculty teaching them and a list of students and their sponsors, two published pieces stand out as sources of information. Jane Nichols Swift '39 "Mount Holyoke in Hartford A 'Noble Experiment,'" *Mount Holyoke Alumnae Quarterly* (Fall 1984), 20–22; and Roger W. Holmes "Mount Holyoke-in-Hartford:," *Journal of Education* 115 (Jan 1935), 39–40.

40. See Brochure for Mount Holyoke-in-Hartford, 1938–39, in Hartford College for Women, Hartford Ct. Descriptive Materials, MHA.

41. See Levin, 134.

42. Laird had earned a Ph.D. from Bryn Mawr in 1901. See "Elizabeth Rebecca Laird, 1874–1969," http://www.physics.ucla.edu/~cwp/Phase2/Laird,_Elizabeth_Rebecca@944123456.html. In 1905–06 she took advantage of Woolley's leave policy to study at the Cavendish Laboratory in Cambridge, England. In 1919, she studied at the University of Chicago.

43. In two separate letters, Allen refers to "faculty legislation" that presumably requires such consultation. See Allen, letter to her mother, 15 Dec 1939 and Allen, letter to her father, 9 Dec 1939, Mount Holyoke College—Faculty and Staff, Allen, Mildred Papers, Series A. Correspondence, Box 7 Folder 100. MHA.

44. Allen, letter to her mother, 15 Dec. 1939.

Apparently, Rusk's argument was that though Laird was only sixty-four in 1937, her twenty-five-year tenure at Mount Holyoke permitted early forced retirement. When Laird retired at the end of 1939, she had already turned sixty-five.

45. Allen, letter to her father, 17 March 1943, Mount Holyoke College—Faculty and Staff, Allen, Mildred Papers, Series A, Correspondence Box 8, Folder 108, MHA.

46. Allen, letter to her mother, 18 March 1945, Mount Holyoke College—Faculty and Staff, Allen, Mildred Papers, Series A, Correspondence Box 8, Folder 113, MHA.

47. Allen wrote to her mother (Allen, letter to mother, 3 March 1946): "Apparently, Mr. Ham was not in the least willing to reappoint Mr. Rusk" Mount Holyoke College—Faculty and Staff, Allen, Mildred Papers, Series A. Correspondence. Box 8, Folder 116. MHA

48. Allen, letter to her father, 6 Feb. 1947. Mount Holyoke College—Faculty and Staff, Allen, Mildred Papers, Series A, Correspondence Box 8, Folder 118, MHA.

49. Allen, letter to her mother, 18 Jan. 1948, Mount Holyoke College—Faculty and Staff, Allen, Mildred Papers, Series A, Correspondence. Box 8, Folder 121. MHA

50. Allen, letter to her father, 16 Feb. 1947. Mount Holyoke College—Faculty and Staff, Allen, Mildred Papers, Series A. Correspondence Box 8, Folder 118, MHA

51. Allen, letter to her mother, 23 Feb. 1941, Mount Holyoke College—Faculty and Staff, Allen, Mildred Papers, Series A, Correspondence Box 7, Folder 103, MHA

52. See John G. Reid, *Viola Florence Barnes, 1885–1979: A Historian's Biography* (Toronto: University of Toronto Press, 2005), 94, for general corroboration.

53. See Barnes, letter to RGH, 5 Feb. 1937, RGH Papers, Series A, Sub-Series 1, Folder 8.

54. Reid, 90.

55. See Reid, 93.

56. Both Barnes quotes from Reid, 94.

57. MHTC (Viola Barnes), 27, also available in Viola Barnes Papers, Box 16, Folder 17, MHA.

58. Quoted in Wells, 253–254.

59. Nowhere was this more apparent than in his treatment of Marks. In 1937, she was chair of the department and director of the Laboratory Theatre, a successful program that she created in playwriting and play production. Marks knew that Ham was determined to remove her from both positions as soon as possible. She was openly disdainful and uncooperative, early on, refusing to participate in a joint Mount Holyoke/Amherst summer school in 1938. (On Marks' relationship with Ham see Wells, 242–244.) By 1940, Ham

succeeded in taking away the chairmanship. She held on to the directorship of the Lab Theatre until 1941, her retirement year, when she was faced with the prospect that Ham planned to hire a man to replace her. Though Woolley never publicly criticized any of Ham's actions, the affront to Marks was too much to ignore. Woolley appealed to Perkins, who was still a trustee, to attempt to stop the appointment, but Ham had his way. (See MEW, letter to Perkins, 19 Dec. 1940, MEW Papers, Series 1, Correspondence, available in Meeropol Research Findings, Folder 1, MHA.) He hired two men as director and technical director of Marks' theatre. "I have been," Marks wrote to Woolley, "completely isolated by Mr. Ham ... as this 'deal' has been put through" (JM, letter to MEW, 1 Feb. 1941).

60. MHTC (Olive Copeland), 4.

61. Seventeen pages from Ham's FBI file were declassified and supplied to a Mount Holyoke College employee in 1988. The earliest entry is from 1943, the last from 1952. Some of the pages are heavily redacted, almost certainly to protect the identity of confidential informants. One memo from V. P. Keay to D. M. Ladd dated 16 Dec. 1952 lists ten "cited organizations" with which Ham was "affiliated." This file is available in Meeropol Papers, Roswell Ham—FBI File. MHA. I am indebted to Professor Daniel Czitrom of Mount Holyoke College for making a copy of this file available to me.

62. See Levin, 149.

Bibliography

Manuscript Collections

Adams, A. Elizabeth Papers. Mount Holyoke College Archives.

Administrative Records, 1920–1976. American Association of University Women Archives.

Allen, Mildred Papers. Mount Holyoke College Archives.

Ball, Margaret Papers. Mount Holyoke College Archives.

Barnes, Viola Papers. Mount Holyoke College Archives.

Board of Trustees Records, Committee of Nine Records. Mount Holyoke College Archives.

Columbia University Oral History Research Office Collection.

Edwards, Boyd Papers. Mount Holyoke College Archives.

Faculty Conference Committee Papers. Mount Holyoke Archives.

Green, Elizabeth. *Mount Holyoke in the Twentieth Century: Oral History Interviews, 1971–*. Mount Holyoke College Archives.

Ham, Roswell G. Papers. Mount Holyoke College Archives.

Hartford College for Women, Hartford, Ct. Descriptive Material. Mount Holyoke College Archives.

Marks, Jeannette Collection. Wellesley College Special Collections.

Marks, Jeannette Papers. Mount Holyoke College Archives.

Meeropol, Ann Karus Research Findings. Mount Holyoke College Archives.

Morgan, Ann Haven Papers. Mount Holyoke College Archives.

Mount Holyoke Alumnae Directory. Mount Holyoke College Archives.

Mount Holyoke College Centenary: Records. Mount Holyoke College Archives.

Mount Holyoke College History Collection. Mount Holyoke College Archives.

Mount Holyoke College Scrap Books Collections. Mount Holyoke College Archives.

Neilson, William Papers. College Archives Smith College.

Nicolson, Marjorie Hope Papers, 1892–1981. College Archives Smith College.

Office of the President, Mary Emma Woolley Records, 1901–1946.

Park Place Congregational Church Archives. Pawtucket, Rhode Island.

Pawtucket Congregational Church Archives. Pawtucket, Rhode Island.

Perkins, Frances Papers. Mount Holyoke College Archives.

Trustees Biographical Files. Mount Holyoke College Archives.

Woolley, Mary Emma Biographical Files. Wellesley College Archives.

Woolley, Mary Emma Papers Mount Holyoke College Archives.

Writings of Mary Emma Woolley

"Achievement versus Possibility." *Journal of the American Association of University Women* 22 (1928–1929): 169–173.

"Address of Congratulations at Inauguration of President Small, Lake Erie College, October 27, 1909." *The Mount Holyoke* 19 (1909–1910): 266–270.

"The American Association of University Women—a Brief Review of Fifty Years." *Journal of the American Association of University Women* 24 (1930–1931): 170–172.

"Character Sketch from 'Adam Bede.'" *The Brown Magazine* 5 (1893–1894): 26–28.

"The Civic Responsibility of the College Woman," *Journal of the Association of Collegiate Alumnae* 7 (1914): 11–16.

"Closing Plea of the Plaintiffs in the Court Held June Thirteenth in Seminary Hall." *Rushlight* 29.3 (June 1884): 26–35.

"Dedication of the Library." *The Mount Holyoke* 13 (1903–1904): 132–138.

"The Development of the Love of Romantic Scenery in America." *American Historical Review* 3 (1897): 56–66.

"Early History of the Colonial Post Office." *Publications of the Rhode Island Historical Society,* New Series 1 (1893–1894): 270–291.

"Editorial." *Rushlight* 29.1 (Dec. 1883): 73–5.

"Education and the Missionary Spirit." *The Mount Holyoke* 18 (1908–1909): 242–244.

"Educational Ideals for the Pupil." *Harper's Bazar* 43 (1909): 754–758.

"Free Press." *The Wellesley Magazine* 8 (1900): 331–333.

"Greetings from Our New President." *Journal of the American Association of University Women* 20 (1926–1927): 99.

Hope Springs Eternal. Ms. Mary Emma Woolley Papers. Autobiographical Materials. Box 1. Mount Holyoke Archives.

Introduction to My Career as a Diplomat. Ms. Mary Emma Woolley Papers. Autobiographical Materials. Box 1. Mount Holyoke Archives.

"Mary Lyon." *The Mount Holyoke* 14 (1904–1905): 231–241.

"A Message from President Woolley." *Journal of the American Association of University Women* 26 (1932–1933): 1.

"New England Etchings." *The Brown Magazine* 5 (1893–1894): 63–65.

Notes on "Autobiography." Ms. Mary Emma Woolley Papers. Autobiographical Materials. Box 1. Mount Holyoke Archives.

"Our Legendary Patrimony." *Rushlight* 29.3 (June 1884): 42–52.

"The Passover Scandal." *The Brown Magazine* 4 (1892–1893): 219–228.

"Portraits of our Grandmothers." *Rushlight* 29.2 (March 1884): 22–28.

"The President's Address." *Journal of the American Association of University Women* 26 (1932–1933): 217–219.

"A Redefinition of Fraternity." *Mount Holyoke Alumnae Quarterly* 2 (1918–1919): 86–91.

"The Social Responsibility of the Educated Christian Woman." *The Congregationalist and Christian World* 89 (1904): 1001–1002.

"Socialistic Schemes." *The Rushlight* 34.5 (March 1890): 75–78.

"Some Results of Higher Education for Women." *Harper's Bazar* 43 (1909): 586–589.

"Value of the Constructive." *The Journal of the Association of Collegiate Alumnae* 9 (1916): 78–82.

"Values of College Training for Woman." *Harper's Bazar* 38 (1904): 836–837.

"The Vocational Power of the Women's College." *The Mount Holyoke* 19 (1909–1910): 165–172.

"What Happened at Geneva?" *Journal of the American Association of University Women* 16 (1932–1933): 67–70.

"What I Owe to My Father." In *What I Owe to My Father,* Sidney Strong, ed. New York: Henry Holt, 1931.

"What's Wrong with Women Teachers?" *Pictorial Review,* 13 March 1929, 22 +.

"The Woman's Club Woman." *Good Housekeeping.* May 1910, 559–565.

"The Women's College." *The Brown Magazine* 6 (1894–1895): 376–381.

Primary Sources

"About Mary Lyon." *The Mount Holyoke* 14 (1904–1905): 288–290.

Addams, Jane. "Commencement Address." *The Mount Holyoke* 17 (1907–1908): 43–7.

Alumnae Association of Mount Holyoke College. *One Hundred Year Biographical Directory of Mount Holyoke College 1837–1937.* Bulletin Series 30, no. 5 South Hadley, MA: Mount Holyoke College, 1937.

"Alumnae Department." *The Mount Holyoke* 12 (1911–1912): 173–184.

"Alumnae Notes," *The Mount Holyoke* 9 (1899–1900): 320–322. 12 (1902–1903): 39–47. (1902–1903): 216–23. 17 (1907–1908): 355. 18 (1908–1909): 122–128. 19 (1909–1910): 364–370. 20 (1910–1911): 458. 21 (1911–1912): 312–320. 22 (1912–1913): 61–67. 23 (1913–1914): 284–297.

American Association of Collegiate Alumnae. *Contributions towards a Bibliography of the Higher Education of Women.* Boston, 1897.

Annual Reports of the President and Treasurer of Wellesley College. 1900. Boston: Wellesley College, 1901.

[Anonymous student, class of] 1918. "Is College Different?" *The Mount Holyoke* 27 (1917–1918): 110–112.

[Anonymous student, class of] 1919. "Summer Work of Mount Holyoke College Girls." *The Mount Holyoke* 29 (1919–1920): 1–2.

Balch, Emily Greene. "College Settlements and the Opportunity to Gain Social Intelligence." *The Mount Holyoke* 24 (1915–1916): 400–404.

Bergeron, Carlisle. "A Person Named Perkins: After Five Years in Office, the Secretary of Labor Is Still Public Puzzle Number One." *The Commentator*, February 1938, 106.

Booth, Alice. "America's Twelve Greatest Women: Mary E. Woolley." *Good Housekeeping*, March 1931, 200–204.

Camp, Dorothy, and Margaret Conrad. "The *Vassar* Training Camp for Nurses." *Mount Holyoke Alumnae Quarterly* 2 (1918–1919): 180–2.

Carter, Edward C. Biography, http://cdi.uvm.edu/findingaids/collection/carter.ead.xml#Biography.

"Christian Association Notes." *The Wellesley Magazine* 4 (1896): 283–284.

"College News." *Mount Holyoke Alumnae Quarterly* 1 (1917–1918): 237–243. 2 (1918–1919): 33–38.

"College Settlements Notes." *The Mount Holyoke* 18 (1908–1909): 397.

"The Complete Roster of America's Greatest Women." *Good Housekeeping*, March 1931, 342.

Cook, Mary Ann. "Saratoga's Cassa Tierra: At One with the Earth." *Saratoga News*, 23 Oct. 2002, www.community-newspapers.com/archives/sratoganews/2002.

Davis, J. Merle "The Institute of Pacific Relations." *International Conciliation*, no. 218 (March 1926): 125–146.

"Disarmament, Four Powers Agree on Geneva Resolution." *Canberra (Australia) Times*, 22 July 1932, http://trove.nla.gov.au/ndp/del/article/2292634.

"Dr. Mary Woolley, Educator, 84, Dead." *New York Times*, 6 Sept. 1947, 17.

Eastman, Rebecca H. "Seven Presidents at Home." *Ladies' Home Journal*, Dec. 1929, 60.

"Editorials." *Journal of the American Association of University Women* 24 (1930–1931): 203–2066.

_____. *Journal of the American Association of University Women* 27 (1933–1934): 167–174.

_____. *The Wellesley Magazine* 7 (1899): 367–369.

Hazard, Caroline. "President's Annual Report." *Annual Reports of the President and Treasurer of Wellesley College. 1900.* Boston: Wellesley College, 1901.

Hinsdale, Ellen C. "The New Plan of Admission." *Mount Holyoke Alumnae Quarterly* 1 (1917–1918): 4–7.

Hyde, William Dewitt. "The Worth of the Womanly Ideal." *The Mount Holyoke* 15 (1905–1906): 127–132.

"Intercollegiate." *The Wellesley Magazine* 7 (1899): 379–381.

"Intercollegiate Debating." *Mount Holyoke Alumnae Quarterly* 17–19: 240.

"International School of Peace." *The Mount Holyoke* 19 (1909–1910): 505.

K., M. C., 1915. "War Relief Work." *The Mount Holyoke* 25 (1915–1916): 44–45.

Laird, Elizabeth Rebecca, 1874–1969, http://www.physics.ucla.edu/~cwp/

Phase2/Laird,_Elizabeth_Rebecca@ 944123456.html.

Lansing, Marion F. "The Curriculum Today." *The Mount Holyoke* 22 (1912–1913): 81–82.

Larcom, Lucy. *Wheaton Seminary: A Semi-Centennial Sketch.* Cambridge: Riverside, 1885.

Lawrence, Henry W. "The Business Man and the Liberal College." *Journal of the American Association of University Women* 25 (June 1932): 213–214.

L.B.D., M.E.G., R.E.K., M.C.M., M.P.S., M.T., M.M., 1916. "Our Money—What We Do with It." *The Mount Holyoke* 25 (1916–1916): 595–599.

Mead, Belle. "The College Woman and the Social Settlement." *The Mount Holyoke* 14 (1904–1905): 191–194.

"Miss Woolley at Geneva—Now It Has Been Told!" *Journal of the American Association of University Women* 27 (1934): 170–171.

"Molly Make-Believe" [anonymous student, class of] 1914. "Extracts from Molly's Diary." *The Mount Holyoke* 23 (1912–1913): 231–237.

Morgan, Ann Haven. "Mount Holyoke's Next President." "Comments and Discussion." *Mount Holyoke Alumnae Quarterly* 19, no. 1 (May, 1935): 28–29.

Morrison, Alva. "The Succession to the Presidency." *Mount Holyoke Alumnae Quarterly* 20 (August 1936): 67–70.

Mount Holyoke Alumnae Directory.

Mount Holyoke College. *Bulletin of Mount Holyoke College: The Catalogue 1910–11.* South Hadley, MA: Mount Holyoke College, 1910.

_____. *Catalogue of Mount Holyoke College, 1904–1905.* South Hadley, MA: Mount Holyoke College, 1904.

_____. *Catalogue of Mount Holyoke College, 1907–1908.* South Hadley, MA: Mount Holyoke College, 1907.

_____. *Catalogue of Mount Holyoke College, 1938.* South Hadley, MA: Mount Holyoke College, 1938.

_____. *Catalogues of Mount Holyoke College* (intermediate years 1939–1949).

_____. *Catalogue of Mount Holyoke College, 1950.* South Hadley, MA: Mount Holyoke College, 1950.

_____. *The Centenary of Mount Holyoke College.* South Hadley, MA: Mount Holyoke College, 1937.

_____. *Reports of the President, 1903–1907.* South Hadley, MA: Mount Holyoke College, 1907.

_____. *The Seventy-Fifth Anniversary.* South Hadley, MA: Mount Holyoke College, 1913.

"News of the International Federation." *Journal of the American Association of University Women* 24 (1930–1931): 25–26.

Nicolson, Marjorie Hope. "The Rights and Privileges Pertaining Thereof." Address (condensed) delivered at the celebration of the centennial of the establishment of the University of Michigan, 14 – 17 June 1937. *Journal of the American Association of University Women* 31 (April 1938): 135–142.

One Hundred Year Biographical Directory of Mount Holyoke College 1837–1937, Bulletin Series 30, no. 5. South Hadley, MA: Alumnae Association of Mount Holyoke College, 1937.

Park Place Congregational Church, a Record of 50 Years. Pawtucket, RI: Park Place Congregational Church, 1932.

Pease, Harriet R. "Report of the Second Annual Meeting of the Graduate Council of Mount Holyoke College." *The Mount Holyoke* 25 (1915–1916): 417–461.

"Picks Miss Woolley as Arms Delegate." *New York Times*, 24 Dec. 1931, 1 +.

"Public Opinion." *The Mount Holyoke* 18 (1908–1909): 103–105, 172–177, 238–243. 19 (1909–1910): 298–304. 20 (1910–1911): 495–496.

Record, Mary Louise. "Half a Century Ago Brown Said It Was an Experiment." *Providence Sunday Journal*, 21 Sept. 1941, section 6, 3.

Report of Mary Emma Woolley President Emeritus of Mount Holyoke College 1936–1937. South Hadley, MA: Mount Holyoke College, 1937.

"Rules, Regulations and Revolution." *The Mount Holyoke* 1920: 156–166.

Seelye, L. Clark. "Founder's Day Address." *The Mount Holyoke* 13 (1903–1904): 188–189.

Smith, Judson. "Mount Holyoke College and Its Alumnae." *The Mount Holyoke* 17 (1907–1908): 1–4.

Stewart, Jane A. "Women's Colleges and Their Women Executives." *Booklovers Magazine* 2 (1903): 341–353.

Stimson, Henry A. "Is Woman's Suffrage an Enlightened and Justifiable Policy for the State." *Biblioteca Sacra* 67 (April 1910): 335–346.

Stowe, Sarah D. (Locke). *History of Mount Holyoke Seminary, 1837–1887.* South Hadley, MA: Mount Holyoke Seminary, 1887.

Thorpe, Anne. "The Social Side of Domestic Service at Vassar." *The Mount Holyoke* 25 (1916–1917): 364–370.

Truesdell, Marion. "Student Government at Mount Holyoke College." *The Mount Holyoke* 25 (1915–1916): 301–309.

United States Department of Labor, Women's Bureau. *Economic Status of University Women in the U.S.A. Report of the Committee on Economic and Legal Status of Women* by Susan Kingsbury (Bulletin of the Women's Bureau, No. 170). Washington, DC: Government Printing Office, 1939.

_____. *Women at Work, a Century of Industrial Change* (Bulletin of the Women's Bureau, No. 161). Washington, DC: Government Printing Office, 1939.

Warner, Frances Lester. *On a New England Campus.* Cambridge: Riverside-Houghton, 1937.

Wellesley College. Wellesley College Calendar, 1897–1898. Boston: Wellesley College, 1897.

Wheaton Female Seminary. *48th Annual Catalogue of Wheaton Female Seminary 1882–83.* Norton, MA: Wheaton Female Seminary, 1882.

_____. *Fifty-fifth Annual Catalogue, 1889–90.* Norton, MA: Wheaton Female Seminary, 1889.

Williston, A. Lyman. "Library Notes." *The Mount Holyoke* 13 (1903–1904): 395.

Woolley, Mary E. *Annual Reports of the President, 1902–1935.* South Hadley, MA : Mount Holyoke College,

Woody, Thomas. *A History of Women's Education in the United States* Vol. 2. New York: The Science Press, 1929.

Secondary Sources: Books

Anouilh, Jean. *Antigone* London: Methuen, 1985.

Berkin, Carol, and Mary Beth Norton, eds. *Women of America: Original Essays and Documents.* Boston: Houghton, 1979.

Burstyn, Joan N. *Victorian Education and the Ideal of Womanhood* London: Croom Helm, 1980.

Chafe, William H. *The American Woman: Her Changing Social, Economic, and Political Role, 1920–1970.* Oxford: Oxford University Press, 1974.

Chambers- Schiller, Lee Virginia. *Liberty a Better Husband. Single Women in America: The Generations of 1780–1840.* New Haven, CT: Yale University Press, 1984.

Clifford, Geraldine Joncich, ed. *Lone Voyagers Academic Women in Coeducational Universities, 1869–1937.* New York: Feminist Press, 1989.

Colman, Penny. *A Woman Unafraid: The Achievements of Frances Perkins.* New York: Atheneum, 1993.

Condliffe, J. B., ed. *Problems of the Pacific, Proceedings of the Second Conference of the Institute of Pacific Relations, Honolulu, Hawaii, July 15 to 29, 1927.* Chicago: University of Chicago Press, 1928.

Conway, Jill K. (with Linda Kealey and Janet E. Schulte). *The Female Experience in Eighteenth- and Nineteenth-Century America.* New York: Garland, 1982.

Coontz, Stephanie. *A Strange Stirring: The Feminine Mystique and American Women at the Dawn of the 1960s.* New York: Basic Books, 2011.

Cott, Nancy F. *The Grounding of Modern Feminism.* New Haven, CT: Yale University Press, 1987.

Degler, Carl. *At Odds: Women and the Family in America from the Revolution to the Present.* Oxford: Oxford University Press, 1980.

Dobkin, Marjorie *Housepian: The Making of a Feminist.* Kent, OH: Kent University Press, 1979.

Douglas, Ann. *The Feminization of American Cultures.* New York: Anchor-Doubleday, 1988.

Downey, Kristin. *The Woman Behind the New Deal*. New York: Anchor Books, Random House, 2009.

Dubois, Ellen Carol, and Lynn Dumenil. *Through Women's Eyes: An American History,* 3rd edition. Boston and New York: Bedford/St. Martin's, 2012.

Edmonds, Anne Carey. *A Memory Book: Mount Holyoke College 1837–1987.* South Hadley, MA: Mount Holyoke College, 1988.

Eisenmann, Linda. *Higher Education for Women in Postwar America, 1945–1965.* Baltimore: Johns Hopkins Press, 2007.

Faderman, Lillian. *Surpassing the Love of Men: Romantic Friendship and Love between Women from the Renaissance to the Present.* New York: William Morrow, 1981.

Forster, Margaret. *Significant Sisters: The Grassroots of Active Feminism, 1839–1939.* New York: Knopf, 1985.

Foucault, Michel. *The History of Sexuality: An Introduction.* New York: Pantheon, 1979.

Frankfort, Roberta. *Collegiate Women, Domesticity and Career in Turn-of-the-Century America.* New York: New York University Press, 1977.

Glascock, Jean, ed. *Wellesley College, 1875–1975: A Century of Women.* Wellesley, MA: Wellesley College, 1975.

Glazer, Penina Migdal, and Miriam Slater. *Unequal Colleagues: The Entrance of Women into the Professions, 1890–1940.* New Brunswick, NJ: Rutgers University Press, 1987.

Gordon, Lynn D. *Gender and Higher Education in the Progressive Era.* New Haven, CT: Yale University Press, 1990.

Green, Elizabeth Alden. *Mary Lyon and Mount Holyoke.* Hanover, NH: University Press of New England, 1979.

Hackett, Alice Payne. *Wellesley: Part of the American Story.* New York: Dutton, 1949.

Ham, Roswell Gray. *Otway and Lee, Biography from a Baroque Age.* New Haven, CT: Yale University Press, 1931.

Handy, Robert T. ed. *The Social Gospel in America 1870–1920.* New York: Oxford University Press, 1966.

Hareven, Tamara K., and Maris A. Vinovskis, eds. *Family and Population in Nineteenth-Century America.* Princeton: Princeton University Press, 1978.

Harris, Barbara. *Beyond Her Sphere: Women and the Professions in American History.* New York: Greenwood, 1978.

Hawk, Grace E. *Pembroke College in Brown University: The First Seventy-Five Years, 1891–1966.* Providence, RI: Brown University Press, 1967.

Heilbrun, Carolyn G. *Writing A Woman's Life.* New York: Norton, 1988.

Helmreich, Paul C. *Wheaton College, 1834–1912: The Seminary Years.* Norton, MA: Class of 1949 Wheaton College, 1895.

Horowitz, Helen Lefkowitz. *Alma Mater: Design and Experience in the Women's Colleges from Their Nineteenth-Century Beginnings to the 1930s.* New York: Alfred A. Knopf, 1984.

_____. *The Power and Passion of M. Carey Thomas.* New York: Alfred A. Knopf, 1994.

Howard, Suzanne. *But We Will Persist: A Comparative Research Report on Status of Women in Academe.* Washington, DC: American Association of University Women, 1978.

Howe, Florence. *Myths of Coeducation.* Bloomington: Indiana University Press, 1984.

Kelley, Mary, ed. *Woman's Being, Woman's Place.* Boston: G. K. Hall, 1979.

Kelly, Joan. *Women, History and Theory: The Essays of Joan Kelly.* Chicago: University of Chicago Press, 1984.

Kendall, Elaine. *Peculiar Institutions.* New York: Putnam, 1975.

Kendall, Paul Murray. *The Art of Biography.* New York: Norton, 1965.

Kerber, Linda K., Alice Kessler-Harris and Kathryn Kish Sklar, eds. *U.S. History and Women's History: New Feminist Essays.* Chapel Hill: University of North Carolina Press, 1995.

Kessler-Harris, Alice. *In Pursuit of Equity: Women, Men and the Quest for Economic Citizenship in 20th-Century America.* Oxford: Oxford University Press, 2001.

_____. *Out to Work: A History of Wage-Earning Women in the United States.* New York: Oxford University Press, 1982.

Kleinberg, S. Jay, Eileen Boris and Vicki L.

Ruiz, eds. *The Practice of U.S. Women's History: Narratives, Intersections, and Dialogues.* New Brunswick, NJ: Rutgers University Press, 2007.

Lasser, Carol, ed. *Educating Men and Women Together: Coeducation in a Changing World.* Urbana and Chicago: University of Illinois Press with Oberlin College, 1987.

Levin, Miriam R. *Defining Women's Scientific Enterprise: Mount Holyoke Faculty and the Rise of American Science.* Hanover, NH, and London: University Press of New England, 2005.

Levine, Susan. *Degrees of Equality: The AAUW and the Challenge of Twentieth-Century Feminism.* Philadelphia: Temple University Press, 1995.

Marks, Jeannette. *The Life and Letters of Mary Emma Woolley.* Washington, DC: Public Affairs Press, 1955.

Martin, George W. *Madam Secretary, Frances Perkins.* Boston: Houghton Mifflin, 1976.

Martin, Jane Roland. *Reclaiming a Conversation: The Ideal of the Educated Woman.* New Haven, CT: Yale University Press, 1985.

Miller, Ann, ed. *A College in Dispersion, Women of Bryn Mawr 1896–1975.* Boulder, CO: Westview Press, 1976.

Mitchell, Robert Morgan. *This Branch of His Planting.* Pawtucket, RI: Park Place Congregational Church, 1982.

Notable American Women 1607–1950. Cambridge, MA: Belknap Press, 1971.

Oates, Stephen B. ed. *Biography as High Adventure.* Amherst: University of Massachusetts Press, 1986.

Palmer, George Herbert. *The Life of Alice Freeman Palmer.* Boston: Houghton, 1908.

Palmieri, Patricia Ann. *In Adamless Eden: The Community of Women Faculty at Wellesley.* New Haven, CT: Yale University Press, 1985.

Pollard, Lucille Addison. *Women on College and University Faculties: A Historical Survey and a Study of Their Present Academic Status.* New York: Arno, 1977.

Reid, John G. *Viola Florence Barnes, 1885–1979: A Historian's Biography.* Toronto: University of Toronto Press, 2005.

Rockwell, George L. *The History of Ridgefield, Connecticut.* Ridgefield: Privately Printed by the Author, 1927.

Rosen, Ruth *The World Split Open, How the Modern Women's Movement Changed America.* New York: Viking Penguin, 2000.

Rosenberg, Rosalind. *Beyond Separate Spheres: Intellectual Roots of Modern Feminism.* New Haven, CT: Yale University Press, 1982.

Rossi, Alice S. *Essays on Sex Equality.* Chicago: University of Chicago Press, 1970.

_____. *Gender and the Life Course.* New York: Aldine, 1985.

Scharf, Lois, and Joan M. Jensen, eds. *Decades of Discontent: The Woman's Movement, 1920–1940.* Westport, CT: Greenwood Press, 1983.

Scott, Anne Firor. *Making the Invisible Woman Visible.* Urbana: University of Illinois Press, 1984.

Sicherman, Barbara, and Carol Hurd Green, eds. *Notable American Women: The Modern Period.* Cambridge, MA: Belknap Press, 1980.

Simeone, Angela. *Academic Women, Working towards Equality.* South Hadley, MA: Bergin and Garvey, 1987.

Solomon, Barbara Miller *In the Company of Educated Women: A History of Women and Higher Education in America.* New Haven, CT: Yale University Press, 1985.

Starkey, Marion L. *The Congregational Way.* New York: Doubleday, 1966.

Stock, Phyllis. *Better than Rubies: A History of Women's Education.* New York: Putnam's, 1978.

Talbot, Marion. *The Education of Women.* Chicago: University of Chicago Press, 1910.

Taylor, Frederick W. *Principles of Scientific Management.* New York and London: Harper & Brothers, 1911.

Teller, Daniel W. *History of Ridgefield.* Danbury, CT: 1878.

VanBurkleo, Sandra F. *"Belonging to the World": Women's Rights and American Constitutional Culture.* Oxford: Oxford University Press, 2001.

Ware, Susan. *Beyond Suffrage: Women and the New Deal.* Cambridge, MA: Harvard University Press, 1981.

_____. *Letter to the World: Seven Women Who Shaped the American Century*. New York: Norton, 1998.

Wells, Anna Mary. *Miss Marks and Miss Woolley*. Boston: Houghton Mifflin, 1978.

Williams, William A. *The Tragedy of American Diplomacy*. New York: Dell, 1972.

Woloch, Nancy. *Women and the American Experience*, 5th edition. New York: McGraw-Hill, 2011.

Woody, Thomas. *A History of Women's Education in the United States*, vol. 2. New York: Science Press, 1929.

Secondary Sources: Articles

Beard, Mary R. "The Second Century Faces the First. Is It Time to Choose New Goals in Higher Education of Women?" "Some Answers to These Questions." *Journal of the American Association of University Women* 31, no. 4 (June 1938): 213–214.

_____. "University Discipline for Women—Asset or Handicap?" *Journal of the American Association of University Women* 25 (1931–1932): 130–131.

Carter, Susan. "Academic Women Revisited: An Empirical Study of Changing Patterns in Women's Employment as College and University Faculty, 1890–1963." *Journal of Social History* 14 (1981): 675–699.

Celello, Kristin. "A New Century of Struggle: Feminism and Antifeminism in the United States, 1920-Present." In *The Practice of U.S. Women's History: Narratives, Intersections, and Dialogues*, edited by S. Jay Kleinberg, Eileen Boris and Vicki L. Ruiz (New Brunswick, NJ: Rutgers University Press, 2007), 333–334.

Cook, Blanche Wiesen. "The Historical Denial of Lesbianism." *Radical History Review* 20 (1979): 60–65.

Dzuback, Mary Ann. "Gender and the Politics of Knowledge." *History of Education Quarterly* 43 (2003): 171–195.

Freedman, Estelle. "Separatism as Strategy: Female Institution Building and American Feminism, 1870–1930." *Feminist Studies* 5 (1979): 512–529.

_____. "Separatism Revisited: Women's Institutions, Social Reform, and the Career of Miriam Van Waters." Chapter 8 in *U.S. History and Women's History: New Feminist Essays*, edited by Linda K. Kerber, Alice Kessler-Harris, and Kathryn Kish Sklar (Chapel Hill: University of North Carolina Press, 1995), 173–175.

Gordon, Lynn D. "Annie Nathan Meyer and Barnard College: Mission and Identity in Women's Higher Education, 1889–1950." *History of Education Quarterly* 26 (1986): 503–522

_____. "Co-Education on Two Campuses: Berkeley and Chicago, 1890–1912." In *Woman's Being, Woman's Place*, edited by Mary Kelley (Boston: G. K. Hall, 1979), 171–195.

_____. "Education and the Professions." In *A Companion to American Women's History*, edited by Nancy A. Hewitt (Oxford: Blackwell, 2002), 239.

McAfee, Mildred H. "Segregation and the Women's College." *American Journal of Sociology*, 43 (1937): 16–22.

Olsen, Deborah M. "Remaking the Image: Promotional Literature of Mount Holyoke, Smith, and Wellesley Colleges in the Mid-to-Late 1940s." *History of Education Quarterly* 40 (2000): 418–459.

Palmieri, Patricia. "Here Was Fellowship: A Social Portrait of Academic Women at Wellesley College, 1895–1920." *History of Education Quarterly* 23 (1983): 195–214.

Reconstructing the Academy, a full issue of *Signs* (Winter 1987).

Rice, Joy K., and Annett Hemmings. "Women's Colleges and Women Achievers: An Update." *Signs* 13 (1988).

Rossi, Alice. "Coeducation in a Gender-Stratified Society." In *Educating Men and Women Together: Coeducation in a Changing World*, edited by Carol Lasser (Urbana: University of Illinois Press, 1987).

Rossiter, Margaret. "Sexual Segregation in the Sciences: Some Data and a Model." *Signs* 4 (1978): 146–151.

Rury, John, and Glenn Harper. "The Trouble with Coeducation: Mann and Women at Antioch, 1953–1860." *History of Education Quarterly* 26 (1986): 481–502.

Smith-Rosenberg, Carroll. "The Female World of Love and Ritual: Relations between Women in Nineteenth-Century America." In *A Heritage of Her Own*, edited by Nancy Cott and Elizabeth Pleck (New York: Simon, 1979), 311–342.

Tayler, Edward W. "In Memoriam: Marjorie Hope Nicolson (1894–1981)." *Journal of the History of Ideas* 42, no. 4, 665–667.

Tuchman, Barbara W. "Biography as a Prism of History." In *Biography as High Adventure*, edited by Stephen B. Oates (Amherst: University of Massachusetts Press, 1986).

Wein, Roberta. "Women's Colleges and Domesticity, 1875–1918." *History of Education Quarterly* 14 (1974): 31–47.

Unpublished Dissertations and Manuscripts

Maglin, Nan Beaver. "Female Friendship: Vida D. Scudder and Florence Converse." Ms. N.d.

Meeropol, Ann Karus. *A Practical Visionary: Mary Emma Woolley and the Education of Women.* Diss. University of Massachusetts, 1992. Ann Arbor: UMI, 1992.

Palmieri, Patricia Ann. *In Adamless Eden: A Social Portrait of the Academic Community at Wellesley College 1975–1920.* Diss. Harvard University, 1981. Ann Arbor: UMI, 1981.

Rota, Tiziana. *Between "True Women" and "New Women": Mount Holyoke Students, 1837 to 1908.* Diss. University of Massachusetts, 1983.

Index

Numbers in ***bold italics*** indicate pages with photographs.